TRUST MATTERS: CROSS-DISCIPLINARY ESSAYS

This volume collects original essays on trust. It examines the role of trust in public life and places analytic questions about the attitude of trust at the centre of a cross-disciplinary inquiry into its value. Bringing together contributors from across the social, historical and political sciences, this edited collection seeks to contribute to a more nuanced understanding of fundamental concepts in political and legal theory by furnishing and sharpening our concepts of trust and trustworthiness.

Trust Matters: Cross-Disciplinary Essays

Edited by
Raquel Barradas de Freitas
and
Sergio Lo Iacono

• HART •
OXFORD • LONDON • NEW YORK • NEW DELHI • SYDNEY

HART PUBLISHING

Bloomsbury Publishing Plc

Kemp House, Chawley Park, Cumnor Hill, Oxford, OX2 9PH, UK

1385 Broadway, New York, NY 10018, USA

29 Earlsfort Terrace, Dublin 2, Ireland

HART PUBLISHING, the Hart/Stag logo, BLOOMSBURY and the Diana logo are trademarks of Bloomsbury Publishing Plc

First published in Great Britain 2021

A catalogue record for this book is available from the British Library.

A catalogue record for this book is available from the Library of Congress.

ISBN: HB: 978-1-50993-525-3
ePDF: 978-1-50993-527-7
ePub: 978-1-50993-526-0

Typeset by Compuscript Ltd, Shannon
Printed and bound in Great Britain

To find out more about our authors and books visit www.hartpublishing.co.uk. Here you will find extracts, author information, details of forthcoming events and the option to sign up for our newsletters.

In memory of John Gardner (1965–2019)

FOREWORD

TIMOTHY ENDICOTT

I am not so sure that we should trust ourselves. And as for trusting *others* … well, on that score I find it quite sobering to read the essays in this remarkable book. Traversing the widest terrain of human experience from different directions, the authors show again and again that trusting others can be the right thing to do. Their essays make sobering reading because they also show, again and again from diverse perspectives, that it is dangerous to trust anyone. The justification for trusting someone always lies in need and vulnerability. But to trust someone is to make your vulnerability into an opportunity for exploitation. It makes betrayal possible.

By probing this central irony in human interaction from such diverse perspectives and in different directions, these essays make a large-scale contribution to the study of humanity. I congratulate and thank Raquel Barradas de Freitas and Sergio Lo Iacono and all the authors.

Readers will seek out particular essays for particular reasons; I especially recommend the project of reading them together. For the multiply ramified complexity of trust can only be disclosed through the work of different people who focus varied gifts on this dangerous and essential relationship, through varied methods. The book is a contribution to legal and economic and political theory, to cognitive and behavioural science, to the philosophy of the emotions, to intellectual history and to cultural studies. The authors apply the methods of all of those fields of study and more to the most diverse array of relationships in which it might be wise and necessary for a person or a group or the public to adopt an attitude of trust toward someone, or alternatively might be reckless and self-destructive. Children toward parents, parents toward babysitters, citizens toward representatives, drivers toward each other, jurors toward witnesses, indigenous peoples toward colonisers, the public toward the state and toward public agencies (the European Food Safety Agency, the London Underground), members of the public toward other members of the public and toward voluntary associations, the faithful toward religious leaders, beneficiaries toward trustees in private law, European Union Member States toward each other, members of the public toward seismologists.

In the resulting complex group discourse concerning trust, the authors light up a wide array of concepts that are related to the concept of trust by one form or another of alliance or antithesis: risk, expectation, reliance, vulnerability, suspicion, exploitation, goodwill, love, anxiety, agency, solidarity, credibility, mutuality, authority, cooperation, delegation, accountability, authenticity, expertise, integrity, virtue, and of course trustworthiness and betrayal. In my view, it is a strength of the book that you will find respectful but deep disagreements among the authors, even as to how to hone the term 'trust' into a useful tool for the human empirical and normative sciences. For the project of articulating an understanding of trust implicates deep and controversial problems of human understanding and human action.

So I recommend this book heartily. It is a library of the human condition. The stories of betrayal that you will find in this book about trust are simply harrowing. There are wrongs that can only be committed where one person trusts another – they are the ironic, painful, reflexively barbed wrongs. If your purpose is to wound someone, it will be so useful for your malign purpose if they trust you. If you love someone, it is (it hurts to say this) dangerous to your loving purpose if they trust you. Without being trusted, you cannot betray them. Betrayal, after all, is the tribute that vice pays to trust.

Timothy Endicott

ACKNOWLEDGEMENTS

This volume emerged from the Trust Matters Workshop, which took place at the European University Institute in April 2018. We are grateful to all participants at the workshop for their papers, intellectual generosity, and openness to new ideas. Our special thanks to our colleagues Marta Morvillo and Carolin Schmitz, who co-organised the workshop.

We are very grateful to the Max Weber Programme and the hardworking team who assisted us in the preparation of the Workshop with great competence, professionalism, and unlimited patience: Karin Tillmans, Ognjen Aleksic, Valeria Pizzini Gambetta, Francesca Grassini, and Anna Sullivan. A particular word of thanks to the Programme Director, Richard Bellamy, who provided advice and encouragement and participated in the Workshop as a commentator. The Workshop was funded by the Law Department, the History and Civilization Department, and the Department of Political and Social Sciences of the EUI. We thank them for their generous support.

A particular word of thanks to Sinead Moloney, whose interest in this project and belief in its potential gave us the energy to believe that we could turn it into a book that Hart would want to publish. We also thank Sasha Jawed, Tom Adams, Richard Cox, Rosamund Jubber, and all involved in the production of this volume.

Most importantly, we are grateful to our contributors, who devoted so much time and intellectual energy to writing their essays. Their ideas, talent, and collegiality have made work on this volume truly enjoyable.

Raquel Barradas de Freitas writes: I am very grateful for the kindness, encouragement, and support of many colleagues, friends, and family during the time I have spent working on this project. Jeff McMahan generously let me use his beautiful office in Corpus Christi College for several weeks (while away from Oxford) – a place where I was able to work surrounded by wonderful music, books, and infinite quantities of the finest green tea. Timothy Endicott has been an unfailingly supportive mentor and friend. William Twining has taught me so much about the common law, legal reasoning, and the challenges of editing a book. I am so grateful for my wonderful parents, Margarida and Carlos, for Zequinha – always wise, always loving, always there – and for my kind, thoughtful, bright daughter Francisca.

Sergio Lo Iacono writes: I would like to sincerely thank my former fellows at the European University Institute for supporting and contributing to this edited collection, providing insightful feedback and lively discussions. I am very grateful to Neli Demireva for her mentorship and guidance in every step of my academic career, and to Burak Sonmez and Federico Brandmayr for their acute comments and friendship. Also, I would like to thank Martina Testori for the stimulating intellectual debates and the unwavering emotional support, which always helps me through the most difficult times.

CONTENTS

LIST OF CONTRIBUTORS

BIRGIT AASA, Department of Law, European University Institute

ANNALISE ACORN, Faculty of Law, University of Alberta

RAQUEL BARRADAS DE FREITAS, Balliol College, University of Oxford

PAUL C. BAUER, Manheim Centre for European Social Research

FEDERICO BRANDMAYR, MacMillan Center, Yale University

ACHAS BURIN, Somerville College, University of Oxford

NELI DEMIREVA, Department of Sociology, University of Essex

CHIARA DESTRI, Centre of Political Research (CEVIPOF), Sciences Po, Paris

TIMOTHY ENDICOTT, All Souls College, University of Oxford

MAX HARRIS, All Souls College, University of Oxford

SERGIO LO IACONO, Department of Social and Behavioural Sciences, Utrecht University

GIULIANO MORI, Philosophy Department, University of Milan

MARTA MORVILLO, Amsterdam Centre for European Law and Governance (ACELG), University of Amsterdam

BURAK SONMEZ, Department of Sociology, London School of Economics

MARTINA TESTORI, Faculty of Social Sciences, Vrije Universiteit Amsterdam

WILLIAM TWINING, Faculty of Laws, University College London

LIST OF FIGURES

1

Introduction: The Virtue of Trust

RAQUEL BARRADAS DE FREITAS

Look around you: trust and distrust are everywhere, from political speeches to newspaper headlines, from public demonstrations to marketing campaigns, from politics to the judiciary, from competitive sports to public health, from the banking system to self-driven cars and big data.[1] Trust is necessary to life in society. It is central to human relationships – the trust we place in others signals how much we value them. Displaying trust in someone adds value to both their life and our own. We often respond to others' trust in us with enhanced engagement and commitment. When we fail to be responsive to trust, we fail to be responsive to moral reasons. When we are incapable of trusting others, we are limited in our capacity to realise a certain kind of value in our lives, and we deprive others of the opportunity to be valued in a distinctive way. Trustworthiness is a virtue, but so is trust.

As we see a revival of interest in trust in public life, politics and the media, this is a good moment to look closely at and reflect about trust and trustworthiness. It matters what they are, how they relate to and differ from one another, and what their role is in complex societies. In an age of post-truth, alternative facts, populism, manipulation, disenchantment and uncertainty, it becomes urgent to shed light on the logic and value of trust. The current revival of interest in trust is a reaction to the various crises of trust in government, in the press, in science (scepticism about climate science), in medicine (scepticism about vaccines), and in expertise of all forms that we currently face. Distrust has driven some significant political shifts of the last few years in countries such as the United Kingdom and the United States.[2] It is also a driving force behind a wave of social conflict and unrest currently sweeping across the world, recently displayed in the 2016 Brexit referendum campaign and, even more dramatically, in the insurrection by supporters of President Trump in Washington DC on 6 January 2021. In general, people have become more suspicious of foreigners, immigrants and anyone outside the groups of which they are members and within which there is a shared sense of collective

[1] See, for instance, the European Commission's White Paper, *Artificial Intelligence: A European Approach to Excellence and Trust* (Brussels, February 2020).

[2] For an analysis of the relation between mistrust and the dark side of meritocracy, see Michael Sandel, *The Tyranny of Merit: What's Become of the Common Good?* (Penguin, 2020).

identity. Such conspicuous weakening of trust is accompanied by a dangerous vast misplacing of trust in the claims of those who share one's prejudices or identity. The proliferation of conspiracy theories and misinformation on the internet and social media is both a cause and a symptom of this form of pathologically unwarranted trust.

In the last year, the Coronavirus pandemic has exposed fissures in the social tissue of countries around the world, including deeply rooted, abhorrent forms of inequality. It has also laid bare our need to rely on those who hold power over us, including those who have access to knowledge and resources which we are unable to access ourselves. Understanding trust and what justifies it allows us to strengthen our grasp of both its value and the limits of and alternatives to it in our personal, social and political lives. As individuals and members of political communities, we are vulnerable to betrayal.[3] Placing trust in someone is a delicate thing to do: it can empower a person, but also expose them to harm. We need tools for determining when trust is warranted, and when it ought to be withheld.[4]

It has been said that superstition brings bad luck.[5] So does the inflation of concepts. Trust, like other concepts such as interpretation, justice, or the rule of law, is currently at risk of overuse and overreach.[6] The first aim of this volume is to reduce this risk by critically examining and sharpening our concept of trust. Recent philosophical literature shows us that there is a difference between relying and trusting, between distrusting and not trusting, between trusting someone and engaging in probabilistic reasoning about what they will do, between trusting someone and believing what they say or believing that they will do what we would like them to do, and so on. Despite the differences between trust and so many other things, we ordinarily use the word 'trust' to refer to all these many other things. And when we do so, as we often do, we do not make a linguistic mistake. The reader may wonder what justifies sharpening a concept which we all use successfully to communicate with one another in ordinary life, in different areas of public discourse, and in academic debate.

[3] Annette Baier notes that betrayal, not disappointment, lies at the heart of the moral relation of trust ('Trust and Anti-Trust', (1986) 96.2 *Ethics* 231–60).

[4] Martin Luther King, *Why We Cannot Wait* (Penguin, 2018). The interesting (and important) issue of the democratic value of distrust is a separate question which deserves attention. Distrust is not the absence of trust. Distrust is not the absence of a belief in a person's trustworthiness or a lack of optimism about their motives. For a view according to which expressing distrust can be a powerful social and political tool in the face of tyranny, see Meena Krishnamurthy, '(White) Tyranny and the Democratic Value of Distrust' (2015) 98. 4 *The Monist* 391–406. See also Trudy Govier, 'Distrust as a Practical Problem' (1992) 23.1 *Journal of Social Philosophy* 52–63, and Katherine Hawley, 'Trust, Distrust, and Commitment' (2014) 48.1 *Nous* 1–20. For a similar analysis of the moral emotion of anger and its place in politics, and an account of the distinctive wrong of 'affective injustice', see Amia Srinivasan, 'The Aptness of Anger' (2017) 26.2 *Journal of Political Philosophy*.

[5] Raymond Smullyan, *5000 B.C., and Other Philosophical Fantasies* (1983), quoted by Umberto Eco in *Foucault's Pendulum* (Secker & Warburg, 1989).

[6] On the pathology of conceptual overreach, see John Tasioulas' recent essay 'The Inflation of Concepts', aeon.co (29 January 2021). Tasioulas explains that conceptual overreach occurs 'when a particular concept undergoes a process of expansion or inflation in which it absorbs ideas and demands that are foreign to it.'

The answer is simple. What justifies sharpening the concept of trust is the value of trust. Trust is not only a conceptual tool for making sense of and improving our social, legal and political institutions; it is also an attitude that defines and gives shape to relationships and ways of life. Because trust is valuable, both intrinsically and instrumentally, we ought to understand it and its place in both personal relationships and public life much better than we currently do. We must clarify the role it plays in different domains of social life, the reasons for action and belief that it gives us, and the moral implications of both its presence and its absence. This volume aims to make a start by giving the reader a set of sharp conceptual tools to use across domains.

Many of our pre-theoretical understandings of what makes relationships healthy and good indicate that trust is valuable. Yet we find it challenging to explain why trust is good, why it is more desirable to trust than to distrust, to be trustworthy rather than unresponsive to trust, to be trusting rather than suspicious. When we attempt to transfer our intuitions about the desirability of trust in personal relationships to the relationship between citizens and political institutions, or between individuals or social groups and big corporations, we face additional challenges – such relationships differ from interpersonal ones in significant ways.[7] We increasingly hear about a crisis of trust in governments, politicians, experts and in the institutional arrangements that we have come to take for granted. Yet public discourse continues to rely on a shared language of trust.

This volume collects original essays on trust. It examines the role of trust in public life and places analytic questions about the attitude of trust at the centre of a cross-disciplinary inquiry into its value. Most contributions to this volume are developed versions of papers presented at an international workshop organised by four Max Weber Fellows at the European University Institute in April 2018. Two of the organisers of that workshop are the editors of this volume, the other two were Marta Morvillo and Carolin Schmitz. Other chapters were commissioned in the following year and the collection expanded beyond the group of scholars who gathered at the Badia Fiesolana for the workshop. From the outset, the aim of this project has been to collect a cross-disciplinary sample of essays reflecting on the concepts of trust and trustworthiness, as used and applied by scholars across the social and cognitive sciences and in the humanities. The impulse was to fill a void in the jurisprudential literature, following the publication of *The Philosophy of Trust* in 2017,[8] which remedied the relative neglect of trust by anglophone philosophers and paved the way for more new, interesting philosophical work on trust.[9]

[7] In *How to Be Trustworthy* (OUP, 2019), 16–20, Katherine Hawley suggests, for example, that trust in intimate relationships, unlike trust in professionals and organisations, is sensitive to the motives of those in whom trust is placed but points out that motives are neither necessary nor sufficient for either trustworthy action or warranted trust.

[8] Paul Faulkner and Thomas Simpson (eds) *The Philosophy of Trust* (OUP, 2017).

[9] An example of the renewed philosophical interest in trust that ensued is the very recent *Routledge Handbook of Trust and Philosophy* edited by Judith Simon (2020). Other examples of recent contributions to the philosophy of trust are *Epistemic Authority: A Theory of Trust, Authority, and Autonomy in*

However, with very few exceptions,[10] no corresponding interest in trust has been forthcoming from those working in the philosophy of law or, more broadly, in legal theory.

The theory according to which the role of trust in public law and in politics ought to be explained by an analogy with fiduciary duties in private law has become influential in Anglo-American scholarship. Legal philosophers and constitutional theorists have developed various forms of the fiduciary theory of government and adjudication, addressing central questions in legal theory from new angles and engaging directly with the concepts of trust and trustworthiness and their role in public life. Timothy Endicott (Oxford) is one example. His recent essay 'The Public Trust'[11] engages critically with the fiduciary theory of government and provides an alternative view of the role of trust in the relationship between citizens and the state, one which denies the power of an analogy with private fiduciary duties in understanding the role of trust in public law. Such questions have important ramifications, among other things, for questions about relations among legal and political authorities in a constitutional setting. Thinking rigorously about trust helps us to think rigorously about fundamental questions in both public and private law, including questions about the nature of the duties that the state and other legal and political authorities have to those whose lives they purport to legitimately regulate. These are important questions with direct implications for how one chooses to live one's life.

Eight of the thirteen essays in this volume address the role of trust in politics, the constitutional arena and the life of legal institutions. One motivation for structuring the volume in a way that emphasises legally relevant themes has been to show lawyers, legal theorists and a more general readership that: (i) we can learn much about law and its limits by learning more about the logic and justification of power and authority; (ii) we can learn much about power and authority by learning more about the attitude of trust; and (iii) we can learn much about trust by talking to scholars working in other disciplines. The volume has been structured in such a way as to encourage contributors and readers alike to seek, identify and articulate connections among the various issues addressed in the essays. The index has been designed to identify points of contact among chapters. The thread running through the volume is the question of what, if any, role trust plays in making sense of and shaping various aspects of the life of social and political communities, including those aspects which are regulated by law.

Belief, by Linda Zagzebski (OUP, 2012), *Testimony, Trust, and Authority*, by Benjamin McMyler (OUP, 2011) and *Knowledge on Trust*, by Paul Faulkner (OUP, 2011).

[10] Evan Fox-Decent, *Sovereignty's Promise: The State as Fiduciary* (OUP, 2011); Gerald J Postema 'Fidelity, Accountability and Trust: Tensions at the Heart of the Rule of Law', in T Bustamante and T Lopes Decat (eds), *Philosophy of Law as an Integral Part of Philosophy: Essays on the Jurisprudence of Gerald J. Postema* (Hart, 2020), 33–60; Paul B Miller and M Harding (eds) *Fiduciaries and Trust: Ethics, Politics, Economics and Law* (CUP, 2020).

[11] Evan J Criddle, Evan Fox-Decent, Andrew S Gold, Sung Hui Kim and Paul B Miller (eds) *Fiduciary Government* (CUP, 2018).

Lawyers and legal theorists tend to take the necessity of law for social cooperation as a fact and give other mechanisms of coordination relatively short shrift. Trust has been thoroughly studied by sociologists, psychologists, cognitive scientists and behavioural economists as a mechanism of social cooperation. Social cooperation was also the starting point of philosophical work on trust, which has since expanded to the epistemology of testimony and to practical philosophy. However, legal theorists have not relied enough on the work on trust produced in the social, cognitive, economic and political sciences or in philosophy. Philosophers of law, more specifically, have not engaged with the philosophical literature on trust when addressing fundamental questions about the nature of law, including questions about the logic and justification of legal authority. Yet law and trust are not obviously mutually exclusive mechanisms of social cooperation. A clearer understanding of trust as a tool of cooperation and as a social virtue provides insight into the nature and limits of law as a social practice and as a means of social control and coordination. This volume's distinctive contribution to the literature is to bring philosophical, sociological and legal conceptual tools together into a rigorous analysis of trust across domains.

Trust is often referred to as an affective attitude,[12] and some philosophers have claimed that we understand trust, at least in part, by understanding the moral emotions we experience when our trust is misplaced or betrayed. We currently witness a growing interest in the role of the emotions in politics and public life, as well as in theories of legal reasoning and argument, with an increasing openness to an interdisciplinary methodology. This goes hand in hand with a richer and more abundant literature on the moral emotions, the rationality of emotions, and on the contribution of the affective sciences to the study of law, legal reasoning and legal practices.[13] In addition to these, greater attention is being paid to work in virtue ethics and virtue epistemology by legal scholars seeking an alternative to mainstream views on legal normativity, reasoning, deliberation and judgment. This volume fits into this new set of directions in legal theory by offering a selection of views on trust as an attitude with both cognitive and affective dimensions, a social and political virtue, a social practice, and a source of reasons for belief and action. Reflecting on the different dimensions of trust encourages us to think about emotion as continuous with perception and cognition and, more specifically, about the moral emotions. Such themes cut across theories of punishment (sanctions may have an expressive function and can convey moral norms; the moral emotions may have an important role to play both in communicating moral judgments and in the repair of broken trust relations), accounts of legal reasoning and adjudication (which in turn inform views on the limits of and relations between legal and moral reasoning and of the scope of the judicial role), and the philosophical foundations of different branches of law.

[12] Karen Jones, 'Trust as an Affective Attitude' (October 1996) 107 *Ethics* 4–25.

[13] See, for example, Amalia Amaya and Maksymilian del Mar (eds) *Virtue, Emotion and Imagination in Law and Legal Reasoning* (Hart, 2020).

Notwithstanding a significant increase of interest in the topic of trust among philosophers in the last few years, there remains a gap between available scholarly work on trust in the social sciences, economics, the cognitive sciences, and political science, on the one hand, and the philosophical literature, on the other. The gap is particularly surprising given the relevance of the notion of trust in addressing fundamental questions in epistemology, moral philosophy, political philosophy and the philosophy of law. This volume aims to bridge that gap by starting a conversation between legal scholars and scholars working in other disciplines, who might not otherwise talk to each other. In addition to this, it seeks to start a much wider conversation between trust scholars and the general public.

I. Chapter Summary

Paul Bauer opens Part I of the volume with an essay titled 'Conceptualising Trust and Trustworthiness'. Bauer's contribution is one of three different proposed formalisations of trust included in this volume, informed by social sciences methodology and, more specifically, by empirical trust research. The aim of the chapter is to give theoretical sharpness to the concepts of trust and trustworthiness, noting that the latter has been relatively neglected in the sociology and political science literature. Bauer concludes, after carefully surveying the literature, that the concepts of trust and trustworthiness designate probabilities. Trust, on Bauer's view, is a probabilistic expectation.

The same concern to sharpen our concept of trust can be seen in Sergio Lo Iacono and Martina Testori's contribution to this volume. Their analysis in chapter three focuses on what they call the 'classic formalisation' of trust as a three-place relation (A trusts B to do X). They question the explanatory power of this formalisation, both for particular and general forms of trust. Lo Iacono and Testori propose a category-based formalisation of the trust relation. They assume that people typically adopt a deductive, top-down approach when responding and relating to their social surroundings and classify others on the basis of a set of properties which then serve as a foundation for expectations about their reliability. The notions of expectation, reliability and probabilistic reasoning reappear as the kernel of the formalisation of trust they propose.

There is a conceptual connection between trust and vulnerability,[14] in particular vulnerability to betrayal. This connection is noted and emphasised throughout the volume. We see the concept of trust furnished in different ways, but the link with vulnerability is explicitly referred to by Annalise Acorn, Max Harris,

[14] For a recent contribution to the literature on the ethics of vulnerability, from the perspective of feminist philosophy, see C Mackenzie, Wendy Roges, Susan Dodds (eds) *Vulnerability: New Essays in Ethics and Feminist Philosophy*. For a proposed re-imagining of law in terms of a relational understanding of the self, including an account of the vulnerable self, see Jonathan Herring *Law and the Relational Self* (CUP, 2020).

Chiara Destri, Achas Burin, Neli Demireva and Birgit Aasa. In chapter four, Burak Sonmez takes the connection between vulnerability and trust as the central concern of his essay. Sonmez suggests that there is a causal connection between the mutual vulnerability of individuals and their willingness to cooperate with one another in the absence of legal mechanisms of enforcement and control. The essay focuses on the question of how typically mistrusted communities, such as refugees and their host populations, may enhance their chances of cooperation by conditioning their own vulnerability to the vulnerability of others in small steps. Sonmez argues that status differences drive expectations of vulnerability to the actions of others in trusting relationships. The essay proposes that we understand the place of trust in cooperative social scenarios in terms of an inverse relation between the scope of action of the trusted and the degree of their vulnerability to those who trust them.

The essays in Part II of the volume are devoted to the theme of the value of trust. Max Harris (chapter five) begins by alerting us to what he calls 'the problem of social relations in contemporary societies'. Harris believes that the pattern of pernicious individualism, in particular, calls for both rigorous thought and vigorous action. Harris considers trust ('a well founded absence of suspicion about another person's motives or likely patterns of behaviour; a goodwill that entails vulnerability and particular expectations') as one possible model of social relations that we might consider as a guide to political life. The other is love ('a deep warmth that varies with the needs of another and involves specific qualities of hospitality, attention, and affection, amongst others'). The essay compares trust and love as possible ethical frameworks for political activity. Harris carefully considers what conceptually distinguishes trust from love, and also what role each can have in social relations. He concludes that love, as a value and as a relational ethic (that is, a body of norms which regulate how we relate to one another), is more appealing than trust. Love, unlike trust, has a connection to justice and can justify conflict. According to Harris, trust is 'colder' and unequipped to serve as a foundation for solidarity, cooperation, and collective action in the political domain.

In chapter six, Chiara Destri takes up the point of view of democratic politics. The starting point of Destri's analysis is the claim that trust plays a significant role in democratic politics, a claim which we are invited to unpack carefully. The relationship between trust and democracy, Destri signals, is more complex, nuanced, and much less straightforward than it may seem. Two questions are addressed in the essay: one asks whether citizens' trust in their representatives is warranted; the other asks what follows from the fact that such trust is often unwarranted. There are two empirical assumptions behind these questions: the first is that citizens trust their representatives; the second is that citizens' trust in their representatives is frequently misplaced. The kernel of the essay, however, is the classic political philosophy problem of the nature of the relationship between individuals (and political communities) and the state (or, in an increasingly global landscape, the political institutions which regulate life in society). Destri engages with the philosophical literature on trust and formulates a working notion, which she then goes on to use surgically to argue that trust in political representatives is only very weakly justifiable. The essay argues that the use of the language of trust is an important means of signalling both the discretionary character of the power of representatives and the vulnerability of individuals within representative democracies. The use of the language of trust, Destri suggests, contributes to an enhanced culture of political accountability. This view may be in line with Onora O'Neill's claim[15] that demands for accountability tend to stem from distrust, and, more significantly, that a culture of accountability gives rise to a culture of suspicion. It may also very well be, as some scholars suggest,[16] that democratic politics is particularly vulnerable to certain forms of wrongful manipulation,[17] understood as one of many ways of betraying trust.

Betrayal is one of the themes addressed in Annalise Acorn's contribution to this volume (chapter seven). Acorn's essay looks closely at the place of trust in the relationship between Indigenous people and the Canadian state since the mid-eighteenth century. There is a combined focus on the history of the relationship and on conceptual questions about trust. Four concerns stand out from among the rich fabric of Acorn's chapter. The first is the question of what the colonial history of Canada can tell us about the ways in which Indigenous people have been induced to trust the state. The second is the question of what reasons people have (deliberately been offered) for trusting the state. The third question is what is required when trust is betrayed. The final concern is one about the value of being precise and specific about objects of trust. An important distinction between the use of the language of trust, on the one hand, and genuine trust or responsiveness to the trust of others, on the other, surfaces at the outset and remains present throughout the chapter, calling our attention to the difference between trusting someone and wanting to believe that they will do what they promise to do. It is possible to use the language of trust to signal both that one deeply values and wants to cultivate a genuinely trusting relationship, and that one feels betrayed and justified in one's distrust of another. The essay ends by suggesting that the key to a solid foundation for a future relationship of trust between Indigenous people and the Canadian state is a clear body of evidence of the state's trustworthiness. The mere appearance of being responsive to the trust of others is not enough.

In chapter eight, Achas Burin argues that trust is an enabling condition for the existence of common property. The essay puts strong emphasis on the conceptual link between trust and vulnerability, as well as on the idea of cooperation in the presence of risk. Burin notes that the predominant scholarly focus on private property is distorting and limiting. In order to provide a trust-based account of common property, Burin looks closely at the legal doctrine of the Public Trust (not to be confused with the political philosophy question of what, if anything,

[15] Onora O'Neill, *A Question of Trust* (CUP, 2002).

[16] Eric Beerbohm and Ryan Davis, 'Gaslighting Citizens', a paper delivered at the NYU Colloquium in Legal, Political and Social Philosophy in 2018 (available at www.law.nyu.edu).

[17] For a selection of philosophical accounts of the logic and moral implications of manipulation, see Christian Coons and Michael Weber (eds) *Manipulation: Theory and Practice* (OUP, 2014).

grounds the trust of individuals in their political representatives; or with the fiduciary theory of government), which is pervasive across the Commonwealth. The essay proposes to remedy a mistake perpetuated in discussions of property: the mistake of assuming, as Burin puts it, that cooperative behaviour is impossible and private property the only feasible option. The central aim of Burin's chapter is to offer the reader reasons for accepting the claim that the role of trust in spaces subject to the Public Trust shows that trust is as plausible a way of understanding common property as any rights-based accounts.

Neli Demireva's contribution to this volume (chapter nine) invites us to think about the role of trust in the life of community organisations (also known as voluntary associations), from a sociological point of view. The particular focus of Demireva's essay is on the possible causal link between governmental funding cuts to voluntary associations and a weakening of social trust. Demireva uses the United Kingdom as a source of empirical evidence on the basis of which the essay outlines a research agenda. For example, Demireva notes that deprived areas in which there is a high number of individuals who declare themselves not to be inclined to trust others have experienced a significant decrease in services in the last 10 years. While noting, with Fukuyama, that it is difficult for public policy to shape social capital, Demireva claims that there is strong evidence that funding cuts to community organisations undermine, reduce and even eliminate opportunities for spontaneous, self-selecting social groups which both reflect and enhance the value of social trust.

Part III of this volume includes five essays on trust, evidence, authority and the law. The first essay (chapter ten), by William Twining, examines key concepts in the literature on evidence and testimony, in common law contexts. Twining looks closely at the place of trust and trustworthiness in making sense of certain standard legal distinctions on the issue of the credibility of witnesses and witness testimony. It is precisely in the domain of witness testimony that some crucial questions about the value of epistemic trust have been raised in the philosophical literature. Some have noted[18] that a particular form of injustice is committed against a person when their credibility as a knower is undermined by prejudice. In such instances of epistemic/testimonial injustice a person is deprived of their epistemic self-trust and also of the sense of being believed and trusted as a knower. These philosophical questions are not addressed by Twining in his essay, but the distinctions drawn clarify the legal and moral considerations involved in assessing the credibility of witnesses both in a court setting and in extra judicial proceedings. The essay focuses mainly the concepts of competency and credibility, and Twining devotes special attention to the development of the concept of competence in English law. According to Twining, the history of the development of common law evidence discourse has moved from focus on excluding general types of evidence (eg hearsay) and classes of witnesses (eg, non-Anglicans,

[18] Miranda Fricker, *Epistemic Injustice: Power and the Ethics of Knowing* (OUP, 2007).

women, children, convicted felons, the accused) towards admitting most relevant evidence and types of witness and testing credibility by reference to the particular circumstances of a specific case. Twining notes that in the early nineteenth century Jeremy Bentham attacked all exclusionary rules of evidence, with special emphasis on the ones making many kinds of witness incompetent. Twining's essay notes that 'trustworthiness' is no longer a term of art in this context because the concept of credibility allows us to see more clearly the range of ways in which testimonial evidence may be doubted. For example, Twining tells us that veracity is only one of the tests of credibility. The essay notes that, though Bentham's views eventually triumphed, his analysis of trustworthiness is still worthy of attention.

Giuliano Mori assumes that trusting is a choice, an act of will. But the central view in his essay (chapter Eleven) is that trusting someone and believing that they are trustworthy are conceptually different things. Mori's analysis illuminates relations among trust, truth, veracity, authenticity and canonical (as opposed to apocryphal) authority, from the perspective of cultural and intellectual history (from Late Antiquity to the Middle Ages). His particular interest is in instances in which trust is mediated by a particular object (eg, a relic or a text). The central (descriptive) claim of Mori's essay, which is supported by various examples, is that trust can precede evidence of trustworthiness and can, in fact, be highly resistant to evidence of untrustworthiness. Conceptually speaking, Mori invites us to question two things: the idea that a belief in trustworthiness is constitutive of the attitude of trust, and the suggestion that a claim to authority entails a claim to trustworthiness.

Chapter Twelve examines the way in which public trust in science and in scientific experts was framed, exemplified and theorised during the 2012 criminal court proceedings which took place in the city of L'Aquila, in central Italy, in the aftermath of a violent and destructive earthquake which caused the deaths of 300 people. At the end of the trial, a group of seismologists and civil protection experts were found guilty of manslaughter. Federico Brandmayr's choice of case study is explained by a tension of two different narratives when public trust in science (in particular where risk assessment is involved) is considered: on the one hand, there is a narrative of betrayal, according to which experts have failed to live up to the legitimate expectations of the addressees of their scientific accounts; on the other hand, there is a narrative according to which the defendants were the victims of a campaign which actively enhanced distrust in them, either purely out of ignorance of the role and limits of scientific knowledge or for politically motivated reasons. Brandmayr unpacks and analyses both the trial and its media coverage and looks closely at how the different legal actors (judges, prosecutors, counsel, witnesses and defendants) articulated and negotiated the meaning of 'trust', how they assessed social and behavioural scientific evidence about trust in science, and how they structured and used different arguments in favour of or against particular legal outcomes.

Marta Morvillo's essay (chapter Thirteen) takes the question of the relationship between authority (epistemic and practical) and trust in science into the domain of food governance in the EU. Assuming that there is a coessential relationship between expertise and trust in this field, Morvillo reflects on the role of regulatory experts in risk regulation and analyses the ways in which the law itself (more specifically, the General Food Law – Regulation 178/2002) presents itself as a purported source of reasons for citizens to place their trust on EU regulatory expertise. Significantly, Morvillo notes that the terms 'trust' and 'confidence' are used interchangeably in discourse around the Regulation. Public confidence in the functioning of the legal structures of EU food governance is considered essential to the sound functioning of the internal market. The broad political theory question at the heart of Morvillo's essay is the difficult but urgent question of the place, status and justification of regulatory expertise in a democratic polity. The boundaries between theoretical authority and practical authority are particularly difficult to trace when it is not clear where the 'knowledge provider' status of experts ends and their 'science policy-making' role begins. Such blurred boundaries give rise to complex issues of accountability and responsibility which it is in our best interest to identify and address. Morvillo argues that the fact of legal formalisation in the field of EU food governance gives trust scholars a reason to take legal analysis and authoritative legal justifications seriously when addressing the issue of public trust in expertise. Morvillo puts special focus on the trust-enhancing aspects of the Regulation and argues that epistemic delegation (which, on her view, defines the relationship between citizens and experts) is, by definition, a manifestation of trust which, in the EU food regulation setting, is institutionally and legally mediated. The central aim of the essay is to clarify and articulate the meaning of 'trusted science' both generally and in the normative practices of the European Food Safety Authority.

One particularly noteworthy example of an increased interest in and reliance on the concepts of trust and trustworthiness in legal practice, doctrine and scholarship is the development of the principle of mutual trust as a constitutional principle of EU Law, by the Court of Justice of the European Union (CJEU) in the last decade or so. The jurisprudence of the court is accompanied by a growing body of scholarly literature on the meaning of 'trust', and on the scope of the principle in EU law, its application and its limits. The increasingly central role given to trust by both the CJEU and EU law scholars also partly explains why constitutional and public law theorists are becoming more interested in trust both as an attitude and as a political virtue. It also further encourages us, following Max Harris's invitation in chapter five, to seriously ask the question of the desirability of a political ethics of trust. In the final essay of this volume (chapter Fourteen), Birgit Aasa takes on the task of unpacking the EU principle of mutual trust. Aasa focuses on the often overlooked EU policy area of judicial cooperation in civil justice matters. One underlying assumption of Aasa's essay is that the judiciary has a role to play (perhaps a decisive, distinctive one) in promoting 'systemic trust' both in the law and in the constitutional project of the EU. Aasa argues that a sharper concept of trust can help to improve legal analysis of the (purportedly legal and constitutional) principle of mutual trust and that 'genuine trust-building' in the EU is a necessary and urgent concern. If mutual trust among member states is to be taken as a presumption in the EU constitutional setting (in particular, in the crucial Area of Freedom, Security and Justice), and if courts have a distinctive role to play in fostering public trust in the legal system, what gives the principle of mutual trust its conceptual edge? Is there a distinction with a difference between fostering public trust in legal institutions and protecting and defending the rule of law? Do we need trust at all if we have the rule of law?[19]

II. Invitation to Readers

Each contributor to this volume has developed a set of conceptual tools which can be used to reflect on, and make sense of, the relationship between trust and various aspects of social life and political institutions, including the law. The authors and I invite the readers to use the essays collected in this volume as a source of ideas for reflecting on the value of trust in personal relationships and in public life. But the choice of a particular view of society, law and politics by reference to which the virtues of trust and trustworthiness can be understood and organised is left to readers. Trust and trustworthiness are virtues, not remedies.[20] The answer to the question of why trust matters is for readers themselves to seek, find and articulate.

References

Amaya, A and Del Mar, M (eds) (2020). *Virtue, Emotion and Imagination in Law and Legal Reasoning*. Hart Publishing.

Anonymous Iamblichus (1995). 'Exhortation to Philosophy.' In M Gagarin and P Woodruff (eds), *Early Greek Political Thought from Homer to the Sophists*. Cambridge University Press.

Bagnoli, C (ed) (2011). *Morality and the Emotions*. Oxford University Press.

Baier, A (1985). *Postures of the Mind: Essays on Mind and Morals*. University of Minnesota Press.

Baier, A (1986). 'Trust and Anti-Trust', *Ethics* 96 (2): 231–60.

Beerbohm, E and Davis, R (2018). 'Gaslighting Citizens', a paper delivered at the NYU Colloquium in Legal, Political and Social Philosophy in 2018 (available at www.law.nyu.edu).

Coons, C and Weber, M (eds) (2014). *Manipulation: Theory and Practice*. Oxford University Press.

Criddle, E J, Fox-Decent, E, Gold, A S, Kim, S H and Miller P B (eds) (2018). *Fiduciary Government*. Cambridge University Press.

D'Arms, J and Jacobson, D (eds) (2014). *Moral Psychology and Human Agency: Philosophical Essays on the Science of Ethics*. Oxford University Press.

Eco, U (1989) *Foucault's Pendulum* London: Secker & Warburg.

[19] Anonymous Iamblichus, *Exhortation to Philosophy*, in M Gagarin and P Woodruff (eds), *Early Greek Political Thought from Homer to the Sophists* (CUP, 1995): 'The first result of lawfulness [*eunomia*] is trust'.

[20] In her review of *Epistemic Injustice: Power and the Ethics of Knowing*, by Miranda Fricker (OUP, 2007), (2010) 25.2 *Hypathia* 559–464, Rae Langton raises the question of whether cultivating certain virtues can correct wrongs, including injustices (462). Unlike Fricker, Langton is sceptical about the corrective or remedial power of virtue.

Faulkner, P (2011). *Knowledge on Trust.* Oxford University Press.
Faulkner, P and Simpson, T (eds) (2017) *The Philosophy of Trust.* Oxford University Press.
Fox-Decent, E (2011). *Sovereignty's Promise: The State as Fiduciary.* Oxford University Press.
Fricker, M (2007). *Epistemic Injustice: Power and the Ethics of Knowing.* Oxford University Press.
Gardner, J (2018). *From Personal Life to Private Law.* Oxford University Press.
Gardner, J (2019). *Torts and Other Wrongs.* Oxford University Press.
Govier, T (1997). *Social Trust and Human Communities.* McGill-Queen's University Press.
Govier, T (1992). 'Distrust as a Practical Problem', *Journal of Social Philosophy* 23 (1): 52–63.
Hawley, K (2019). *How to Be Trustworthy.* Oxford: Oxford University Press.
Hawley, K (2014). 'Trust, Distrust, and Commitment', *Nous* 48 (1): 1–20.
Herring, J (2020). *Law and the Relational Self.* Cambridge University Press.
Jones, K (1996). 'Trust as an Affective Attitude.' October, *Ethics* 107 (1): 4–25.
King, M L (2018). *Why We Cannot Wait.* Penguin.
Krishnamurthy, M (2015). '(White) Tyranny and the Democratic Value of Distrust.' *The Monist* 98 (4): 391–406.
Langton, R (2007). Review of *Epistemic Injustice: Power and the Ethics of Knowing*, by Miranda Fricker *Hypatia* 25 (2) 459–64.
MacKenzie, C, Rogers, W and Dodds, S (eds) (2014). *Vulnerability: New Essays in Ethics and Feminist Philosophy.*
Miller, P B and Harding, M (eds) (2020). *Fiduciaries and Trust: Ethics, Politics, Economics and Law.* Cambridge University Press.
McMyler, B (2011). *Testimony, Trust, and Authority.* Oxford University Press.
Nussbaum, M (2013). *Creating Capabilities: The Human Development Approach.* Harvard University Press.
Postema, G J (2020). 'Fidelity, Accountability and Trust: Tensions at the Heart of the Rule of Law.', In T Bustamante and T Lopes Decat (eds), *Philosophy of Law as an Integral Part of Philosophy: Essays on the Jurisprudence of Gerald J. Postema.* 33–60, Hart.
O'Neil, O (2002). *A Question of Trust.* Cambridge University Press.
Owens, D (2017). *Normativity and Control. Oxford University Press.*
Sandel, M (2020). *The Tyranny of Merit: What's Become of the Common Good?* Penguin.
Simon, J (ed) (2020). *Routledge Handbook of Trust and Philosophy.*
Smullyan, R (1983). *5000 B.C. and Other Philosophical Fantasies.* New York: St Martin's Press.
Srinivasan, A (2018). 'The Aptness of Anger.' *Journal of Political Philosophy*, 26 (2): 123–44.
Strawson, P (1974). *Freedom and Resentment and Other Essays.* London: Methuen.
Tasioulas, J (2021). 'The Inflation of Concepts.' *Aeon Magazine* (aeon.co), 29 January.
Tilly, C (2005). *Trust and Rule.* Cambridge University Press.
Weatherhill, S (2016). *Law and Values in the EU.* Oxford University Press.
Williams, B (2002). *Truth and Truthfulness.* Princeton University Press.
Zagzebski, L (2012). *Epistemic Authority: A Theory of Trust, Authority, and Autonomy in Belief.* Oxford University Press.

PART I

Formalising Trust

2

Clearing the Jungle: Conceptualising Trust and Trustworthiness

PAUL C BAUER

I. Introduction[1]

The concepts of trust and trustworthiness are widely studied across disciplines such as sociology, political science, psychology, economics, management studies, philosophy, and anthropology. Debates are taking place in parallel, different schools of thought have developed, and anyone interested in the subject matter will encounter a massive number of – partly ambiguous – definitions. Many scholars lament this situation (Bigley and Pearce 1998; Hardin 2006; Hoffman 2002; Hosmer 1995; Lewicki and Bunker 1995; Luhmann 1988; McKnight and Chervany 1996; Nannestad 2008; Rousseau et al. 1998; Shapiro 1987). It has also led to various noteworthy attempts to classify definitions of and research on trust (Bromiley and Cummings 1995; Hosmer 1995; Lewicki and Bunker 1995; McKnight and Chervany 1996; Mishra 1996; Sitkin and Roth 1993). Adding to this unique conceptual complexity, scholars have coined many subconcepts such as 'particularised trust' or 'knowledge-based trust'. To illustrate this profusion of definitions, Table 2.1 gives an overview of a collection of influential definitions. Notably, the number found in the literature is much more significant. For instance, only in the field of organisational trust, Seppänen et al. (2007) have identified over 70 different definitions of trust.

This lack of conceptual agreement has several adverse effects on trust research, particularly in sociology and political science. First, it is challenging to structure

[1] This study is a revised version of an earlier manuscript, of which different versions have been published online (SSRN) and in the Political Concepts Working Paper Series. Some of the ideas presented here mirror ideas in my dissertation (Bauer 2015). I would like to thank the participants of various panels (ECPR Graduate Conference 2012, ECPR General Conference 2013, SVPW conference 2014) and the workshop 'Challenges of civil society in modern democracies' 2012 (Uppsala), as well as anonymous reviewers for their input. I am also grateful to Ryan Carlin, Matthias Fatke, Oscar Gabriel, Diego Gambetta, Birte Gundelach, Richard Traunmüller, Andrej Tusicisny, Didier Ruedin, Max Schaub and anonymous reviewers for discussions and feedback. Most importantly, I would like to thank the two editors Raquel Barradas De Freitas and Sergio Lo Iacono, for stimulating and excellent feedback.

and compare research carried out thus far. While many studies carry the label 'trust' in their title, the concept has lost its theoretical sharpness. We encounter an immense variety of theoretical arguments and empirical measures, eg, trust survey questions behind it. Hence, it would be useful to have a conception that allows us to classify research meaningfully. Second, debates that revolve around these concepts are at cross-purposes. For instance, scholars debate how many forms of trust there are. However, in doing so, they disagree about whether forms of trust designate the considerations on which a trustor's expectations are based, eg, strategic considerations, or about types of different trustees at whom the expectations may be directed, eg, a government or a party (cp Fisher, Heerde-Hudson, and Tucker 2011; Fisher, Heerde, and Tucker 2010; Hooghe 2011). One finds similar debates in the domain of social trust (Freitag and Traunmüller 2009; Freitag and Bauer 2013). Third, scholars blur the distinction between trust and trustworthiness, both in conceptual discussions and studies that link these concepts to other phenomena. The concept of trustworthiness has received much less attention in sociology and political science than the concept of trust. It is rarely defined in the literature, despite being trust's twin concept.

The present chapter pursues the following question: *How can we define the concepts of trust and trustworthiness?* Previous attempts to summarise the conceptual literature on trust have at least to a certain extent embraced the underlying conceptual complexity (eg, Bromiley and Cummings 1995; Hosmer 1995; Lewicki and Bunker 1995; McKnight and Chervany 1996; Mishra 1996; Rousseau et al. 1998; Sitkin and Roth 1993). For instance, Rousseau et al. (1998) survey understandings of trust across disciplines. They conclude that risk and interdependence between trustor and trustee reappear as essential aspects of trust identified across disciplines. Moreover, disciplines 'share the root assumptions that trust is psychological and important to organizational life' (Rousseau et al. 1998, 395).[2] Rousseau et al. (1998, 395) suggest that a widely held view of trust is trusting as a 'psychological state comprising the intention to accept vulnerability based upon positive expectations of the intentions or behavior of another.' In the present study, I would like to take a step further and provide a more systematic definition of trust (and trustworthiness). Rather than providing a classification that accepts the conceptual diversity one finds in trust research or coming up with a completely new account of trust, I aim to systematically analyse leading definitions of trust and trustworthiness and distil some shared criteria. Using those criteria, I will present a unifying view of trust and trustworthiness.

In Section 2, I derive a definition of trust and trustworthiness. Section 3 serves to clarify the difference between trust and trustworthiness and closely linked concepts such as trusting behaviour, cooperation, confidence, and mistrust. The conclusion in Section 4 summarises the chapter. It suggests that it is indeed

[2] See, eg, Owens (2017) for a different view.

possible to derive a more unified understanding of trust from the various conceptual contributions made in the past. This unified understanding, so it seems, is beneficial for analysing trust in daily situations as required of any useful conception in sociology, political science, and related disciplines.

II. Deriving a Definition of Trust and Trustworthiness

First, several scholars agree that trust and trustworthiness play a role in situations that can be described using few parameters (Baier 1986; Hardin 1992, 154, 2002; Luhmann 1979, 27; Sztompka 1999, 55). For instance, Baier (1986) points to the importance of differentiating between different trustees and the expected behaviour in this relation, thus, 'taking trust to be a three-place predicate (A trusts B with valued thing C)' (Baier 1986, 236). Slightly reformulated, when speaking about trust, we essentially speak about a trustor A_i that trusts (judges the trustworthiness of) the trustee B_j with regard to some behaviour X_k (X_k is often called the object to trust). Turning this statement around, we may reason about a trustee B_j who is trustworthy with regard to some behaviour X_k and judged by trustor A_i. These three parameters are subtle and may be replaced with different real-life trustees and behaviours, as indicated by the indices i, j, and k. This formulation also illustrates that differentiating between trust and trustworthiness is of fundamental importance. A trustee could be trustworthy, eg, never lie, independently of whatever level of trust the trustor has in him, in fact, independently of whether he is trusted by anyone (Levi and Stoker 2000, 476). For Yamagishi et al. (1994), a trustor's overestimation of a trustee's trustworthiness is part of the concept of trust. Importantly, the term behaviour above subsumes both situations in which someone is trusted to do something or trusted not to do something (eg, Offe 1999, 47).

Table 2.1 Various influential definitions of trust

Author(s)	Definition
Baier (1986)	Baier (1986, 235) asserts that '[t]rust … is accepted vulnerability to another's possible but not expected ill will (or lack of good will) toward one'.
Barber (1983)	Barber (1983, 96–98) outlines that trust describes various types of expectations that social actors have of one another in social relationships and social systems and differentiates between general and specific subtypes.
Dasgupta (1988)	'In defining trust I have spoken of one's expectations regarding others' choice of actions that have a bearing on one's own choice of action' (Dasgupta 1988, 53).

(continued)

Table 2.1 ***(Continued)***

Author(s)	Definition
Deutsch (1960)	Deutsch (1960, 124) describes the essential features of trust situations: an individual is confronted with 'a choice to trust or not in the behaviour of another person', namely that the 'individual is confronted with an ambiguous path, a path that can lead either to an event perceived to be beneficial or to an event perceived to be harmful'.
Gambetta (1988)	'trust (or, symmetrically, distrust) is a particular level of the subjective probability with which an agent assesses that another agent or group of agents will perform a particular action, both before he can monitor such action (or independently of his capacity ever to be able to monitor it) and in a context in which it affects his own action' (Gambetta 1988, 217).
Hardin (2002)	'trust as encapsulated interest' (Hardin 2002, 1); 'I trust you because I think it is in your interest to take my interests in the relevant matter seriously' (Hardin 2002, 1); 'incentive compatibility, while necessary, is not sufficient for that account, which further requires that the trusted values the continuation of the relationship with the trustor and has compatible interests at least in part for this reason' (Hardin 2002, 5).
Luhmann (1988)	'trust is a solution for specific problems of risk' (Luhmann 1988, 95); 'Both concepts [trust and confidence] refer to expectations which may lapse into disappointments' (Luhmann 1988, 97); 'Trust, on the other hand, requires a previous engagement on your part. It presupposes a situation of risk' (Luhmann 1988, 97); 'If you choose one action in preference to others in spite of the possibility of being disappointed by the action of others, you define the situation as one of trust' (Luhmann 1988, 97).
Mayer, Davis and Schoorman (1995)	Trust is the 'willingness of a party to be vulnerable to the actions of another party based on the expectation that the other will perform a particular action important to the trustor, irrespective of the ability to monitor or control that other party' (Mayer, Davis, and Schoorman 1995, 712).
Offe (1999)	'Trust is the belief concerning the action that is to be expected from others. The belief refers to probabilities that (certain categories of) others will do certain things or refrain from doing certain things, which in either case affects the well-being of the holder of the belief, as well as possibly the well-being of others or a relevant collectivity' (Offe 1999, 47).
Sztompka (1999)	'Trust is a bet about the future contingent actions of others' (Sztompka 1999, 25); 'trust consists of two main components: beliefs and commitment' (Sztompka 1999, 25); 'Trust is more than just contemplative consideration of future possibilities. We must also face the future actively, by committing ourselves to action […] trust involves commitment through action' (Sztompka 1999, 26).

(continued)

Table 2.1 *(Continued)*

Author(s)	Definition
Yamagishi, Toshio, and Midori (1994)	'Trust can thus be defined as a bias in the processing of imperfect information about the partner's intentions. A trusting person is the one who overestimates the benignity of the partner's intentions beyond the level warranted by the prudent assessment of the available information' (Yamagishi, Toshio, and Midori 1994, 136).
Rotter (1967)	'Interpersonal trust is defined here as an expectancy held by an individual or a group that the word, promise, verbal or written statement of another individual or group can be relied upon' (Rotter 1967, 651).

Second, both concepts are related to the idea of probability. The idea of trust as a subjective probability – a belief formed as a result of probabilistic reasoning – is fairly common (cp Hoffman 2002, 379). Several authors directly refer to 'probability' in their definitions. For instance, Gambetta (1988, 217) asserts that trust 'is a particular level of the subjective probability with which an agent assesses [...] another agent'. Similarly, Offe (1999, 47) writes that trust is a belief that 'refers to probabilities that [...] others will do certain things or refrain from doing certain things'. Dasgupta (1988, 62, 65–66) uses the example of a customer who is unsure whether a salesman is trustworthy or untrustworthy and 'imputes a (subjective) probability p to the salesman being honest'. Coleman (1990, 99) does not explicitly define trust as a subjective probability; however, he develops a formal model for the 'placement of trust' in which the mentioned subjective probability appears as an expectation. The above definitions are widely cited by other scholars in the field, who also seem to have embraced the idea of trust as a probability. This probability quantifies the belief that the trusted person will do what one is expecting her to do.

The idea of trustworthiness as a probability is seldomly explicitly stated in the literature. For instance, Rotter and Stein (1971, 335) mention a probability in their discussion of trustworthiness: '[T]rust and trustworthiness are closely related. The less trusting an individual, the more he is likely to lie or to deceive others'. Here trustworthiness describes the probability of lying or deceiving others. Commonly, scholars discuss attributes or factors that may raise trustworthiness, ie, the probability that one behaves according to the trustor's expectations. According to Mayer, Davis, and Schoorman (1995, 716–17), a trustee's most essential characteristics, which consistently reappear, are ability, benevolence, and integrity. Likewise, Levi and Stoker (2000, 476) define trustworthiness referring to attributes a trustee B_j might possess: 'a commitment to act in the interests of the trustor because of moral values [...], caring about the trustor, incentive compatibility, or some combination of all three' and second, 'competence in the domain over which trust is being given'. McKnight and Chervany (1996, 34–35), Hardin (2002, 28–29) and Bacharach and Gambetta (2001, 153) provide similar arguments. Hence, although seldomly explicitly stated, the idea that trustworthiness also describes a probability, namely the probability that a trustee acts as expected by the trustor, seems implicit behind many theoretical elaborations. Different attributes of trustworthiness, eg, moral values, may raise this probability. And as mentioned, a trustor's trust and a trustee's trustworthiness may be aligned or not. Importantly, trustworthiness aka trustworthy behaviour as defined here may be the result of a trustee's benevolence, but it might just as well come about because a trustee is selfish, but his interest aligns with that of the trustor, ie, the trustee does not have to be a 'good' person. In a single situation, a trustee can behave trustworthily (1) or not (0), ie, fulfil a trustee's expectation or not (Ermisch et al. 2009). We may then conceive trustworthiness as a probability in two ways, first, as the probability that a trustee will behave trustworthily in the future. Importantly, this probability does not need to be equal to the trustor's subjective estimate but should instead be understood as the 'correct' belief, the 'correct' probability that she will do – in the future – what she is being trusted to do. Second, trustworthiness can be seen as the probability of trustworthy behaviour across situations, ie, the frequency of trustworthy behaviour. Such situations may concern repeated behaviour by a single trustee, one-off behaviour by a group of people, or repeated behaviour by a group of people. For instance, if a trustee returns a loan to a trustor (eg, a friend or the employee of a bank) ten out of ten times, we will say that her trustworthiness is one. If six out of a group of ten debtors return their loan, this group's trustworthiness will be 0.6.

Third, there is also a temporal dimension to the concepts. When we speak about trust, it is a generally accepted notion that trust refers to an individual's expectation at a particular point in time t_0 about a trustee's future behaviour at t_1. Many authors follow this idea, even if their definitions differ in many other respects (Bacharach and Gambetta 2001, 150; Baier 1986, 235; Barber 1983, 96:8–9; Dasgupta 1988; Gambetta 1988, 217; Hoffman 2002, 378; Luhmann 1988, 712; Offe 1999, 47, 25). Expectations held in the present at t_0 that concern behaviour in the future t_1 are often related to past expectations at t_{-1}, which may be revised after collecting relevant experiences. Similarly, most scholars do not directly define trustworthiness with regard to time but instead discuss factors that might impact the future behaviour of someone, eg, the willingness and ability to behave in a certain way (McKnight and Chervany 1996, 34).

Fourth, trust situations are also defined by A_i's preference with regard to a trustee's behaviour. A_i prefers that B_j displays trustworthy behaviour X_k (eg, keeps the secret) rather than the corresponding untrustworthy behaviour $\neg X_k$ (eg, does not keep the secret). By adding this assumption to the definition, trust is set apart from A's simple expectations. And trustworthiness (the trustee's behaviour) is set apart from simple behaviours since the trustor's perspective defines it, ie, trustworthy behaviour is what the trustor views as trustworthy. This idea is reflected in many accounts of trust and trustworthiness, mostly because authors refer to the fact that trust and trustworthiness are related to the interest of the trustor (eg, Hardin 2002; Levi and Stoker 2000; McKnight and Chervany 1996), which we would probably argue is linked to the trustor's preference. Others do so more directly by restricting X to behaviour that at least seems to be in the interest of the trustor. For instance, Rotter (1967) refers to truth-telling. However, trust definitions that only refer to a trustor's interest fail to specify the perspective from which they define trustworthiness. Hence, I prefer referring to a trustor's preference because it is the subjective nature of a trustor's preferences that matters in trust situations. From the perspective of an outside observer, a trustee could act in the trustor's interest because he lied to her for her own good. However, from the trustor's perspective, this would still feel like a betrayal because the trustee acted against the trustor's preference. Importantly, the definition provided here does not preclude the possibility that a trustor, while feeling cheated or betrayed at first, changes their perspective later on.

Relatedly, linked to the point above, different positions exist on whether a trust definition should include the fact that the trustee has to be aware of the trustor's preference, ie, on whether the trustee has to know the trustor's preference (eg, Ermisch et al. 2009; Hardin 2002). I think this should not be a requirement. Take the following example: A_i takes B_j out to dinner and pays for it. The next time A_i and B_j go out to dinner, A_i expects that B_j will pay, an expectation that seems warranted as mutual invitations are a norm; failure for B_j to do so makes A_i worse off and B_j better off. A_i might not have gone to dinner with B_j if she had known about B_j's behaviour in advance. Trust is A_i's probabilistic expectation P_{Ai} that B_j will pay. Subsequently, B_j can behave trustworthily (pay for the dinner) or not (not pay). If B_j does not pay, B_j does not behave trustworthily in A_i's view.

As a consequence, A_i may adapt her level of trust accordingly. Importantly, this adaption is independent of B_j's knowledge of A_i's preferences since A_i does not need to communicate them to B_j. In other words, trust is related to trustor A_i's subjective perception of the situation, ie, what A_i regards as trustworthy behaviour. Naturally, a third party may conclude that A_i's expectation was exaggerated or that B_j is a good person but could not pay for some unrelated reason. However, this does not matter for the situation and the involved actors since A_i's perception of having been cheated is what matters. Necessitating a trustee's awareness of a trustor's preferences would force us not to use the concepts when discussing trust in and the trustworthiness of trustees that are potentially unaware of the trustor (eg, a car and its owner, a government and its citizens, etc). Naturally, A_i may communicate their preferences to B_j, assuming that knowledge of A_i's preference will increase B_j's trustworthiness. However, B_j's awareness of A_i's preference is not a requirement to speak of trust and trustworthiness. For the same reason, it is also problematic to qualify trustworthy behaviour with adjectives such as 'benevolent' because any such qualification depends on the trustor's perception. It might exclude trust situations that concern the competence of a trustee ('He is the nicest guy on earth, but you can't trust him to return your stuff because he is disorganised').

Fifth, trust and trustworthiness are at stake in all sorts of situations; In their research, scholars of various disciplines differ in how they specify which trustors (A), trustees (B), and behaviours (X) they investigate. Researchers investigate trust judgments of individuals generally, but also those made by more specific groups such as patients (Mechanic and Schlesinger 1996), criminals (Gambetta 2006), and taxi drivers (Gambetta and Hamill 2005). Trustees in empirical research cover strangers but also more specific trustees such as the police or the courts (Tyler and Huo 2002), political parties (Carlin 2014), partisans (Carlin and Love 2013), science and technology (Roberts et al. 2011), sellers (Doney and Cannon 1997) and investments (Bottazzi, Da Rin, and Hellmann 2011) just to name a few. Finally, researchers name a wide variety of behaviours, such as truth-telling (Rotter 1971), concerning which trustees are assessed. An applicable and general conception should be flexible enough to encompass a wide variety of behaviours as well as non-human trustees. This flexibility can be achieved by keeping the abstract placeholders ABX in our conception and replacing them with specific content depending on our research question or the situation we study. For the social sciences, we can generally agree that A should encompass single individuals or groups of individuals. B, in turn, should be a placeholder that can be filled with different content, certainly with single individuals and groups of individuals (eg, a government), but also with physical objects (eg, a dice, a car, a plane) or institutions (eg, a particular law, democracy as a set of institutions, the legal system). X, in turn, may refer to behaviour (or effects) of a different sort, such as 'does not steal my bike', 'protects human rights' and 'won't crash'. As long as researchers clearly state the substance of the elements ABX, this flexibility is very useful. Importantly, the context Y of a situation should matter for trust and trustworthiness (eg, a meeting a stranger in a dark street rather than during the daytime). Accordingly, context Y could either be added to the definition itself or regarded as a cause investigated independently, for instance, if certain behaviours may occur in different contexts.

To sum up, situations of trust and trustworthiness can be described using parameters (normally A_i = trustor; B_j = trustee; X_k = behaviour) and concern trustee's behaviour to which a preference by the trustor A_i is attached. Both concepts designate probabilities. Trust equals a trustor's subjective estimate of the probability that B_j will behave as preferred by A_i. Trustworthiness corresponds either to the 'correct' probability (as belief) or a probability in the frequentist sense, namely the share of trustworthy vs untrustworthy behaviour across a series of situations either by a single or several trustees. Generally, a useful conception should be flexible enough to encompass all sorts of situations. These characteristics may be used to derive the following definition:

Trust P_{A_i} is trustor A_i's estimate of the probability P_{B_j} that B_j will display A_i's preferred behaviour X_k, ie, of B_j's trustworthiness.

To give a concrete example: On Monday, Peter (A_{Peter}) may estimate that the probability ($P_{B_{John}}$) that his brother John (B_{John}) returns a borrowed loan at the end of the week is relatively high, eg, 0.7. Peter does not know that John lost his job Monday morning, so a correct guess of John's trustworthiness ($P_{B_{John}}$) would be 0.3. On learning this information on Tuesday, Peter will adapt his expectation, ie, his level of trust ($P_{A_{Peter}}$).

Trust is situational, that is P_{A_i} and P_{B_j} potentially depend on all three elements of the relationship (ABX), and since they are probabilities, they may take on values from 0 to 1. Moreover, P_{A_i} is not necessarily related to P_{B_j} since A_i may over- or underestimate B_j's trustworthiness. Nonetheless, A_i's preference regarding B_j's behaviour is essential. We can use P_{A_i} to designate a single trustor's trust and P_A for several trustors. Analog, P_{B_j} may designate a single trustee's trustworthiness and P_B the trustworthiness of a group of trustees. The term subjective emphasises that A_i's judgment may be wrong and may deviate from some 'correct' probability.

When studying trust and trustworthiness, we should follow Barber's advice (1983, 96:17) and 'specify the social relationship or social system of reference'. This step details trustors A, trustees B, and behaviours X and thereby defines the situations we are theorising about and the units with which we may try to measure trust and trustworthiness. Clearly, there is a trade-off: The fewer situations are subsumed under the chosen categories for ABX, ie, the fewer situations we theorise about, the more precise our theories about P_A and P_B will probably be.

III. Trusting Behaviour, Cooperation, Confidence, Mistrust, and Risk

The conception derived here can be used to discuss several related conceptual aspects. First, the above understanding establishes that trust is a cognitive attitude (a belief)[3] and not a decision/choice or a behaviour (cp Rousseau et al. 1998, 395).[4] Hardin (2002, 58–60) regards this position as 'trivially evident'; however, some researchers tend to mix expectations and ensuing decisions or behaviours in their theories and definitions. Since trust is an expectation about future behaviour, it is not necessary that some exchange or action takes place. 'Trusting behavior' (Barr 2003) or 'behaviorally exhibited trust' (Fehr et al. 2002), eg, A_i lends 20 euros to B_j, may be a consequence of a certain level of trust, ie, the trustor's subjective probability (eg, $P_{A_i} > 0.7$). Sometimes alleged 'trusting behavior' results from the absence of other behavioural options, coercion, or indifference rather than a high level of trust.[5] In other words, it may be consistent with many alternative specifications of expectations (Manski 2004, 1330).

Differentiating trust from trusting behaviour also helps us to avoid mixing the concept of trust with the concept of cooperation (Cook and Cooper 2003, 213). It is precisely the interest in the latter concept that motivates many researchers to study trust. Cooperation describes situations in which an individual willingly acts in a manner that contributes to the others' welfare (Diekmann and Lindenberg 2001), ie, a trustor engages in cooperative behaviour when she acts in a way that benefits

[3] While being a cognitive attitude, trust is not a conative attitude (an intention) or an affective attitude (an emotion) (cf. Faulkner and Simpson 2017, Jones 1996).

[4] Interestingly, when queried about their level of trust in a survey, respondents may have to decide between scale points on a trust scale.

[5] At times individuals may act as if they did trust (exhibiting trusting behaviour) for moral, didactic, or prudential reasons. There is also the notion of therapeutic trust (cf. Acorn 2021, same volume).

the trustee or both. If we do not differentiate the two concepts, it leads to circular arguments when relating the concept of trust to the concept of cooperation. In how far trust (as a subjective probability) is related to trusting or cooperative behaviour (ie, what is the threshold?) is a question that can be studied empirically (Bauer et al. 2019).

Second, the difference between trust and confidence can be clarified. Following Luhmann (1988, 97) and Deutsch (1960, 124), we can sensibly argue that the term 'confidence' represents a narrower understanding of trust, namely the case in which the trust judgment exceeds a certain threshold (eg, $P_{A_i} > 0.5$ or 0.8). Deutsch (1960, 124) describes confidence as 'the individual's assumption that the event he desires rather than the event he fears will occur', which would correspond to a value above 0.5 on a probability scale. In principle, one could add that confidence not only implies that the trust judgment exceeds a certain threshold but also that the uncertainty interval around this judgment is tiny (see below).

Third, I suggest not treating trust and mistrust/distrust as distinct concepts (see Cook, Hardin and Levi 2005, 33f; Hardin 2002, 89f; Lagace and Gassenheimer 1989 for opposing opinions; Lewicki and Brinsfield 2012; Wrightsman and Wuescher 1974). Rather than providing an independent definition and measurement of mistrust/distrust, I would simply reverse the scale, eg, a trust level of 0.8 corresponds to a mistrust level of 0.2 (eg, Carlin 2014; Gambetta 1988; Luhmann 1980). For instance, if we ask someone on election day, 'What do you think is the probability that an elected conservative government would decrease unemployment?' then the lower an individual's estimated probability (eg, $P_{A_i} = 0.3$), the higher their level of mistrust and the lower their level of trust. If the probability is low, we would expect individuals to behave as suspicious, distrustful individuals do. For instance, a voter may choose not to vote for a conservative government and abstain from voting if he assumes that it is unlikely that this government would decrease unemployment.

Fourth, contested concepts related to our discussion of trust and trustworthiness are risk and uncertainty. Rousseau et al. (1998, 395) define risk as 'the perceived probability of loss, as interpreted by a decision maker'.[6] In the present account, this perceived probability of loss is nothing else than the complementary probability to a trustor's level of trust P_{A_i}, ie, $R_{A_i} = 1 - P_{A_i}$. When A_i has a high level of trust in B_j, eg, to invite him to a dinner they are having together (eg, $P_{A_i} = 0.9$), then A estimates the risk that B does not invite him as very low (eg, $R_{A_i} = 0.1$ and $P_{A_i} = 0.9$). In that sense, risk as the complementary probability would be the same as mistrust in our conception.

Uncertainty usually describes a situation where we do not know the probabilities attached to outcomes, eg, I do not know with what probability B_j will act trustworthily or untrustworthily. In the present conception, trustor A may be uncertain about his trust judgment, ie, A_i finds himself unable to come up

[6] Citing Chiles and McMackin (1996) and MacCrimmon and Wehrung (1986).

with a precise point estimate of P_{A_i}. Therefore, as depicted in Figure 2.1, trustor A_i may indicate that the probability that B_j is trustworthy lies anywhere within a specific interval. The bigger this interval, the more uncertain A_i is about their trust judgment.

There are some interesting scenarios on such scales. If my trust judgment is 0 per cent or 100 per cent (without any uncertainty), it means that I am sure about how the trustee will behave. However, it is still trust because I do not know what will happen in the end. Adding uncertainty to a conception of trust complicates things. If we compare two persons with the same trust judgment, eg, 70 per cent, but one is very certain about his judgment (no uncertainty interval), and the other is very uncertain about it (eg, an uncertainty interval going from 40% to 100%) we might conclude that the latter has a lower level of trust. However, what is happening is that we redefine the ABX trust situation, which is now about judging, ie, trusting one's own trust judgment.[7] Bacharach and Gambetta (2001) make a similar step in their discussion of trust as a second-order problem.

Figure 2.1 Example of A_i's trust judgement and A_i's potential uncertainty about it

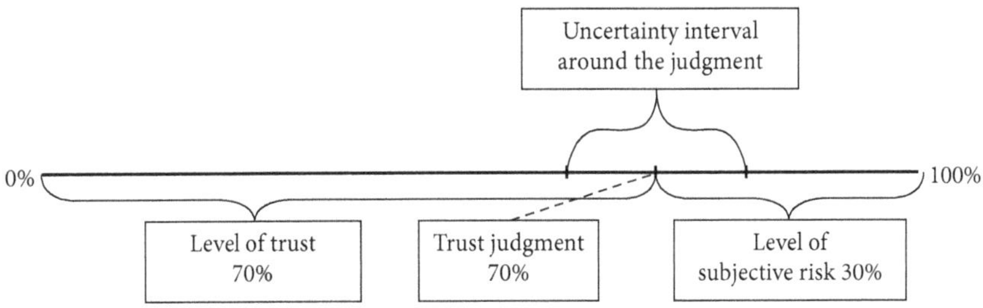

Fifth, when we define trust as a probabilistic expectation, we must specify how it is related to trust decisions, ie, trusting behaviour. In our view, the relation between trust (as a subjective probability) and resulting trusting behaviour is a relation that we have to investigate empirically. To start, trust as a subjective probability is likely to be influenced by different factors (costs, signals, etc). Subsequently, people might act on different thresholds of trust (and conversely subjective risk). However, trusting behaviour might also depend on how certain A_i is about his trust judgment. Suppose A_i is unable to give a precise point estimate such as 0.6 but instead opts for a range of values such as 0.5 to 0.8. In that case, this uncertainty may render A unable to engage in any trusting/cooperative behaviour. Empirically, we would need to query both A_i's trust judgment, how certain A is about his/her judgment and subsequently see if A_i decides to behave accordingly (eg, send the money in a binary trust game) or not. We would expect to find that different trustors need

[7] Importantly, the step from conceptualising trust on such scales and measuring it on such scales is potentially a large one. While such scales are used in practice, they may prove challenging for many individuals (eg, one would assume that exposition to the concept of probability is necessary).

different trust thresholds to engage in trusting behaviour. Importantly, trust as an expectation and precursor to cooperative behaviour may interact with other thought processes or heuristics that may matter in such situations.

IV. Conclusion

The field of trust research has produced an enormous number of conceptualisations. Empirical trust research departs from a smaller set of definitions, but those definitions often do not seem to be very well aligned with the measures used in applied research. The present study was guided by the following question: *How can we define the concepts of trust and trustworthiness?* Building on previous scholarly accounts of trust, I derived the following definition:

> *Trust P_{A_i} is trustor A_i's estimate of the probability P_{B_j} that B_j will display A_i' preferred behaviour X_k, ie, of B_j's trustworthiness.*

The definition presented here is more formal as compared to various earlier ones. I tried to argue that it may function as a systematic umbrella for trust research. I suggest that the definition may serve as a conceptual tool that provides a reliable and useful foundation for future research on trust and trustworthiness. Because of the abstraction, it can apply to various empirical situations by specifying the elements A, B, and X. It compels us to precisely describe what situations we investigate, ie, who the trustors (As) and trustees (Bs) are and what behaviours (Xs) we deem relevant. For instance, studies based on student samples will be marked as such (eg, Glaeser et al. 2000). Also, it should help in clearly delineating the causes and consequences of trust from the concept itself. It also has the potential to lead to more precise ways of measurement. For instance, it compels us to formulate survey questions that refer to specific trustees and an expected behaviour rather than more abstract and vague survey items such as the 'most people' question (Bauer and Freitag 2018).[8] A further contribution lies in the clear distinction between trust and trustworthiness. Trust and trustworthiness may not be aligned because trustors over- or underestimate the trustworthiness of a trustee.

Following previous conceptions, the definition conceptualises trust as a subjective probability. In principle, we could replace 'subjective estimate of the probability P_{Bj}' with the more general terms 'belief' or 'expectation'. This raises the question of why adding the probability notion is useful. The idea that humans pursue probabilistic reasoning in their everyday lives is questionable. Still, a probabilistic conception is a more precise, helpful model to describe trust situations. To what extent we can measure trust as a subjective probability, ie, ask people for the

[8] Most versions of the most-people survey measure are similar to the following question, which is followed by different answer scales: 'Generally speaking, would you say that most people can be trusted, or that you can't be too careful in dealing with people?'

subjective probabilities, is another kettle of fish (Bauer and Freitag 2018). In doing so, we should consider recent advances in this area (eg, Leeman et al. 2021, Delavande and Rohwedder 2008, Manski 2004).

Moreover, I would assume that humans often cooperate with others following simple heuristics ('my doctor is trustworthy'), rather than weighing different factors that may affect others' trustworthiness. And, across repeated social interactions, trust judgments that were not falsified may turn into simple heuristics. For instance, when we make new friends, we will initially make trust judgments, eg, when it comes to sharing delicate information, but after many, repeated interactions information sharing may become a 'rule'. In my view, to speak of trust, there must be a conscious thought process, ie, an individual arriving at an estimate. While cooperative behaviour based on heuristics may appear to be based on trust, I would differentiate such situations from situations that involve trust.

This essay provides multiple avenues for future research. First, just as earlier accounts of trust and trustworthiness, the conception presented here should be critically assessed regarding its practicality. Any conception of trust needs to be battle-tested in terms of its theoretical but also empirical usefulness. One idea is to devise and test measures that closely reflect the presented trust conception, eg, the idea of trust as a subjective probability. Within trust research, such measures are used rarely. Such data is collected indirectly in experimental research (eg, Ermisch and Gambetta 2010, 370). Second, while current empirical research relies mostly on broad and somewhat vague concepts, such as generalised trust, there is ample research investigating specific situations (eg, Carlin 2014; Gambetta and Hamill 2005; Mechanic and Schlesinger 1996). A fruitful avenue could be to explore cross-situational trust–understood as an individual's average trust score across her judgments of many different situations–as an alternative to generalised trust (Bauer and Freitag 2018, Robbins 2016). Moving into this direction, scholars recently started to investigate the relationship between generalised trust and more specific forms of trust that fall under the suggested definition (eg, Robbins 2015, 2019). Such investigations seem worthwhile since research on the causes and consequences of trust and trustworthiness and measures of the same concepts will benefit when we set clear boundaries regarding the situations we study.

References

Acorn, Annalise. 2021. 'The Language of Trust Without the Attitude of Trust: Repairing Relations Between Indigenous People and the Canadian State.' In *Trust Matters: Cross-Disciplinary Essays*, edited by Raquel Barradas De Freitas and Sergio Lo Iacono. Hart Publishing.

Bacharach, Michael, and Diego Gambetta. 2001. 'Trust in Signs.' In *Trust in Society*, edited by Karen S Cook, 148–84. New York: Russell Sage Foundation.

Baier, Annette. 1986. 'Trust and Antitrust.' *Ethics* 96: 231–60.

Barber, Bernard. 1983. *The Logic and Limits of Trust* Vol 96. New Brunswick, NJ: Rutgers University Press New Brunswick, NJ.

Barr, Abigail. 2003. 'Trust and Expected Trustworthiness: Experimental Evidence from Zimbabwean Villages.' *The Economic Journal of Nepal* 113 (489): 614–30.

Bauer, Paul C 2015. 'Three Essays on the Concept of Trust and Its Foundations.' PhD thesis, University of Bern, Switzerland.

Bauer, Paul C and Markus Freitag. 2018. 'Measuring Trust.' In Eric M Uslaner (Ed), *The Oxford Handbook of Social and Political Trust*, 1–27. Oxford: Oxford University Press.

Bauer, Paul C, Florian Keusch and Frauke Kreuter. 2019. 'Trust and Cooperation: Evidence from the Realm of Data-Sharing.'

Bigley, Gregory A and Jone L Pearce. 1998. 'Straining for Shared Meaning in Organization Science: Problems of Trust and Distrust.' *Academy of Management Review. Academy of Management* 23 (3): 405–21.

Bottazzi, Laura, Marco Da Rin and Thomas F Hellmann. 2011. 'The Importance of Trust for Investment: Evidence from Venture Capital.' National Bureau of Economic Research.

Brewer, Marilynn B 1981. 'Ethnocentrism and Its Role in Interpersonal Trust.' In Marilyn B Brewer (Ed), *Scientific Inquiry and the Social Sciences: A Volume in Honor of Donald T. Campbell* 214–31. San Francisco: Jossey-Bass.

Bromiley, Philip and Larry L Cummings. 1995. 'Transactions Costs in Organizations with Trust.' *Research on Negotiation in Organizations* 5: 219–50.

Carlin, Ryan E 2014. 'What's Not to Trust? Rubrics of Political Party Trustworthiness in Chile and Argentina.' *Party Politics* 20 (1): 63–77.

Carlin, Ryan E and Gregory J Love. 2013. 'The Politics of Interpersonal Trust and Reciprocity: An Experimental Approach.' *Political Behavior* 1–21.

Chiles, Todd H and John F McMackin. 1996. 'Integrating Variable Risk Preferences, Trust, and Transaction Cost Economics.' *Academy of Management Review. Academy of Management* 21 (1): 73–99.

Coleman, James S 1990. *Foundations of Social Theory*. Cambridge: Harvard University Press.

Colquitt, Jason A, Brent A Scott and Jeffery A LePine. 2007. 'Trust, Trustworthiness, and Trust Propensity: A Meta-Analytic Test of Their Unique Relationships with Risk Taking and Job Performance.' *The Journal of Applied Psychology* 92 (4): 909–27.

Cook, Karen S and Robin M Cooper. 2003. 'Experimental Studies of Cooperation, Trust, and Social Exchange.' In Elinor Ostrom and J. Walker (Eds), *Trust and Reciprocity: Interdisciplinary Lessons for Experimental Research*, 209–44. New York: Russell Sage Foundation.

Cook, Karen S, Russell Hardin and Margaret Levi. 2005. *Cooperation Without Trust?* New York: Russell Sage Foundation.

Dasgupta, Partha. 1988. 'Trust as a Commodity.' In *Trust: Making and Breaking Cooperative Relations*, edited by Diego Gambetta, 49–72. New York: Basil Blackwell.

Delavande, Adeline, Susann Rohwedder. 2008. 'Eliciting Subjective Probabilities in Internet Surveys.' *Public Opinion Quarterly* 72 (5): 866–91.

Delhey, Jan, Kenneth Newton and Christian Welzel. 2011. 'How General Is Trust in 'Most People'? Solving the Radius of Trust Problem.' *American Sociological Review* 76 (5): 786–807.

Deutsch, Morton. 1960. 'The Effect of Motivational Orientation Upon Trust and Suspicion.' *Human Relations; Studies Towards the Integration of the Social Sciences* 13 (2): 123–39.

Dinesen, Peter Thisted. 2011. 'When in Rome, Do as the Romans Do? An Analysis of the Acculturation of Generalized Trust of Non-Western Immigrants in Western Europe.' PhD thesis, Aarhus Universitet.

Doney, Patricia M and Joseph P Cannon. 1997. 'An Examination of the Nature of Trust in Buyer-Seller Relationships.' *The Journal of Marketing* 35–51.

Erikson, Emily and Joseph M Parent. 2007. 'Central Authority and Order.' *Sociological Theory* 25 (3): 245–67.

Erikson, Erik H 1959. 'Growth and Crisis of the Healthy Personality.' In Erik H Erikson (Ed), *Psychological Issues: Selected Papers* 1 (1) 51–107. New York: International Universities Press.

Ermisch, John and Diego Gambetta. 2010. 'Do Strong Family Ties Inhibit Trust?' *Journal of Economic Behavior & Organization* 75: 365–76.

Ermisch, John, Diego Gambetta, Heather Laurie, Thomas Siedler and S C Noah Uhrig. 2009. 'Measuring People's Trust.' *Journal of the Royal Statistical Society* 172 (4): 749–69.

Faulkner, Paul and Thomas Simpson. 2017. 'Introduction.' In *The Philosophy of Trust*. Oxford: Oxford University Press.

Fehr, Ernst, Urs Fischbacher, Bernhard von Rosenbladt, Jürgen Schupp and Gert G Wagner. 2002. 'A Nation-Wide Laboratory. Examining Trust and Trustworthiness by Integrating Behavioral Experiments into Representative Surveys.' *Schmollers Jahrbuch* 122 (4): 519–42.

Fisher, Justin, Jennifer van Heerde-Hudson and Andrew Tucker. 2011. 'Why Both Theory and Empirics Suggest There Is More Than One Form of Trust: A Response to Hooghe.' *British Journal of Politics and International Relations* 13: 276–81.

Fisher, Justin, Jennifer van Heerde and Andrew Tucker. 2010. 'Does One Trust Judgement Fit All? Linking Theory and Empirics.' *British Journal of Politics and International Relations* 12 (2): 161–88.

Freitag, Markus and Richard Traunmüller. 2009. 'Spheres of Trust: An Empirical Analysis of the Foundations of Particularised and Generalised Trust.' *European Journal of Political Research* 48: 782–803.

Freitag, M and P C Bauer. 2013. 'Testing for Measurement Equivalence in Surveys: Dimensions of Social Trust Across Cultural Contexts.' *Public Opinion Quarterly* S1: 24–44.

Fukuyama, Francis. 2001. 'Social Capital, Civil Society and Development.' *Third World Quarterly* 22 (1): 7–20.

Gambetta, Diego. 1988. 'Can We Trust Trust?' In Diego Gambetta (Ed), *Trust: Making and Breaking Cooperative Relations*, 213–37. Cambridge, Massachusetts: Basil Blackwell.

——. 2006. 'Trust's Odd Ways.' *Understanding Choice, Explaining Behaviour. Essays in Honour of Ole-Jorgen Skog, Oslo Academic Press, Oslo.*

Gambetta, Diego and Heather Hamill. 2005. *Streetwise: How Taxi Drivers Establish Customer's Trustworthiness*. Russell Sage Foundation.

Glaeser, Edward L, David I Laibson, Jose A Scheinkman and Christine L Soutter. 2000. 'Measuring Trust.' *The Quarterly Journal of Economics* 115 (3): 811–46.

Glanville, Jennifer L and Pamela Paxton. 2007. 'How Do We Learn to Trust? A Confirmatory Tetrad Analysis of the Sources of Generalized Trust.' *Social Psychology Quarterly* 70 (3): 230–42.

Hardin, Russell. 1992. 'The Street-Level Epistemology of Trust.' *Analyse & Kritik* 14: 152–76.

——. 2002. *Trust and Trustworthiness*. New York: Russell Sage Foundation.

——. 2006. *Trust*. Cambridge: Polity.

Harrison, Lawrence E 1985. *Underdevelopment Is a State of Mind: The Latin American Case*. New York: Madison Books.

Harriss, John. 2003. "Widening the Radius of Trust': Ethnographic Explorations of Trust and Indian Business.' *The Journal of the Royal Anthropological Institute* 9 (4): 755–73.

Hetherington, Marc J and Jason A Husser. 2012. 'How Trust Matters: The Changing Political Relevance of Political Trust.' *American Journal of Political Science* 56 (2): 312–25.

Hoffman, Aaron M 2002. 'A Conceptualization of Trust in International Relations.' *European Journal of International Relations* 8 (3): 375–401.

Hooghe, Marc. 2011. 'Why There Is Basically Only One Form of Political Trust.' *British Journal of Politics and International Relations* 13 (2): 269–75.

Hosmer, Larue T 1995. 'Trust: The Connecting Link Between Organizational Theory and Philosophical Ethics.' *Academy of Management Review. Academy of Management* 20 (2): 379–403.

Jones, Karen. 1996. 'Trust as an Affective Attitude.' *Ethics* 107 (1): 4–25.

Karakayali, Nedim. 2009. 'Social Distance and Affective Orientations.' *Sociological Forum* 24 (3): 538–62.

Kramer, Roderick M 1999. 'Trust and Distrust in Organizations: Emerging Perspectives, Enduring Questions.' *Annual Review of Psychology* 50: 569–98.

Lagace, Rosemary R and Jule B Gassenheimer. 1989. 'A Measure of Global Trust and Suspicion: Replication.' *Psychological Reports* 65 (2): 473–74.

Leemann, L, Stoetzer, L and Traunmüller, R (2021). 'Eliciting Beliefs as Distributions in Online Surveys.' *Political Analysis*.

Levi, Margaret and Laura Stoker. 2000. 'Political Trust and Trustworthiness.' *Annual Review of Political Science* 3: 475–507.

Lewicki, Roy J and Chad Brinsfield. 2012. 'Measuring Trust Beliefs and Behaviours.' In Fergus Lyon, Guido Mollering and Mark N K Saunders (Eds), *Handbook of Research Methods on Trust*, 29–39. Edward Elgar Publishing.

Lewicki, Roy J and Barbara B Bunker. 1995. 'Trust in Relationships: A Model of Development and Decline.' In Barbara B Bunker and Jeffrey Z Rubin *Conflict, Cooperation, and Justice: Essays Inspired by the Work of Morton Deutsch*, edited by. San Francisco, CA: Jossey-Bass.

Lo Iacono. 2020. 'Who Are You Trusting? A Group-Based Formalisation of Trust.' In Trust Matters.

Luhmann, Niklas. 1979. *Trust and Power*. Chichester: Wiley.

——. 1980. 'Trust: A Mechanism for the Reduction of Social Complexity.' In *Trust and Power*. New York: Wiley.

——. 1988. 'Familiarity, Confidence, Trust: Problems and Alternatives.' In Diego Gambetta (Ed), *Trust: Making and Breaking Cooperative Relations*, 94–107. Cambridge, Massachusetts: Basil Blackwell.

MacCrimmon, Kenneth R and Donald A Wehrung. 1986. 'Taking Risks: The Management of Uncertainty.' New York, NY: Free Press.

Manski, Charles F 2004. 'Measuring Expectations.' *Econometrica: Journal of the Econometric Society* 72 (5): 1329–76.

Mayer, Roger C, James H Davis and F David Schoorman. 1995. 'An Integrative Model of Organizational Trust.' *Academy of Management Review. Academy of Management* 20 (3): 709–34.

McCrae, Robert R and Paul T Costa Jr 2003. *Personality in Adulthood: A Five-Factor Theory Perspective*. New York: The Guilford Press.

McKnight, D Harrison and Norman L Chervany. 1996. 'The Meanings of Trust.'

Mechanic, David and Mark Schlesinger. 1996. 'The Impact of Managed Care on Patients' Trust in Medical Care and Their Physicians.' *JAMA: The Journal of the American Medical Association* 275 (21): 1693–7.

Michel, Torsten. 2013. 'Time to Get Emotional: Phronetic Reflections on the Concept of Trust in International Relations.' *European Journal of International Relations* 19 (4): 869–90.

Mishra, Aneil K 1996. 'Organizational Responses to Crisis: The Centrality of Trust.' In *Trust in Organizations: Frontiers of Theory and Research* 261–87.

Mooradian, Todd, Birgit Renzl and Kurt Matzler. 2006. 'Who Trusts? Personality, Trust and Knowledge Sharing.' *Management Learning* 37 (4): 523–40.

Nannestad, Peter. 2008. 'What Have We Learned About Generalized Trust, If Anything?' *Annual Review of Political Science* 11: 413–36.

Offe, Claus. 1999. 'How Can We Trust Our Fellow Citizens?' In Mark E Warren (Ed), *Democracy and Trust*, 42–87. Cambridge: Cambridge University Press.

Owens, David. 2017. 'Trusting a Promise and Other Things.' In *The Philosophy of Trust*. Oxford: Oxford University Press.

Putnam, Robert David. 2000. *Bowling Alone: The Collapse and Revival of American Community*. New York: Simon & Schuster.

Rathbun, Brian C 2011. 'Before Hegemony: Generalized Trust and the Creation and Design of International Security Organizations.' *International Organization* 65 (2): 243–73.

Realo, Anu, Jüri Allik and Brenna Greenfield. 2008. 'Radius of Trust: Social Capital in Relation to Familism and Institutional Collectivism.' *Journal of Cross-Cultural Psychology* 39 (4): 447–62.

Reeskens, Tim. 2013. 'But Who Are Those 'Most People' That Can Be Trusted? Evaluating the Radius of Trust Across 29 European Societies.' *Social Indicators Research* 114 (2): 703–22.

Robbins, Blaine G 2015. 'From the General to the Specific: How Social Trust Motivates Relational Trust.' *Social Science Research*.

Robbins, Blaine G 2016. 'What Is Trust? A Multidisciplinary Review, Critique, and Synthesis.' *Sociology Compass* 10 (10): 972–86.
Robbins, Blaine G 2019. 'Measuring Generalized Trust: Two New Approaches.' *Sociological Methods & Research* 1–52.
Roberts, Mary Roduta, Grace Reid, Meadow Schroeder and Stephen P Norris. 2011. 'Causal or Spurious? The Relationship of Knowledge and Attitudes to Trust in Science and Technology.' *Public Understanding of Science.*
Rotter, Julian B. 1967. 'A New Scale for the Measurement of Interpersonal Trust.' *Journal of Personality* 35 (4): 651–65.
Rotter, Julian B. 1971. 'Generalized Expectancies for Interpersonal Trust.' *The American Psychologist* 26 (5): 443.
Rotter, Julian B, and Donald K Stein. 1971. 'Public Attitudes Toward the Trustworthiness, Competence, and Altruism of Twenty Selected Occupations.' *Journal of Applied Social Psychology* 1 (4): 334–43.
Rousseau, Denise M, Sim B Sitkin, Ronald S Burt, and Colin Camerer. 1998. 'Not so Different After All: A Cross-Discipline View of Trust.' *Academy of Management Review*. 23 (3): 393–404.
Seppänen, Risto, Kirsimarja Blomqvist and Sanna Sundqvist. 2007. 'Measuring Inter-Organizational Trust–a Critical Review of the Empirical Research in 1990–2003.' *Industrial Marketing Management* 36 (2): 249–65.
Shapiro, Susan P. 1987. 'The Social Control of Impersonal Trust.' *The American Journal of Sociology* 93 (3): 623–58.
Sitkin, Sim B, and Nancy L Roth. 1993. 'Explaining the Limited Effectiveness of Legalistic 'Remedies' for Trust/ Distrust.' *Organization Science* 4 (3): 367–92.
Stolle, Dietlind. 2002. 'Trusting Strangers: The Concept of Generalized Trust in Perspective.' *Österreichische Zeitschrift Für Politikwissenschaft* 31: 397–412.
Sztompka, Piotr. 1999. *Trust: A Sociological Theory*. Cambridge, UK: Cambridge University Press.
Tajfel, Henri. 1974. 'Social Identity and Intergroup Behaviour.' *Social Sciences Information. Information Sur Les Sciences Sociales* 13: 65–93.
Tajfel, Henri, and John C Turner. 1979. 'An Integrative Theory of Intergroup Conflict.' In William G Austin and Stephen Worchel (Eds), *The Social Psychology of Intergroup Relations* 33–48. Pacific Grove, CA: Brooks/Cole.
Tyler, Tom R and Yuen J Huo. 2002. *Trust in the Law: Encouraging Public Cooperation with the Police and Courts* Vol 5. Russell Sage Foundation.
Welch, Michael R, David Sikkink, and Matthew T Loveland. 2007. 'The Radius of Trust: Religion, Social Embeddedness and Trust in Strangers.' *Social Forces; a Scientific Medium of Social Study and Interpretation* 86 (1): 23–46.
Wrightsman, Lawrence S, and M Leslie Wuescher. 1974. *Assumptions About Human Nature: A Social Psychological Approach*. Monterey, CA: Brooks/Cole.
Yamagishi, Toshio, Yamagishi Toshio, and Yamagishi Midori. 1994. 'Trust and Commitment in the United States and Japan.' *Motivation and Emotion* 18 (2): 129–66.

3

Who are We Trusting? A Category-Based Formalisation of Trust

SERGIO LO IACONO, MARTINA TESTORI

I. Introduction

Over the last 30 years, the interest in trust has grown greatly across different disciplines. From economics, psychology and sociology to philosophy and political science, the notion of trust has gained a central position in current academic debates, enriching our understanding of various social phenomena. In 2020 alone, the number of academic publications on trust was about 2,400, in line with a general increase over the years (see Figure 3.1).

Figure 3.1 Number of publications on trust, generalised/social trust and institutional/political trust from 1990 to 2020. Data source: Web of Science[1]

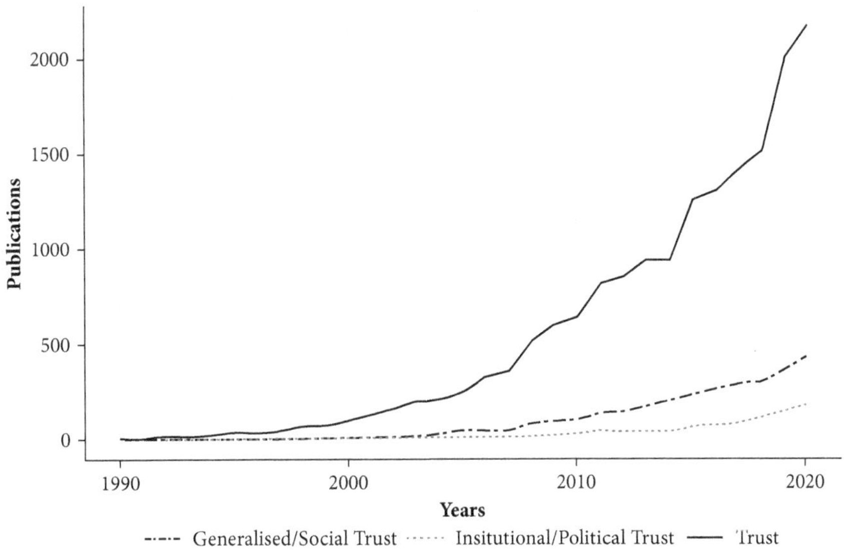

[1] Data collected from Web of Science (https://clarivate.com/products/web-of-science/). Key terms for trust: AK (Author's Keyword) = trust AND KP (Keyword Plus) = trust. For generalised/social trust: AK = (generalised trust OR generalised trust OR social trust) AND KP = (generalised trust OR

The data show that the increasing interest in trust is fairly common across different fields. In Figure 3.2, we show the percentage of academic publications on trust for the following disciplines: sociology, political science, management, psychology, philosophy and economics. Management records the largest growth rate over the past 30 years. In 2020, roughly 2.5% of all management publications concerned trust (the largest percentage among the fields considered). Trust-related publications in political science recorded a spike in the in the last couple of years, reaching 2% of the total publications in the field. Other disciplines also confirm the growing trend since the 1990s, and today trust publications account for roughly 1% of the total publications in economics, sociology, philosophy and psychology.

Figure 3.2 Percentage of publications on trust by discipline from 1990 to 2020. Data source: Web of Science[2]

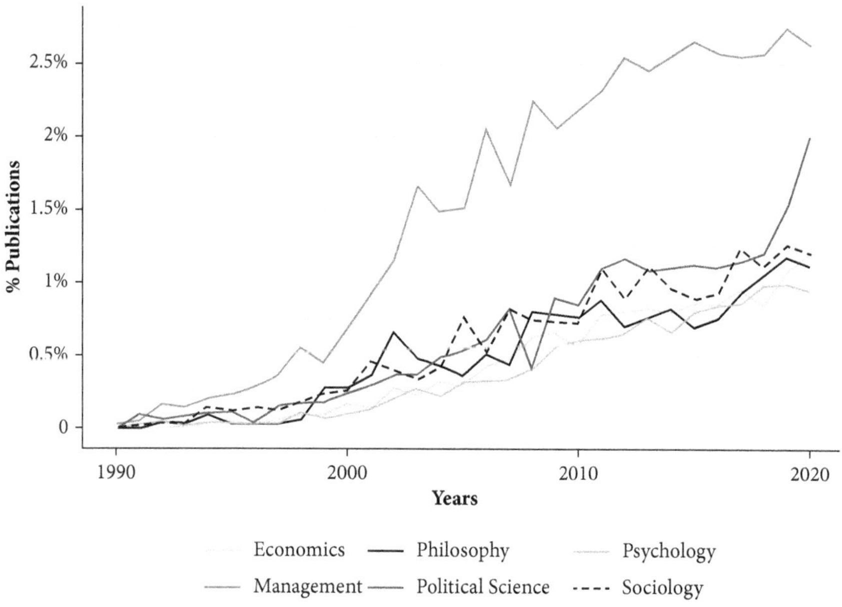

generalised trust OR social trust). For institutional/political trust: AK = (institutional trust OR political trust) AND KP = (institutional trust OR political trust). Timespan: 1990–2020; WC (Web of Science Category): Management, Sociology (including Social Work, Family Studies and Ethnic Studies), Economics, Political Science (including International Relations), Philosophy (including Ethics), Psychology (including P. Developmental, P. Multidisciplinary, P. Applied, P. Social, P. Educational, P. Clinical and P. Experimental).

[2] Data collected from Web of Science (https://clarivate.com/products/web-of-science/).
Key terms: AK(Authors Keyword)=trust AND KP(Keyword Plus)=trust. Timespan: 1990–2020; WC (Web of Science Category): Management, Sociology (including Social Work, Family Studies and Ethnic Studies), Economics, Political Science (including International Relations), Philosophy (including Ethics), Psychology (including P. Developmental, P. Multidisciplinary, P. Applied, P. Social, P. Educational, P. Clinical and P. Experimental).

The popularisation of the notion of trust in the social sciences can be traced back to Niklas Luhmann. In his book *Trust and Power*, published in 1979,[3] the German sociologist emphasised that trust covers an important function in our society (Luhmann, 1979). Luhmann argued that contemporary societies depend strongly on people's positive expectations about others and institutions: in our daily life we are overwhelmed by information that is relevant with regard to the uncertainty characterising the world around us, and that allows us to make informed decisions. However, no individual can exhaustively evaluate such information. To manage this complexity, we need to rely on others. That is, given the impracticability of carefully assessing all facts available, we simply assume that other people, institutions or collective actors will behave as we presume they should, making the uncertainty that surrounds us bearable (at least on psychological grounds). Thus, trusting is not associated with an effective reduction of risk but rather with an increase in our tolerance towards it. In Luhmann's words: '[trust] does not consist in an increase of security with a corresponding decrease in insecurity; it lies conversely in an increase of bearable security at the expense of security' (Luhmann 1979: 79–80). From this perspective, trust accompanies us continually: leaving our children at school, voting in local elections, giving our house keys to a friend are very different actions but they all imply the placing of trust on some actors to do something. We trust the teacher to educate our children properly, the elected representatives to deliver on their campaign promises, and our friend to return the house keys when we need them.

Luhmann's ideas have been well received in the academic community and greatly expanded across fields. In 1986, with the article 'Trust and Antitrust', Annette Baier prompted a discussion on the notion of trust in moral philosophy and greatly influenced Karen Jones' later account of trust as an affective attitude (Baier, 1986; Jones, 1996). Russel Hardin, James Coleman and Diego Gambetta focused on the cognitive and rational dimension of trust, while emphasising its sociological implications (Gambetta, 1988; Hardin, 1993, 2002; Coleman, 1990). In political science, Robert Putnam and Francis Fukuyama further revisited the notion, emphasising its potentially wide and long-lasting effects on a variety of social and political outcomes, such as democratic institutions, social cohesion and institutional performances (Fukuyama, 1995; Putnam, 2000; Putnam, Leonardi and Nanetti, 1993). Progressively, economists also gained interest in how trusting beliefs can affect social exchanges and community wealth (Williamson, 1993). In this regard, Joyce Berg and colleagues devised the so-called 'trust game' to provide an objective measure of trusting behaviours solidly based on game theory (J. Berg, Dickhaut and McCabe, 1995).

Empirical research has also shown a growing interest for trust towards general categories of actors (see Figure 3.1, generalised/social trust and political/institutional trust), indicating its relevance in relation to several social phenomena.

[3] The original years of publication of the book *Trust and Power* are 1973 (*Vertrauen*) and 1975 (*Macht*) in German. In 1979, the book was published in English as *Trust and Power*.

For instance, political trust (ie, trust towards the government) has been carefully monitored over the years and its slow decline in Western societies has been associated with the rise of populism in recent years (Algan, Guriev, Papaioannou and Passari, 2017; Berg, 2021; Newton, Stolle and Zmerli, 2018; Van der Meer, 2017; Van der Meer and Zmerli, 2017). Social trust (ie, trust towards unknown fellow citizens) has been shown to positively correlate with individuals' well-being, social cohesion, more impartial political institutions and lower crime levels (Charron, Dijkstra and Lapuente, 2014; Freitag and Bühlmann, 2009; Helliwell and Putnam, 2004; Kawachi, Kennedy and Wilkinson, 1999; Kennedy, Kawachi, Prothrow-Stith, Lochner and Gupta, 1998; Knack and Keefer, 1997; Lederman, Loayza and Menendez, 2002; Levi, 1998; Lo Iacono, 2019; Lo Iacono and Quaranta, 2019; Messner, Rosenfeld and Baumer, 2004; Putnam, 2000; Putnam et al, 1993; Zak and Knack, 2001). A meta-analysis of 212 effect sizes in the literature indicates that trust is indeed positively intertwined with cooperation, especially in situations where there is a larger conflict of interest between actors (Balliet and Van Lange, 2013). Taken together, such evidence has led several scholars to see trust as a crucial component of democratic, prosperous and cooperative societies (Levi, 1998; Offe, 1999; Ostrom, 1990, 2003; Putnam, 2000).

When we graphically represent the most influential scholars[4] on the topic of trust in the last 30 years alone, we can observe a complex network of authors who have studied and developed the concept as we know it to date; see Figure 3.3. The figure has been constructed by computing the author co-citation network of scholars that have received the highest number of citations in the last 30 years. Different colours indicate different co-citation clusters,[5] which seem to correlate to specific research areas. The network highlights some of the core scholars responsible for the development and the advancement of the work on trust, such as Robert Putnam in political science, James Coleman in sociology, Oliver Williamson in economics, Roger C Mayer and David Gefen in management, Philip M Posdakoff in business, and Ernst Fehr in behavioural economics (Fehr, 2009; Gefen, Karahanna and Straub, 2003; Coleman, 1990; Kosfeld, Heinrichs, Zak, Fischbacher and Fehr, 2005; Podsakoff, MacKenzie, Moorman and Fetter, 1990; Putnam, 2000; Schoorman, Mayer and Davis, 2007; Williamson, 1993). Also, the network depicts a dense grid of connections between scholars from different clusters of research, suggesting the strong interdependency between disciplines studying trust.

[4] Author co-citation network created through VOSviewer (1.6.16) (www.vosviewer.com). Co-citation analysis 'is a method that may be useful for avoiding isolation in scholarship, expediting knowledge integration, and, ultimately, building consilience across disciplines … This method may be useful for strategically selecting information that can build consilience about ideas and constructs that are relevant across a range of disciplines.' (Trujillo and Long, 2018:1). Unit of analysis: cited authors. Counting methods: full counting. Minimum number of citations of an author: 400. Co-citation links are created between two authors that are both cited by the same document. The thicker the link between two authors, the larger the number of articles that cite both authors together.

[5] A co-citation cluster is formed by those authors that are co-cited by a large number of papers. The denser the cluster, the more papers cited those authors together. Cluster normalisation: association strength (parameters: attraction=2, repulsion=1). Note that Web of Science data only includes the first authors of the cited papers, thus limiting the co-citation analysis of authors to the first authors.

Figure 3.3 Author co-citation network on trust publications from 1990 to 2020. Data source: Web of Science. Data analysed with VOSviewer

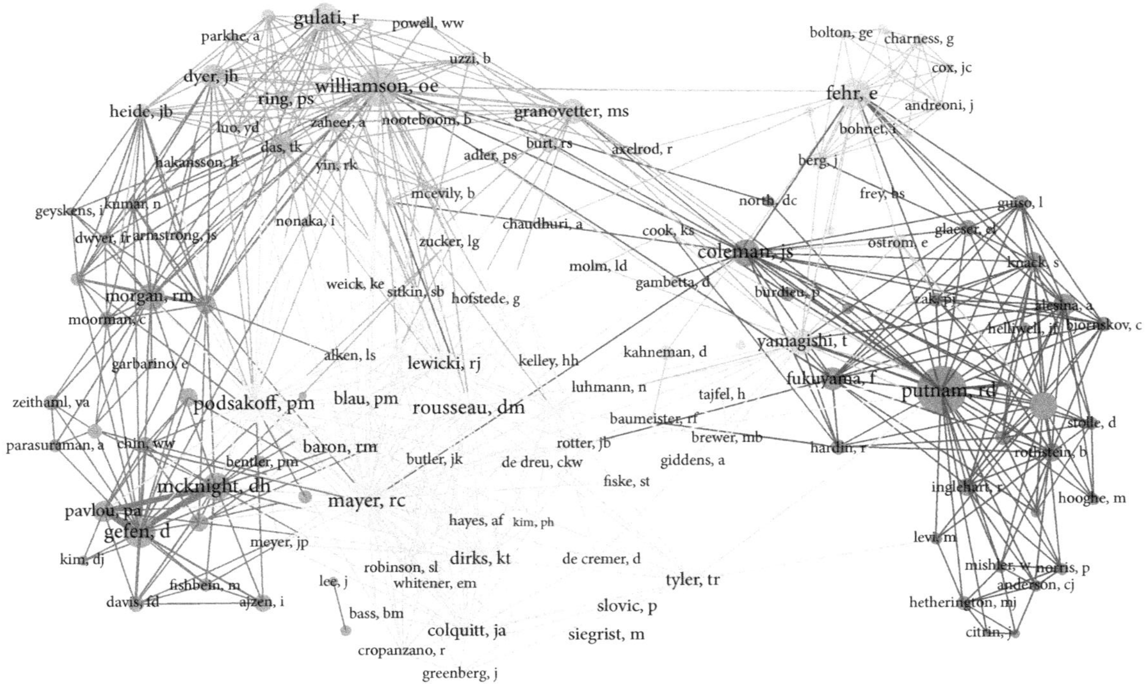

Such a wide-ranging interest on the notion of trust has encouraged productive and stimulating interdisciplinary academic debates over time. However, it has also nourished a proliferation of trust definitions. Even within the same field, trust is often defined in different ways with stronger (or weaker) emphases on certain dimensions of the notion. In this regard, Paul Bauer notices that when approaching the topic of trust, social scientists face nothing short of a jungle of definitions, which it is difficult to clear (see Bauer, this volume; Destri, this volume).

Nevertheless, while conceptual clarity on the meaning of trust seems far from being achieved, it appears that there is some level of convergence in the literature on how the structure of the trust relation can be formalised. Indeed, despite the different understandings of what trusting means, the structure of the trust relation is consistently formalised as a three-part relation where an individual trusts another individual to perform a certain action. However, the increased complexity of the notion across fields and the specification of different forms of trust have pointed out relevant inconsistencies between such annotation and some of the most widespread conceptualisations of trust (eg, social trust). In the next sections, we discuss these inconsistencies and propose a way to revise the current formalisation to overcome such issues.

II. The Classic Formalisation and the Generalisation Problem

Trust is often formalised as a three-part relation of the following form:

A trusts B to do X,

where trust can be defined as the expected trustworthiness or reliability of another individual B to perform an action X (Baier, 1986; Gambetta, 1988; Hardin, 1993; Luhmann, 1979; Offe, 1999). A trust relation therefore involves two actors (a trustor and a trustee) in which the trustor evaluates, on a case-by-case basis, the likelihood that the trustee will dependably perform a certain act. Different instances can be considered within this framework: I might trust a caregiver to look after my grandfather, but I might not trust him/her in respect of other actions, such as taking care of my grandfather's plants in the garden. I could trust my friend Mike to do so, though he would be one of the last persons to call to look after my grandfather. While trust is often regarded as a belief, it is well-acknowledged that it also has a behavioural dimension (see Bauer, this volume): by deciding to act upon our trusting beliefs, we rely on another individual to do something. Such action of reliance entails vulnerability; if the action we rely on others to do is not fulfilled, this may cause us harm, discomfort, feelings of betrayal, or disappointment. In this sense, when we act in a trusting manner, we expose ourselves to the risk that the trustee will not comply with our expectations (see Sonmez, this volume). To illustrate, let us go back to the case of the caregiver. Since I expect him/her to take good care of my grandfather, I could reasonably leave the two of them alone in the house while I go out to do some grocery shopping. My action relies on the expectation that the caregiver will be trustworthy while exposing me to the risk that he/she might fail to meet my expectations and treat my grandfather poorly. Such a vulnerability towards the trustee is a feature often cited as crucial in the definition of a trusting action (Buskens and Raub, 2002; Buskens, Raub and van der Veer, 2010). Note, furthermore, that while in conversational language we often state that we simply 'trust someone' with no reference to the action to be performed, it has been argued that it is quite implausible to trust someone in respect to all matters – instead, we are likely to implicitly apply some sort of modifier when stating our trust towards someone. As Hardin puts it 'only a small child, a lover, Abraham speaking to god, or a rabid follower of a charismatic leader might be able to say "I trust you" without implicit modifier' (Hardin 1993: 506–07).

The above formalisation, which we will refer to as the 'classic formalisation' (ie, A trusts B to do X), was first suggested by Niklas Luhmann in 1979 and then reproposed, most noticeably, by Annette Baier and Russel Hardin. The literature on trust has greatly developed since then and scholars have put forward multiple definitions of trust (see Bauer, this volume). In economics, political science, sociology and psychology, trust is commonly seen as a set of expectations or beliefs directed towards specific individuals (eg, family members, friends) as well as collective entities or general categories of actors (eg, the legal system, politicians, fellow citizens, neighbours, strangers). The complexity of the notion has greatly grown, and various conceptualisations of trust have been at the centre of heated academic debates (eg, out-group vs in-group trust, particularised vs generalised trust, and so on). On the other hand, the formalisation of the trust relation has remained mostly unchanged over the years (see Uslaner, 2002 and 2008 for an exception[6]), while being widely adopted across disciplines.

However, not all conceptualisations of trust can be reconciled with the classic formalisation of the trust relation. In this regard, Cook, Hardin and Levi (2005) point out that while conceptualisations of trust referring to specific individuals (such as a friend or a stranger we meet down the street) work well with the classic formalisation, conceptualisations of trust referring to general categories of people do not. The core of the problem can be summarised as follows: if trust is understood as the expected reliability of another actor B in respect to a specific action X, and B comprises a large group of individuals (eg, our neighbours), then it becomes almost impossible to evaluate whether all or the vast majority of the individuals

[6] Uslaner argues that the annotation 'A trusts B to do X' refers to strategic (or knowledge-based) trust, while more general forms of trust, such as moralistic trust, could be formalised as follows '∀ B and ∀ X: A trusts B to do X'. This annotation has some clear shortcomings as Uslaner himself acknowledges: 'it is foolish to trust all of the people all of the time. Moralistic trust doesn't demand that. But it does presume that we trust most people under most circumstances (where most is widely defined)' (Uslaner, 2008: 33). This creates an inconsistency between the formalisation and the definition of moralistic trust, making the suggested annotation problematic.

within that group are going to be trustworthy. Thus, trust towards general categories of actors can hardly occur. This is particularly problematic when we consider Hardin's definition of trust, thereby we trust B because we believe that B takes our interests at heart and encapsulates our interests in their own (Hardin, 1993, 2002). How can we reasonably believe that the vast majority of people in our neighbourhood (or in any other large group) are going to have our interests at heart? From this point of view, forms of trust directed towards general categories of people are seen as implausible, and trust is regarded as an attitude mostly directed towards specific actors. For instance, according to Cook, Hardin and Levi (2005) citizens cannot assess the trustworthiness of the government because it is unfeasible to assess whether each single employee of the government has our interests at heart. On the other hand, distrust towards large groups can exist as it is easier to assume that the vast majority of actors in a group does not have our interests at heart (Cook et al., 2005; Hardin, 1993, 2002).

This line of reasoning leads Cook, Hardin and Levi (2005) to conclude that the notion of generalised or social trust (ie, trust towards unknown fellow citizens) is a by-product of poorly devised survey questions, which force respondents to say that they are either generally trusting or generally untrusting – eg 'Generally speaking, would you say that most people can be trusted, or that you can't be too careful in dealing with people?'. However, if trust towards broad categories of actors was truly an empty concept, measures of these notions should perform poorly and weakly correlate with other theoretically relevant concepts. Indeed, we should expect survey respondents to answer questions on trust towards fellow citizens or the government almost randomly, as they should find them meaningless or misleading. Consequently, finding statistically significant correlations with close notions (eg, optimism, cooperation, risk-aversion, etc.) would be unlikely. Nevertheless, empirical evidence on the matter supports the opposite conclusion: a vast body of research in sociology, economics and political science shows that questions on social, political and institutional trust perform relatively well in terms of measurement validity and reliability, while correlating meaningfully with theoretically pertinent concepts (Hout and Hastings, 2016; Lundmark, Gilljam and Dahlberg, 2016; Nannestad, 2008).

For instance, trust towards politicians, government and legal institutions is shown to correlate well with indicators of institutional quality, performance and fairness (Hooghe, Marien and Oser, 2017; Khan, 2016; Lo Iacono, 2019; You, 2018; Zmerli and Van der Meer, 2017). Similarly, social trust associates with measures of optimism, risk-aversion and pro-social behaviours and attitudes, both in observational and experimental studies. Discriminated minorities report lower levels of trust towards their fellow citizens in comparison to the rest of the population, while positive social interactions seem to foster trust towards others (Abascal and Baldassarri, 2015; Buskens et al., 2010; Delhey and Newton, 2003; Glanville, Andersson and Paxton, 2013; Lo Iacono, 2018; Lo Iacono and Sonmez, 2021; Uslaner, 2002). Furthermore, despite the heavy criticisms, the standard survey question on social trust displays a strong test-retest reliability, and it is consistent with alternative and more specific measurements (attitudinal or even behavioural in some instances) of the notion, especially when the 11-point scale version of the question is employed (instead of its dichotomous version)[7] (Fehr, Fischbacher, Von Rosenbladt, Schupp and Wagner, 2003; Hout and Hastings, 2016; Lundmark et al., 2016; Nannestad, 2008; Sapienza, Toldra-Simats and Zingales, 2013).

Another problematic point of the classic formalisation of the trust relation is that it heavily relies on an inductive approach whereby general constructs of trust can only be produced as a sum or a combination of individual-level experiences (see also Bauer, 2015). That is, according to Hardin and colleagues, the only way we can place trust in broad groups is to evaluate the expected trustworthiness of every element or the vast majority of the elements (eg, the employees) in the group (eg, the government). This, however, is in contrast with evidence from cognitive and social psychology showing that individuals also adopt top-down, deductive approaches when relating to their surroundings (Devine, 1989; Fiske and Neuberg, 1990; Gelman and Davidson, 2013; Liberman, Woodward and Kinzler, 2017; Sutherland, Cimpian, Leslie and Gelman, 2015; Weisman, Johnson and Shutts, 2015). As argued by Liberman and colleagues,

> a large body of work suggests that the tendency to conceive of people as belonging to social categories is automatic. Indeed, the ability to group instances into categories and to use category-based knowledge to generate novel inductive inferences is a powerful aspect of human cognition. In particular, the capacity to view category members as sharing important, unchanging, and possibly unobservable similarities allows people to efficiently, and perhaps even spontaneously, learn a property of a category and apply it to novel category members. When applied to the social domain, forming conceptually-rich categories has obvious functional value – social categories organize our vast knowledge about human attributes and about the complex relationship networks that comprise human social life.
>
> Liberman et al (2017: 556)

Within this line of reasoning, trust towards general categories of actors (eg, neighbours, strangers, government, etc) appears to be very much possible from both a theoretical and an empirical point of view.

The inconsistencies between the classic formalisation and the empirical evidence outlined above call for a revision of the current approach. Adopting different annotations for different forms of trust (as proposed by Uslaner 2002, 2008) may produce a variety of trust formalisations as vast as the number of definitions prosed in the literature so far, generating further misunderstandings. Instead, we argue that different types of trust relations can share the very same general structure. Hence, we present a unifying annotation that can accommodate conceptualisations of trust referring to either specific individuals or general categories of actors.

[7] Nevertheless, alternative measures of the concept might be performing better and should be perhaps adopted more widely – see, for instance, Blaine Robbins' recent contributions (Robbins, 2019, 2020).

III. A Category-based Formalisation of Trust

As discussed above, the classic formalisation postulates that 'A trusts B to do X'. Below, in line with evidence from cognitive and social psychology, we assume that individuals employ complex categorisation systems to relate with their social surroundings. Based on these theories, we ask ourselves how B and X should be redefined in order to include such an intricate element of human cognition in the formalisation of the trust relation. In other words, if we accept that individuals use category-based knowledge to evaluate others' expected trustworthiness, how should B and X be formally constructed? How can we determine who is being evaluated (ie, B)? For what sort of actions are others deemed as reliable (ie, X)? We employ simple concepts from set theory (Foreman and Kanamori, 2009) to expand the classic formalisation of trust and illustrate how B and X can be defined in a manner that is consistent with the category-based approach. Finally, we discuss how both trust towards specific individuals and large groups of actors unfold from our formalisation.

A. What is B?

Typically, B represents the individual in which A is placing his/her trust. However, if people automatically conceive others as belonging to certain categories, then B should be more accurately depicted as a group or a set of people, which can include any given number of individuals.

In order to identify who belongs to each category, we need to determine what common traits are shared by the people within each category. We will call these traits 'properties'.

First, let us define H as the set of all individuals, $H=\{A_1, A_2, \ldots, A_n\}$, $n \in \mathbb{N}$, and P as the set of all properties through which an individual classifies others, $P_{A_i}=\{p_1, p_2, \ldots, p_m\}$, $m \in \mathbb{N}$. Note that each individual might classify others based on a different set of properties, thus P depends on the individual A_i.

Second, for each individual A_i we define the set B_{A_i} containing all the categories in which other individuals are classified according to A_i's properties P_{A_i} (B_{A_i} is therefore a set of sets[8]). More specifically, a category in B_{A_i} is defined as follows:

$$B_{\{A_i,j\}}=\left\{b \mid b \in H,\ b \text{ holds } P_{\{A_i,j\}}\right\} \subseteq H$$

where $P_{\{A_i,j\}}$ belongs to the powerset of P_{A_i}, $P_{\{A_i,j\}} \in \mathcal{P}\left(P_{A_i}\right)$.[9] In other words, each category $B_{\{A_i,j\}}$ contains all individuals that A_i classifies as holding the properties $P_{\{A_i,j\}}$.

[8] A set of sets is a set whose elements are themselves sets. In this case, the elements of B_{A_i} are the sets $B_{A_i,j}$ that contain all individuals that A_i categorises as holding the set of properties $P_{A_i,j}$.

[9] The powerset of a set S is the set of all subsets of S, including the empty set (ø) and S itself. A subset of S is a set that only contains elements that belongs to S. For example, if we consider S = {1,2,3}, then the powerset of S is $\mathcal{P}(S)=\{\varnothing,\{1\},\{2\},\{3\},\{1,2\},\{1,3\},\{2,3\},\{1,2,3\}\}$.

To illustrate, let us suppose that individual $\tilde{A}$ classifies other people based only on the following properties: kindness, strength and politeness.[10] Then, $\tilde{A}$'s set of properties is $P_{\tilde{A}} = \{kind,\ strong,\ polite\}$. $\tilde{A}$ categorises others based on these three properties and places each individual in one of the possible subsets of the powerset of $P_{\tilde{A}}$. The powerset of the properties $P_{\tilde{A}}$ is:

$$\mathcal{P}(P_{\tilde{A}}) = \{\emptyset, \{kind\}, \{strong\}, \{polite\}, \{kind,\ strong\}, \{kind,\ polite\}, \{strong, polite\}, \{kind, strong, polite\}\}$$

where $\emptyset$ is the empty set (that is, a set without any elements).Thus, $\tilde{A}$ organises each individual in one of the following eight categories: neither kind, nor strong, nor polite; only kind; only strong; only polite; kind and strong; kind and polite; strong and polite; kind, strong and polite. Each one of these categories is contained in $B_{\tilde{A}}$. For example, $B_{\{\tilde{A},1\}}$ contains all people that $\tilde{A}$ categorises as neither kind, nor strong nor polite, while $B_{\{\tilde{A},8\}}$ contains all people that $\tilde{A}$ categorises as kind, strong and polite.[11]

The example presented here illustrates the classification for a set of only three properties. However, individuals employ complex set of properties to classify others, creating multiple and overlapping categories. Even if we assume that the overall set of properties used to classify others is the same, each individual might differ in the way he/she constructs each category. For example, some individuals might categorise police officers as people sharing the following properties: law-enforcer, honest; while other individuals might categorise police officers as people sharing the properties: law-enforcer, dishonest. The two categories might even include the same set of individuals, but the two classifications imply two different worldviews.

Furthermore, scholars argue that individuals are not fully aware of the set of properties defining each category, which therefore tend to have blurred and muddy boundaries – see literature on fuzzy theory on categorisation processes (Belohlavek, Klir, Lewis III and Way, 2009). Nevertheless, individuals can refer to the same group of people when there is a minimum common ground in the way they are defined. Indeed, even if categories are unlikely to be identical across individuals, they can share a minimum set of properties allowing people to communicate and share opinions about them. To illustrate, in the example presented above, police officers were categorised in both cases as law-enforcers, enabling people with radically different views on police officers to identify the same category of individuals and exchange their ideas. Similarly, other groups of people can be classified as belonging to the same categories (such as our fellow

[10] Let us call $\tilde{A}$ a specific individual. The notation simply refers to a specific individual that we use for the example.

[11] $B_{\{\tilde{A},2\}}$ contains all people that $\tilde{A}$ categorises as only kind; $B_{\{\tilde{A},3\}}$ contains all people that $\tilde{A}$ categorises as only strong; $B_{\{\tilde{A},4\}}$ contains all people that $\tilde{A}$ categorises as only polite; $B_{\{\tilde{A},5\}}$ contains all people that $\tilde{A}$ categorises as both kind and strong; $B_{\{\tilde{A},6\}}$ contains all people that $\tilde{A}$ categorises as both kind and polite; $B_{\{\tilde{A},7\}}$ contains all people that $\tilde{A}$ categorises as both strong and polite.

citizens, our neighbours, the government and so on) by different individuals once a minimum set of common properties is identified. As a result, we can formulate a variety of beliefs and expectations about groups of people, including their expected reliability or trustworthiness.[12]

B. What is X?

In the classic formulation, X represents the action that A trusts B to do. In our formalisation, X strictly depends on the set B created by A. Once the set B is defined, A places in X all the actions that he/she expects B to be reliable for. That is, given the set $B_{\{A_i,j\}}$ of people holding the properties $P_{\{A_i,j\}}$ (in the eyes of A_i), $X_{\{A_i,j\}}$ defines the set of actions that A_i expects individuals in $B_{\{A_i,j\}}$ to be trustworthy or reliable for:

$$X_{\{A_i,j\}} = \left\{ x \middle| x \text{ is an action, } A_i \text{ expects } B_{\{A_i,j\}} \text{ to be reliable for } x \right\}.$$ [13]

For example, individuals that categorise police officers as people that are law-enforcer and honest should define a set of actions that they expect the police officers to be trustworthy or reliable for, based on the properties used to construct the category. Thus, they could expect the police officers to dependably protect them in case of immediate danger or to patrol the neighbourhood to guarantee everyone's safety, but they would not expect the police officers to paint their garden's fence, look after their children, or help an old woman to cross the street.

Clearly, the properties that we use to categorise others strongly affect the set of actions that we expect them to be reliable for. That is, the set of actions X can be expanded or restricted by the set of properties P that we ascribe to a group. For instance, individuals that categorise police officers as people that are law-enforcer, honest and kind might presume that a police officer will help the old woman to cross the street. On the other hand, individuals that categorise police officers as people that are law-enforcer and dishonest are likely to have a very limited set of actions whereby police officers are seen as trustworthy, and they would not perhaps expect them to guarantee their safety, let alone help the old woman to cross the street.

[12] Note that our goal here is not to disentangle how the categorisation processes work (this is the core of the research agenda of an entire branch of psychology and cognitive science). Rather, we are building upon prior theoretical and empirical contributions to define some essential elements to construct the category-based formalisation of trust.

[13] Note that, when *A* conceptualises the set of actions that he/she deems the group *B* to be reliable for, this might differ from the set of actions *A* thinks is *B*'s duty to do. *A* might recognise a set of actions that *B* should do given the properties it holds (police officers should enforce the law) but still not trust *B* to carry out such actions.

In other words, if we attribute negative properties to a group of people, the set of actions that we would trust them to do should be rather restricted. However, if we attribute positive properties to a group of people, then the set of actions we will be willing to trust them to do should be larger.[14]

C. The Revised Formalisation

To sum up, our category-based formalisation can be expressed as follows:

$$A \text{ trusts } B_{\{A,j\}} \text{ to do } X_{\{A,j\}}$$

where $B_{\{A,j\}} = \left\{ b \mid b \in H,\ b \text{ holds } P_{\{A,j\}} \right\}$ is the set of individuals that A categorises as sharing the set of properties $P_{\{A,\ j\}} = \{P_1, P_2, \ldots, P_m\}$, $m \in N$, and $X_{\{A,j\}} = \left\{ \text{x} \middle| \text{x is an action, } A \text{ expects } B_{\{A,j\}} \text{ to be reliable for x} \right\}$ is the set of actions that A deems people in $B_{\{A,j\}}$ to be reliable for. In other words, A trusts a group of people ($B_{\{A,j\}}$) in which all members share the same properties ($P_{\{A,j\}}$) to do a certain number of actions ($X_{\{A,j\}}$).

Figure 3.4 Graphical representation of the classic and the category-based formalisations

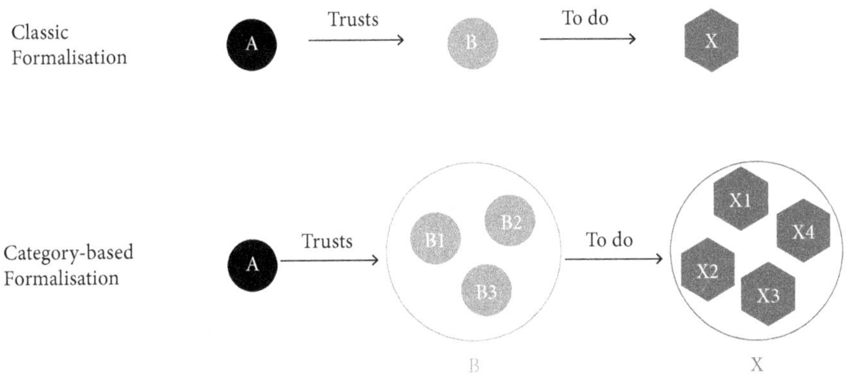

D. Individual Level Trust

Our category-based formalisation provides the tools to conceptualise trust towards groups of people that usually comprise a great variety of individuals

[14] As an extreme case, X might comprehend all actions that A can conceive. That is, A could trust B in respect to all matters. This kind of trust resembles what Hardin describes as 'trust without implicit modifiers' (Hardin 1993: 507).

(eg, neighbours, fellow citizens, the government etc). However, we often refer to trust as a relation that happens towards one specific individual and one specific action. For example, we trust our mother/father to take care of us, we trust our partners to be faithful, we trust our doctor to provide us the best treatment when we are sick, and so on. Hence, how does our approach relate to trust towards specific individuals and actions? In the category-based formalisation of the trust relation, people classify others on the basis of a set of properties P and formulate expectations about them. In such a way, we can determine for what set of actions X the category of people B can be trusted according to A. This approach does not prevent us from identifying specific trust relations. As a matter of fact, we can define sets of properties to identify few particular individuals (eg, my family members) or only one single individual (eg, my best friend from high school, my maths teacher in elementary school, and so on). If the set of properties $P_{\{A,j\}}$ is constructed in such a way that it identifies one specific person, then our category-based formalisation is equivalent to the classic one.

Figure 3.5 Category-based formalisation of trust towards one single individual towards one single action

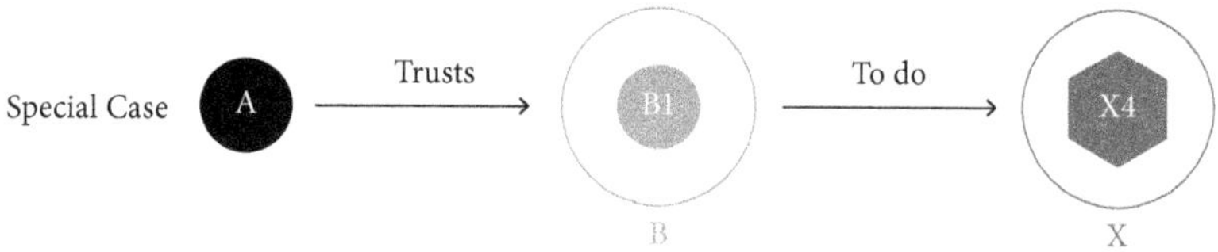

That is, once the set $B_{\{A,j\}}$ comprises only one individual, our classification allows us to define the trust relation towards one single individual. Furthermore, by defining the set $X_{\{A,j\}}$, we define the set of all actions that we trust the group $B_{\{A,j\}}$ to do. When we express our trust towards $B_{\{A,j\}}$ for a specific action, we simply consider the specific element $x_{j,t}$ belonging to $X_{\{A,j\}} = \{x_{j,1}, x_{j,2}, \ldots, x_{j,s}\}, s \in N$. Thus, the classic formalisation is a special case of the category-based one in which the category $B_{\{A,j\}}$ only comprises one individual and the action is one specific element of the set X. In this sense, the classic formalisation can be expressed as a special case of our category-based formalisation.

IV. Conclusions

The classic formalisation of the trust relation relies on a case-by-case approach whereby we trust one individual at the time in regard to one specific action. As a result, trust towards groups of people can be established only by evaluating the expected trustworthiness of the vast majority of individuals in the group, which is often unfeasible. Given this framework, one may infer that trust towards general categories of actors (eg, neighbours, fellow citizens, the government, police officers etc) is a rare event in our society and that our attempts to measure such an unlikely phenomenon would perform poorly. However, as discussed above, empirical evidence suggests that the opposite is true: trust towards general categories of people appears to be a sound and measurable concept, widely applied by people in their daily life.

To overcome this inconsistency, we extended the classic three-part annotation of the trust relation. Relying on the assumption that people adopt a deductive, top-down approach to relate with their social surroundings, we developed a category-based formalisation of the trust relation (building upon prior work in cognitive and social psychology – Belohlavek, et al, 2009; Devine, 1989; Fiske and Neuberg, 1990; Gelman and Davidson, 2013; Liberman et al, 2017; Sutherland et al, 2015; Weisman, et al, 2015). In our formalisation, people classify others on the basis of a set of properties P and formulate expectations about them and the actions they should be reliable to do. As such, our formalisation encapsulates and expands the classic formalisation (instead of rejecting it), suggesting an annotation of the trust relation that encompasses both particular and general forms of trust. In this sense, our category-based formalisation is meant as a tool for other researchers to facilitate the study of trust and avoid the proliferation of different and conflicting annotations. With this goal in mind, we propose a unifying and flexible annotation, which allows scholars to formalise different types of trust (eg, generalised and particularised trust, in-group and out-group trust etc), in the attempt of structuring current debates with further rigour.

Our formalisation also provides an opportunity to re-think how we measure trust. If we consider current survey questions according to the category-based formalisation, it emerges that such questions tend to specify the category of actors B towards which trust is placed, but not the type of action X to be performed. For instance, let us consider some of the standard trust questions: 'Generally speaking, would you say that most people can be trusted, or that you can't be too careful in dealing with people?' or 'On a scale of 1 to 5 (1= cannot be trusted at all, 5 = can be trusted a lot), how much do you trust each of the following groups of people: … people in your family; … people in your neighbourhood; … strangers'. According to our formalisation, specifying only the category of actors B should not pose a problem per se. Indeed, once respondents can determine a category of actors B,[15] a set of actions X will also be defined.

[15] The assumption here is that respondents can agree on the category of actors B the question is referring to. For certain survey questions, this might be easier (eg, when the question refers to well-established social categories, or professions such as police officers), but it could be harder in case of very broad categories. In this regard, some studies have shown that there is relevant heterogeneity in what respondents mean by 'most people' in the standard social trust question (Bauer and Freitag, 2018; Sturgis and Smith, 2010).

However, this lack of specification might reduce precision, creating significant heterogeneity in our measurements of the concept (see Bauer, this volume). More broadly, it would be interesting to see (1) if respondents think of a set of actions implicitly associated with B, and (2) to what extent respondents agree on the set of actions they would trust B with. This would provide us a more fine-grained understanding of what current indicators of trust are measuring, while also testing the empirical validity of our formalisation.

On the other hand, some survey questions on trust do specify both the category B and the action X to be performed: – eg 'If you lost a wallet or purse that contained two hundred dollars, how likely is it to be returned with the money in it, if it was found: by someone who lives close by? by a stranger?' (see, for instance, Freitag and Bauer, 2016). Such sorts of questions offer an interesting opportunity to evaluate how people trust different categories of people while keeping the action constant. A different approach would be to keep the category of actors B constant while changing the type of action X to be performed (eg, returning a lost wallet or purse, giving correct directions etc.). This would allow us to explore the boundaries of people's trust towards certain categories of actors in relation to the deeds to be performed, and answer several relevant questions, such as for what sort of actions are we willing to rely on our neighbours? On the police officers? On our fellow citizens?

Finally, while survey-questions tend to assume X and specify B, behavioural measurements of trust tend to specify X and leave B unspecified. As a matter of fact, in experiments participants have a clear understanding of the task to perform, but the person they are playing with (ie, the category of actors B) can change greatly depending on the type of experiment (eg, in-lab experiment, field experiment, web experiment), and the sample pool used (eg, student sample, web sample, representative sample from the general population). For instance, assuming that participants are matched at random and individual identities or behaviours are not revealed, participants in an in-lab experiment using a student sample pool will be likely playing with other fellow students (hence, B would be the group of fellow students). Differently, participants in a web experiment using a US sample pool will be playing with other fellow citizens (hence, B would be the group of fellow citizens) (Levine and Palfrey, 2007). Whether such a difference is relevant (or not), either from a theoretical or empirical point of view, should be evaluated case-by-case.

To summarise, our category-based formalisation not only provides a tool to encompass both particular and generalised trust within the three-part relation of trust, but it also offers a framework to better assess how individuals place their trust in others. By evaluating B and X in a consistent manner across a variety of cases, we prompt researchers to pay greater attention to which parts of the trust relation are being measured (in either survey or experimental research), ultimately encouraging a more rigorous and precise understanding of trust.

References

Abascal, M and Baldassarri, D (2015). 'Love thy Neighbor? Ethnoracial Diversity and Trust Reexamined.' *American Journal of Sociology* 121 (3): 722–82.

Algan, Y, Guriev, S, Papaioannou, E and Passari, E (2017). 'The European Trust Crisis and the Rise of Populism.' *Brookings Papers on Economic Activity* 48 (2): 309–400.

Baier, A (1986). 'Trust and Antitrust.' *Ethics* 96 (2): 231–60.

Balliet, D and Van Lange, P A (2013). 'Trust, Conflict, and Cooperation: A Meta-Analysis.' *Psychological Bulletin* 139 (5): 1090.

Bauer, P C (2015). 'Negative Experiences and Trust: A Causal Analysis of the Effects of Victimization on Generalized Trust.' *European Sociological Review* 31 (4): 397–417.

Bauer, P C and Freitag, M (2018). 'Measuring Trust.' *The Oxford Handbook of Social and Political Trust, 15.*

Belohlavek, R, Klir, G J, Lewis III, H W and Way, E C (2009). 'Concepts and Fuzzy Sets: Misunderstandings, Misconceptions, and Oversights.' *International Journal of Approximate Reasoning 51* (1): 23–34.

Berg, M (2021). 'The Decline of Political Trust and the Rise of Populism in the United States.' In *Authority and Trust in US Culture and Society* (37–60): transcript-Verlag.

Berg, J, Dickhaut, J and McCabe, K (1995). 'Trust, Reciprocity, and Social History.' *Games and Economic Behavior* 10 (1): 122–42.

Buskens, V and Raub, W (2002). 'Embedded Trust: Control and Learning.' In *Advances in Group Processes* (167–202): Emerald Group Publishing Limited.

Buskens, V, Raub, W and Van Der Veer, J (2010). 'Trust in Triads: An Experimental Study.' *Social Networks* 32 (4): 301–12.

Charron, N, Dijkstra, L and Lapuente, V (2014). 'Regional Governance Matters: Quality of Government within European Union Member States.' *Regional Studies* 48 (1): 68–90.

Coleman, J (1990). *Foundations of social theory.* Cambridge, MA: Belknap.

Cook, K S, Hardin, R and Levi, M (2005). *Cooperation without Trust?* Russell Sage Foundation.

Delhey, J and Newton, K (2003). Who Trusts? The Origins of Social Trust in Seven Societies. *European Societies* 5 (2): 93–137.

Devine, P G (1989). 'Stereotypes and Prejudice: Their Automatic and Controlled Components.' *Journal of Personality and Social Psychology* 56 (1): 5.

Fehr, E (2009). 'On the Economics and Biology of Trust.' *Journal of the European Economic Association* 7 (2–3): 235–66.

Fehr, E, Fischbacher, U, Von Rosenbladt, B, Schupp, J and Wagner, G G (2003). A Nation-wide Laboratory: Examining Trust and Trustworthiness by Integrating Behavioral Experiments into Representative Survey. *Available at SSRN 385120.*

Fiske, S T and Neuberg, S L (1990). 'A Continuum of Impression Formation, from Category-Based to Individuating Processes: Influences of Information and Motivation on Attention and Interpretation.' *Advances in Experimental Social Psychology 23*: 1–74.

Foreman, M and Kanamori, A (2009). *Handbook of Set Theory.* Springer Science and Business Media.

Freitag, M and Bauer, P C (2016). 'Personality traits and the Propensity to Trust Friends and Strangers.' *The Social Science Journal* 53 (4): 467–76.

Freitag, M and Bühlmann, M (2009). 'Crafting Trust: The Role of Political Institutions in a Comparative Perspective'. *Comparative Political Studies* 42 (12): 1537–66.

Fukuyama, F (1995). *Trust: The Social Virtues and the Creation of Prosperity*: Free Press Paperbacks.

Gambetta, D (1988). Trust: Making and Breaking Cooperative Relations.

Gefen, D, Karahanna, E and Straub, D W (2003). 'Trust and TAM in Online Shopping: An Integrated Model.' *MIS Quarterly* 51–90.

Gelman, S A and Davidson, N S (2013). 'Conceptual Influences on Category-Based Induction.' *Cognitive Psychology* 66 (3): 327–53.

Glanville, J L, Andersson, M A and Paxton, P (2013). 'Do Social Connections Create Trust? An Examination Using New Longitudinal Data.' *Social Forces* 92 (2): 545–62.

Hardin, R (1993). 'The Street-Level Epistemology of Trust.' *Politics and Society* 21 (4): 505–29.
Hardin, R (2002). *Trust and Trustworthiness*. Russell Sage Foundation.
Helliwell, J F and Putnam, R D (2004). 'The Social Context of Well-Being.' *Philosophical Transactions of the Royal Society of London. Series B: Biological Sciences* 359 (1449): 1435–46.
Hooghe, M, Marien, S and Oser, J (2017). 'Great Expectations: The Effect of Democratic Ideals on Political Trust in European Democracies.' *Contemporary Politics* 23 (2): 214–30.
Hout, M and Hastings, O P (2016). 'Reliability of the Core Items in the General Social Survey: Estimates from the Three-Wave Panels, 2006–2014.' *Sociological Science* 3: 971–1002.
Jones, K (1996). 'Trust as an Affective Attitude.' *Ethics* 107 (1): 4–25.
Kawachi, I, Kennedy, B P and Wilkinson, R G (1999). Crime: Social Disorganization and Relative Deprivation.' *Social Science and Medicine* 48 (6): 719–31.
Kennedy, B P, Kawachi, I, Prothrow-Stith, D, Lochner, K and Gupta, V (1998). 'Social Capital, Income Inequality, and Firearm Violent Crime.' *Social Science and Medicine* 47 (1): 7–17.
Khan, H A (2016). 'The Linkage Between Political Trust and the Quality of Government: An Analysis.' *International Journal of Public Administration* 39 (9): 665–75.
Knack, S and Keefer, P (1997). 'Does Social Capital have an Economic Payoff? A Cross-Country Investigation.' *The Quarterly Journal of Economics* 112 (4), 1251–88.
Kosfeld, M, Heinrichs, M, Zak, P J, Fischbacher, U and Fehr, E (2005). 'Oxytocin Increases Trust in Humans.' *Nature* 435 (7042): 673–76.
Lederman, D, Loayza, N and Menendez, A M (2002). 'Violent Crime: Does Social Capital Matter?' *Economic Development and Cultural Change* 50 (3): 509–39.
Levi, M (1998). 'A State of Trust.' In V. Braithwaite and M. Levi (Eds.), *Trust and Governance* 1: 77–101.
Levine, D K and Palfrey, T R (2007). 'The Paradox of Voter Participation? A Laboratory Study.' *American Political Science Review* 101 (1): 143–58.
Liberman, Z, Woodward, A L and Kinzler, K D (2017). 'The Origins of Social Categorization.' *Trends in Cognitive Science* 21 (7): 556–68.
Lo Iacono, S (2018). 'Does Community Social Embeddedness Promote Generalized Trust? An Experimental Test of the Spillover Effect.' *Social Science Research* 73: 126–45.
Lo Iacono, S (2019). 'Law-Breaking, Fairness, and Generalized Trust: The Mediating Role of Trust in Institutions.' *PloS one* 14 (8): e0220160.
Lo Iacono, S and Quaranta, M (2019). 'Contextual Economic Conditions, Institutions and Social Trust: Trends and Cross-National Differences in Europe, 2002–2017.' *Polis* 33 (2): 185–214.
Lo Iacono, S and Sonmez, B (2021). 'The Effect of Trusting and Trustworthy Environments on the Provision of Public Goods.' *European Sociological Review*. 37 (1): 155–68.
Luhmann, N (1979). *Trust and Power Chichester*. UK: John Wiley and Sons, Inc.
Lundmark, S, Gilljam, M and Dahlberg, S (2016). 'Measuring Generalized Trust: An Examination of Question Wording and the Number of Scale Points.' *Public Opinion Quarterly*, 80 (1): 26–43.
Messner, S F, Rosenfeld, R and Baumer, E P (2004). 'Dimensions of Social Capital and rates of Criminal Homicide.' *American Sociological Review* 69 (6): 882–903.
Nannestad, P (2008). 'What have We Learned about Generalized Trust, if Anything?' *Annual Review of Political Science* 11: 413–36.
Newton, K, Stolle, D and Zmerli, S (2018). 'Social and Political Trust.' *The Oxford Handbook of Social and Political Trust* 37: 961–76.
Offe, C (1999). 'How Can We Trust our Fellow Citizens.' *Democracy and Trust* 52: 42–87.
Ostrom, E (1990). *Governing the Commons: The Evolution of Institutions for Collective Action*. Cambridge University Press.
Ostrom, E (2003). 'Toward a Behavioral Theory Linking Trust, Reciprocity, and Reputation.' *Trust and Reciprocity: Interdisciplinary Lessons from Experimental Research* ch 6, 19–79.
Podsakoff, P M, MacKenzie, S B, Moorman, R H and Fetter, R (1990). 'Transformational Leader Behaviors and their Effects on Followers' Trust in Leader, Satisfaction, and Organizational Citizenship Behaviors.' *The Leadership Quarterly* 1 (2): 107–42.
Putnam, R D (2000). *Bowling Alone: The Collapse and Revival of American Community*. Simon and Schuster.

Putnam, R D, Leonardi, R and Nanetti, R Y (1993). *Making Democracy Work: Civic Traditions in Modern Italy*. Princeton University Press.
Robbins, B G (2019). 'Measuring Generalized Trust: Two New Approaches.' *Sociological Methods and Research* 0049124119852371.
Robbins, B G (2020). An Empirical Comparison of Four Generalized Trust Scales: Tests-retest Reliability, Measurement Invariance, Predictive Validity, and Replicability.
Sapienza, P, Toldra-Simats, A and Zingales, L (2013). 'Understanding Trust.' *The Economic Journal* 123 (573): 1313–32.
Schoorman, F D, Mayer, R C and Davis, J H (2007). *An Integrative Model of Organizational Trust: Past, Present, and Future*. In Academy of Management Briarcliff Manor, NY 10510.
Sturgis, P and Smith, P (2010). 'Assessing the Validity of Generalized Trust Questions: What Kind of Trust are We Measuring?' *International Journal of Public Opinion Research* 22 (1): 74–92.
Sutherland, S L, Cimpian, A, Leslie, S J and Gelman, S A (2015). 'Memory Errors Reveal a Bias to Spontaneously Generalize to Categories.' *Cognitive Science* 39 (5): 1021–46.
Trujillo, C M and Long, T M (2018). 'Document Co-Citation Analysis to Enhance Transdisciplinary Research.' *Science Advances* 4 (1): e1701130.
Uslaner, E M (2002). *The Moral Foundations of Trust*. Cambridge University Press.
Uslaner, E M (2008). 'Trust as a Moral Value.' *The Handbook of Social Capital* 101–21.
Van der Meer, T W (2017). 'Political Trust and the "Crisis of Democracy".' In *Oxford Research Encyclopedia of Politics*.
Van der Meer, T W and Zmerli, S (2017). 'The Deeply Rooted Concern with Political Trust.' In *Handbook on Political Trust*. Edward Elgar Publishing.
Weisman, K, Johnson, M V and Shutts, K (2015). 'Young Children's Automatic Encoding of Social Categories.' *Developmental Science* 18 (6): 1036–43.
Williamson, O E (1993). 'Calculativeness, Trust, and Economic Organization.' *The Journal of Law and Economics* 36 (1, Part 2): 453–86.
You, J s (2018). Trust and Corruption. *The Oxford Handbook of Social and Political Trust*, 473.
Zak, P J and Knack, S (2001). 'Trust and Growth.' *The Economic Journal* 111 (470): 295–321.
Zmerli, S and Van Der Meer, T W (2017). *Handbook on Political Trust*. Edward Elgar Publishing.

4

The Double-Edged Sword of Cooperation

The Vulnerability of Trusting and Trustworthy Behaviour

BURAK SONMEZ

In situations where personal interests are particularly at odds with collective interests, trust is central to understanding cooperation. Since societies' dependence on cooperation in providing public goods grows incrementally in physical and virtual environments (eg, online petitions, open-access digital archives and online crowdsourcing), we are (unsurprisingly) witnessing the need for trust as a prerequisite for cooperation. In practice, individuals or entities are frequently protected by laws (*legal central authorities*) or *private ordering* to deal with free-riding in collective actions. Some scholars, for instance, show that individuals are willing to incur a small cost to punish free riders (Fehr and Gächter 2000; Fehr and Gächter 2002). However, how is it possible to encourage people to contribute to the provision of public goods in the absence of enforcement? It is particularly pivotal to identify the causal mechanism of cooperative behaviour through *learning, reliability, strategies or goodwill* when sanctions are unconvincing and costly to ensure public goods. In this vein, even though there is no clear-cut understanding of how trust and trustworthiness drive collective actions (for further discussions, see Bacharach et al 2007; Coleman 1994), scholars from different disciplines have sought to conceptualise and explain the fundamentals of how trust and cooperation go hand in hand (Buskens and Raub 2002; Gächter et al 2004; Gambetta 1988; J Jordan et al 2015; J Jordan et al 2016; Ledyard 1995; Lo Iacono and Sonmez 2021; Rigdon et al 2007; Rothstein 2000; Uslaner 2002).

Much of the social sciences literature on trust suggests that the concept of trust has been formulated in multiple ways. For instance, there are two broadly defined views of trust: affective- and cognitive-based. Affective-based trust is considered interpersonal and emphatic concern towards others, while cognitive-based trust is conceptualised as a rational assessment of beliefs about reliability, strategies, credibility, and competence (McAllister 1995; Uslaner 2002). Following this distinction, affective trust is also considered the willingness of an individual (the trustor) to be vulnerable to the actions of other(s) (the trustee) because the emotional bond between the trustee and trustor assures that the trustor's concern for the trustee is reciprocated. On the other hand, cognitive trust primarily relates to the willingness to be vulnerable to the actions of the trustee, determined by direct or indirect interactions with the trustee, such as learning about their reputation (McAllister, 1995). Scholars also define these vulnerabilities as some sort of expectations that the trustee will engage in the trusting behaviour even in the absence of an authority monitoring the actions (Colquitt et al 2007; Dirks and Ferrin 2002; Ho and Weigelt 2005; Montgomery et al 2008; Rousseau et al 1998).

Following such definitions in the literature, it is argued that individuals hold differential expectations of trust through their attitudes and information on others' reputation. People often hold and update these expectations unconsciously through their socialisation and interpersonal interactions. Relatedly, the greater people's expectations that their trusting behaviour will be honoured by trustees, the more vulnerable they become against the betrayal of trustees. However, this relational understanding between trust and vulnerability is often conceptualised through the lens of the trustor but not the trustee in the social sciences literature. In addition, this type of vulnerability predominantly focuses on expectations rather than actual structural vulnerability. For instance, status characteristics theory (STC) suggests that status differences between individuals (eg, refugees as low-status and citizens as high-status) in collective actions may create certain expectations where higher-status group members are expected to be more influential (Ridgeway 1991). Following the STC theory, I argue that the vulnerability of low-status groups in trusting relationships is structurally embedded, thereby leading to relatively unmalleable expectations on their trusting or trustworthy behaviour. Given the impact of roles (trustor vs trustee) and structural differences in the relationship between vulnerability and trust, there is a bourgeoning literature on to what extent the current understanding of trust and trustworthiness through vulnerability is limited, especially when individuals have greater action spaces and different payoff structures in alternative Trust games than in the typical Trust games[1] (Cox et al 2016; Keser and Özgümüs 2018; Engler et al 2018). That is, scholars found that the trustor becomes more discouraged to send any amount if their actions become more vulnerable to the second mover's betrayal (Keser and Özgümüs 2018). On the other hand, if the trustor decides to accept a set of opportunities with a high risk of being betrayed by the trustee, the trustee might see this intention-based social preference as a strong, trusting signal (Engler et al 2018).

[1] The most popular forms of Trust games are known as either investment or trust games (Berg et al 1995), where two players–a trustor and a trustee–start with identical initial endowments (ε). As a first step, the trustor chooses to transfer the amount $\theta \in [0, \varepsilon]$ to the trustee, and the amount sent is multiplied by γ before the trustee receives–conventionally, $\gamma > 1$. In the final stage, the trustee decides on whether to return the amount $\lambda \in [0, \theta\gamma]$ back to the trustor. Scholars, in general, consider the trustor as trusting if they send more than the 'minimum' amount, and defines the trustee as trustworthy if they return more than the 'minimum' amount or more than the amount sent to them (Chaudhuri and Gangadharant 2007; Ben-Ner and Putterman 2009).

In the following, I will consider different causal explanations to understand people's willingness to cooperate in collective actions where trust and trustworthiness are subject to various types of vulnerability. In addition, I will revisit the paradigmatic designs in understanding cooperation to discuss to what extent reputational information constructs expectations in trusting relationships and how vulnerability as both relational and structural concept is ignored in these designs. In doing so, the chapter will also shed some light on the challenges in establishing social cooperation between vulnerable groups, such as asylum seekers or refugees and host populations, in the absence of legal regulations.

I. Trust and Cooperation

The questions of whom I should trust, to what extent I can trust, and why I should trust become salient in revealing how much trust is required to sustain or engage in cooperation, especially when central authority and monitoring are deficient or non-existent. Scholars have shown that enforcement strategies for cooperation may actually backfire since the existence of institutional enforcement can motivate people to think that others cooperate to avoid punishment rather than their own goodwill or moral responsibility (Bowles 2008; Fehr and Rockenbach 2003; Mulder et al 2006). Therefore, once the enforcement or contractual obligation is no longer available, individuals may be more likely to free ride on the cooperation of others.

On the one hand, tackling global challenges such as humanitarian crises, climate change and health crises urges countries to cooperate to alleviate the dire impacts of these crises. On the other, the standard game-theoretic assumption is that cooperation across populations in contributing to a common resource (the public good) is implausible when the dominant strategy is to free ride on the contribution of others (Kollock 1998). Studying how to solve social dilemmas, Kollock categorised them into three broad groups: *motivational*, *strategic*, and *structural*. Motivational solutions are related to other-regarding preferences by which individuals are concerned about their own payoffs and others' gains (for reviews, see *social value orientation*, Van Lange 1999). However, I am more interested in focusing on strategic and structural solutions where social conditions (eg, social learning) and structural mechanisms (eg, reputation systems) highlight the conceptual salience of trust in cooperation. Individuals with a strong incentive to protect their reputation, for instance, are considered trustworthy in cooperative interactions (Diekmann et al 2014; Kuwabara 2015; Milinski 2016; Przepiorka et al 2017; Przepiorka and Berger 2017; Yamagishi et al 2009). Given the development of trust between particular groups or individuals, such as neighbours, co-workers and online community members over repeated interactions, scholars also examine how individuals extrapolate from their experiences in dyadic interactions to establish certain trust-related expectations in similar or different cooperative contexts (Glanville 2004; Glanville and Paxton 2007; Lo Iacono and Sonmez 2021). Another explanation to understanding why people avoid free-riding among group members, irrespective of enforcement mechanisms, is status hierarchies. Individuals, who contribute more to the group, may be regarded as *higher status people* since the contributions to public goods determine one's ranking in relation to the social hierarchy (Flynn et al 2006; Milinski et al 2002). High contributors are considered to be concerned with group welfare (Ridgeway 1978; 1982). From this point of view, they are highly expected to comply with the moral obligation of being honourable in cooperating with low-status individuals (Homans 1958). Taken together, they seem to signal more trustworthiness while exerting greater influence over other group members. In that vein, individuals are more likely to cooperate with high contributors, even in the situation where high contributors are more vulnerable to exploitation (Willer 2009). However, none of these studies has examined to what extent vulnerability embedded in social interactions and structural mechanisms influences trusting and trustworthy behaviour and, eventually, cooperation. The next section delves into understanding the juxtaposition of trust and vulnerability.

II. Trust and Vulnerability

In cooperating with others, individuals are exposed to specific uncertainties and vulnerabilities because of their trusting and trustworthy actions. Accordingly, trust is considered a *relational risk* where individuals are willing to engage in a social exchange by accepting the vulnerability to the actions of others based on the expectations about the others (Rousseau et al 1998). In our everyday life, we often think of vulnerability with negative connotations as an unfavourable condition that needs to be alleviated immediately. However, at the same time, we often voluntarily put ourselves into such situations where we fall in love or gossip about someone or rely on other drivers at the traffic light, thereby becoming vulnerable to others' failures to comply with our trusting or trustworthy actions. Individuals are willing to accept vulnerability to a certain extent in social exchanges to gain some emotional or material payoffs. Another strand of the literature focuses on the fact that the trustor has to accept their vulnerability in a *leap of faith* based on the goodwill of others rather than calculated expectations of trustworthiness. Notably, early sociological studies (see Georg Simmel 1950) distinguish one type of trust, in which the element of faith towards a stranger is beyond knowledge or particular reasons and combined with a sort of transcendent conception (Möllering 2006).

Rather, I reflect on the conventional notion that a trustor expects a trustee to honour the trusting act because the expected outcome with this social exchange outweighs the uncertainty of their vulnerability to the trustee. Following this line of thought, I first suggest that this conception of trust has been predominantly considered relational between the trustor and the trustee in the empirical studies, and often assumes that a trustor is vulnerable to a trustee's failure to honour, yet the fact that the trustor has the *structural advantage* to reserve the right not to initiate trusting behaviour is underexamined. Elaborating on what I define as the structural advantage, I stress that structural vulnerability entails a contextual dimension in trust-building processes, in which expectations of vulnerability to one's action are hardly independent of variances in status hierarchies. Those status differences, in general, drive interpersonal perception and behaviour in social contexts (Ridgeway and Berger 1986).

In a typical Investment or Trust Game studied by (Berg et al 1995; Kreps, 1990), a player has no control over which role (*sender or receiver*) they will be assigned. Player_i is assigned to the sender role, while player_j is assigned to the receiver role with probability p and the reverse allocation with probability $1 - p$. After the roles are randomly allocated, the trustor (sender) moves first to decide whether or not to trust the trustee (receiver) with a given endowment, x amount, before the trustee decides whether or not to reciprocate. Summarising the game accordingly, when the game is played only once (one round), the action set for the trustor is {Trust, Not trust}, and the action set for the trustee is {Reciprocate, Not reciprocate}. If the game is played for one round–not conditional on player's past interactions–the role-contingent strategies to cooperate could be interpreted as unconditional affective trusting behaviour that suggests a moral obligation to trust and expect reciprocity rather than betrayal, even though traditional game theory predicts that trust and reciprocity are not sustainable in finite durations (Olson 2012). On the other hand, in the repeated interactions, it is assumed that people make their best decision on whether to trust or not, relying on their most recent belief from the interactions (eg, see individual learning theories Buskens and Raub 2002; Skyrms 1990). Thus, in the repeated interactions, the trustee could have an opportunity in their action set to change the trustor's prior probability on the belief that the trustee will not betray.

However, one caveat in these games is that the trustee cannot take any action to challenge the trustor, who does not give any opportunity to entail a possibility of betrayal. In contrast to the limited action space in these games, the most recent literature on experimental economics shows that the structure of the game itself can modulate the expectations of the actors on what norms apply to the particular situation (Keser and Özgümüs 2018; List 2007). If the trusted actor also has an opportunity to take money away from the trustor, as well as the amount received, the trustor may expect less trustworthiness because of the increased vulnerability to the actions of the trustees, thereby trusting less. On the other hand, Engler et al (2017) show that when the trustor chooses an action space where the trustee can cause a potential loss for her, the trustee interprets this choice as a signal of enhanced vulnerability and performs in a more trustworthy manner in turn. This growing literature taken together implies that trusting and trustworthy behaviours may foster cooperation if the degree of vulnerability is determined by the trustor rather than imposed by a third party. Given this structural dynamic between vulnerability and trusting behaviour, it is important to examine how one's place in status hierarchies may modulate the expectations of being vulnerable to others' actions. That is, people in higher status positions expect more honouring behaviour than those in lower status positions (Berger et al 1995). These status characteristics, eg, become concrete when disadvantaged group members believe that most people perceive their group to be less competent and less trustworthy (Ridgeway 1997). Relatedly, one may further question whether informal status hierarchies naturally occurring through repeated interactions among individuals and dictated hierarchies would lead to different expectations of vulnerability in trusting relationships.

Reflecting on the status hierarchies in interpersonal interactions, I contend that the conventional operationalisation of trust through Trust games does not account for the variation in trustee's or trustor's prior expectations about their future interactions, which stem from their status position. Therefore, researchers should also disentangle to which extent people's expectations of vulnerability to one's action in trusting relationships derive from status characteristics, as well as their roles and dyadic interactions. In building trusting relationships in real-world social dilemmas, status hierarchies of both trustees and trustors are often signalled or visible to each other. For instance, Falk and Zehnder (2013), using a Trust game in a field experiment, show that individuals tend to invest more money (placing more trust) into the residents of the districts characterised by higher socioeconomic status rather than those living in the districts affiliated with lower socioeconomic status. Similarly, Trifiletti and Capozza (2011) found that in a Trust game, participants from Southern Italy characterised as low status in relation to participants from Northern Italy trusted the high-status participants from Northern Italy more than their own group. Following this reflection, people's expectations of vulnerability to trustee's or trustor's action are not only influenced by one's reputation based on personal interactions but also by their social status. In this regard, the following section discusses why a traditional causal pathway of reputational formation in interpersonal trust to sustain cooperation may mislead researchers to resolve social dilemmas.

III. Reconsidering the Paradigms in Cooperation

Traditional causal pathway to study cooperation through trust between host populations and identified vulnerable aliens, such as refugees, may be confounded. For example, in the conventional causal paths, a stranger is expected to cooperate or help if the other actor has established a positive (eg, cooperative) reputation. Nonetheless, individuals do not know about all interactions among actors in reality since tracing back to all relational interactions of the other actor(s) is unfeasible (Milinski 2016). Instead, people may rely on status-based characteristics to approximate someone's trustworthiness based on their social status and related performance expectations. That is, if social images exist in a population where greater competences and trustworthiness are associated with certain groups (eg, native population) in relation to lower social status (eg, refugees), people may infer a positive/negative reputation based on strangers' apparent status so that the level of trust can differ in favour of trustees perceived as higher status. Relatedly, Zhang and colleagues (2019), through a field experiment demonstrate that native people are more likely to offer help (being more prosocial) to high-status immigrants than low-status immigrants, characterised based on their language skills.

Drawing on the status characteristics theory (Ridgeway 1991), I focus on a few points where the effect of reputational information on trusting and trustworthy behaviour in *one-shot* and *indirectly observable social dilemma settings* may be confounded by social status, thereby influencing expectations of vulnerability to one's actions in cooperation. In explaining this confounding bias, I delve into the *assumption of excludability* in the conventional causal path of cooperation through reputational information, which ensures that exogenous variation created by a random assignment influences the outcome through only the variable of interest (eg, availability of reputational information). Otherwise, the estimated treatment effect cannot be regarded as causal. In particular, the treatment assignments using the observability or availability of reputational information in different contexts (Chu et al 2019; Resnick et al 2006; Yoeli et al 2013) do not only lead to belief updating on reputations to understand the variation in outcomes (eg, cooperation for public goods provision) but also affect people's prior beliefs interacted with various omitted factors. For instance, Yoeli et al (2013) collaborated with a utility company for a demand response programme to prevent blackouts because of excessive use of electricity. The demand response programme requires residents to voluntarily sign up to authorise the company to restrict their central use of air conditioners via a remote switch-in-line during peak hours. Participation in this programme by residents in the city is socially optimal because the inconvenience is minimal for households, compared to the societal cost of blackouts. In doing so, the main experimental treatment was to randomly vary whether residents' neighbours could tell who signed up for the programme, looking at publicly available sheets in a communal area near their home. Their study found that making participation in a public good observable by neighbours in a field experiment renders people three times more likely to cooperate. Nonetheless, this conventional design may not strictly hold the *assumption of excludability*.

More precisely, the excludability violation in this design may occur because people's previous interactions with neighbours are entangled with their social status in the community. That is, random assignment to treatment might also be triggering other possible causes to the outcome. For example, if neighbour$_i$ (high-status) is aware of the social status of the neighbour$_j$ (low-status), the reputational information on neighbour$_j$'s choice to participate in a collective action could influence neighbour$_i$'s vulnerability updating through neighbour$_i$'s expectations about how the community perceives the social status of neighbour$_j$ rather than only the reputational information itself. Even if the reputational information on neighbour$_j$ is positive, lower expectations on neighbour$_j$'s contribution due to the social status of $neighbour_j$ may still lead $neighbour_i$ to remain vulnerable to the defection of $neighbour_j$. In addition, $neighbour_i$ (high-status) is vulnerable to incurring reputational cost if they choose not to contribute to public goods since the community primarily expects high-status neighbours to contribute.

In elaborating on the excludability violation, one's expectation of vulnerability to others' free-riding behaviour is not only affected by how most people perceive the position and characteristics of one's social status but also one's identity[2] (eg, political identity). That is, if $neighbour_i$ were informed that the specific collective action at hand is coordinated by a specific third party (eg, a political party) or $neighbour_i$ was aware of the political identity of $neighbour_j$, it is expected that $neighbour_i$ would question the trustworthiness of the given reputational information and update their expectation of vulnerability to $neighbour_j$'s action accordingly. Together, social norms are not homogeneous across community or even different political identities in the same community (Ellingsen et al 2013). For instance, previous research showed that political conservatives are more likely to refuse the availability of reputational information in the context of energy conservation (Costa and Kahn 2013).

Overall, the direct effect of the availability of reputational information may boil down to the extent to which the information on actors (eg, their social status and identity) is incomplete among individuals in a certain social dilemma. For example, Yoeli et al (2013) found that homeowners living in the apartments are significantly influenced by the availability of reputational information on whether their neighbours participated in the energy-saving programme, while renters are not responsive to the same indirect reciprocity to contribute to the public good. Researchers interpreted that renters are more temporary than homeowners and, therefore, less likely to invest in long-term relationships with other neighbours. If I am allowed to counterfactually assert that if the social status of renters and homeowners were visible across the participants in the same building, then we would be able to better comprehend the limitation with the assumption of excludability in the study at hand. In line with the status characteristic theory, the renters (eg, low-status) would be expected to contribute less to the public good compared to their homeowners because of their hierarchical status by which higher-status members (eg, homeowners) are expected to be more influential in participation (Ridgeway 1991), regardless of the duration of interactions. Thus, it is a strong assumption that exposure to reputational information directly causes cooperation in large-scale collective actions. Rather, I emphasise that the effect of reputational information becomes heavily contingent on status characteristics of individuals in collective actions. Individuals in different social status positions have distinct expectations of being vulnerable to untrustworthy or distrusting action. In contrast

[2] In line with the social identity theory (Tajfel et al 1971), trust can also be influenced by identity-related characteristics of a trustor and a trustee, as well as status-based characteristics. For instance, if a trustee and a trustor share the same salient social categories, it is expected that the level of trust will be biased towards in-group members and biased against out-group members.

to field experiments, the laboratory setting enables researchers to anonymise the participants regarding their social cues in the Trust game to better isolate the effect itself, yet the structure of the game still holds the fact that if the trustee is aware that the trustor can give no opportunity to entail any possibility of betrayal (not sending any amount), trustee's expectation of being vulnerable to the trustor is contingent on their position with respect to the hierarchy of the game.

IV. Reputation, Vulnerability, and Mistrusted Communities

Given the aforementioned theoretical reconsiderations, I highlight the potential challenges for researchers and policymakers in social justice and refugee studies to disentangle how reputational information may backfire or help refugees and host populations to cooperate. Refugees are often perceived and represented as 'economic burden', 'culturally incompatible' or 'mistrusting for security reasons' in the public sphere through media or political institutions (Dempster & Hargrave 2017). Such crystallised stereotypes may operate as cognitive shortcuts[3] (cue-taking) in signalling a social status or social identities that undermine the positive impact of reputational information on mistrusted communities when host populations engage in trustworthy or trusting behaviour with them. That is, if the host population receives communications through media channels about positive contributions of refugees to their host communities (eg, helping the rejuvenation of local parks), this reputational information contradicting the expectations on refugees based on their social status characteristics may not entirely update the host population's expectations of vulnerability to refugees' actions in trusting relationships since most perceive low-status groups to be less trustworthy (Ridgeway, 1997). In addition to this challenge, previous research also shows that when people are exposed to negative reputational information, this strengthens their existing biases if the given reputation does not contradict their prior expectation (*confirmatory bias*) (Chu et al 2019). This may explain how the host population polarises their expectations about refugee communities over time when they receive negative reputational information on refugees. The other side of the coin is that refugees are in a certain social position to expect trusting behaviour of the host communities with a greater degree of vulnerability in the first place. This asymmetry is akin to the structure of the binary Trust game where the trustee cannot take any action to challenge the non-cooperative trustor, who provides no opportunity to entail a possibility of betrayal.

[3] I refer to the bounded rationality account of cue receptivity, which assumes that people avoid costly cognitive efforts for belief formation. Instead, they base their expectations on value-consistent positions (eg, social status) (Bakker et al 2019).

In light of the aforementioned discussion, let us consider an asylum seeker who hopes for cooperation to grant protection in another country–*impersonal trust* arises here. This refers to an indirect trusting relationship, in which trusting action is mediated by an agent or structure (Shapiro 1987). Let's assume that there is no binding or functional international treaty to urge countries to accept each asylum seeker. Impersonal trust is mostly perceived as shared norms rather than an individually calculated phenomenon (Hosmer 1995) and yields a humanitarian expectation that others will trust asylum seekers. However, host populations have a structural opportunity to move first to decide on whether to trust or not to welcome asylum seekers into the country.[4] This influences the vulnerability of asylum seekers to the betrayal of impersonal trust, while the countries or host populations build up their trusting relationships with other populations and countries, relying on interdependence, familiarity and known reputation with whom they have had past interactions rather than one-shot interactions (Granovetter 1985). That said, an asylum seeker who is not trusted may incur reputational harm against the host populations through international or domestic humanitarian organisations. Hendrix and Wong (2013), for instance, showed that operating reputational concerns by international human rights organisations could explain larger effects on altering human rights abusing behaviour in autocracies. Hence, the larger action space of asylum seekers in an impersonal trusting relationship with host populations may change the degree of vulnerability of the host population in cooperation in spite of status hierarchies between host populations and asylum seekers.

After discussing the challenges for asylum seekers in their initial one-off impersonal trusting relationship with host populations, let us continue with their probationary period[5] if refugee status is granted. Theoretically, trust and reciprocity can lead to sustainable cooperation when an interaction is repeated among strangers in interpersonal relationships if they particularly think that they may encounter each other in the future (Bicchieri et al 2004). Nonetheless, in many circumstances, keeping track of repeated interactions to develop a rationally optimal strategy in trusting relationships among actors is cognitively exhaustive and costly. Alternatively, researchers have therefore drawn attention to individual learning theories (Buskens and Raub 2002; Skyrms 1990) or how disclosing reputational information may serve as a form of forging trust and cooperation through reciprocal *self-closure*, thereby making themselves willingly vulnerable to each other (Feinberg et al 2012; Kopányi-Peuker et al 2017; Sommerfeld et al 2007; 2008; and many others). Given these considerations, I choose to engage in how the availability of reputational information may enhance the vulnerability of refugees

[4] Asylum seeking applicants will not be granted asylum if the government believes that the applicant may render the country vulnerable to potential threats (Home Office 2019).

[5] For instance, after the initial asylum application, an applicant can be recognised as a refugee or granted asylum with five years' leave to remain in the UK in order to be able to apply later for indefinite leave to remain (Home Office 2019). This process is defined as a transition/interim period.

(low-status) and host populations (high-status) to each other in inducing impersonal trust and cooperation through counterfactual examples.

Let us imagine a refugee (a former political prisoner in country Y) who has just gained initial trust from the host country X to resettle. Once refugee status is granted by the host country, the refugee as a trustee is expected to submit confidential personal information and evidence to the host country X, even though discouraged to disclose such information to strategically minimise the likelihood of betrayal and exploitation in trusting relationships. In sum, the host country X is only vulnerable to the degree where reputational information provided by the refugee is inaccurate, thereby abusing the trust. By contrast, the refugee enters into a social contract–it is controversial to define whether this contract is voluntarily or forced–accepting a higher level of vulnerability. In this case, to sustain cooperation, the refugee is obliged to reciprocate given trust, taking a leap in the dark without the possibility to enhance an impact on the host country's vulnerability to their trusting relationship. In addition to this structural asymmetry in self-closure, refugees are also represented as low-status in social hierarchies. This situation strongly signals that the wider population expects refugees to be less trustworthy vis-à-vis sustaining cooperation. Taken together, the asymmetric enhanced vulnerability and social status of the trustee in the trusting relationship may inevitably underpin the expectation that the capacity of refugees' trustworthiness is undermined by the culture of suspicion towards them (Hynes 2009).

Let us reconsider the same refugee, holding the characteristics of the host country X and time constant, with regular assistance by international or domestic human rights organisations throughout the resettlement period. Instead of exposing their reputational information to the host country rapidly, these organisations can act as the guardian of trust (a third party) in order to respect what and when the refugee is willing to disclose information and attempt to build trust gradually. In sharing reputational information with the organisations, the refugee, in turn, is given an opportunity to spread some reputational information about their host country to public spheres where companies, customers and tourists, for instance, make their humanitarianly conscious decisions with the host country (eg, cultural boycotts). Note that the role of these organisations is not to punish norm violation but to coordinate norm enforcement, assisting refugees to communicate reputational information on the host country to the wider public spheres. As outlined earlier, if the trustor becomes aware of the possibility that the trusted actor (refugee) has an opportunity to incur reputational harm, the trustor may expect less trustworthiness because of their increased vulnerability to the actions of the trustees in one-off interactions. In contrast, the impersonal trust relationship coordinated through a third party described above entails a variant where both refugees and host countries may have the possibility to build trust by conditioning their enhanced vulnerability on the other's enhanced vulnerability in small steps, thereby transforming themselves into successful cooperators. Therefore, given that refugees are trapped in their lower social position and mistrusting status characteristics when building trust relationships with such mistrusted communities, host populations need to recognise that enhancing their vulnerability towards refugees may help alleviate lower expectations on the trustworthiness of refugees in cooperation.

V. Implications and Conclusion

The implications of this chapter centre around that (1) the conventional frameworks in understanding social dilemmas undertheorise the endogeneity of social status and structural vulnerability in trusting and trustworthy behaviours, drawing attention to the limited action space of trustees; (2) the enlarged action space of asylum seekers in host countries might resolve free-riding in cooperation if the host country's vulnerability to the actions of asylum seekers is enhanced; (3) refugees and host countries may have the possibility to build trust by conditioning one's own enhanced vulnerability through reputational information on the other's enhanced vulnerability in small steps rather than in leaps and bounds; (4) the exposure to or communicating reputational information in promoting cooperation across individuals may be confounded by social status and identities to sustain cooperation when someone's social status or identities carry contrary evidence against provided reputational information.

First, these implications highlight that further research in behavioural social sciences should experimentally examine how the enlargement of action space for trustees in different social dilemmas influences trustor's expectation about their vulnerability to trustees in both one-off and repeated interactions. In doing so, further studies can also measure trustee's beliefs about trustor's vulnerability and trustee's beliefs about trustor's guesses of the trustee's vulnerability. This would help us better interpret to what extent expectations on vulnerabilities affect trusting and trustworthy behaviour. Second, policymakers in refugee-hosting countries responsible for social justice should keep in mind that asylum seekers may become more cooperative in application processes if the rapport with them relies on a gradual mechanism where reciprocal vulnerabilities develop in small steps rather than stigmatising asylum seekers with suspicion in the first place. In this regard, the first interactions with asylum seekers can be conducted by professional refugee care providers with whom they can regain a sense of security. Third, a clear causal identification and designing interventions are important when researchers deal with certain vulnerable groups. To my knowledge, the majority of studies using reputational information have not unveiled the role of vulnerability in understanding how expectations of being vulnerable to one's action help or undermine cooperation. Relevantly, in future studies, scholars should account for heterogonous characteristics of people's social status moderating the effect of reputational information. That is, communicating positive reputational information on the social image of low-status communities in collective actions may not simply lead people to update their expectations on the trustworthiness of those communities.

Therefore, one approach to improve the causal identification of reputational information in solving social dilemmas is to curb the impact of people's social status by either statistical controls or ideally manipulating the perceived social status of people. Overall, I hope this chapter clarifies some issues on the causal identification caveats in dealing with the endogeneity of vulnerability through trusting and trustworthy behaviour and helps researchers and policymakers clearly understand how they can improve their interventions to facilitate cooperation in relevant social dilemmas.

References

Ananish, Chaudhuri and Lata, Gangadharant. (2007). 'An Experimental Analysis of Trust and Trustworthiness.' *Southern Economic Journal* 27.

Bacharach, M, Guerra, G and Zizzo, D J (2007). 'The Self-fulfilling Property of Trust: An Experimental Study.' *Theory and Decision* 63 (4): 349–88.

Bakker, B, Lelkes, Y and Malka, A (2019). *Understanding Partisan Cue Receptivity: Tests of Predictions from the Bounded Rationality and Expressive Utility Perspectives.*

Ben-Ner, A and Putterman, L (2009). 'Trust, Communication and Contracts: An Experiment.' *Journal of Economic Behavior & Organization*, 70 (1–2): 106–21.

Berg, J, Dickhaut, J and McCabe, K (1995). 'Trust, Reciprocity, and Social History.' *Games and Economic Behavior* 10 (1): 122–42.

Bicchieri, C, Duffy, J and Tolle, G (2004). 'Trust Among Strangers.' *Philosophy of Science* 71 (3): 286–319.

Bowles, S (2008). 'Policies Designed for Self-interested Citizens may Undermine "the Moral Sentiments": Evidence from Economic Experiments.' *Science* 320 (5883): 1605–09.

Buskens, V and Raub, W (2002). 'Embedded Trust: Control and Learning.' *Advances in Group Processes*, 19: 167–202.

Chaudhuri, A (2011). 'Sustaining Cooperation in Laboratory Public Goods Experiments: A Selective Survey of the Literature.' *Experimental Economics* 14 (1): 47–83.

Chu, J, Li, G, Loyalka, P, Liu, C, Rosa, L & Li, Y (2019). 'Stuck in Place? A Field Experiment on the Effects of Reputational Information on Student Evaluations.' *Social Forces*.

Coleman, J S (1994). *Foundations of social theory*. Harvard University Press.

Colquitt, J A, Scott, B A and LePine, J A.(2007). 'Trust, trustworthiness, and trust propensity: A meta-analytic test of their unique relationships with risk taking and job performance.' *Journal of Applied Psychology* 92 (4): 909.

Costa, D L and Kahn, M E (2013). 'Energy Conservation "Nudges" and Environmentalist Ideology: Evidence from a Randomized Residential Electricity Field Experiment.' *Journal of the European Economic Association* 11 (3): 680–702.

Dempster, H and Hargrave, K (2017). 'Understanding Public Attitudes Towards Refugees and Migrants.' *London: Overseas Development Institute & Chatham House.*

Deutsch, M (1962). *Cooperation and Trust: Some Theoretical Notes.*

Diekmann, A, Jann, B, Przepiorka, W and Wehrli, S (2014). 'Reputation Formation and the Evolution of Cooperation in Anonymous Online Markets.' *American Sociological Review* 79 (1): 65–85.

Dirks, K T and Ferrin, D L (2002). 'Trust in Leadership: Meta-nalytic Findings and Implications for Research and Practice.' *Journal of Applied Psychology* 87 (4): 611.

Ellingsen, T, Herrmann, B, Nowak, M, Rand, D G and Tarnita, C (2013). 'Civic Capital in Two Cultures: The Nature of Cooperation in Romania and USA.' *Available at SSRN 2179575.*

Ermisch, J, Gambetta, D, Laurie, H, Siedler, T and Noah Uhrig, S C (2009). 'Measuring People's Trust.' *Journal of the Royal Statistical Society: Series A (Statistics in Society)*, 172 (4): 749–69.

Falk, A and Zehnder, C (2013). 'A City-Wide Experiment on Trust discrimination.' *Journal of Public Economics* 100: 15–27.
Fehr, E, Fischbacher, U, Von Rosenbladt, B, Schupp, J and Wagner, G G (2003). *A Nation-Wide laboratory: Examining Trust and Trustworthiness by Integrating Behavioral Experiments into Representative Survey.*
Fehr, E and Gachter, S (2000). 'Cooperation and Punishment in Public Goods Experiments.' *American Economic Review* 90 (4): 980–94.
Fehr, E and Gächter, S (2002). 'Altruistic Punishment in Humans.' *Nature* 415 (6868): 137–40.
Fehr, E and Rockenbach, B (2003). 'Detrimental Effects of Sanctions on Human Altruism.' *Nature* 422 (6928): 137–40.
Feinberg, M, Willer, R, Stellar, J and Keltner, D (2012). 'The Virtues of Gossip: Reputational Information Sharing as Prosocial Behavior.' *Journal of Personality and Social Psychology* 102 (5): 1015.
Fischbacher, U and Gachter, S (2010). 'Social Preferences, Beliefs, and the Dynamics of Free Riding in Public Goods Experiments.' *American Economic Review* 100 (1): 541–56.
Gächter, S, Herrmann, B and Thöni, C (2004). 'Trust, Voluntary Cooperation, and Socio-Economic Background: Survey and Experimental Evidence.' *Journal of Economic Behavior & Organization* 55 (4): 505–31.
Gambetta, D. (1988). *Trust: Making and Breaking Cooperative Relations.*
Glanville, J L (2004). 'Voluntary Associations and Social Network Structure: Why Organizational Location and Type are Important.' *Sociological Forum* 19 (3): 465–91.
Glanville, J L and Paxton, P. (2007). 'How Do We Learn to Trust? A Confirmatory Tetrad Analysis of the Sources of Generalized Trust.' *Social Psychology Quarterly* 70 (3): 230–42.
Granovetter, M (1985). 'Economic Action and Social Structure: The Problem of Embeddedness.' *American Journal of Sociology* 91 (3): 481–510.
Hendrix, C S and Wong, W H (2013). 'When is the Pen Truly Mighty? Regime Type and the Efficacy of Naming and Shaming in Curbing Human Rights Abuses.' *British Journal of Political Science* 43 (3): 651–72.
Ho, T-H and Weigelt, K (2005). 'Trust Building Among Strangers.' *Management Science* 51 (4): 519–30.
Homans, G C (1958). 'Social Behaviour as Exchange.' *American Journal of Sociology.*
Home Office. (2019). *User Guide to Home Office Immigration Statistics.* 133.
Hosmer, L T (1995). 'Trust: The Connecting Link Between Organizational Theory and Philosophical Ethics.' *Academy of Management Review* 20 (2): 379–403.
Hynes, P (2009). 'Contemporary Compulsory Dispersal and the Absence of Space for the Restoration of Trust.' *Journal of Refugee Studies* 22 (1): 97–121.
Lo Iacono, S and Sonmez, B (2021). 'The Effect of Trusting and Trustworthy Environments on the Provision of Public Goods.' *European Sociological Review* 37 February (1):155–68.
Jordan, J J, Hoffman, M, Nowak, M A and Rand, D G (2016). 'Uncalculating Cooperation is Used to Signal Trustworthiness.' *Proceedings of the National Academy of Sciences* 113 (31): 8658–63.
Jordan, J, Peysakhovich, A and Rand, D G (2015). 'Why We Cooperate.' *The Moral Brain: A Multidisciplinary Perspective* 87.
Keser, C and Özgümüs, A (2018). 'Trust, Vulnerability and Trustworthiness.' *Economics Letters* 163: 149–51.
Kiyonari, T, Yamagishi, T, Cook, K S and Cheshire, C (2006). 'Does Trust Beget Trustworthiness? Trust and Trustworthiness in Two Games and Two Cultures: A Research Note.' *Social Psychology Quarterly* 69 (3): 270–83.
Kocher, M G, Martinsson, P, Matzat, D and Wollbrant, C (2015). 'The Role of Beliefs, Trust, and Risk in Contributions to a Public Good.' *Journal of Economic Psychology* 51: 236–44.
Kollock, P (1998). 'Social Dilemmas: The Anatomy of Cooperation.' *Annual Review of Sociology* 24 (1): 183–214.
Kopányi-Peuker, A, Offerman, T and Sloof, R (2017). 'Fostering Cooperation Through the Enhancement of own Vulnerability.' *Games and Economic Behavior*, 101: 273–90.
Kreps, D M (1990). *Game Theory and Economic Modelling.* Oxford University Press.

Kuwabara, K. (2015). 'Do Reputation Systems Undermine Trust? Divergent Effects of Enforcement Type on Generalized Trust and Trustworthiness.' *American Journal of Sociology* 120 (5): 1390–428.
Ledyard, O (1995). 'Public Goods: Some Experimental Results.' *Handbook of Experimental Economics* 1.
List, J A (2007). 'On the Interpretation of Giving in Dictator Games.' *Journal of Political Economy* 115 (3): 482–93.
Luhmann, N (2018). *Trust and Power*. John Wiley & Sons.
Mayer, R C, Davis, J H and Schoorman, F D (1995). 'An Integrative Model of Organizational Trust.' *Academy of Management Review*, 20 (3): 709–34.
McAllister, D J (1995). 'Affect-and Cognition-Based Trust as Foundations for Interpersonal Cooperation in Organizations.' *Academy of Management Journal* 38 (1): 24–59.
Milinski, M (2016). 'Reputation, a Universal Currency for Human Social Interactions.' *Philosophical Transactions of the Royal Society B: Biological Sciences* 371 (1687): 20150100.
Möllering, G (2006). 'Trust Beyond Risk: The Leap of Faith.' *Trust: Reason, Routine, Reflexivity* 105–26.
Montgomery, K, Jordens, C F C and Little, M (2008). 'How Vulnerability and Trust Interact During Extreme Events: Insights for Human Service Agencies and Organizations.' *Administration & Society* 40 (6): 621–44.
Mulder, L B, Van Dijk, E, De Cremer, D and Wilke, H A (2006). 'Undermining Trust and Cooperation: The paradox of Sanctioning Systems in Social Dilemmas.' *Journal of Experimental Social Psychology* 42 (2): 147–162.
Olson, M (2012). 'The Logic of Collective Action' [1965]. *Contemporary Sociological Theory*, 124.
Przepiorka, W and Berger, J (2017). 'Signalling Theory Evolving: Signals and Signs of Trustworthiness in Social Exchange.' *Social Dilemmas, Institutions and the Evolution of Cooperation. Berlin: De Gruyter Oldenbourg* 373–92.
Przepiorka, W, Norbutas, L and Corten, R (2017). 'Order without law: Reputation Promotes Cooperation in a Cryptomarket for Illegal Drugs.' *European Sociological Review* 33 (6): 752–64.
Resnick, P, Zeckhauser, R, Swanson, J and Lockwood, K (2006). 'The Value of Reputation on eBay: A Controlled Experiment.' *Experimental Economics* 9 (2): 79–101.
Rigdon, M L, McCabe, K A and Smith, V L (2007). 'Sustaining Cooperation in Trust Games.' *The Economic Journal* 117 (522): 991–1007.
Ridgeway, C L (1978). 'Conformity, Group-Oriented Motivation, and Status Attainment in Small Groups.' *Social Psychology* 175–88.
Ridgeway, C L (1982). Status in groups: 'The Importance of Motivation.' *American Sociological Review* 76–88.
Ridgeway, C L and Berger, J (1986). 'Expectations, Legitimation, and Dominance Behavior in Task Groups.' *American Sociological Review* 603–17.
Ridgeway, Cecilia L (1991). 'The Social Construction of Status Value: Gender and Other Nominal Characteristics.' Social Forces 70 (2): 367–86.
Ridgeway, C L (1997). 'Where Do Status Value Beliefs Come From? New Developments.' *Status, Network, and Structure* 137–58.
Robertson, R, Gockel, C and Brauner, E (2013). 'Trust your Teammates or Bosses? Differential Effects of Trust on Transactive Memory, Job Satisfaction, and Performance.' *Employee Relations.*
Romano, A, Balliet, D, Yamagishi, T and Liu, J H (2017). 'Parochial Trust and Cooperation Across 17 Societies.' *Proceedings of the National Academy of Sciences* 114 (48): 12702–07.
Rothstein, B (2000). 'Trust, Social Dilemmas and Collective Memories.' *Journal of Theoretical Politics* 12 (4): 477–501.
Rousseau, D M, Sitkin, S B, Burt, R S and Camerer, C (1998). 'Not so Different After All: A Cross-Discipline View of Trust.' *Academy of Management Review* 23 (3): 393–404.
Shapiro, S P (1987). 'The Social Control of Impersonal Trust.' *American Journal of Sociology* 93 (3): 62–658.
Simmel, G (1950). 'The Sociology of Georg Simmel. Transl., ed and intr. by K H Wolff.' New York: Free Press.

Simpson, B and Eriksson, K (2009). 'The Dynamics of Contracts and Generalized Trustworthiness.' *Rationality and Society* 21 (1): 59–80.

Skyrms, B (1990). *The Dynamics of Rational Deliberation*. Harvard University Press.

Sommerfeld, R D, Krambeck, H-J and Milinski, M (2008). 'Multiple Gossip Statements and their Effect on Reputation and Trustworthiness.' *Proceedings of the Royal Society B: Biological Sciences* 275 (1650): 2529–36.

Sommerfeld, R D, Krambeck, H-J, Semmann, D and Milinski, M (2007). 'Gossip as an Alternative for Direct Observation in Games of Indirect Reciprocity.' *Proceedings of the National Academy of Sciences* 104 (44): 17435–40.

Tajfel, H, Billig, M G, Bundy, R P and Flament, C (1971). 'Social Categorization and Intergroup Behaviour.' *European Journal of Social Psychology* 1 (2): 149–78.

Trifiletti, E and Capozza, D (2011). 'Examining Group-Based Trust with the Investment Game.' *Social Behavior and Personality: An International Journal* 39 (3): 405–09.

Uslaner, E M (2002). *The Moral Foundations of Trust*. Cambridge University Press.

Van Lange, P A (1999). 'The Pursuit of Joint Outcomes and Equality in Outcomes: An Integrative Model of Social Value Orientation.' *Journal of Personality and Social Psychology* 77 (2): 337.

Willer, R (2009). 'Groups Reward Individual Sacrifice: The Status Solution to the Collective Action Problem.' *American Sociological Review* 74 (1): 23–43.

Yamagishi, T, Matsuda, M, Yoshikai, N, Takahashi, H & Usui, Y (2009). 'Solving the Lemons Problem with Reputation.' *ETrust: Forming Relationships in the Online World* 73–109.

Yoeli, E, Hoffman, M., Rand, D G and Nowak, M A (2013). 'Powering up with Indirect Reciprocity in a Large-Scale Field Experiment.' *Proceedings of the National Academy of Sciences* 110 (Supplement 2), 10424–29.

Zhang, N, Aidenberger, A, Rauhut, H and Winter, F (2019). 'Prosocial Behaviour in Interethnic Encounters: Evidence from a Field Experiment with High-and Low-Status Immigrants.' *European Sociological Review* 35 (4): 582–97.

PART II

The Value of Trust

5

How Should We Relate to Each Other Politically?

Love and Trust as Relational Ethics in the Political Realm

MAX HARRIS*

I. Introduction

There are pernicious patterns in how human beings interact with one another in societies all over the world. Some individuals, including a significant number of young people, are lonely – and constantly experience a gap between their desired and actual levels of meaningful social contact.[1] Others face regular marginalisation even when interacting with other people, with such marginalisation often building on long histories of particular groups being demonised, exploited, or excluded.[2] Others still, holding themselves out (knowingly or unknowingly) in positions of superiority, face damaged relationships. This is to say nothing of the experience of entire communities that are isolated from others, or of experiences

* Examination Fellow in Law, All Souls College, University of Oxford. My thanks to Richard Bellamy, Linda Eggert, Paul Billingham, Christine Hobden and all participants at the 'Trust Matters' workshop, organised through the Max Weber Programme for Postdoctoral Studies at the European University Institute in Florence, for feedback on drafts of this chapter. My particular thanks to Raquel Barradas de Freitas for her helpful comments and organisation of that workshop. All errors, as always, are my responsibility alone.

[1] New Zealand has begun collecting statistics on loneliness. Those between the age of 15 and 24 have the highest levels of loneliness in the general population (16.8%): see New Zealand Ministry of Social Development, *The Social Report 2016*, available online at http://socialreport.msd.govt.nz/social-connectedness/loneliness.html. There are different ways of defining loneliness. It could be defined as a gap between desired and actual social connection (a subjective definition). It could alternatively be defined as a sense of dislocation from one's social world (a less precise, more objective definition). There may different ways of understanding the connection between a lack of trust and loneliness, which I do not pursue in this chapter.

[2] As Elizabeth Anderson says, 'Across the world, the most profound and systematic inequalities track such identities as gender, class, race, caste, ethnicity, national citizenship, sexual orientation, and religion': Elizabeth Anderson, 'Toward a Non-Ideal, Relational Methodology for Political Philosophy: Comments on Schwartzman's *Challenging Liberalism*' (2009) 24(4) *Hypatia* 130, 133.

of exploitation at work or structural exclusion from the economy. The problem of social relations in contemporary societies – not a new problem – requires urgent attention and action.

This chapter addresses that problem, and asks what kind of social relations we should aspire to build in the political realm. In particular, it compares love and trust as models for social relations that we might seek to realise in political activity. The chapter is split into four following sections. Section II makes some points about the methodology and conceptual framework of the chapter. Section III, the longest of the chapter, aims to throw greater light on the nature of trust and love in the context of social relations. Section IV compares trust and love, and explains why love is more appealing as a relational ethic in the political realm. The final section of the chapter considers objections and implications.

Generally there is little to be gained by attempting to fit a piece of work into a disciplinary pigeonhole. But it is worth noting at the outset that this chapter, while primarily an attempt to theorise an aspect of politics, has continuities with – and implications for – legal theory. Relational ethics in the political realm, such as love or trust, provide a guide for everyday behaviour. But they also might underpin, and inform, a legal order. I return at the close of this chapter to how legal scholars might take forward the theoretical analysis in what follows.

To be clear, this chapter does not offer an account of how love and trust are to be realised within the political realm. That is a different project. But it is worth underscoring that both love and trust have material preconditions. Neither would be capable of becoming a dominant relational ethic in the political realm without significant changes to economic and social structures. This chapter presumes that such changes are possible, and that there is value in considering how we should relate to each other in a society that has secured those changes. It aims to provide both careful analysis of theoretical work on love and trust, and a more creative inquiry into the basis of a possible shared political future.

II. Methodology, Context and Concepts

Good theorising about politics (as well as legal theory) should be sensitive to, and self-aware about, the social context in which a theorist is situated. By 'social context', I mean both the theorist's own positioning in a community (including membership or non-membership in relevant social groups, and level of ascribed power) and the social conditions discernible by the theorist. At one level, such context matters because it can, knowingly and unknowingly, shape the perspective and intuitions of the theorist. Social context here includes a theorist's social and intellectual world, and the literature with which they are familiar (which will often relate to the institutions at which they have been trained and are employed). As Lorna Finlayson puts it, 'political philosophy is not an isolated field … but a human institution, overlapping with other human institutions – all of which bear traces of the social world in which they are embedded.'[3] Charles Mills puts the point even more precisely: 'all theorizing, both moral and non-moral, takes place in an intellectual realm dominated by concepts, assumptions, norms, values and framing perspectives that reflect the experience and group interests of the privileged group (whether the bourgeoisie, or men, or whites).'[4] Awareness of social context can also help a theorist to make a good faith effort to make their work useful to the communities around them. It allows a theorist to do their best to identify pressing social challenges and to orient their work to address those challenges accordingly.[5] I take it to be part of the duty of anyone theorising politics to endeavour to see what is wrong with contemporary political arrangements and to imagine alternative political futures.

Sometimes an approach that acknowledges the rootedness of theorising within a social context is associated with nonideal theory. I do not, however, think this grounded methodology precludes some consideration of ideals. I take theorising to involve, in part, the construction of slightly stylised categories that aim to have some greater applicability beyond a specific historical moment; normative theorising involves shaping those categories into norms. But what is important is what is claimed for these norms, and how far they purport to rise above a specific historical moment. Norms will inevitably be informed by the social context of a theorist. They should therefore be constructed with care, without pretensions to timelessness, and with an acknowledgment that they might reflect the biases, blindspots and blinkers of a particular theorist and a particular time.

These three propositions – that a theorist should be aware of social context, committed to identifying what is wrong with societies and what can be done about it, and able to deploy ideals or norms inevitably informed by that social context – underpin the analysis that follows. Nothing seems to me to turn on whether these propositions, taken individually or separately, are seen as forming part of ideal or nonideal theory; the distinction appears to me to be unhelpful.[6] The approach shares some of the features of Iris Marion Young's method: like Young, I reject any 'effort to construct a universal normative system insulated from a particular society', insist on the value of 'normative reflection that is historically and socially contextualized',[7] and seek to 'reveal moral deficiencies … in contemporary … societies and at the same time to envision transformative possibilities'.[8]

[3] Lorna Finlayson, *The Political is Political: Conformity and the Illusion of Dissent in Contemporary Political Philosophy* (Rowman and Littlefield, 2015) 3.

[4] Charles W Mills, *Black Rights/White Wrongs: The Critique of Racial Liberalism* (Oxford University Press, 2017) 82.

[5] This does not mean that theorists should be deluded about the potential impact of political theory on, say, contemporary politics.

[6] As many others have said, there are multiple senses in which a theory can be 'ideal' or 'nonideal'; the distinction confuses more than it clarifies.

[7] Iris Marion Young, *Justice and the Politics of Difference* (Princeton University Press, 1990) 5.

[8] Iris Marion Young, *Inclusion and Democracy* (Oxford University Press, 2000) 8–9. I first came across this quotation, and the quotation from *Justice and the Politics of Difference* above n 7, in Alison M Jaggar's excellent chapter on Iris Marion Young's method: Alison M Jaggar, '*L'imagination Au Pouvoir*: Comparing John Rawls' Method of Ideal Theory with Iris Marion Young's Method of Critical Theory'

One further assumption should be articulated at the outset: the assumption of a relational worldview. I assume that human beings are social creatures. This means that human beings need social connection and a sense of belonging in broader communities. It means that we misunderstand individuals when we regard them apart from their relationships, associations and communities. It also means that human beings are deprived of an important feature of their identities and existence when they are disconnected from their relationships, associations and communities. Kimberley Brownlee puts the point well when noting that, on this view, everyone ought to have 'minimal opportunities for non-threatening, decent, or supportive social interaction.'[9] And Elizabeth Anderson is right to note that a relational methodology pays particular attention to 'hierarchical social relations among people, organized along lines of group identity such as race, class and gender.'[10]

It is important to set out these preliminary points for reasons of transparency and clarity: they help to indicate where value judgments might lie beneath the argument of this chapter, and to explain why certain claims are not taken further. These preliminary points also attempt to offer some justification for the orientation of this chapter. Furthermore, these assumptions are important for the chapter's argument: when love and trust are compared in the third part of the chapter, they are compared in light of the social challenges of our contemporary world, and in light of human beings' relationality.[11]

With this framework explained, some comments can be made about the specific social context to which this chapter responds. This chapter emerges out of my experiences in English-speaking 'high-income' countries (in particular, New Zealand, the United Kingdom and the United States),[12] and understands pervasive and pernicious individualism to be a problem with which theorists should engage.[13] By 'pervasive and pernicious individualism' I mean the widespread, harmful phenomenon where the individual is viewed as the fundamental unit of social life,[14] where it is thought that greater action should be taken to entrench this

in Ann Nagel and Methchild Nagel (eds), *Dancing with Iris: The Philosophy of Iris Marion Young* (Oxford University Press, 2009) 95, 97.

[9] Kimberley Brownlee, 'A Human Right Against Social Deprivation' (2013) 63 *Philosophical Quarterly* 199, 206.

[10] Anderson, above n 2, 132.

[11] I should add that I would accept that the comparison will also be inflected by my own experiences of love and trust; a different writer might make different observations.

[12] I use inverted commas because these countries have, on average, high incomes, but they are also well-known for high levels of inequality – and the measure of incomes, gross domestic product per capita, is notoriously inadequate as a metric.

[13] This chapter was also originally written in early 2018, being revisited in late 2020 before publication. In the intervening years there have already been developments that have compelled me to revise my views and assessment of salient social conditions; to some extent I have attempted to incorporate those developments into this chapter, but only so much revision is possible.

[14] Jeremy Gilbert makes a similar comment in *Common Ground: Democracy and Collectivity in an Age of Individualism* (Pluto Press, 2013) 31, when describing the dominant norm of our time: 'the singular human being [is seen] as the basic unit of all experience'.

position, and where collective and relational actions are maligned or marginalised. I regard pervasive and pernicious individualism as a summary of a set of facts about the contemporary world, rather than as a theoretical position (though certain intellectual frameworks may have contributed to these aspects of the contemporary world). Pervasive and pernicious individualism produces a way of being in, and way of seeing, the world. This is not the place to provide a genealogy of those facts about the contemporary world, though I aim to be accommodating of different theoretical traditions, including anti-capitalist traditions that trace such pervasive and pernicious individualism back to the reigning economic system. I take it that, as Indigenous writers have noted,[15] this phenomenon has existed for many decades in English-speaking 'high-income' countries (as well as elsewhere), in part as a product of colonisation. But in the last 20–30 years, such pervasive and pernicious individualism has worsened through a series of public policy interventions: including the cutting of taxes, the weakening of trade unions and the privatisation of public services.[16] Evidence of such individualism is easy to find. The Hofstede measure of 'individualism' ranks New Zealand, Australia, Canada, the United Kingdom and the United States as individualist cultures.[17] Nelson Maldonado-Torres has described 'the lonely subject' in settler-colonial countries, implying that this is the result of individualised societies.[18] Nicos Poulantzas describes a process of 'individualization' produced by the contemporary structures of state and law.[19]

Against this backdrop of pervasive and pernicious individualism, the dominant way of thinking about relating to one another is in terms of mutual benefit, or each individual's self-interest being advanced through an exchange or interaction.

The primary challenge, in my view, for theorists and citizens living in those countries, is how to move towards a society in which relationships are rebuilt, and some ideal of interdependent or collective existence can be secured. I understand Immanuel Wallerstein to be grasping for the words to express that challenge when writing, 'Fraternity or … comradeship is a construction to be pieced together with enormous difficulty, and yet this fragile prospect is in fact the underpinning of the achievement of liberty/equality.'[20]

[15] See, for example, Taiake Alfred, 'Wasase: Indigenous Resurgences', in Jacob T Levy and Iris Marion Young, *Colonialism and its Legacies* (Lexington, 2011).

[16] These are often described together as 'neoliberalism', which is variously understood to be this policy package or a broader order of reason ushered in by these policies: David Harvey, *A Brief History of Neoliberalism* (Oxford University Press, 2007); Michel Foucault, *The Birth of Biopolitics: Lectures at the College de France, 1978–1979* (Palgrave Macmillan, 2010).

[17] Their scores are 79, 90, 80, 81 and 91 respectively. The Hofstede Index is based on Professor Geert Hofstede's work: see www.hofstede-insights.com/models/national-culture/.

[18] See Nelson Maldonado-Torres, *Against War* (Duke University Press, 2008).

[19] See Nicos Poulantzas, *State, Power, Socialism* (tr Patrick Camiller, first published 1978, Verso 2014) 87 and 104. At 87: 'Law participates in this process by helping to establish and consecrate the new great Difference: *individualization*.' At 104: 'The individualization of the body-politic – as an ensemble of identical monads separated from the State – rests on the state framework that is inscribed in the spatial matrix implied by the labour process.'

[20] Immanuel Wallerstein, *Unthinking Social Science: The Limits of Nineteenth Century Paradigms* (Temple University Press, 2001), quoted in Maldonado-Torres, above n 17, at 199–200. I prefer not to use the language of 'fraternity', partly because of its gendered and patriarchal connotations.

One question, by no means the only question, that arises out of this challenge, is how should we characterise the ethic – described by Wallerstein as '[f]raternity … or comradeship' – that ought to govern in a world that overcomes pervasive and pernicious individualism? The aim of this chapter is to attempt, with some degree of precision, to specify some candidates for that ideal and to consider their merits.

I would describe the category of ideal that is needed as a relational ethic for the political realm. A relational ethic is a norm, or a body of norms, concerning how we ought to relate to one another. It can be used as a standard against which to measure the state of social relations; it could also serve, secondarily, as a common goal and basis for mobilising people into action to transform social relations.[21] A relational ethic will not necessarily always be honoured in practice, but ought to be widely valued. A relational ethic applies not just to interactions between individuals, but also to interactions between collectives, or between collectives and individuals. What is meant by 'the political realm' is more complex. I understand 'the political' to be the struggle by which ideas, individuals, institutions and identities gain or lose power – and 'the realm' of the political to be the arena (physical, cultural, economic, legal and intellectual) in which that struggle takes place. This definition deliberately leaves open the possibility that 'the political realm' is expansive and porous, since it is conceivable that the struggle by which ideas, individuals, institutions and identies extends into many conversations and activities in everyday life, as well as arenas explicitly dedicated to activist and electoral politics. But the definition still serves to delimit the space in which a relational ethic might apply.

III. Trust and Love

There are multiple possible candidates for a relational ethic for the political realm. To take just a few examples, other theorists have explored sympathy, friendship and care.[22] I do not want to presume that it is only one relational ethic that must

[21] In saying this I think it is important to heed Robin Kelley's comment: 'Without new visions we don't know what to build, only what to knock down.' See Robin Kelley, *Freedom Dreams: The Black Radical Imagination* (Beacon Press, 2002) vii. In this chapter I have largely avoided the language of rights and duties when considering love. That is a deliberate move, since I aim in this chapter to consider a different kind of register in which we might express the needs and aspirations for our shared social life, which is less cold than the language of rights or duties. (I do not deny that it might be possible to reproduce and adapt some of the propositions I present below in terms of the language of rights or duties.) I share Angela Davis's view that '[o]ne of the great challenges of any social movement is to develop new vocabularies': see Angela Y Davis, 'Marcuse's Legacies', https://pages.gseis.ucla.edu/faculty/kellner/Illumina%20Folder/Angela_Davis%5B1%5D%5B1%5D.pdf.

[22] See, respectively: David Hume, *An Enquiry Concerning the Principles of Morals* (London, A. Millar, 1751) on sympathy; Danielle Allen, *Talking to Strangers: Anxieties of Citizenship Since* Brown v Board of Education (Chicago, University of Chicago Press, 2004) on friendship; Joan Tronto, *Moral Boundaries: Political Argument for an Ethic of Care* (New York, Routledge, 1993) on care.

be settled upon, but I do want to consider the strengths and weaknesses of various relational ethics in order to achieve some clarity and depth of analysis.

I compare trust and love in what follows, drawing on general accounts of these values to develop accounts relevant to the political realm. I consider trust because some thinkers have suggested that trust across citizens is the essential element of a successful society.[23] Other indices of successful government use 'broad social trust' as their key measure.[24] Such theories and quantitative measures would imply that trust is the key relational ethic towards which we should all aspire. I analyse love, meanwhile, because it is a relational ethic not often considered in either theoretical or empirical literature. It appears to offer promise as a political idea around which diverse groups – Indigenous peoples, religious thinkers, liberals, socialists – have rallied.[25] I hope, too, that contrasting trust and love will help to illuminate what we are seeking, and not seeking, in a relational ethic for the political realm. To draw this contrast well we have to begin with conceptual accounts of these two forms of relational ethic in the political realm. I want to try to sketch the most attractive accounts of each of these concepts as possible, before comparing them.

We can build up an account of trust in the political realm by considering the work of Annette Baier and David Owens. Both have developed fine-grained frameworks for thinking about trust that can provide at least a starting point for conceiving of trust in the political realm. It goes without saying that consideration of Baier and Owens' is by no means a proxy for a full review of the literature; it is merely assumed in what follows that their work provides a good prompt for deeper thinking about trust.

Baier begins her widely cited 1986 article by suggesting that trust is 'reliance on another's goodwill'.[26] In this way, trust can leave one vulnerable. But she adds that trust goes beyond unfocused reliance on another's goodwill; it involves leaving people with things we value. This gives some discretionary power to the person in whom we are reposing trust.[27] A person who is trusted with something that we value cannot act in a way that goes beyond the scope of the task they are entrusted with, either: the example she gives is that a babysitter asked to take care of a baby cannot paint the nursery the baby is in.

Baier also makes trust subject to a test of moral decency: a trust relationship must 'not rely on successful threats held over the trusted, or on her successful cover-up of breaches of trust'.[28] She states the point more generally, as a test of expressibility, by saying that 'knowledge of what the other party is relying on for

[23] See, for example, Francis Fukuyama, *Trust: The Social Virtues and the Creation of Prosperity* (The Free Press, 1996).

[24] See 'Special Report: The Secret of their Success', *The Economist*, 2 February 2013, www.economist.com/news/special-report/21570835-nordic-countries-are-probably-best-governed-world-secret-their.

[25] See, for example, the diverse bodies of work produced by Moana Jackson, Cornel West, Martha Nussbaum and Che Guevara, respectively, all of whom have written about love.

[26] Annette Baier, 'Trust and Antitrust' (1986) 96(2) *Ethics* 231, 234.

[27] Ibid, 237.

[28] Ibid, 255.

the continuance of the trust relationship' should not 'destabilize the relation'.[29] In other words, the reasons parties have for maintaining a trust relationship do not necessarily need to be disclosed, but they should be such that if they were disclosed the relationship would not be damaged. Baier accepts that her test is 'noncommittal as to what cases of reliance on another's psychology will be acceptable [or unacceptable]'.[30] Fear is not always unacceptable, according to Baier; what is unacceptable 'will vary from context to context, depending on the nature of the goods entrusted and on other relationships', as well as variations in individual psychology.[31]

She acknowledges that her test emerges out of contractarian morality, and in closing she expresses concern that her account is focused on 'two-party trust relationships', with 'the same individualist limitations' found 'in contractarianism'.[32] In an interesting comment, relevant to some of the methodological reflections made at the outset of this chapter, Baier observes that '[m]odern moral philosophy has concentrated on fairly cool relationships between those who are deemed to be roughly equal in power'.[33] This approach is borne of the fact that '[t]he great moral theorists in our tradition are … mostly men who had minimal adult dealings with (and so were then minimally influenced by) women', and leads to an excessive focus on contract as a model for social relations.[34] Baier implies that there is a need to break from this dominant approach.

Owens takes a different approach, with some overlap. In his contribution to one of the only edited collections on the philosophy of trust, Owens begins by claiming that trust is essential to sociality: 'society could not exist in its present form', he writes, 'unless both trusted one another and showed themselves worthy of that trust'.[35] But Owens doubts that there is one general attitude of trust that underpins all of society; instead, he believes different kinds of trust exist for different objects. He calls for a shift of focus, away from trust as a concept, towards the objects of trust. He sets out to answer three kinds of questions: a 'modal question' about what kind of thing trust is; a 'motivational question' about the characteristic content of trust; and a 'question of justification' about what justifies trust.[36]

In following his professed commitment to focus on objects of trust, Owens notes that trust helps to realise the distinctive form of value in an object. It need not be interpersonal, he notes: we can trust a car or an apple, as well as other people. As well, trust is not the only way we can realise the distinctive value of objects: respect might serve the same function. But trust involves an active realisation of

[29] Ibid.
[30] Ibid, 256.
[31] Ibid.
[32] Ibid, 258.
[33] Ibid, 247–48.
[34] David Owens, 'Trusting a Promise and other Things', in Paul Faulkner and Thomas Simpson, *The Philosophy of Trust* (Oxford University Press, 2017), 214–29.
[35] Ibid, 214.
[36] Ibid, 215.

the value of objects. Laughter might help to realise the value of an object, but trust involves 'a more positive engagement … involving the expenditure of energy or one's undergoing a significant change'.[37] Trust in a person is always shorthand, says Owens, for 'trust in something that a person is or does'.[38]

Owens goes on to examine trust in a promise, in an attempt to shed light on trust and different objects of trust. We rely on promises because the other person is aware of an obligation to perform and because their obligation has a non-instrumental value, according to Owens.[39] But Owens also is at pains to emphasise the importance of relationships for trust, and uses the case study of a promise to illuminate this broader point. 'Trusting relationships', he writes, 'are human connections with a certain normative character, namely connections that involve a network of reciprocal rights and obligations'.[40] Obligations within relationships of trust are valuable for their own sake, argues Owens, and they bind parties because of this value. Owens concludes, though, by reiterating that '[t]rust is as various as the objects of trust', and emphasises that he has offered no account of trust for all times and for all contexts.[41]

There is much that is illuminating about Baier and Owens' accounts, which we will return to shortly. But two shortcomings are worth pointing out. First, it is striking that neither Baier nor Owens says much about the phenomenon of distrust. Owens concedes at the outset of his article that distrust would dissolve social bonds, but this is his only reference to distrust. There are a few more references to distrust in Baier's article, but these are only made in passing. Her lyrical final sentence encourages us all to 'trust not only our trust but, even more vitally, our distrust' – and yet there is no sustained analysis in her article of how distrust comes about, or when trust is suspended or withheld.[42] Relatedly, though Baier notes that there has been a historical focus on trust in relations of equal power, she does not spend much time discussing trust where unequal relations subsist. Second, Baier and Owens are notably narrow in how they define the scope of trust. Though Baier starts by talking about trust as reliance on another's goodwill, she confines this claim over the course of her article, referring to the way in which a person can exceed the bounds of the trust reposed in them. She also understands trust to involve leaving people with things that we value; it is not clear that trust always needs to be so focused on things, or what people are left with. Similarly, Owens wants to reduce general trust in a person to trust pertaining to a particular way that a person is, or a particular activity that a person does. In both contributions, what is offered is a task-based account of trust, and a relatively transactional task-based account of trust at that. Baier goes some way to admitting this when

[37] Ibid, 216.

[38] Ibid, 217. In this reference Owens is referring to how an activity might reveal how a person is, or what a person does.

[39] Ibid, 225.

[40] Ibid, 226.

[41] Ibid, 229.

[42] Baier, above n 26, at 60.

saying that she is concerned that she has focused on 'two-party trust relationships', with all 'the same individualist limitations' that go with this approach.[43]

Nevertheless there are insights from these articles that should be taken forward to any new attempt to sketch an account of trust (including trust in the political realm). Owens' suggested architecture for a good account of trust is instructive: it should explain what kind of thing trust is; what the characteristic content of trust is; and what justifies trust. This is a clear structure for any account of trust, and captures important aspects of a full explanation of trust. Baier appears right to say that the intellectual history of sociality or cooperation has tended to concentrate on overly cool relationships between people, and that the background of philosophers might have something to do with this. (The reference to philosophers' background here might relevantly be thought to include not only their gender and social circles, as Baier notes, but also their class background and how they have been racialised.) The comment invites us not to be so cool in our own analyses. It accords with intuition to say, as Owens does, that trust varies with context: there does seem to be some variation in what trust is when I am with my family, compared to when I hand a book to a friend and entrust a friend with that book. Baier's references to vulnerability and goodwill also seem worth returning to: goodwill, on first impression, seems either to be a basis for trust or a consequence of it, and trust (at least in some contexts, including the example of handing over a book, mentioned above) involves some degree of vulnerability.

In developing an account of trust in the political realm, rooted in the conditions of our world today, it is helpful to begin with political contexts where trust is suspended or withheld or refused, including in situations of unequal power relationships. It would seem this might help with understanding some conditions for trust in the political realm. A majority of black young people in America, to take one example, do not trust the police.[44] There are different reasons for this. But a refusal to trust an institution such as the police seems to involve a well-founded suspicion of the motives or likely behaviour of individuals in that institution (as well as the institution as a whole). In the case of black young people, there is a suspicion that they will be subject to racial profiling and violence at the hands of the police. We might also think of other examples: Indigenous individuals referring to distrust of the state, in light of repeated acts of dispossession and marginalisation; or women, who have experienced sexual violence, speaking of distrusting men.[45]

From this, two points might be extrapolated. Trust is not isolated from social structures and individuals' positioning in social groups; indeed, such positioning

[43] Above n 32.

[44] University of Chicago, 'Young People of Color Mistrust Police, Report Finds', https://news.uchicago.edu/story/young-people-color-mistrust-police-and-legal-system-report-finds. The levels of mistrust may have worsened since this chapter was first drafted, and this report first cited, in 2018.

[45] It is worth mentioning that there is a difference between *not trusting* a person or institution, and actively distrusting that person or institution; Raquel Barradas de Freitas has highlighted this distinction to me.

can inform trust and distrust. Trust might well depend on particular individual and group histories of interaction. Accordingly, in giving a partial answer to Owens' question of justification, we might regard trust (at least in some circumstances) as being a result of past experiences or relationships. This is a partial answer because I consider that past experiences or relationships are a primary basis for extending trust, but I do not want to preclude the possibility that trust or distrust has other bases.[46] Second, if distrust involves well-founded suspicion of the kind described above, it would appear that trust, at a minimum (and at least when it involves human-human interaction), ought to involve a well-founded absence of suspicion about the motives or likely behaviour of another person or institution.

To say that trust involves a well-founded absence of suspicion seems insufficient, however.[47] So what more does trust entail? It is important to point out here that, contrary to some of the suggestions of Baier and Owens, trust and distrust can relate to a person as a whole, and might not be reducible to trust in a trait or activity of that person. When a person says to me, 'I distrust you', that might be a judgement based on activities or experiences, but it can still be a conclusion about that person's view of my character that goes beyond particular activities or experiences. Trust, in other words, need not be task-based or transactional. It can be reduced to tasks or transactions – trust might be inhibited in particular respects – but it doesn't have to be so cramped in its focus. In circumstances where there is a refusal to trust a person as a whole, there is not merely a refusal to rely on someone's word or undertaking. It might be a refusal to count on a person in a more general sense. In contrast, trusting someone – not just with my keys, or my possessions, or my family, but in some wider sense – involves a general goodwill towards that other person (which might necessitate believing that a promise will be fulfilled), which implies a set of expectations about that person's future conduct as well as a willingness to make oneself vulnerable to that person to the extent that the person has any power. That goodwill is a particular orientation towards another, a way of relating or being open to a person or community or institution. This is more than an attitude, which is a psychological state of affairs, and different in character to a speech act.

This account of trust in the political realm is necessarily brief and imprecise. My attempt has been to refine accounts already presented in order to derive at least an account that is attractive, as a basis for discussion. No doubt it requires further specification and qualification. To sum up: trust might vary in different contexts. But in the political realm, to address Owens' three concerns:

1. The mode of trust is the following: trust is a disposition or orientation towards others.

[46] By 'bases' I mean something like foundations for a view.

[47] It must also, at the very least, be more than a mere probabilistic judgment of the likelihood of an occurrence. I am grateful to Raquel Barradas de Freitas for drawing this point to my attention.

2. The content of trust (what Owens calls 'the motivation', which might well be a misnomer) is a well-founded absence of suspicion, as well as a generalised goodwill, implying expectations and a capacity for vulnerability.
3. The justification of trust lies, at least primarily, in past experiences and relationships.

We turn now to the meaning of love in the political realm, as an alternative relational ethic. Because I have traced aspects of the intellectual history of a politics of love elsewhere,[48] I will spend less time than I have done in the foregoing section on trust providing commentary on the work of others, though I will engage in particular with the work of bell hooks, Harry Frankfurt, Emmanuel Levinas and Niko Kolodny.

It is worth beginning, as we did with trust, by considering in passing, and impressionistically, the absence of love and what that can tell us about what love means. The aim is to generate cognate concepts and experiences that help to explain what love is. Because love can be given as well as received, we have to draw a further distinction – we will need to consider what it means for someone to feel unloved, as well as what it means for someone to be incapable of loving. As bell hooks has noted, the scant literature that does exist on love (perhaps because it is dominated by male authors who have often led comfortable lives in receipt of love) tends to pay little attention to the feeling of being unloved.[49] Lack of receipt of love can result in a sense of being unworthy, isolated, or lonely. The inability to love, meanwhile, is a somewhat different phenomenon. It can be a product of low self-esteem. Alternatively, as Franz Fanon has written, it can be because the objects of love have made no effort to resolve injustices that present barriers to love.[50] What all of this suggests is that there are some preconditions to love being realised. bell hooks has said, '[w]ithout justice there can be no love';[51] a more muted claim is simply that without the complete realisation of justice, there may be some impediments to the ability of some people to love.

What, then, is love itself? Harry Frankfurt has offered one of the more philosophically textured efforts to define it. In a line that recalls (and contrasts with) Owens' account of trust, Frankfurt contends that love is not only a response to the value of the object of love.[52] Instead, love may make an object valuable. Love is connected to care, according to Frankfurt. It involves viewing objects of love as ends in themselves, through a particular 'configuration of the will'.[53] He resists

[48] See, for example, Max Harris and Philip McKibbin, 'The Politics of Love', *The Aotearoa Project*, 20 May 2015, https://theaotearoaproject.wordpress.com/2015/05/20/the-politics-of-love-max-harris-and-philip-mckibbin/; Max Harris, 'Join the Party of Love,' *Aeon*, 24 April 2017, https://aeon.co/essays/it-is-time-for-love-to-become-a-radical-force-in-politics; and Max Harris, *The New Zealand Project* (Bridget Williams Books, 2017).

[49] bell hooks, *All About Love: New Visions* (William Morrow, 2000) xx–xvii.

[50] See Franz Fanon, *Black Skin, White Masks* (Penguin, 1952).

[51] bell hooks writes: 'Without justice there can be no love' in *All About Love*, above n 48, 30.

[52] Harry Frankfurt, *The Reasons of Love* (Princeton University Press, 2009), 23.

[53] Ibid, 25.

viewing romantic or sexual relationships as a paradigm of love, suggesting that these relationships have distracting features that do not assist in defining what love is. Instead, he holds that love is a 'mode of disinterested concern'.[54] The concern is directed towards an object that is 'ineluctably particular'; love cannot involve merely an object that is an 'instance or exemplar' of something else, says Frankfurt.[55] Love is 'not under our direct and immediate voluntary control',[56] and imposes constraints on our will.

Love is related to care, and must involve some particular attention to a specific object. But Frankfurt does not explain how love is different from care, and does not say how some general categories within relationships (such as a parent-child relationship) relate to the particularity of a loving relationship. As well, his claim that love is a 'mode of disinterested concern' that constrains the will does not sufficiently capture the intensity or depth of feelings of love. Love requires, and entails, more than concern. We must therefore extract some of what is valuable about Frankfurt's account, while jettisoning the rest.

Emmanuel Levinas emerges from a different philosophical tradition, and focuses less on what reasons we have to love – but offers (perhaps more elliptical) reflections on love that are worthy of consideration as we seek to develop an attractive account of love in the political realm. In *Totality and Infinity*, Levinas outlines an approach that views individuality not as a starting point, but as something that is achieved through sociality. This background view informs his understanding of love. Levinas emphasises that love involves an orientation towards the Other: 'To love is to fear for another, to come to the assistance of his [or her] frailty'.[57] He goes on to say: 'The *way* of the tender consists in an extreme fragility, a vulnerability' that 'manifests itself at the limit of being and non-being, as a soft warmth where being dissipates into radiance … dis-individualising and reliving itself of its own weight of being.'[58] He discusses how the caress expresses love. But he suggests that love cannot be exercised in a broader public context. It is 'the very contrary of the social relation':[59] Love 'excludes the third party … [and] remains intimacy, dual solitude, closed society, the supremely non–public.'[60] Levinas seeks, as well, to distinguish love from friendship. In his conclusions to *Totality and Infinity*, Levinas returns to the notion that social relations in a broader public involve a flattening of people so that their particularities are not recognised. 'In political life,'

[54] Ibid, 26.
[55] Ibid.
[56] Ibid.
[57] Emmanuel Levinas, *Totality and Infinity: An Essay on Exteriority* (Martinus Nijhoff Publishers, 1979, first published 1961) 256.
[58] Ibid. Some closely connected ideas are explored by Jackie Wang, albeit not under the rubric of 'love' but instead within the framework of exploring 'oceanic feeling', in: Jackie Wang, 'Oceanic Feeling and Communist Affect', 2020 Riga Biennial, www.rigabiennial.com/en/riboca-2/programme/event-dreams-jackie-wang.
[59] Ibid, 264–65.
[60] Ibid, 265.

Levinas writes, '… humanity is understood from its works – a humanity of interchangeable men [*sic*].' He adds: 'The substitution of men [*sic*] for one another … makes possible exploitation.'[61]

This brief summary of Levinas on love does not adequately contextualise his position, or explain its links to Jewish history and philosophy, or other intellectual traditions. But some tentative comments might be made by way of evaluation. His account, while less clean and analytical than Frankfurt's, highlights some important features of love not present in Frankfurt's writing. The notion that love might involve an alignment with another's interests and experiences ('to fear for another') gets closer to capturing the intensity of love, as does Levinas' description of love as a 'vulnerability' and 'soft warmth'. What is less clear is why it must be inherent in love that it must be 'supremely non-public', or what Levinas means by 'public'. Levinas does not specify whether love is extinguished when there is a lack of private intimacy, when there is an inability to appreciate the singularity of heterogeneous members of the public, or for some other reason.

I would suggest that it is possible for love to exist beyond familial or romantic relationships; it is necessary for me to establish this in order for love to be eligible to be a relational ethic in the political realm. (Such a position may be consistent or inconsistent with Levinas, depending on how his work is interpreted.) This view follows from my understanding of love. Love is a deep sense of warmth directed towards another; generally another person, but possibly an object or idea or institution.[62] Warmth, whilst in one sense a metaphorical concept, is not easily reducible to other elements but entails hospitality, listening, patience, generosity, attention and affection.[63] It is variegated: love should be supplied with more depth and intensity when people face particular need or absence of self-worth. Love involves a recognition of the norms and needs of a particular relationship, while at the same time involving a particular focus on the singularity of the object of love. It also need not be inconsistent with conflict or anger. Whilst I share Levinas' view of love as 'warmth' and tenderness, I would not use the phrase 'soft warmth', since on some occasions it may be that love is a disposition that requires firm anger, even outrage.[64]

[61] Ibid, 298.

[62] The focus on another, or the other, echoes Levinas' account, but it also echoes the approach of a range of writers concerned with love. Iris Murdoch says that love 'is the extremely difficult realization that something other than oneself is real': Iris Murdoch, 'The Sublime and the Good' (1959) 13(3) *The Chicago Review* 42–55, 51.

[63] Simone Weil has focused on attention and generosity as a part of love, and I share her view that love, generosity and attention are related. She writes that love is 'intense, pure, disinterested, gratuitous, generous attention:' Simone Weil, *Selected Essays, 1934–1943: Historical, Political and Moral Writings* (Eugene, Wipf and Stock, 2015) 28. In my view, however, generosity and attention are manifestations of love, rather than being love itself.

[64] When I describe love as a disposition, I have in mind something not far from what I think Baldwin is conveying when he describes love as a 'state of grace', a particular way of being in the world: James Baldwin, *The Fire Next Time* (New York, Penguin, 1963) 95.

Love in the political realm is the expression of this deep sense of warmth in the process by which ideas, institutions and individuals gain or lose power. This requires that in political conversations, actions, or activities, love is a motivating force – a lodestar for decision-making. It also requires that love be embodied in political practice, and secured in the outcomes of politics. There is nothing in the nature of love, that deep sense of warmth manifested in different ways, that precludes it from applying in the realm of the political. Love in the realm of the political must certainly be adapted from love in other contexts. However, the same approach adopted elsewhere can be used, of identifying the nature of a particular relationship (say, citizen-citizen, or citizen-government), and attempting to address the singular other, in a manner that is modulated to the norms and obligations of that relationship.[65] The only other modification in the political realm is that love could be additionally variegated in the sense that the needs of the other in light of their membership in a social group should be identified, and addressed accordingly, in a way that might require more love in particular contexts. How such love is varied and directed is a matter of judgment for particular cases.

Niko Kolodny draws attention to the question, why do we love?[66] For Kolodny, it is the relationship to a person that is the reason for love.[67] He contrasts this with Frankfurt's claim that few reasons for love can be given, since love is so particular in each case. Kolodny contends that love is rendered normatively appropriate in particular settings by a relationship. It should be clear, based on what I have said thus far, that I share some of Kolodny's views about the importance of a relationship as a basis for love. However, I would offer a slightly more expansive account of the reasons for love, and would attempt to accommodate both Kolodny and Frankfurt's approaches. Simplifying slightly, my suggestion is that there are reasons for love. Those reasons include the category of relationship in which two or more people find themselves; the singularity of the other person, the object of love; that other person's need for love, which might vary depending on that person's social positioning and membership in social groups; and our own need to be constituted as individuals by the objects of our love. The further qualification I would add is that the relationships that provide some of our reasons for love are not pre-ordained or static, and their bounds and concomitant obligations can evolve over time. These relationships, along with their attendant obligations, are rooted in the histories and conditions of particular societies.

[65] This emphasis on the singularity of the other is also reminiscent of Martin Buber's discussion of the I-Thou relationship. See Martin Buber, *I and Thou* (Simon & Schuster, 2000, first published 1923). I accept that a fuller moral and political theory would have to explain how love interrelates with the norms of a particular relationship, and how to determine which types of relationship involve different norms.

[66] Niko Kolodny, 'Love as Valuing a Relationship' (2003) 112(2) *The Philosophical Review* 135–89.

[67] Ibid, at 136.

IV. Comparing Love and Trust as Relational Ethics in the Political Realm

With workable accounts of love and trust in the political realm now outlined, we can bring these concepts alongside each other and compare their merits. I have already said that we are seeking a relational ethic for the political realm, which overcomes the pervasive and pernicious individualism that exists in some societies. In comparing love and trust, then, I suggest it is important that we consider their coherence as concepts, as well as their appropriateness as a response to pervasive and pernicious individualism. Consideration of appropriateness for context may raise empirical questions and questions about how these ideals might be operationalised; I will try to indicate where these questions arise.

An initial worry, as we set out towards a comparison, is that the accounts we have developed of love and trust in the political realm essentially render them equivalent concepts. Trust has been defined as a general goodwill, whereas love is a deep warmth. Are these not just two dispositions towards essentially being good, expressed in slightly different language? It is correct that trust and love share some important features. But to say that they are the same is to caricature the accounts that have been sketched. To recapitulate a little: trust involves a well-founded absence of suspicion about another person's motives or likely patterns of behaviour (which can be bounded, or confined to a specific sphere), and a goodwill that entails vulnerability and particular expectations. It is extended towards another based on past experiences and relationships, and might be inhibited by those past experiences and relationships.[68] Love, in contrast, has a connection to justice, and might be inhibited by the failure to realise the demands of justice. The deep warmth of love is different from the expectations and vulnerability that follow from trust; it varies with the needs of another and involves specific qualities of hospitality, attention and affection, amongst others. It can justify conflict. It should be clear that when fuller accounts are given of these concepts, rather than one-sentence summaries, there is conceptual distance between them – and enough for a comparison, and contrast, to be drawn.

The first point to be made in comparison is that trust is a colder kind of relation than love, and could be insufficient as a basis for solidarity, cooperation and collective action.[69] By 'cold' I mean that trust is a little more distant, more detached, and less intense than love. If Baier's characterisation of the intellectual history of cooperation and cognate concepts is accepted, as a gradual move away from the 'cool, distanced relations between more or less free and equal adult strangers, say, the members of an all male club',[70] trust is closer to earlier contractarian accounts of

[68] I do not take a position here on whether, or the extent to which, trust is a matter of will.

[69] To be clear, I am only comparing here love and trust's possible role as a relational ethic in the political realm, where I consider them to be distinct from each other; love and trust may have a different relationship in other domains, but I do not consider the point in this chapter.

[70] Baier, above n 26, 248.

cooperation-like concepts than is love. Why, though, is this a problem? Perhaps in the political realm what is needed is a relational ethic that secures bonds between people in a firm but careful way. The answer to this is that it is a problem because it is not sufficiently distinct from pervasive and pernicious individualism. At least in English-speaking 'high-income' countries, with which I am familiar, there has been a visible shift in values in recent decades. Different countries have experienced, variously, a significant decline in cooperative activities, with detrimental implications for the social support people are able to gain when experiencing trauma or other challenges;[71] greater championing of fame, financial success and achievement, at the expense of communitarian ideals;[72] and the persistence of inequality, with associated effects on mental health and wellbeing.[73] An ambitious ideal – distinct from pervasive and pernicious individualism – is needed. Against that backdrop, it seems reasonable to err on the side of the relational ethic that is less distant and detached: love in the political realm.

It might be wondered, though, whether love is too demanding – and whether its ambition and intensity as a relational ethic is at once its greatest strength as well as its greatest shortcoming. The argument of over-demandingness might be specified in the following way. Requiring that all those engaged in the political realm – individuals speaking to their families about politics, activists developing a new campaign, politicians passing laws – be motivated by love, embody love, and secure love in outcome is either impossible, or so challenging that it would likely incur exhaustion and a loss of the energy needed to tackle endemic individualism. In these circumstances, seeking trust appears to be more feasible and sustainable. As intuitively appealing as these claims might sound, there are two responses in defence of love as a relational ethic in the political realm. First, the visceral intensity of intimate love need not be replicated exactly in interactions between activists, or between a constituent and a politician. The requirements of love are, as already discussed, modulated depending on the relationship. This slightly softens the force of the claim that a love-based ethic is over-demanding. Second, perhaps more importantly, over-demandingness is not a slam-dunk objection on its own account, unless the charge is that an ethic is so over-demanding to be impossible, an empirical claim for which there is not yet any available evidence. Instead, what must be assessed is whether an ethic is over-demanding relative or proportionate to its function and the needs that it serves. Building a society that can sustain a political order distinctive from the pervasiveness and perniciousness of individualism in our time requires a demanding ethic (which might be underpinned by

[71] Robert Putnam, *Bowling Alone: The Collapse and Revival of American Community* (Simon & Schuster, 2001).

[72] Yalda T Uhls and Patricia M Green, 'The Rise of Fame: An Historical Content Analysis', *Cyberpsychology: Journal of Cybersocial Research on Cyberspace*, 5, 1 (2011), www.cyberpsychology.eu/view.php?cisloclanku=2011061601.

[73] Kate Pickett and Richard G Wilkinson, *The Spirit Level: Why Equality is Better for Everyone* (Allen Lane, 2009).

other collective economic structures). Love as a relational ethic for the political realm is therefore appropriate.

Finally, for the purposes of this comparison, love in the political realm seems better able, than trust, to serve as an appropriate relational ethic across a range of political contexts. It is not clear that an exhortation – to all involved in political practice, in all its forms – to trust is conducive to improved politics when the reality of unequal power relations is acknowledged. This is because in some circumstances the opposite of trust, distrust, is healthy and defensible in a way that the opposite(s) of love (which I take to be fear and hate, amongst others) are not. It is legitimate for African-American young people to show some suspicion towards the police. It is useful for citizens to query and interrogate the agendas and values lying behind, say, some politicians' comments or lobbyists' public statements. Indeed, it might be not only a justified, but also an essential, part of good political practice for political actors (such as activists in Black Lives Matter, or campaigners seeking to hold lobbyists to account) to suspend their trust – and to confine their trust to a small number of allies. Workers might be right not to trust employers; renters might be right not to trust landlords, given in both cases their positioning within the economy and likely interests. An overly quick willingness to trust might result in naivety towards the operation of power. Accordingly, mandating that trust be a model relational ethic for the political realm could be misleading and unhelpful, even in a world no longer governed by pervasive and pernicious individualism.

To this, several things might be said. It could be said that what is needed is simply a more sophisticated account of trust in the political realm, which delineates how it applies, to whom, and for what purposes; a more delineated account – which says, for example, that in a relationship of unequal power trust can be withheld – might accommodate the settings where distrust is justified and necessary. But even notwithstanding this point, there remains a lingering doubt that to specify trust as the optimal relational ethic in the political realm is to encourage too much trust, and to create political practices that might in particular serve the needs of the powerful at the expense of the powerless. It also might be said that love shares the same deficiency. To call on all in politics to love could be said to be implausible, when love has been long withheld by governments and others from groups such as Indigenous peoples and ethnic minorities for decades, even centuries; it is to make a mockery of the struggle of these peoples and to cajole these groups into a premature reconciliation. But the key response here is that there are resources within the account given of love in the political realm to address this criticism. Love – which, as I have said, entails hospitality, listening, patience, generosity, attention and affection – does not have to be offered by all. There are preconditions to love being directed towards others, and love can also be varied depending on the context. Overall, whilst another account of trust (not yet imagined in this chapter) might better address this criticism, it appears that love as a relational ethic in the political realm is more capable than trust of responding to situations of unequal power relations, and of contributing to a model of social relations appropriate to the needs of different political actors.

Transforming social relations is not a matter of urging cooperation in all contexts. Love as a relational ethic is better able to respond to this nuance, and to contribute to a model of social relations that is less individualistic while also being sensitive to context and history.

V. Objections and Implications

There are multiple possible objections that might be mounted at the account I've given here. I sketch only two, before turning to one important implication of preferring love to trust as a relational ethic for the political realm.

The first objection is methodological, and is drawn from the work of Charles Mills. In his brilliant critique of idealisation in political theory, he acknowledges that in the field of normative concepts, idealisation might appear to be the least problematic.[74] But he describes three risks in the idealisation of normative concepts related to whether they are legitimate, the way the concept is applied, and the absence of other concepts. The first and third points are connected: Mills notes that questions should be asked about where a concept has been drawn from, and why one concept has been chosen for analysis over another. He says: 'the non-ideal perspective of the socially subordinated is necessary to generate certain critical evaluative concepts in the first place.'[75] This point can be applied to the discussion of love and trust above, since we have tried to idealise these normative concepts. Why have these concepts been chosen over others? Do they suit the interests of some over others? Whilst I accept that these concepts are proximate to my study and experiences, and that such proximity may say something about these concepts suiting the interests of people like me,[76] it is relevant that love in particular has been generated as a concept by people in socially subordinated positions: including Indigenous writers, feminists of colour and African-American writers.[77] Love, therefore, might be said to have some legitimacy as a concept, to use Mills' term, as long as accounts of love are informed by and duly acknowledge those writers in socially subordinated positions who have helped to generate its content. (I have attempted to do that in this chapter.) However, Mills' second risk remains: attention must be paid to how a concept is applied or operationalised. My response

[74] Mills, above n 4, 84.

[75] Ibid, 85.

[76] Namely, economically comfortable cis white men.

[77] These include, most prominently, Moana Jackson, bell hooks and James Baldwin, amongst many others. See, for example: Moana Jackson, 'How about a politics that imagines the impossible?', *e-tangata*, 23 September 2017, https://e-tangata.co.nz/comment-and-analysis/moana-jackson-how-about-a-politics-that-imagines-the-impossible/; bell hooks, *All About Love: New Visions* (William Morrow, 2000); James Baldwin, *The Fire Next Time* (Penguin, 1990).

would be to accept Mills' point completely. Theorising about love grounded in nonideal conditions should continue to show how love might be dependent on other concepts, and those who are socially subordinated must be given a central role in determining love's application in the political realm to ensure that its meaning is not hijacked or distorted by the powerful.

A second objection to the foregoing analysis is: why can't trust and love both be parts of a relational ethic for the political realm, especially if (as was observed earlier in the chapter) a relational ethic can be a body of norms, rather than a single norm? Trust and love might be on different planes, or occupy different parts of the social space. Again, I would want to accept the force of at least part of this objection. I have not meant to create an antagonistic run-off between love and trust. Instead, I have aimed to throw light on each of them, and to explore their various attractions and shortcomings. I do think I have explained that isolating trust as the relational ethic for the political realm may be unhelpful in some significant ways, and that love does not share the same shortcomings as trust. But I would leave open the possibility that trust has some important role to play in the architecture of social relations. It is for another chapter to examine what role this is. It may be, for example, that trust in some relationships in politics is necessary for love to operate across the political realm: minimal trust in some functions of the state might be a precondition for love to serve as a relational ethic,[78] though further analytical work would be needed to substantiate that claim.

With these objections considered and (I hope) addressed, I want to set out one principal implication of accepting love as a relational ethic in the political realm. In light of the account of love in the political realm given in this chapter, it is incumbent upon all societies that seek to advance love as a relational ethic in the political realm to act urgently to remove barriers or inhibitions to love. And the removal of barriers might entail significant commitments of resources, time and political will. Recalling bell hooks' line that '[w]ithout justice there can be no love',[79] societies might be obliged to take transformative steps in order to create the conditions for love. Erich Fromm expresses a similar thought in his writing, noting that the 'social structure of Western civilization and the spirit resulting from it' are not 'conducive to the development of love' – and that the social structure of Western civilisation might need to be changed to produce a more conducive context for love.[80] In English-speaking high-income societies (and perhaps in other societies, too), steps necessary might include decolonisation (where societies remain stained by imperialism), radical redistribution and collectivisation of resources, and transformation of legal, social and economic structures to put an end to patriarchy. A commitment to love demands such action.

[78] Annette Baier's work might provide some basis for this position. She suggests that 'morality … requires trust to thrive' in: above n 26, 232.

[79] Above n 50.

[80] Erich Fromm, *The Art of Loving* (Harper & Row, 1956), 83.

VI. Conclusion

This chapter has ranged widely, in offering some comments on methodology in political theory, evaluating accounts of trust and love, building alternative accounts, and comparing the merits of these accounts. For some readers this might appear scattered, perhaps incoherent in its attempt to draw from different theoretical traditions. But one of the most valuable things theorising about politics can do (if I can count this chapter in that category), I think, is to be generative of future thought and work. I hope I have at least prompted some further questions and lines of inquiry. I share Lorna Finlayson's view: 'I don't see any reason, in philosophy, to abide by the principle of not starting what we cannot finish – a principle which would probably preclude ever starting anything – and anyway … philosophical projects are necessarily incomplete and open-ended.'[81] Pretentions to anything close to completeness and perfection in philosophical work seem to me to be exactly what we should be escaping. For those not convinced of the prospects of love as a relational ethic, or the concept of a relational ethic itself, it is hoped that this chapter has made some useful, generative contribution to the understanding of work by Baier, Owens, hooks, Frankfurt, Levinas, Kolodny and others.

In underscoring the need for further work in this area, given the open-endedness of what has been presented here, it is important to note that I have considered the merits of love and trust only for the purposes of serving as a relational ethic in the political realm. And I have only considered their merits in certain societies; I do not want to overstate their relevance beyond these societies, or claim to know more about the conditions of societies in which I have not spent extended periods of time. As well, I have not considered other ideals, or how love and trust might compare to other ideals, including solidarity, or *ubuntu*, or friendship.[82] I have assumed that a relational ethic is something to which we should aspire (when it might be that such a unifying ethos is not desirable, or a distraction from the immediate conflicts in our lives in this time). A further reason for necessary humility is that the conceptual content of these ideals, and in particular relational ethics, can be illuminated further through experience – and few societies have great experience placing love as a lodestar for social relations. As Lisa Stevenson says in her magisterial anthropological work on care: 'the ethical work of caring for ourselves and for others as imaginative beings … [is] a task whose outlines cannot be traced in advance' in any complete way.[83] The same is true of

[81] Finlayson, above n 3, 7.

[82] Further work is needed to theorise solidarity in full; that theorising would be a useful contribution to a range of contemporary political debates. My provisional view is that solidarity requires something like a shared political relationship and orientation, as well as a willingness to act appropriately to sustain and strengthen that shared political relationship and orientation; this is distinct in emphasis from my account of love.

[83] Lisa Stevenson, *Life Beside Itself: Imagining Care in the Canadian Arctic* (Oakland, University of California Press) 209. My understanding of these concepts, and the limits of my understanding, are shaped by my personal and political experiences,

love: the ethical work of loving others and ourselves in societies riven by pervasive and pernicious individualism is a task whose outlines cannot be traced fully in advance. What I hope I have done, at least, is focused the mind on the question of how we should relate to each other politically in a world that moves beyond pervasive and pernicious individualism, and suggested that 'with love' might be one viable answer.

It is worth noting, finally, that further work in the field of law could usefully deepen and develop the lines of inquiry sketched out, very provisionally, in this chapter. If love is indeed a preferable relational ethic for the political realm, it might reasonably be asked what the role of law is in advancing or maintaining this relational ethic. Ought politicians to bear love in mind as they pass legislation – as a foundational value that should be realised through, or at least not contradicted by, parliamentary law? Should judges have regard to love as a relational ethic in their reasoning – if so, how? And does the claim that love is an attractive relational ethic in the political realm relate in any meaningful way to former Justice of the High Court of Australia Michael Kirby's view that love is the foundation of human rights, properly understood?[84] This is not the place for answers to any of these difficult questions. Suffice to say: fruitful work remains to be done on how a relational ethic in the political realm can be scaffolded and operationalised;[85] scholars in the overlapping disciplines of political theory and law will have much room for further inquiry if these are questions to which they choose to turn their minds.

References

Alfred, Taiake. 'Wasase: Indigenous Resurgences', in Jacob T. Levy and Iris Marion Young, *Colonialism and its Legacies* (Lexington, 2011).

Allen, Danielle. *Talking to Strangers: Anxieties of Citizenship Since* Brown v Board of Education (University of Chicago Press, Chicago, 2004).

Anderson, Elizabeth. 'Toward a Non-Ideal, Relational Methodology for Political Philosophy: Comments on Schwartzman's *Challenging Liberalism*' (2009) 24(4) *Hypatia* 130.

Baier, Annette. 'Trust and Antitrust' (1986) 96(2) *Ethics* 231.

Baldwin, James. *The Fire Next Time* (Penguin, New York, 1963).

Brownlee, Kimberley. 'A Human Right Against Social Deprivation' (2013) 63 *Philosophical Quarterly* 199.

Davis, Angela Y. 'Marcuse's Legacies', https://pages.gseis.ucla.edu/faculty/kellner/Illumina%20Folder/Angela_Davis%5B1%5D%5B1%5D.pdf.

Fanon, Franz. *Black Skin, White Masks* (Penguin, 1952).

Finlayson, Lorna. *The Political is Political: Conformity and the Illusion of Dissent in Contemporary Political Philosophy* (Rowman and Littlefield, 2015).

[84] See Ben Knight, 'Justice Kirby Warns of the Death Penalty', *ABC*, 7 October 2003, www.abc.net.au/am/content/2003/s961254.htm: 'If you ask what is the essence of human rights, I think it's love, that you can love another person, even a person who's done very wrong things, because you realise you share with them the phenomenon of the common existence of our species.'

[85] One very limited way love might be operationalised as a relational ethic through law is as a guide to law-making and as a standard against which law is judged, though this may be an overly narrow approach that ignores the ways in which a broader collective ethos can be cultivated.

Foucault, Michel. *The Birth of Biopolitics: Lectures at the College de France, 1978–1979* (Palgrave Macmillan, 2010).
Frankfurt, Harry. *The Reasons of Love* (Princeton University Press, 2009).
Fromm, Erich. *The Art of Loving* (Harper & Row, 1956).
Fukuyama, Francis. *Trust: The Social Virtues and the Creation of Prosperity* (The Free Press, 1996).
Gilbert, Jeremy. *Common Ground: Democracy and Collectivity in an Age of Individualism* (Pluto Press, 2013).
Harris, Max. 'Join the Party of Love,' *Aeon*, 24 April 2017, https://aeon.co/essays/it-is-time-for-love-to-become-a-radical-force-in-politics.
Harris, Max. *The New Zealand Project* (Bridget Williams Books, 2017).
Harris, Max and Philip McKibbin, 'The Politics of Love', *The Aotearoa Project*, 20 May 2015, https://theaotearoaproject.wordpress.com/2015/05/20/the-politics-of-love-max-harris-and-philip-mckibbin/.
Harvey, David. *A Brief History of Neoliberalism* (Oxford University Press, 2007).
Hofstede Index, www.hofstede-insights.com/models/national-culture/.
hooks, bell. *All About Love: New Visions* (William Morrow, 2000).
Hume, David. *An Enquiry Concerning the Principles of Morals* (A. Millar, London, 1751).
Jackson, Moana. 'How about a politics that imagines the impossible?', *e-tangata*, 23 September 2017, https://e-tangata.co.nz/comment-and-analysis/moana-jackson-how-about-a-politics-that-imagines-the-impossible/.
Jaggar, Alison M. '*L'imagination Au Pouvoir*: Comparing John Rawls' Method of Ideal Theory with Iris Marion Young's Method of Critical Theory' in Ann Nagel and Methchild Nagel, *Dancing with Iris: The Philosophy of Iris Marion Young* (Oxford University Press, 2009).
Kelley, Robin. *Freedom Dreams: The Black Radical Imagination* (Beacon Press, 2002).
Knight, Ben. 'Justice Kirby Warns of the Death Penalty', *ABC*, 7 October 2003, www.abc.net.au/am/content/2003/s961254.htm.
Kolodny, Niko. 'Love as Valuing a Relationship' (2003) 112(2) *The Philosophical Review* 135–189.
Levinas, Emmanuel. *Totality and Infinity: An Essay on Exteriority* (Martinus Nijhoff Publishers, 1979, first published 1961).
Maldonado-Torres, Nelson. *Against War* (Duke University Press, 2008).
Mills, Charles W. *Black Rights/White Wrongs: The Critique of Racial Liberalism* (Oxford University Press, 2017).
Murdoch, Iris. 'The Sublime and the Good' (1959) 13(3) *The Chicago Review*, 42–55.
New Zealand Ministry of Social Development, *The Social Report 2016*, http://socialreport.msd.govt.nz/social-connectedness/loneliness.html.
Owens, David. 'Trusting a Promise and other Things', in Paul Faulkner and Thomas Simpson, *The Philosophy of Trust* (Oxford University Press, 2017), 214–29.
Pickett, Kate and Richard G Wilkinson, *The Spirit Level: Why Equality is Better for Everyone* (Allen Lane, 2009).
Poulantzas, Nicos. *State, Power, Socialism* (tr Patrick Camiller, first published 1978, Verso 2014).
Putnam, Robert. *Bowling Alone: The Collapse and Revival of American Community* (Simon & Schuster, 2001).
Stevenson, Lisa *Life Beside Itself: Imagining Care in the Canadian Arctic* (University of California Press, Oakland).
The Economist, 'Special Report: The Secret of their Success', 2 February 2013, www.economist.com/news/special-report/21570835-nordic-countries-are-probably-best-governed-world-secret-their.
Tronto, Joan. *Moral Boundaries: Political Argument for an Ethic of Care* (Routledge, New York, 1993).
Uhls, Yalda T. and Patricia M. Green, 'The Rise of Fame: An Historical Content Analysis', *Cyberpsychology: Journal of Cybersocial Research on Cyberspace*, 5, 1 (2011), www.cyberpsychology.eu/view.php?cisloclanku=2011061601.
University of Chicago, 'Young People of Color Mistrust Police, Report Finds', https://news.uchicago.edu/story/young-people-color-mistrust-police-and-legal-system-report-finds.

Wang, Jackie. 'Oceanic Feeling and Communist Affect', 2020 Riga Biennial, www.rigabiennial.com/en/riboca-2/programme/event-dreams-jackie-wang.
Weil, Simone. *Selected Essays, 1934–1943: Historical, Political and Moral Writings* (Wipf and Stock, Eugene, 2015).
Young, Iris Marion. *Justice and the Politics of Difference* (Princeton University Press, 1990).
Young, Iris Marion. *Inclusion and Democracy* (Oxford University Press, 2000).

6

Democratic Politics and the Circles of Trust

CHIARA DESTRI*

I. Introduction

Trust seems to play a significant role in democratic politics. It has been observed that democratic governments are associated with higher levels of social and political trust when contrasted with nondemocratic systems.[1] Trust and democracy appear to be linked in a self-reinforcing circle whereby higher levels of trust are conducive to more desirable forms of democracy, and democratic institutions preserve trust relationships and allow them to thrive.[2] Thus, on the one hand, trust is vital for democracy to maintain 'stability, viability and legitimacy',[3] while on

* Earlier drafts of this chapter have been presented at the Max Weber June Conference and the Braga Meetings in Ethics and Political Philosophy in 2019. I thank all participants there for their comments. Special thanks go to the editors of this volume, Raquel Barradas de Freitas and Sergio Lo Iacono for their excellent and helpful feedback, and to Carlo Burelli for his continuous intellectual support. This research has been made possible by a Marie Curie Fellowship, project number 836571.

[1] See Kenneth Newton, Dietlind Stolle and Sonja Zmerli, 'Social and Political Trust' in Eric M Uslaner (ed), *The Oxford Handbook of Social and Political Trust* (Oxford, Oxford University Press, 2018), 37–56.

[2] The connection is more generally established between trust and fair and impartial institutions. See again, Newton, Stolle and Zmerli 'Social and Political Trust' but also Bo Rothstein and Dietlind Stolle,' The State and Social Capital: An Institutional Theory of Generalized Trust' (2008) 40 *Comparative politics*, 441–59; Markus Freitag and Marc Bühlmann, 'Crafting Trust: The Role of Political Institutions in a Comparative Perspective' (2009) 42 *Comparative Political Studies*, 1537–66; Blaine G Robbins, 'A Blessing and a Curse? Political Institutions in the Growth and Decay of Generalized Trust: A Cross-National Panel Analysis 1980–2009' (2012) 25 *PloS one*, https://doi.org/10.1371/journal.pone.0035120; Robert D Putnam, *Making Democracy Work: Civic Traditions in Modern Italy* (Princeton, Princeton University Press, 1993); Eric M Uslaner, 'Democracy and Social Capital' in Mark E Warren (ed), *Democracy and Trust* (Cambridge, CUP, 1999), 121–50.

[3] Tom W G van der Meer and Sonja Zmerli, 'The Deeply Rooted Concern with Political Trust' in Tom W G van der Meer and Sonja Zmerli (eds), *Handbook on Political Trust* (Cheltenham, Edward Elgar, 2017), 1–18, 1.

the other, by protecting associative rights, democracies let people organise and engage in cooperative schemes that enhance their mutually trusting relations.[4] As a result, democracies see high levels of horizontal trust, ie trust that individuals have among themselves.[5]

However, the relationship between trust and democracy is less straightforward than it seems. Firstly, some have denounced a progressive decline of social and political trust in some democratic countries such as the United States, Portugal and Spain, showing that democratic institutions may coexist with low levels of horizontal trust.[6] Secondly, and more importantly, democracy and *vertical* trust, which is trust in political institutions and government, might be *inherently* at odds, as Mark Warren suggests. He argues that democracies 'emerged from' and 'were founded on' *distrust* towards those in government,[7] so much so that constitutional arrangements democracies endowed themselves with services to enable citizens to control, monitor and make them accountable. One might think that only horizontal trust matters to democracy and that as long as citizens trust themselves and one another, they can jointly keep their eye on the government.[8] The problem is that if, by definition, a democratic form of government requires that the people rule, in contemporary democracies, citizens only have an indirect role as lawmakers. They can only give a general direction to the political process by selecting representatives, who are the ones tasked with responsibility for elaborating policy proposals and passing the laws for them.[9] If these representatives ought to be distrusted, one might wonder why we should keep the current institutional setting of representative democracies giving representatives such a crucial role as lawmakers.

Some European populist parties, like the Five Star Movement in Italy, have recently advocated in favour of the imperative mandate claiming that citizens cannot trust their representatives anymore. Let us call this stance the 'delegate solution', which aims to submit representatives to constituents' instructions and, in

[4] Mark E Warren 'Trust and Democracy' in Eric M Uslaner (ed), *The Oxford Handbook of Social and Political Trust* (Oxford, Oxford University Press, 2018), 75–94, 77.

[5] Robert D Putnam, *Making Democracy Work*.

[6] See Robert D Putnam, *Bowling Alone: The Collapse and Revival of American Community* (New York, Simon & Schuster, 2000), Mariano Torcal, 'The Decline of Political Trust in Spain and Portugal: Economic Performance or Political Responsiveness?' (2014) 58 *American Behavioural Scientist*, 1542–1567. Against this view on declining horizontal trust, see Uslaner, 'Democracy and Social Capital' and Sergio Lo Iacono and Mario Quaranta, 'Contextual Economic Conditions, Institutions and Social Trust: Trends and Cross-National Differences in Europe, 2002–2017' (2019) 33 *Polis*, 185–214.

[7] Respectively Warren 'Trust and Democracy', 76 and Warren, 'What Kinds of Trust Does a Democracy Need? Trust from the Perspective of Democratic Theory' in Tom GW van der Meer and Sonja Zmerli (eds), *Handbook on Political Trust* (Cheltenham, Edward Edgar, 2017), 33–52, 33.

[8] Republicanism is often associated with this position because it requires horizontal trust and vertical distrust or mistrust. See Philip Pettit, *Republicanism: A Theory of Freedom and Government* (Oxford, OUP, 1997) and Patti Tamara Lenard, 'Trust Your Compatriots, but Count Your Change: The Roles of Trust, Mistrust and Distrust in Democracy' (2008) 56 *Political Studies*, 312–32.

[9] Bernard Manin, *The Principles of Representative Government* (Cambridge, CUP, 1997), Nadia Urbinati, *Representative Democracy: Principles and Genealogy* (Chicago, University of Chicago Press 2006).

so doing, to give citizens a stronger role in decision making. Such a proposal is not new. It resonates well, for instance, with Jean-Jacques Rousseau's notorious scorn of eighteenth-century English people, who believed they were free when they were constantly dominated by their own Parliament, except during the election time.[10] Given that the strong push for the delegate solution comes from citizens' lack of trust in representatives, it is worth investigating vertical trust between citizens and representatives more closely.

This chapter does so by addressing two related questions. The first one concerns whether citizen trust in representatives is warranted. While this is, to a large extent, an empirical question, I argue that there are sound theoretical reasons for being sceptical about vertical trust in representatives. The second question examines what ensues from the fact that citizen trust in representatives is often unwarranted.

In the following section, I briefly introduce the concept of trust with which I work. The third section applies this concept to political representation and explains why vertical trust in representatives is hardly justified. The fourth section illustrates the delegate solution and raises three objections against it. This proposal is not only unfeasible, as it has been argued, but also undesirable because it is based on a mischaracterisation of the representative process. The fifth section identifies two circles of trust, namely two self-reinforcing mechanisms that generate trust, and contends that we should not relinquish the *language* of trust because it serves to express public recognition of representatives' discretionary power and citizens' vulnerability under representative democracies. A language of trust is compatible with *mistrust*, which demands a certain degree of oversight of representatives' activities, or so I claim. The final section wraps up the argument and concludes.

II. An Account of Trust

Trust is a complex phenomenon, which extends to a wide range of human relationships. It has been noted that trust is a 'three-place predicate': A trusts B with valued thing C or to do X.[11] Usually, when citizen Anne trusts MP Barbara, she does so with respect to a specific set of tasks, including looking after her interests, voicing her concerns, informing her of policy proposals currently on the floor, and voting in Parliament to pass or reject laws. Trust in this sense applies to a specific, often implicitly assumed, domain. Anne may trust Barbara as an MP without trusting her as a friend or a babysitter because these roles entail very different tasks.

[10] Jean-Jacques Rousseau, 'The Social Contract' in JJ Rousseau and Susan Dunn (ed), *The Social Contract and The First and Second Discourses* (New Haven, Yale University Press, 2002 [1763]), 149–254, 221.

[11] Annette Baier, 'Trust and Antitrust' (1986) 96 *Ethics*, 231–60, 236. See also Hardin *Trust and Trustworthiness* (New York, Russell Sage Foundation, 2002), 7. For an interesting conceptualization of trust as probability, see Paul Bauer's chapter in this volume.

Following other scholars, such as Russel Hardin, Mark Warren and Paul Bauer in this volume, I define trust as the belief or expectation in the trustee's trustworthiness.[12] Accordingly, when Anne trusts Barbara with her son, she has the belief or expectation that Barbara will be trustworthy in taking care of him. Without such belief, Anne cannot trust Barbara. Of course, she can come to believe that Barbara is a trustworthy babysitter, but she cannot bring herself to have such a belief without evidence.[13] Proper trust is, therefore, not something we can decide on. As Annette Baier observes, an invitation to being trusted cannot be accepted at will.[14]

For this chapter, it suffices to consider trustworthiness as a disposition consisting of (1) competence and (2) willingness to respond to the trustor's trust (3) because this is a compelling reason for action.[15] Accordingly, when Anne trusts Barbara with her son, she believes that Barbara is *competent* and *willing* to take care of him *because* Anne trusts her to do so. This definition of trustworthiness serves to make sense of three important elements. Firstly, we need to believe in the trustee's competence to accomplish the task we trust her to do in order to trust her. It would be unreasonable for Anne to trust her three-year-old son Ben to cook dinner since this would mean that she has the clearly mistaken belief that Ben is competent around the stove. Secondly, we need to believe that the trustee is *responsive* to trust.[16] Anne may believe that her selfish sister Brenda can cook dinner and that she is sometimes willing to do so, yet Anne does not trust Brenda with preparing dinner insofar as she knows that Brenda is not interested in helping Anne out. Thirdly, we need to believe that the trustee takes the trust placed on her as a compelling reason for action. Anne may believe that her colleague Betty is competent and willing to deal with one of her clients, but she cannot trust her to do so if she believes Betty is only moved by her ambition. Betty will respond to Anne's trust for reasons that are entirely independent of the fact that Anne trusts her.[17]

[12] See Hardin, *Trust and Trustworthiness;* Warren, 'Democratic Theory and Trust' in Mark E Warren (ed), *Democracy and Trust* (Cambridge, CUP, 1999), 310–45 and Paul Bauer, 'Conceptualising Trust and Trustworthiness', in Raquel Barradas de Freitas and Sergio Lo Iacono (eds), *Trust Matters: Cross-Disciplinary Essays* (Oxford, Hart Publishing, forthcoming). Against this cognitivist approach to trust, see Karen Jones, 'Trust as an Affective Attitude' (1996) 107 *Ethics*, 4–25.

[13] See Pamela Hieronymi, 'The Reasons of Trust' (2008) 86 *Australasian Journal of Philosophy*, 213–36.

[14] Baier, 'Trust and Antitrust', 244. But compare with Richard Holton, 'Deciding to Trust, Coming to Believe' (1994) 72 *Australasian Journal of Philosophy*, 63–76.

[15] See Karen Jones, 'Trustworthiness' (2012) 123 *Ethics*, 61–85, 70.

[16] According to this view, trustworthiness is a kind of trust-responsiveness. Both Hardin and Jones, for very different reasons and with different qualifications, give accounts of trustworthiness that are as neutral as possible with respect to the trustee's motivational structure: Hardin, 'Trustworthiness' (1996) 107 *Ethics*, 26–42; Jones, 'Trustworthiness', 77. Importantly, while Hardin allows for self-interested people to be trustworthy in the presence of the right institutional constraints, Jones openly rejects this idea and claims that there are things such as fear, indifference and self-interest that are not adequate as a motivational foundation of trustworthiness (Jones, 'Trustworthiness', 68–69). For a different and probabilistic take on trustworthiness, see Bauer in this volume.

[17] This chapter assumes that the trustor is always justified in asking for the trustee's trustworthiness because this seems to be the case with vertical trust in representatives. It is not necessarily the case with all trust relations, though.

Hence, both trust and trustworthiness are domain-specific and person-indexed:[18] Anne trusts MP Barbara, rather than her colleague Betty (different persons), representing her in Parliament, but she does not trust Barbara with taking care of her son Ben (different tasks). Conversely, Barbara is trustworthy as a representative if she is competent and willing to take Anne's trust as a compelling reason for action, even though she may indeed be untrustworthy with kids.

Trust thus involves a form of reliance: when Anne trusts Barbara with looking after her child, she relies on Barbara to take care of him in a certain way.[19] However, trust is different from mere reliance precisely in virtue of its relation to trustworthiness. Firstly, it requires an interaction between people: while I may rely on the sun to come up every morning, I can *trust* the sun to do so only metaphorically.[20] Secondly, trust is more than mere reliance on someone else's 'dependable habits':[21] If Anne knows that Barbara has a sweet tooth, she may expect her to finish her ice cream, but she does not properly *trust* her to do so. In fact, she relies on Barbara's habit without Barbara's having the smallest idea. Similarly, a thief may rely on her forgetful victim to leave the window open out of distraction, but we would not say that the thief *trusts* her victim to do so because the victim can hardly be seen as competent and willing to respond to the thief's trust. Both Barbara and the victim may be reliable in their behaviour, which makes Anne's and the thief's expectation rational, but we would not call them trustworthy. Naturally, making one's trust explicit is not always necessary: I do not need to remind my partner every day that I trust him not to cheat on me. However, trustworthiness requires that the trustee is aware of the trustor's trust in a certain domain so that she can respond to it appropriately. In such a way, a peculiar *circle of trust* can develop. On the one hand, the trustor's trusting behaviour provides the trustee with a reason to appropriately respond to the trust; on the other, the warranted belief that the trustee will be trustworthy grounds the trustor's trusting behaviour.[22]

Finally, virtually all scholars agree that trust always involves the trustor's acceptance of vulnerability to the trustee's discretionary power and hence to the possibility of abuse: by trusting Barbara, Anne is allowing her the opportunity to hurt her. Annette Baier has famously claimed that only trust makes you vulnerable to betrayal rather than mere disappointment.[23] Regardless of what is the appropriate reaction when one's trust is broken, it seems uncontroversial that when Anne trusts Barbara, she gives Barbara a certain amount of discretionary power to do C, meaning that she does not check on Barbara repeatedly, she does not attempt to control how Barbara acts with respect to C and is not vigilant that Barbara will

[18] Jones considers both 'three-place predicates', 'Trustworthiness', 70–73. She further distinguishes between simple and rich trustworthiness, with the latter having a two-place structure, but this goes beyond the scope of this article.

[19] See Pettit, 'The Cunning of Trust', 204 and Baier, 'Trust and Antitrust', 259.

[20] See Pettit, 'The Cunning of Trust', 205 and Hardin, *Trust and Trustworthiness*, 12.

[21] Baier, 'Trust and Antitrust', 234. For a similar point, see also Jones, 'Trustworthiness', 65.

[22] For an analysis of this trust mechanism, see Pettit, 'The Cunning of Trust' and the section after the next.

[23] See Baier, 'Trust and Antitrust', 235.

do C in the exact way she expects her to do. Barbara has leeway to act as she sees fit in virtue of Anne's trust. As has been pointed out, if Anne spends her night monitoring Barbara's babysitting remotely via a 'nanny-cam', she is not properly trusting her.[24] It is not by chance that Baier considers the acceptance of such a state of vulnerability as part and parcel of what it means to trust: 'trust then, on its first approximation, is *accepted vulnerability* to another's possible but not expected ill will (or lack of goodwill) toward one'.[25]

As a belief, trust is not always normatively valuable.[26] Because the trustee can exercise her discretionary power over the trustor, trust is valuable only when warranted, namely when the trustor has good reasons or is justified in believing that the trustee deserves her trust. As already mentioned, the answer to such a question is, to a large extent, empirical: we need evidence to assess the trustor's belief in the trustee's trustworthiness. As Onora O'Neill notes, reasonably placed trust requires information about both the claims of the person who invites us to trust and about the trustee herself.[27]

The trouble with justified trust is that the higher is the trustor's vulnerability, the higher the bar for justified trust will be. If Anne is sitting in the post office, waiting for her turn, and receives a call, she may trust a stranger to keep her seat while she is away. She has virtually no belief concerning the stranger's trustworthiness, but she is also asking very little. If she wrongly trusts the stranger, she will not risk much. Yet, if Anne must choose a babysitter for her son, it is unlikely that she will trust the same stranger without more information about her.

Social and political trust can expand the horizon of possibility for human actions only if they can be safely attributed to strangers when important interactions are at stake.[28] Life without trust would be a nightmare because we would need to closely monitor friends and family we trust to care for us, colleagues we trust to be honest, flatmates we trust not to sneak in our room, and strangers we trust not to threaten or assault us when we get out of the house. Because we are social beings, we need to cooperate with others; we cannot check on everyone we get in contact with because we are finite beings,.[29] Trust is therefore necessary. On the other hand, trust is also risky because it exposes the trustor to someone else's discretionary power. The distinctive vulnerability that trusting entails stems from the fact that the trustee, being a free agent, always has the opportunity to act in unpredictable ways and harm the trustor, especially to the extent that the trustor does not keep the trustee under surveillance. Thus, functioning societies often make trust easier by diminishing the impact of the vulnerability related to trust, hence lowering the cost of misplaced trust.[30]

[24] See Jeremy Wanderer and Leo Townsend, 'Is It Rational to Trust?' (2013) 8 *Philosophy Compass*, 1–14, 1.

[25] Baier, 'Trust and Antitrust', 235, emphasis added.

[26] See Hardin, 'Do We Want Trust in Government?' in Mark E Warren (ed) *Democracy and Trust* (Cambridge, CUP, 1999), 24.

[27] See O'Neill, *A Question of Trust* (Cambridge, CUP, 2002), 64.

[28] See Eric M Uslaner, *The Moral Foundations of Trust* (Cambridge, CUP, 2002).

[29] Jones, 'Trustworthiness'.

[30] Hardin, *Trust and Trustworthiness*.

For this reason, Warren claims that trust 'expands domains of collective self-rule'[31] by enabling people to engage in self-government. The complexities of contemporary societies and the social division of labour notwithstanding, if citizens trust those who vote on binding laws for them, they may be said to remain politically autonomous. Therefore, trust in representatives is a key issue to explore from a democratic point of view. Importantly, it is also a peculiar case of *personal* vertical trust. Since the accountability mechanism that applies to representatives works through the division of the citizenry in constituencies, it seems reasonable to start by looking at the trust relationship between each representative and her constituency.[32] To do so, we need to investigate representatives' roles within modern democratic institutions.

III. Political Representation: Delegates vs Trustees

Under contemporary democracies, citizens do not make the law directly; rather, they do so through elected representatives. Therefore, political representation is at the heart of modern democracy, to such an extent that it almost seems impossible nowadays to think of the latter without reference to the former and vice versa.[33] In her ground-breaking analysis, one of the most important scholars in political representation, Hanna Pitkin, has famously equated the two.[34] However, as she has later observed, democracy and representation are tied together into an 'uneasy alliance'.[35]

As a matter of fact, there is a constant tension between the democratic ideal and its representative institutionalisation. On the one hand, in a democracy, the people should exercise final control over the law or at least, on a very minimalist account of what democracy entails, collective decisions should be responsive to citizens' preferences.[36] On the other, these preferences are formally voiced only through representatives, who deliberate and vote on specific policy proposals. Through general elections, representatives are bestowed the right to vote on legislation, but the way they exercise this right contributes to determining whether the

[31] Warren, 'Trust and Democracy', 75.

[32] To be sure, this approach focuses on electoral rather than nonelectoral representation but given the starting question (ie whether representatives should be a trustee or delegate), such an outlook seems the more appropriate. For an argument against territorial constituencies, which characterise most contemporary democracies, see Andrew Rehfeld, *The Concept of Constituency: Political Representation, Democratic Legitimacy, and Institutional Design* (Cambridge, CUP, 2005). For a shift to nonelectoral representation, see Michael Saward, 'Authorisation and Authenticity: Representation and the Unelected' (2009) 17 *The Journal of Political Philosophy* 1–22.

[33] Plotke, David, 'Representation Is Democracy' (1997) 4 *Constellations*, 19–34.

[34] Hannah F Pitkin, *The Concept of Representation* (Berkeley, University of California Press, 1967).

[35] Pitkin, 'Representation and Democracy: Uneasy Alliance' (2004) 27 *Scandinavian Political Studies*, 335–42, 335.

[36] For contemporary advocates of the former view, see Thomas Christiano, *The Constitution of Equality: Democratic Authority and Its Limits* (Oxford, OUP, 2008) and Philip Pettit, *On the People's Terms: A Republican Theory and Model of Democracy* (Cambridge, CUP, 2012), while an example of the latter is Albert Weale, *Democracy* (Houndmills, Macmillan Press, 1999).

representative system in place is truly a democracy or not. If elected officials do not care about citizens' interests and are unresponsive to them, representative democracy would turn out to be, like Rousseau, for instance, claims, an elected aristocracy, where the people are free only when they vote at elections and then sink back into slavery. At the same time, standards for evaluating the performance of representatives depends on the view of representation one favours, and it is contentious which one is adequate since representation is a 'single, highly complex concept'.[37]

Historically, the literature on political representation has offered two alternative ways in which representatives are expected to act: either as delegates or as trustees.[38] According to the former model, representatives follow the expressed preferences of their constituents, and the key virtue of their role is responsiveness to those preferences. A democratic form of political representation then requires that representatives take their constituents' preferences and bring them to the Parliament untouched. On the latter view, instead, representatives are not mere executors of constituents' will; rather, they are entrusted with their interests, which they ought to pursue according to their conscience.[39] Edmund Burke, who is generally thought to be a champion of the trustee model, put it in a fairly plain way:

> Parliament is not a congress of ambassadors from different and hostile interests, which interest each must maintain, as an agent and advocate, against other agents and advocates; but Parliament is a deliberative assembly of one nation, with one interest, that of the whole.[40]

According to this reading, delegate and trustee are two models for representatives' behaviour. When MPs exercise their functions, they may either act as a delegate, hence follow their constituents' instructions or as trustees, thereby following their conscience. There are various dimensions to these opposing models.[41] For instance, supporters of trusteeship have traditionally claimed, as Burke does in this passage, that representatives should only care for the national interest, while advocates of delegation have been mostly seen as pluralists, according to whom representatives should pursue their own district's local interests.[42] Another example concerns what

[37] See Pitkin, *The Concept of Representation*, 8.

[38] Dovi, S (2018, Fall). Political Representation. Retrieved from Stanford Encyclopedia of Philosophy: https://plato.stanford.edu/archives/fall2018/entries/political-representation

[39] John Berkow, the former Speaker of the House of Commons, makes a similar point in his resignation speech: www.ft.com/content/18f28954-d317-11e9-8367-807ebd53ab77.

[40] Edmund Burke, *Reflections on the Revolution in France* (London, Penguin Books, 1968 [1790]), 115.

[41] In this sense, trustee and delegate are not opposing poles in a continuum of discretion, as Ethan Leib and David Ponet claim, because their distinction involves multiple dimensions. See Ethan J Leib and David L Ponet, 'Fiduciary Representation and Deliberative Engagement with Children' (2012) 20 *The Journal of Political Philosophy*, 178. Pitkin's view also admits degrees of independence, as in Pitkin, *The Concept of Representation*, 146. Against this simplistic view of representation, see Andrew Rehfeld, 'Representation Rethought: On Trustees, Delegates, and Gyroscopes in the Study of Political Representation and Democracy' (2009) 103 *American Political Science Review*, 214–30.

[42] For a similar opposition between state-oriented and district-oriented representatives, see also Heinz Eulau, John C Wahlke, William Buchanan, and Leroy C Ferguson, 'The Role of the Representative: Some Empirical Observations on the Theory of Edmund Burke' (1959) 53 *American Political Science Review* 742.

Andrew Rehfeld calls the sources of judgment: in advancing their aims, whatever these may be, MPs may rely on their own judgment or their constituents'.[43]

Significantly, these two dimensions differ: a representative could follow the common good as she sees it, but she could also follow *her constituents'* view of the common good. Conversely, she could advance her constituents' local interests as she sees them or as *her constituents* see them, and the two perspectives may conflict. Furthermore, these dimensions admit degrees. A representative may follow the common good most of the time but refrain from doing so when this deeply hurts her constituents' interests. Or she can attempt to find a compromise between the two. Similarly, she may rely on her judgment most of the time because she thinks her constituents will be on the same page with her[44] while giving priority to their views if they openly disagree with her.

All these considerations pertain to the way representatives are expected to act and cast their vote in Parliament. However, the opposition between the delegate and trustee is also an opposition between mandate and independence concerning the *right* to decide how to cast a vote.[45] From now on, I will call the *trustee in the proper sense* a representative with the right to decide how to vote, while I will refer to the representative who does not have this right as a *delegate in the proper sense.*[46] In such a way, I intend to separate the question concerning the considerations based on which representatives are expected to act from that concerning *the owner of the right to decide how representatives ought to cast their votes on legislation.* The latter is a dichotomous question: either this right belongs to the representatives or stays with the people. Furthermore, the latter question enjoys priority with respect to the first one: if the right stays with the people, it will be up to each district to decide how a representative should cast each vote. Conversely, if the right is bestowed on the representative, we can further wonder how she should exercise it to be a good representative.[47]

Both options are at first sight consistent with democratic principles. It is true that democracy requires that citizens have final control over the rules they are obliged to follow, or at least that these rules are responsive to their preferences, but such a requirement does not entail that citizens have final authority over how their representatives cast their ballot. Bernard Manin famously pointed out that 'none of the representative governments established since the end of the Eighteenth

[43] Rehfeld, 'Representation Rethought'.

[44] As Congressmen interviewed by Richard Fenno like to say, 'If your conscience and your district disagree too often, you're in the wrong business'. See Richard F Jr Fenno, *Home Style: Members in their Districts* (Boston, Little Brown, 1978).

[45] Pitkin collapses these two different questions in her work, *The Concept of Representation*, 165. For criticism, see Rehfeld, 'Representation Rethought'.

[46] Here I follow Rehfeld's suggestion, but I employ different terms. He uses the adjectives 'mandated' and 'independent' to refer to what I call 'delegate' and 'trustee' in the proper sense. See Rehfeld, 'Representation Rethought', 225.

[47] For a recent attempt to offer inherently democratic standards to evaluate representatives' conduct, see Suzanne Dovi, The Good Representative (Malden, Blackwell Publishing, 2007).

century has authorized imperative mandates or granted a legally binding status to the instructions given by the electorate'.[48] In a 2009 report, the European Commission for Democracy through Law has even defined the prohibition of an imperative mandate as 'a cornerstone of European democratic constitutionalism'.[49] In most Western liberal democracies, then, citizens retain the power to sanction their representatives by ousting them through regular elections, but they *entrust* the power to decide how to vote on legislation to someone else.

However, if citizens do not trust or even distrust their representatives, treating them as delegates may seem a more prudent arrangement. According to two 2020 surveys, 31 per cent of French have trust in the National Assembly, while in the USA, only six and seven per cent of respondents declare that they trust Congress 'a great deal' and 'quite a lot', respectively.[50] In these cases, retaining both the right to sanction representatives and decide how they ought to vote seems a wiser option for suspicious citizens. Constituents of each district would then provide their delegate with strict instructions on how to cast their vote on laws discussed in Parliament. I will call this the delegate solution. Different supporters of this solution can be found in history. When he tried to adapt his democratic principles to a large nation state such as Poland, Rousseau offered a system of delegation similar to the one that the Paris Commune would have implemented almost a century later.[51] Even though this proposal may seem unfeasible, it has been recently advanced by some populist parties, such as the Italian Five Stars Movement, whose main political leaders claimed multiple times that representatives should only act as delegates of the people and new technologies can be employed to convey voters' preferences into a collective ranking that representatives would only be tasked with executing.[52]

Since the argument defended by the advocates of the delegate solution rests on a warranted lack of trust or distrust in representatives, we first need to assess this claim. To be sure, whether constituents are justified in trusting their representative will be a contingent matter, which depends on the context and the representative's character. However, it is important to note that the delegate solution is institutional: we are not wondering whether a single representative should have the right

[48] Bernard Manin, *The Principles of Representative Government*, 163.

[49] European Commission of Democracy through Law, *Report on the Imperative Mandate and Similar Practices*, art 39, www.venice.coe.int/webforms/documents/default.aspx?pdffile=CDL-AD(2009)027-e.

[50] The sources, for France and the USA respectively, are the following: www.sciencespo.fr/cevipof/sites/sciencespo.fr.cevipof/files/Barometre_confiance_vague9.pdf and https://news.gallup.com/poll/1600/congress-public.aspx. Yet, trust in the individual representative seems higher than trust in the entire legislative assembly, according to Fenno, *Home Style*.

[51] See Manin, *The Principles of Representative Government*, 165.

[52] See for instance: Beppe Grillo, 'Circonvenzione di Elettore' [Voter Circumvention] (March 2013) www.beppegrillo.it/circonvenzione-di-elettore/; Giorgio Grasso, 'Mandato Imperativo e Mandato di Partito: il Caso del MoVimento 5 Stelle' [Imperative Mandate and Party Mandate: the 5 Stars Movement Case] (2017) 2 *Osservatorio Costituzionale*, 1–7. The use of blockchain technology to vote would help make proposals like this feasible: Desmond Johnson, 'Blockchain-Based Voting in the US and EU Constitutional Orders: A Digital Technology to Secure Democratic Values?' (2019) 10 *European Journal of Risk Regulation*, 330–58.

to decide how to cast her vote in Parliament or not. We are asking whether any representative *qua representative* should have such a right. Two theoretical reasons cast doubt on citizen trust in representatives.

The first concerns the relationship between citizens and representative. Hardin observes that Madisonian liberalism has always stood up for a default position of distrust of government because of the power public officials hold and the conflict of interests that might divide those officials from citizens.[53] According to Hardin, to assess the justifiability of a trust belief, one needs to know either a political actor's motivation and interests or the structure of incentives within the institution.[54] When we look at representatives, their motivation is opaque because citizens do not often know them personally, and regular elections do not constitute a sufficiently strong incentive to ensure that representatives be trustworthy with their constituents' interests. This assessment is contingent on many factors, among which are the strength and credibility of oversight agencies and other state institutions, such as the media, audit commissions and the judiciary, which can lower the vulnerability related to trust in representatives by ensuring publicity and accountability.[55] However, since citizens' vulnerability to representatives' discretion *between* elections remains high, Hardin supports a default position of 'lack of either trust or distrust because we typically lack the relevant knowledge for going further than that'.[56]

The second reason stems from the relationship among citizens themselves. Warren claims that politics is inherently ridden with conflict among all individuals, in virtue of its relation to disagreement, on the one hand, and coercive power, on the other.[57] As he states, 'when it comes to politics, the basic conditions of warranted trust relationships–convergent interests and institutional roles that predict the goodwill of others–cannot and *should* not be taken for granted'.[58] Warren distinguishes between proper political institutions, such as legislatures and elected executives that citizens ought to distrust, and those ministries and agencies meant to provide citizens with broadly agreed public goods, towards which citizens cannot be suspicious. He claims that while the latter is and ought to be trusted by citizens in a healthy democracy, the former serve the purpose of *channelling distrust away from the latter and it into the political arena.* The way contemporary

[53] See Hardin, *Trust and Trustworthiness*, 153.

[54] Hardin develops his famous 'encapsulated interests account' to identify the conditions under which trustworthiness can correctly be inferred. Accordingly, the trustee need not be altruistic or tied to the trustor in a thick relationship, as long as the trustee's interests encapsulate the trustor's. According to Hardin, knowledge of the trustee's motivation (ie of their interests) and of the structure of incentives within which the trustee acts (affecting their interests) are necessary to assess whether they are trustworthy. See Russell Hardin, 'The Street-Level Epistemology of Trust' (1993) 21 *Politics & Society* 505–l529.

[55] Trust in these other first-order institutions is, therefore, essential, according to Warren, 'Trust and Democracy'.

[56] Hardin, 'Do We Want Trust in Government?', 23.

[57] Warren, 'Democratic Theory and Trust', 311.

[58] Warren, 'Democracy and Trust', 76, emphasis added).

democracies work, with competitive elections, free media and oversight agencies, institutionalises distrust and prevents it from generalising to the rest of society while at the same time empowering citizens to control politicians and public officials in these institutions thanks to the public discourse and voting.[59]

Trust requires that the trustee complies with her task in a way that is acceptable for the trustor. Anne would probably not trust Barbara as a babysitter if she knew that Barbara favours educational strategies that she finds objectionable. Similarly, even though Anne is ignorant concerning the best way to be treated for her cancer, she trusts her doctor insofar as she believes that the doctor will know and follow the most effective therapy available. In these cases, Anne either knows exactly how she wants her trustee to act, like with the babysitter, or shares the goal that the trustee should pursue with her own strategy, like with the doctor. However, when dealing with political representation, shared goals and strategies seem to characterise only the relationship between citizens and the representative *they have voted for*.[60]

Firstly, there is no reason to think that local interests are entirely homogeneous. If Anne is a blue-collar worker, her interests will likely differ from affluent entrepreneurs in her district. If the winning candidate runs on a policy platform that advances these entrepreneurs' interests, it will possibly set back Anne's.[61] Secondly, remember that a representative may intend to advance not only the district's interests, which are not themselves homogeneous but also a specific view of the common good. It is likely that what a disliked candidate considers in line with the common good is not compatible with Anne's views. Moreover, there are reasons to think that any view of the common good will cover conflict of interests and identities still running underneath and, as a result, even those who voted for the winning candidate may come to distrust her if she compromises a certain particularistic view of local interests and group identities based on which she has campaigned.[62] Therefore, while Anne may be justified in trusting some representatives sometimes, it is hard to see how she can be justified in trusting her representative all the time (ie regardless of whether she has voted for her or not).

Both Warren and Hardin fail to draw from this conclusion any implication concerning the institutional setup of representative democracy. If citizens do not trust their representatives, an imperative mandate seems preferable because it compels MPs to yield to the instructions of those who elected them and facilitates oversight from citizens who voted against them. Importantly, in this case, authorised representatives would still retain the right to vote in Parliament; what they

[59] Warren, 'Democracy and Trust', 90–91.

[60] This problem is, of course, more significant in first past the post systems but likely to happen also with proportional representation if citizens do not endorse major parties.

[61] Warren argues something similar: since candidates win by appealing to a community of interests and identities, they likely alienate those who do share them. See Warren, 'Trust and Democracy', 315.

[62] See Warren, 'Democratic Theory and Trust', 316.

would lose is the right to decide how to vote.[63] Two consequences would ensue. First, representatives would be legally bound to enact only those policy proposals that have passed the scrutiny of their voters. Second, since citizens cannot trust their representatives but would still need them to vote in Parliament, they should strictly monitor representatives' activities to be sure that representatives do not act on the basis of their own judgment.

IV. The Problems with the Delegate Solution

The delegate solution has met with many criticisms throughout history. Rather than reviewing these objections, most of which emphasise the unfeasibility of this proposal, I will focus on three objections that directly draw from the nature of political representation and its connection to trust.

The first problem with the delegate solution is that it derives from an essential misconception of the kind of practice that involves political representation. According to this view, citizens are assumed to have fixed interests or preferences *prior* to the representative process and that the representatives' job is just to take them as they are and translate them into coercive laws. This assumption seriously misreads the process of political representation, which is much more complex and articulated.

As Michael Saward observes, representation is better understood as a *process or a practice of claim-making*, where the represented is not simply made present but somehow *constituted* itself by the process.[64] More precisely, Saward distinguishes five components of the claim-making practice:

> A maker of representations ('M') puts forward a subject ('S') which stands for an object ('O') that is related to a referent ('R') and is offered to an audience ('A').[65]

The maker of the claim is someone who presents a subject as representative for something. The maker and subject might be the same when someone makes a claim. The something represented, the object, is the product of the claim-making practice and generally identified by specific features that the maker presents as belonging to a certain referent in the real world. All this happens in front of an audience expected to accept or reject the claim. Saward offers the following example:

> The Liberal Party (maker) offers itself (subject) as standing for the interests of the 'family' (object) to the electorate (audience).[66]

[63] Rehfeld, 'Representation Rethought', 225.
[64] See Saward, *The Representative Claim* (Oxford, OUP 2010), 8.
[65] Saward, *The Representative Claim*, 36.
[66] Saward, *The Representative Claim*, 37.

The 'family' as the *object* of representation differs from the family as the real-world referent. While the latter is the actual families that the Liberal Party claims to represent, the object consists of how the claim-maker describes the family (the Liberal Party). For instance, the Liberal Party may refer to actual families (referent) as loci of traditional values and middle-class aspirations. It is then up to the audience that the claim-maker addresses to accept or reject the claim. In the example, the audience is constituted by the electorate, whose members are expected by the claim-maker to identify with the object (the family) and can accept or reject such an identification.

Although the final say stays with the audience/electorate, candidates present themselves before the electorate as advocates for interests and ideals that they elaborate in the first place. Represented interests and ideals are the *objects* of the claim-making process rather than the referent; they are not predetermined prior to it but constituted in it. This element is what is neglected by an account of representatives as mere delegates. When they compete for office, politicians offer objects of representation that do not simply reflect real-world referents in a neutral way, but they pick out distinctive features to make their claim convincing for their intended audience. To be sure, if a candidate claims to speak for the working class and then her case for it (the object she presents) is weak, the electorate can reject this claim by not voting for her. However, in any representative process, no matter how democratic, there is an important element of inventiveness, construction and agency on the claim-maker's part. Because of this, candidates are responsible for the way they present the interests and ideals they stand for, and they should not avoid such responsibility by claiming that they are simply following their constituency's instructions.

An advocate of the delegate solution could object that this is true for the campaigning preceding elections when candidates compete for office, but this is not the case once they have been elected. Only at that point, they ought to be faithful to the promises they have made during the campaign and have been accepted by the constituency electing them.[67] This counter-objection unveils two further mistakes underlying the delegate solution. Firstly, candidates tend to put together a comprehensive agenda, which systematises multiple values and interests in a coherent policy platform.[68] While voters share aspects of such a programme, it is also well known that they do not often endorse it in its entirety. To the extent that legislative majorities aim to pursue a coherent set of goals, each representative cannot simply refer to its voters to cast her ballot because this would hinder consistent decision making by compelling the representative to vote according to changing majorities in her district.

[67] Voting in Parliament is only one of the many political activities in which a representative is involved. Citizens' control in all other activities is even more difficult to achieve and could hinder the realisation of the MP's programme.

[68] Importantly this is not the candidates' job, but often political parties'. Neglecting parties in representation has serious consequences for the way the relationship between representatives and citizens is conceptualised. Unfortunately, there is no space for further reflections on this topic.

Secondly, and more importantly, a representative who is legally bound to vote as their constituents decide shirks all responsibility for the consequences of their policy proposals. By withholding the right to decide how to vote in Parliament, citizens would assume full responsibility for the laws passed, while representatives would become substantively unaccountable. Firstly, representatives would not be responsible for the policy proposals they put forward in their programme because these have been chosen by those constituents who voted for them. Secondly, representatives would not be responsible for which bits and parts of their programme get realised and which do not, because again, this is their constituents' call. Citizens would then end up with no agenda-setting power because of how representation works but full responsibility for representatives' actions, which according to the delegate solution, they would dictate. The result would be representatives' lack of accountability to citizens.[69]

We seem to have reached an impasse. On the one hand, citizens should suspend their trust in representatives or even endorse a default position of distrust of those representatives they did not vote for because they do not share the same goals and views. On the other hand, delegation cannot work because it neglects and conceals the creative role that candidates as claim-makers have in representation. Even though the audience will adjudicate whether this object convincingly connects to the real-world referent, it is up to the claim-maker to first determine the object of representation. If representatives have this creative role in the representative process, they already enjoy discretionary power to which citizens are vulnerable. Replacing representatives with citizens as final decision-makers has the puzzling result of obliterating representatives' accountability. At the same time, the nature of political representation makes it very difficult for all citizens to trust their representatives all the time, and hence trust *as a belief in the trustee's trustworthiness* seems unwarranted.

V. Trusting Behaviour and Language of Trust

One may think that this conundrum can be solved by calling on what Philip Pettit has labelled the 'cunning of trust'. He argues that even if there may be no reason to believe in others' trustworthiness, we can still rely on their trust-responsiveness. According to Pettit, people are trustworthy when they respond to trust for reasons of loyalty, virtue or prudence. However, these noble motivations are not the only ones who can prompt people to aptly respond to trust. Famously, he asserts that trust-responsiveness may be triggered by more mundane motivations such as the desire to be considered trustworthy and hence enjoy a good reputation among other people. This motivation, which would not be sufficient to qualify someone

[69] Surely they would need to provide reasons if they failed to follow the citizens' will, but they would not be accountable for the consequences of their mandate.

as trustworthy in his account, may still make them trust-responsive. Hence, the trustee can be made aware of the trustor's *presumption* of trust, even though the trustor does not actually trust them, and aptly respond to it in virtue of trust-responsiveness. Knowing that a person may display trust towards strangers by counting on the fact that these persons will be trust-responsive because they want to appear trustworthy. Trust understood as 'manifest reliance', as Pettit defines it, can generate a trustworthy behaviour due to trust-responsiveness, while this, in turn, makes it rational to trust someone even without a belief in her trustworthiness.

I think Pettit's view can be understood better if we clarify a distinction that seems implicit in his article. He separates trustworthiness from trust-responsiveness. However, because he considers trust as 'manifest reliance', he loses sight of another critical distinction between trust *as a belief* and trust *as a behaviour.*

Let us go back to Anne. She can entrust someone with her son in the sense of displaying trusting behaviour towards that person even without trusting that person.[70] If Anne needs to rush to the hospital and by pure chance, her colleague Betty can take care of Ben for the time Anne is at her mother's bedside, Anne can trust Betty with him in the sense of *showing trust* to Betty even though she has no belief concerning Betty's trustworthiness. Given the situation she finds herself in, Anne does not monitor Betty with a 'nanny-cam' and instead acts as if she believed that Betty is trustworthy around children because she accepts to be vulnerable with respect to Ben's health to Betty's discretionary power.

We often have multiple reasons to show such trusting behaviour. That Anne trusts Betty with her child, ie she believes that Betty is a trustworthy babysitter, is only one possible reason for showing Betty that she trusts her.[71] Yet, we often trust for entirely different reasons. When Anne leaves her laptop unattended on a table, she trusts people sipping coffee around her not to steal it. She may act because she sincerely believes that people around her are competent and willing not to break her trust by stealing her laptop. However, she may have no belief of such sort and nevertheless act as if she trusted them because she accepts her vulnerability to their power, the possibility of losing her laptop. Perhaps she does it out of a general attitude of optimism towards strangers,[72] perhaps she thinks it is her civic duty to show trust to her fellow citizens; perhaps she wants to try them. Think of Anne trusting her teenage daughter Becca to stay two nights alone at home: even though Anne does not believe Becca to be trustworthy (she is very much afraid Becca will throw a crowded, alcohol-ridden party); she thinks that showing Becca her trust,

[70] Hardin is keen on distinguishing between trust, which is a belief, and behaviour and claims that 'there is no 'act of trusting'' (Hardin, 'Trust and Trustworthiness', 59). Yet, it makes sense to talk about trusting behaviour to target those actions of reliance without monitoring that can be motivated in various ways. See also Edna Ullman-Margalit, 'Trust, Distrust, and In-Between' in Russell Hardin (ed), *Distrust* (New York, Russell Sage Foundation, 2004), 60–82.

[71] As a belief trust does not necessitate action: Anne may never act on the basis of her trust in Barbara. What matters here is that the converse is also true: a trusting behaviour also does not necessitate trust, in the sense of a belief in the trustee's trustworthiness. See Hieronymi, 'The Reasons of Trust'.

[72] For a study of generalised trust, see Uslaner, *The Moral Foundations of Trust*.

by not checking on her every half an hour, will help her become a more responsible young adult.[73] The possession of a belief in the trustee's trustworthiness is only one of the possible reasons justifying trustful behaviour.

Therefore, Pettit's 'cunning of trust' is better understood as a case of trusting behaviour and trust-responsiveness generating a similar self-reinforcing mechanism to the one engendered by actual trust and trustworthiness. When Anne displays trusting behaviour (without real trust), Becca takes her mother's expression of trust as a compelling reason to act as Anne expects. This helps Anne believe that Becca is indeed trustworthy and hence trust her for real.[74] According to Pettit, only the alternative mechanism of trusting behaviour, trust-responsiveness and actual trust can explain what he calls the 'creativity of trust', namely the fact that trust can be 'built on nothing' and 'establish such relationships in the first place'.[75]

The problem with this alternative circle of trust is that Pettit's definition of trust-responsiveness is too ambiguous. He claims to be 'uncommitted on whether that desire [to a good reputation] is basic or on whether its strength depends on the fact that by getting others to think well of them, people are better able to secure the material goods they pursue'.[76] Accordingly, the reason behind a desire for a good reputation does not matter: Becca would still be trust-responsive even if she had only instrumental reasons to care for her mother's good opinion. Perhaps she wants her mother to trust her with more important things, like driving her car, or perhaps she simply does not want her mother to scold her. Now, individual action is often overdetermined, and we may have multiple reasons for doing the same thing. However, this example highlights that the willingness to respond to trust may be absent from a trustee's motivation set without preventing the trustee's trust-responsiveness. If Becca *only* wants to avoid punishment, she will respond to Anne's trust for the reason that is independent of the fact that she takes Anne's trust as a compelling reason for action (in fact, she takes Anne's threat of punishment as such).

Previously I have defined trustworthiness as the capacity and willingness to take a trustor's trust as a compelling reason for action. Contrary to Pettit, I do not predicate trustworthiness on loyalty, virtue or prudence; hence I include his definition of intrinsic trust-responsiveness (the basic desire for a good reputation) in my definition of trustworthiness. The motivations for trustworthiness may differ and range from love and integrity to an intrinsic desire to be well regarded. However, trustworthiness excludes trust-responsiveness, which is only motivated

[73] For cases of therapeutic trust, see H J N Horsburgh, 'The Ethics of Trust' (1960) 10 *The Philosophical Quarterly*, 343–54.

[74] Wanderer and Townsend have objected to Pettit that the lack of transparency in the trustor's motivation for trust would undermine the trustee's disposition to respond to trust (Wanderer and Townsend, 'Is It Rational to Trust?', 10). In the example, though, Anne does not trust Becca with the intention of exploiting Becca's trust for a good reputation. She does so because she thinks that this will help Becca become a trustworthy person, even though she is currently not.

[75] Pettit, 'The Cunning of Trust', 218.

[76] Pettit, 'The Cunning of Trust', 216.

by *instrumental* desires for a good reputation. If Becca wants her mother to think well of her so she can spend time with her friends on weekends, she is only instrumentally trust-responsive. In other words, she acts as if she was trustworthy (ie taking Anne's trust as a compelling reason for action), while she is only responding to Anne's trust for reasons that have nothing to do with the fact that Anne trusts her.

This distinction between trustworthiness broadly intended and instrumental trust-responsiveness helps us see the problem of Pettit's alternative circle of trust. If the trustee is indeed trustworthy in the sense of taking the trustor's trust as a compelling reason for action, the mechanism of trust is self-reinforcing. However, if the trustee is only instrumentally trust-responsive, what results is a *circle of misplaced trust* because the trustee is not acting in response to the received trust.

Think of Anne's colleague, Betty, who has been trusted with Anne's son, Ben, and let us assume that Betty is an untrustworthy babysitter. Yet, Anne is very influential at work and may play an important role in Betty's future career. Thus, Betty responds to Anne's trust as if she were trustworthy, without considering that Anne has placed trust in her as a compelling reason for action. If Betty intrinsically desired to be well thought of by Anne and this gave her a reason to aptly respond to Anne's trust, she would be trustworthy even without being altruistic. However, since Betty does not care about Anne's trust and simply acts in a way that is more convenient to her, which happens to be trust-responsive, she is not trustworthy even if she responds to Anne's trust. If Anne ends up trusting Betty, her trust will be misplaced.

While a belief in the trustee's trustworthiness is not always necessary to generate a circle of justified trust, a belief in someone's trust-responsiveness can be insufficient. In cases of high vulnerability, this circle of misplaced trust, generating unwarranted trust by the connection of trusting behaviour and instrumental trust-responsiveness, can be worrisome. Citizen trust in representatives is one of such cases.

Take an untrustworthy representative: her only reason for responding to trust is that she wants to be re-elected. Thanks to accountability devices such as free media, periodic elections and an independent judiciary, she seems to have self-interested reasons to act in such a way as to preserve her constituents' trust. The same set of social and political institutions also lower the costs of vulnerability for misplaced trust. Thus, following the 'cunning of trust', constituents would have two reasons to show their trust: the representative is incentivised to be trust-responsive, and they are not fully vulnerable to her power.

Take two possible scenarios. In the first, MP Barbara is untrustworthy, and her constituents do not trust her. They show a trusting behaviour thinking that she is trust-responsive, ie she wants to be re-elected. She acts as if she is trustworthy and manages to convince her constituents that this is the case by hiding away her conflicts of interests and paying off journalists to have flattering press coverage. They end up with a false belief and unwarranted trust. In the second scenario, MP Barbara is also untrustworthy, but she does not convince her constituents otherwise. They still think that she is trust-responsive and, therefore, they do not closely check on her political activities. However, the reason why she responds to their trust is that it is the best way to promote her interests. If other ways that allow her to reach her goal more conveniently, she has no reason not to use them, thus possibly undermining her constituents' interests and ideals. Citizens' trusting behaviour then is also unwarranted.

In both cases, Pettit's alternative circle of trust misfires because it prevents citizens from monitoring representatives by either prompting them to trust or show trust towards them. In these cases, it seems that an attitude of mistrust and careful oversight of one's representative seems a preferable strategy, especially when citizens are dealing with representatives they did not vote for.

I think there are reasons to preserve, nonetheless, a public language of trust. Annalise Acorn, in this volume, explores the persistence of such rhetoric in the relationship between the Canadian State and Indigenous People. As she observes, the language of trust 'plays on the other's desire to be seen by third parties as trustworthy', in a way similar to Pettit's 'cunning of trust'.[77] However, I also think that a public language of trust achieves two essential aims, regardless of whether it manages to produce a circle of justified trust.

Firstly, the rhetoric of trust assigns clear roles to citizens and representatives. As we have seen, representatives claim to speak in the name of certain interests and ideals that they offer as characterising their constituency. Their creative role gives them a certain amount of discretionary power over their constituents because they are responsible for the self-image of the constituency whose interests and ideals they are meant to represent. Therefore, they must also have the right and the responsibility to further these interests and ideals by deciding how to vote in Parliament. What a language of trust contributes to realising is public awareness of citizens' vulnerability and representatives' discretionary power.

Secondly, this awareness may give intrinsically trust-responsive representatives reason to be trustworthy and to take their constituents' interests at heart. Even if representatives are not so moved, the language of trust assigns them clear responsibility for their actions. Although they might try to claim that they are only delegates for their constituents' will, the public awareness of their role as trustees will allow citizens to see more easily through such a claim and acknowledge their related responsibilities. In this sense, a language of trust is compatible with citizens' mistrust in or even distrust of their representatives if and when representatives fail to strike the right balance between local and national interests and their constituents and their own views.[78]

[77] Annalise Acorn's contribution to this volume, p 136.

[78] See Meena Krishnamurthy, '(White) Tyranny and the Democratic Value of Distrust' (2015) 98 *The Monist* 391–406.

VI. Conclusion

The argument presented follows five steps. The first step consisted in identifying trust with a belief in the trustee's trustworthiness. So conceived, well-grounded trust justifies a trusting behaviour, which provides the trustee with a compelling reason to keep that trust. This is what I called the circle of trust and the first self-reinforcing mechanism pinpointed by Pettit.

The second step involved arguing that citizen trust in representatives is often unwarranted because of the distinctive nature of political representation under conditions of conflict of interests. The same nature, however, also undermines what I called the delegate solution, namely the idea that the right to decide how representatives should vote in Parliament should belong to citizens. The third step thus argued that the delegate solution is unconvincing and leaves us with an impasse. On the one hand, political representation is inconsistent with trust in a representative for whom a citizen has not voted because this citizen would likely reject both the activities and goals of their supposed trustee. On the other, political representation inevitably bestows on representatives the discretionary power to select, characterise and even create interests and ideals that they will represent in Parliament. It seems then that representatives must be trustees, in the sense of having the right to decide how to vote in Parliament, without being trusted by citizens.

However, as Pettit and others have observed, trust is not the only reason for acting trustfully. What Pettit calls the 'cunning of trust' is the possibility of another self-reinforcing mechanism that develops from trusting behaviour and trust-responsiveness. Even if the trustor lacks the belief of the trustee's trustworthiness, they may nevertheless act *as if* they trusted because they can count on the trustee's desire for a good reputation. If this mechanism were effective, citizens could act as if they trusted representatives because there are instrumental reasons for representatives to be trust-responsive (ie they want to be re-elected). The fourth step was to argue that this alternative circle of trust risks generating misplaced trust. If the trustee is untrustworthy, their response to the trustor's trust will be completely contingent on the circumstances. If the trustor either comes to trust her or does not check on her as a result, she will be dangerously vulnerable to the trustee's power. Therefore, citizens should not rely on this specific circle of misplaced trust because their trust or trusting behaviour would be unwarranted.

The final step consisted in suggesting that citizens who do not have a specific belief concerning their representatives' trustworthiness (or who believe them to be untrustworthy) should *mistrust* them, which means monitoring their activities to see if they abuse their power. At the same time, the language of trust should not be discarded. In fact, it still serves the purpose of giving public recognition of representatives' discretionary power and citizens' vulnerability. Accountability mechanisms alone allow citizens to oversee representatives, but at the same time, they convey the wrong image of their relationship. If citizens are only seen as the principal and representatives as their agent, the latter appearing under strict control of the former and that the final responsibility only stands with the former. However, while citizens do have ways to check on representatives and replace them if needed (a possibility inherent to any system worthy of the name of democracy), representatives still enjoy wide discretionary power in the claim-making process before elections and in the law-making process after elections. The rhetoric of trust helps publicly remind representatives of their political responsibility and citizens of their vulnerability in their dealings with them.

References

Acorn, A 'The Language of Trust Without the Attitude of Trust: Repairing Relations between Indigenous People and the Canadian State.' In Raquel Barradas de Freitas and Sergio Lo Iacono (eds), *Trust Matters: Cross-Disciplinary Essays*. Oxford: Hart Publishing, 2021.

Baier, A (1986). 'Trust and Antitrust.' *Ethics* 96 (2): 231.

'Baromètre de La Confiance Politique' (CEVIPOF – Sciences Po 2018) Vague 9, www.sciencespo.fr/cevipof/sites/sciencespo.fr.cevipof/files/Barometre_confiance_vague9.pdf.

Bauer, P 'Conceptualising Trust and Trustworthiness', in Raquel Barradas de Freitas and Sergio Lo Iacono (eds), *Trust Matters: Cross-Disciplinary Essays*. Oxford: Hart Publishing, 2021.

beppegrillo.it (2013). 'Circonvenzione di elettore | Il Blog di Beppe Grillo', www.beppegrillo.it/circonvenzione-di-elettore/.

Burke, E (1968). *Reflections on the Revolution in France*. London: Penguin Books.

Christiano, T (2008). *The Constitution of Equality: Democratic Authority and Its Limits*. Oxford: Oxford University Press.

Dovi, S 'Political Representation', https://plato.stanford.edu/archives/fall2018/entries/political-representation/.

Dovi, S (2007). *The Good Representative*. Malden: Blackwell Publishing.

Eulau, H et al. 1959. 'The Role of the Representative: Some Empirical Observations on the Theory of Edmund Burke.' *American Political Science Review* 53 (3): 742.

Fenno, R F (1978). *Home Style: House Members in Their Districts*. Boston: Little, Brown.

Freitag, M and Bühlmann, M (2009). 'Crafting Trust: The Role of Political Institutions in a Comparative Perspective.' *42 Comparative Political Studies* 42 (12): 1537–66.

Gallup, (2007). 'Congress and the Public.' *Gallup.com*, 12 October, https://news.gallup.com/poll/1600/Congress-Public.aspx.

Grasso, G (2017). 'Mandato imperativo e mandato di partito: il caso del MoVimento 5 Stelle.' 2 *Osservatorio Costituzionale* 1.

Hardin, R (1996). 'Trustworthiness.' (1996) *Ethics* 107: 26.

Hardin, R (1999). 'Do We Want Trust in Government?' In Mark E Warren (ed), *Democracy and Trust*, Cambridge: Cambridge University Press.

Hardin, R (2002). *Trust and Trustworthiness*. Vol IV, New York: Russell Sage Foundation.

Hardin, R (2016). 'The Street-Level Epistemology of Trust.' *Politics & Society* 21 (4): 505.

Hieronymi, P (2008). 'The Reasons of Trust.' *Australasian Journal of Philosophy* 86 (2): 213.

Holton, R (1994). 'Deciding to Trust, Coming to Believe.' *Australasian Journal of Philosophy* 72 (1): 63.

Horsburgh, H J N (1960). 'The Ethics of Trust.' *The Philosophical Quarterly* 41 (10): 343.

Iacono, S L, Quaranta, M and Lo Iacono, S (2019). 'Contextual Economic Conditions, Institutions and Social Trust: Trends and Cross-National Differences in Europe, 2002–2017.' *Polis* 33 (2): 185.

Johnson, D, (2019). 'Blockchain-Based Voting in the US and EU Constitutional Orders: A Digital Technology to Secure Democratic Values?' *European Journal of Risk Regulation* 10 (2): 330.

Jones, K (1996). 'Trust as an Affective Attitude.' *107 Ethics* 107 (1): 4.

Jones, K (2012). 'Trustworthiness.' *Ethics* 123 (1): 61.

Meena Krishnamurthy (2015). '(White) Tyranny and the Democratic Value of Distrust.' *The Monist* 98 (4): 391.

Leib, E J and Ponet, D L 'Fiduciary Representation and Deliberative Engagement with Children.' *Journal of Political Philosophy* 20 (2): 178.

Lenard, P T (2008). 'Trust Your Compatriots, but Count Your Change: The Roles of Trust, Mistrust and Distrust in Democracy.' *Political Studies* 56 (2): 312.

Manin, B (1997). *The Principles of Representative Government*. Cambridge: Cambridge University Press.

Newton, K, Stolle, D and Zmerli, S (2018) 'Social and Political Trust.' In Eric M Uslaner (Ed), *The Oxford Handbook of Social and Political Trust*. Oxford: Oxford University Press.

O'Neill, O (2002). *A Question of Trust*. Cambridge: Cambridge University Press.

Pettit, P (1995). 'The Cunning of Trust.' *Philosophy and Public Affairs* 24 (3): 202.

Pettit, P (1999). *Republicanism: A Theory of Freedom and Government*. Oxford: Oxford University Press.

Pettit, P (2012). *On the People's Terms*. Cambridge: Cambridge University Press.

Pitkin, H F (1967). *The Concept of Representation*. Berkeley: University of California Press.

Pitkin, H F (2004). 'Representation and Democracy: Uneasy Alliance.' *27 Scandinavian Political Studies* 27 (3): 335.

Plotke, D (1997). 'Representation Is Democracy.' *Constellations* 4: 19.

Putnam, R (2000). *Bowling Alone: The Collapse and Revival of American Community*. New York: Simon & Schuster.

Putnam, R D (1993). *Making Democracy Work: Civic Traditions in Modern Italy*. Princeton: Princeton University Press.

Rehfeld, A (2005). *The Concept of Constituency: Political Representation, Democratic Legitimacy, and Institutional Design*. Cambridge: Cambridge University Press.

Rehfeld, A (2008). 'Report on the Imperative Mandate and Similar Practices.' (European Commission for Democracy Through Law) Study No 488, www.venice.coe.int/webforms/documents/default.aspx?pdffile=CDL-AD(2009)027-e.

Rehfeld, A (2009). 'Representation Rethought: On Trustees, Delegates, and Gyroscopes in the Study of Political Representation and Democracy.' *American Political Science Review* 103 (2): 214–230.

Robbins, B G (2012). 'A Blessing and a Curse? Political Institutions in the Growth and Decay of Generalized Trust: A Cross-National Panel Analysis 1980–2009.' *PLOS ONE* 7 (4). e35120.

Rothstein, B and Stolle, D (2008). 'The State and Social Capital: An Institutional Theory of Generalized Trust.' *Comparative Politics* 40 (4): 441.

Rousseau, J-J (2002). 'The Social Contract.' In Susan Dunn (ed), *The Social Contract and The First and Second Discourses*. New Haven: Yale University Press.

Saward, M (2009). 'Authorisation and Authenticity: Representation and the Unelected.' *Journal of Political Philosophy* 17 (1).

Saward, M (2010). *The Representative Claim*. Oxford: Oxford University Press.

Torcal, M (2014). 'The Decline of Political Trust in Spain and Portugal: Economic Performance or Political Responsiveness?' *American Behavioral Scientist* 58 (12): 1542.

Ullman-Margalit, E (2004). 'Trust, Distrust, and In-Between.' In Russell Hardin (ed), *Distrust*. New York: Russell Sage Foundation.

Urbinati, N (2006). *Representative Democracy: Principles and Genealogy*. Chicago: University of Chicago Press.

Uslaner, E M (1999). 'Democracy and Social Capital.' In Mark E Warren (ed), *Democracy and Trust*. Cambridge: Cambridge University Press.

Uslaner, E M, (2002). *The Moral Foundations of Trust*. Cambridge: Cambridge University Press.

Van der Meer, T W G and Zmerli, S (2017). 'The Deeply Rooted Concern with Political Trust.' In Sonja Zmerli and Tom W G van der Meer (Eds), *Handbook on Political Trust*. Cheltenham: Edward Elgar Publishing.

Wanderer, J and Townsend, L (2013). 'Is It Rational to Trust?' *Philosophy Compass* 8 (1).

Warren, M (2018). 'Trust and Democracy.' *The Oxford Handbook of Social and Political Trust*.

Warren, M E (1999). 'Democratic Theory and Trust.' In Mark E Warren (ed), *Democracy and Trust*. Cambridge: Cambridge University Press.
Warren, M, (2017). 'What Kinds of Trust Does a Democracy Need? Trust from the Perspective of Democratic Theory.' In Tom W G van der Meer and Sonja Zmerli (Eds), *Handbook on Political Trust*. Cheltenham: Edward Elgar Publishing.
Weale, A (1999). *Democracy*. Houndmills: Macmillan Press.

7

Trust in the Relationship between Indigenous People and the Canadian State

ANNALISE ACORN

I. Introduction

From the time of the Royal Proclamation of 1763 to the present day, the settler government in what is now Canada has consistently claimed to be trustworthy in its relation to Indigenous people and has invited Indigenous people's trust.[1] That state has, however, been equally consistently untrustworthy.[2] In what follows I examine four facets of the history of that relationship, pairing with each an analysis of a conceptual question about trust. My aim in linking these historical

[1] In addition to the Proclamation see the whole of Alexander Morris, *The treaties of Canada with the Indians of Manitoba and the North-West Territories, including the negotiations on which they were based, and other information relating thereto* (Toronto, Belfords, 1880). More recent declarations by state agents of the state's trustworthiness are found in Canadian case law. See, for example, See *R v Sparrow* [1990] 1 SCR 1075; *Delgamuukw v British Columbia* [1997] 3 SCR 1010; *R v Badger* [1996] 1 S.C.R. 771; *Lax Kw'alaams Indian Band v Canada (Attorney General)* [2011] 3 SCR 535 and also in the state's self-description on its websites. See for example the Federal Department of Justice website on the Government of Canada's relationship with Indigenous Peoples, www.justice.gc.ca/eng/csj-sjc/principles-principes.html.

[2] With respect to early breaches of treaties, see *Beardy's & Okemasis Band #96 and #97 v Her Majesty the Queen in Right of Canada*, 2015 SCTC 3, Jim Miller, Arthur J Ray, Frank Tough, *Bounty and Benevolence: a history of Saskatchewan treaties* (Montreal, McGill-Queens, 2000) 187, Hugh A Dempsey *Big Bear: the end of freedom* (University of Regina, 2006), Derek Whitehouse Strong, '"Everything Promised had been Included in the Writing:" Indian reserve farming and the spirit and intent of treaty six reconsidered' (2007) 27(1) *Great Plains Quarterly* 25–37. With respect to the residential schools, see Truth and Reconciliation Commission of Canada, *Final Report Volume One: Summary* (Lorimer, 2015). With respect to the government's refusal to fund Indigenous child welfare proportionately with non-Indigenous child welfare, see *First Nations Child and Family Caring Society of Canada v Attorney General of Canada (Representing the Minister of Indian Affairs and Northern Development Canada)* (2016 CHRT 2) as well as the following non-compliance orders issues against the government by the Canadian Human Rights Tribunal (2016 CHRT 10), (2017 CHRT 14) and (2018 CHRT 4). See also Andrea Gunn, 'Ottawa has spent more than $5 million in legal fees fighting complaints about First Nations child welfare' *The Chronicle Herald* 30 January 2020, www.thechronicleherald.ca/news/canada/ottawa-has-spent-more-than-5-million-in-legal-fees-fighting-complaints-about-first-nations-child-welfare-405103/.

observations to these conceptual questions is not to make any general philosophical claims about the nature of trust. Rather, I look at this story of colonisation in Canada to see what it reveals about how people are induced to trust, what reasons people can have for trusting, what kind of reorientation is required when trust is breached and what might be the ethical benefits of insisting on specificity about the objects of trust.

I begin with 'The Invitation'. Here I examine the rhetoric used by agents of the Canadian state to attempt to induce Indigenous trust at the time of the signing of the Victorian treaties. I place that piece of the story in conversation with the question of whether there is some emotional flavour to trust that distinguishes it from mere reliance. Next, in 'The Entrusting' I examine the Indigenous decision to enter into the treaties. Here I ask whether there might be certain affective states, such as extreme anxiety, that might be incompatible with trust properly so called. Could it be that the state of desperation Indigenous people found themselves in in the second half of the nineteenth century was so severe as to preclude the possibility of true entrusting? This is followed by 'The Betrayal' where I examine the Canadian state's multiple failures of trustworthiness. Here I address another perennial question about trust. Why does breach of trust result in feelings of betrayal rather than just disappointed expectation? And finally in 'The Denial' I show how the Canadian state, despite these betrayals, continues to describe itself as trustworthy in its relations to Indigenous people. I pair this analysis with a conceptual question about whether trust should be understood as having a three place predicate. Why might it be ethically preferable always to insist on specificity about exactly what A trusts B to do?

II. The Invitation

> Criminals, not moral philosophers, have been the experts at discerning different forms of trust.[3]

During the treaty negotiations, the Canadian state through its Lieutenant Governors invited Indigenous people's trust. Here we will look at the language of that invitation and juxtapose that with a question sometimes posed in philosophical discussions of trust. Is it the emotional flavour of trust that makes it different from mere reliance?[4] My aim here is to observe the Canadian state's strategy in persuading Indigenous people to trust them. What emotional state did those agents think would best ease the way toward Indigenous trust? We can learn much about the affective states accompanying trust by looking at the ways in which those seeking to gain others' trust attempt to manipulate the emotions. The agents of the Canadian state seem to have assumed that the best way to convince Indigenous people to trust was to convince them that they were loved, to elicit in them the feeling of being loved.

[3] A Baier, 'Trust and Anti-Trust' (1986) 96 *Ethics* 231, 234.

[4] Karen Jones, 'Trust as an affective attitude' (1996) 107(1) *Ethics* 4–25.

The aim of the Canadian state in entering into the treaties was to secure cessation of Indigenous lands.[5] The proposed consideration for that release was that Indigenous people would retain sufficient lands for themselves, the state would provide yearly payments to each individual and chief, assistance with a transition to agricultural economies as well as health care (including hoped-for vaccinations for smallpox) and optional education for Indigenous people.[6] The nature of the proposed agreement thus created a significant asymmetry as to trust. There was no need for the state to trust Indigenous people past the moment of signing. By contrast, most of the Canadian state's undertakings, aside from immediate money payments, were in the form of ongoing obligations, many of which were to be performed far into the future.

An extensive record of this invitation to trust is found in the papers of Lieutenant Governor Alexander Morris. Let's turn first to Morris's account of what Sir Adams George Archibald, Lieutenant Governor of Manitoba said in his speech during the negotiations leading up to Treaties Nos 1 and 2:

> Your Great Mother, the Queen, wishes to do justice to all her children alike. She will deal fairly with those of the setting sun just as she would with those of the rising Sun ….[7]
>
> She wishes her red children to be happy and contented ….[8]
>
> Your Great Mother therefore will lay aside for you 'lots' of land to be used by you and your children forever. She will not allow the white men to intrude upon these lots. She will make rules to keep them for you so that as long as the sun shall shine, there shall be no Indian who has not a place that he can call his home, where he can go and pitch his camp, or, if he chooses, build his house and till his land.[9]

Lieutenant Governor Alexander Morris reports his own speech in the negotiations for Treaty 4 as follows:

> Now I think that you see that the Queen loves her red children, that she wants to do you good, and you ought to show that you think so. I cannot believe that you will be the first Indians, the Queen's subjects, who will not take her by the hand …[10]
>
> I tell you this, trust my words, they come from the heart of one who loves the Indian people, and who is charged by his Queen to tell them the words of truth …[11]
>
> It is for you to say, not us; we have done all that men who love their red brothers can do; it is for you now to act, on you rests the duty of saying whether you believe our message or not, whether you want the Queen to help you or not, whether or not you will go away

[5] See n 1 above Morris.

[6] Treaty No 6 between Her Majesty the Queen and the Plain and Wood Cree Indians and other Tribes of Indians at Fort Carlton, Fort Pitt and Battle River with Adhesions, www.rcaanc-cirnac.gc.ca/eng/1100100028710/1581292569426#chp1.

[7] See n 1 above Morris, 28.

[8] Ibid.

[9] Ibid, 28–29.

[10] Ibid, 93.

[11] Ibid, 115.

> and let the days and the years go on, and let the food grow scarcer, and let your children grow up and do nothing to keep off the hunger and the cold that is before them.[12]

And Morris tells us that he said this in the negotiations for Treaty 6:

> My Indian brothers, Indians of the plains, I have shaken hands with a few of you, I shake hands with all of you in my heart. God has given us a good day, I trust his eye is upon us, and that what we do will be for the benefit of his children …[13]
>
> What I trust and hope we will do is not for to-day or to-morrow only; what I will promise, and what I believe and hope you will take, is to last as long as the sun shines and yonder river flows …[14]
>
> I have proposed on behalf of the Queen what I believe to be for your good, and not for yours only, but for that of your children's children, and when you go away think of my words. Try to understand what my heart is toward you. I will trust that we may come together hand to hand and heart to heart again. I trust that God will bless this bright day for our good, and give your Chiefs and Councillors wisdom so that you will accept the words of your Governor …[15]
>
> I know that the sympathy of the Queen, and her assistance, would be given you in any unforeseen circumstances. You must trust to her generosity.[16]

Queen Victoria is described as a mother who could be trusted because she cared about and loved the Indigenous people. Within the legal framework of the Canadian state, the 'Crown' as contracting party to the treaties was (and is) an abstraction referring to the bureaucracy and institutions of settler government. Through the rhetorical device of the Great Queen Mother, the Crown, that corporate and impersonal institution, was made to appear personal, feminine, close and individual. A woman who was both powerful and loving was posited as the one accepting immediate responsibility for the state's obligations. The affective state that was sought and invited as a foundation for trust was the feeling of being secure in love, in a mother's love.

We see also that the agents of the Canadian state issued their own declarations of love for the Indigenous people. What the agents of the state appear to have been trying to induce was trust – not just as the belief in the reliability of the Canadian state as regards its treaty promises, but a trust that the state would be a reliable promise maker *for reasons of* a love springing from a deep sense of kinship capable of lasting through generations. Max Harris in his contribution to this collection argues that love is preferable to trust as a 'relational ethic'.[17] He notes, 'in some circumstances the opposite of trust, distrust, is healthy in a way

[12] Ibid, 117.
[13] Ibid 199.
[14] Ibid 202.
[15] Ibid 209.
[16] Ibid 211.
[17] M Harris, 'How Should We Relate to Each Other Politically? Love and Trust as Relational Ethics in the Political Realm' In this volume.

that the opposite(s) of love (which I take to be fear and hate, amongst others) are not'.[18] Harris highlights the way in which these two intersubjective states, while both involve an element of positive affect, can have different valances and ramifications in the political realm. Of course, love and trust need not be intertwined. Just as it is possible to separate the nutrients in the yolk of an egg from the protective layer of the egg white, so one can disentangle the nourishment of love from the security of trust. But, the rhetoric of these Lieutenant Governors suggests the two begin and belong together.

As Harris notes, philosopher Annette Baier grounds trust in the idea of reliance on another's goodwill.[19] But trust, perhaps in its core case, relies on that goodwill toward another that has crossed into an intense and holistic concern for their wellbeing and has become and is experienced as love. Thus, a declaration of love as an inducement to trust makes rational sense. It provides a powerful reason to trust. The affective flavour of trust in its core case; trust grounded in confidence in the other's love, includes the positive self-evaluation entailed in the feeling of being loved. The feeling of being loved can propel trust, suspending one above concern with potential problems and supporting forbearance from critical inquiry.

Canadian politician Bob Rae notes that whereas Indigenous people considered the treaties to be analogous to a marriage (a vision of a shared life into the future) the Canadian state viewed the treaties as a divorce (minutes of settlement sorting out the terms of separation.)[20] Yet the negotiations leading up to the treaties show that whatever plans for separation the agents of the Canadian state had in mind, what they articulated was a vision of mutual and reciprocal love grounding a foundation for both trust and trustworthiness – something deeply familial.

This idea of trust grounded in loving kinship was recognisable within Indigenous traditions. Indeed, it resonated with the (very different) Indigenous legal framework supporting the entering into of the treaties. Indigenous legal scholar James Sákéj Youngblood Henderson notes that performance-based Indigenous laws that underpinned the treaties were of a piece with deeply held spiritual beliefs.[21] Henderson points to the Indigenous legal concept of *wahkohtowin*, or the 'law of good relationships' as key in the Indigenous understanding of the rights and obligations being agreed to under the treaty.[22] Henderson also comingles the language of trust with the language of love in articulating the relevant Indigenous legal concepts: 'The authority to make treaties is transmitted from the source of perfect love.'[23] Eliciting the trust of the Indigenous people had overriding

[18] Ibid at 90.

[19] See n 3 above, Baier at 234.

[20] 'Is It a Divorce or Marriage? Two versions of a treaty narrative' Walrus Talks, 23 April 2015, https://thewalrus.ca/tv-is-it-a-divorce-or-marriage-two-versions-of-a-treaty-narrative/.

[21] JSY Henderson, 'The Indigenous Law Foundation of the Victorian Treaties' Talk delivered at Edmonton, University of Alberta Faculty of Law, 6 March 2018.

[22] Ibid.

[23] Ibid.

legal significance within the Indigenous understanding of *wahkohtowin*. Under Indigenous law, Henderson notes, the legal significance of figure of the 'Queen as a person who cared, as someone who wanted to be a relative and a mother to the Indigenous people and to love them in the way that they wanted to live.'[24] The expression of the desire for kinship relations and willingness to take on the role of mother had significant legal consequences within Indigenous legal traditions. The Indigenous legal and ethical framework therefore was such that the rhetoric of love and kinship based trust would be interpreted as having solemn and binding consequences.

The Lieutenant Governors' monologues are replete with the language of love-based trust. But when put to the test of actual interaction with Indigenous leaders, the façade of loving concern quickly breaks down. For example, consider the following exchange. Having just assured the Chiefs 'they would never be made ashamed of what they then did',[25] Lieutenant Governor Morris had a request from one of the Chiefs that the initial money payment be made up-front prior to signing. The Chief understandably wanted the state's most immediate obligation actually to be performed before signing over the lands. That much power to influence the agents of the state might have been some kind of symbolic surety of the state's current love and future trustworthiness. But Morris replied, 'If you can trust us forever you can do so for half an hour; sign the treaty.'[26] Morris's rebuffing of the Chief's request, the hint of his intention to humiliate, contradicts his earlier tone of loving kinship and foreshadows the sad betrayals that were to come.

III. The Entrusting

> I readily trust others: but I would only do so with difficulty if ever I were to give grounds for thinking that I was acting out of despair … rather than from frankness and trust in a man's word.[27]

Let's turn now to examine the Indigenous decision to trust the agents of the Canadian state enough to enter into the treaties. Here we will ask another conceptual question. Are there some affective states that preclude the possibility of trust?[28] In particular, is it possible to trust in the presence of overwhelming anxiety? Is it possible to trust under duress?

[24] Ibid.

[25] See n 1 above Morris at 123.

[26] Ibid. This seems to have been Morris's line whenever a Chief wanted payment up-front prior to signing. See also Morris n 2 above at 46.

[27] M de Montaigne, 'Whether the governor of a besieged fortress should go out and parley.' In *Michel de Montaigne: the complete essays*. AM Screech translator (London, Penguin Books, 1991) 24.

[28] KF Jones, 'Trust and Terror' in P DesAutels and M Urban Walker (eds) *Moral psychology: feminist ethics and social theory* (Lanham, Rowman & Littlefield, 2004).

At the time of the negotiation of the treaties, Indigenous people knew they were in severe circumstances. First they were facing starvation as a result of the disappearance of the buffalo, brought about by the arrival of the settlers.[29] The buffalo had been the cornerstone of the Indigenous way of life. The buffalo roaming the plains of North America in the 1600s are estimated to have numbered around 30 million. By the time of the signing of Treaty 6 in 1876, the buffalo were facing imminent extinction.[30]

Second, Indigenous people were facing epidemics of infectious diseases introduced by settlers, particularly smallpox, to which they had no immunity.[31] Indigenous people needed and wanted assistance with health care and hoped for provision of smallpox vaccines that had been compulsory for children in England since 1853.[32]

Third, Indigenous people needed and wanted help to establish and enforce rules to protect their people from the ravages of a predatory and exploitative alcohol trade.[33] The use of whisky as a currency in trading in return for furs had broken down the health and wellbeing of many Indigenous people.

Finally, Indigenous people were aware of continuous settler encroachment. They knew that under these weakened circumstances, they would likely not have the power to stop settlers from forcibly taking their lands.[34]

Given this desperation, and given that the ones to be trusted were largely responsible for this state of destitution, was it even possible for Indigenous people to trust in any meaningful sense? Or did the absence of any real choice negate the possibility of trust?

Of course, war is another context in which we can wonder about whether one can be properly said to trust an adversary. Military historian Dennis Showalter for example writes, 'The greatest risk a soldier can take in combat is surrendering. It involves a primal act of trust towards "others" who directly seek your death.'[35]

[29] T Hubbard, 'Buffalo Genocide in Nineteenth Century North America: 'Kill, Skin, and Sell' in AL Hinton, A Woolford, J Benvenuto (eds) *Colonial Genocide in Indigenous North America* (Duke University Press, 2014); MS Taylor, *Buffalo Hunt: International trade and the virtual extinction of the North American Bison*, Working Paper 12969, National Bureau of Economic Research, Cambridge MA, March 2007, www.nber.org/papers/w12969.

[30] Hubbard above n 29 at fn 11 and see P Erasmus and H Thompson, *Buffalo Days and Nights* (Calgary, Glenbow Institute, 1999) 247–48.

[31] C Stuart Houston and S Houston, 'The first smallpox epidemic on the Canadian Plains: In the fur-traders' words' (2000) 11(2) *Can J Infect Dis* 112–15. And see JJ Heagerty, *Four centuries of medical history in Canada: and a sketch of the medical history of Newfoundland*, 1879–1946. Vol 1 (Toronto, The Macmillan Co, 1928) 17–65. And EW Stearn and AE Stearn, *The effect of smallpox on the destiny of the Amerindian.* (Bruce Humphries, 1945) 44–45.

[32] The Vaccination Act 1853. See http://navigator.health.org.uk/content/united-kingdom-vaccination-act-1853-made-vaccination-against-smallpox-compulsory.

[33] HR Johnson, *Firewater: how alcohol is killing my people (and yours)* (Regina, University of Regina Press, 2016). On this point see also n 2 above Morris at p 50 where the Indigenous people were requesting prohibition of sale of alcohol on reserve as a term of the treaty.

[34] See n 30 above Erasmus fn 14.

[35] D Showalter, 'By the Book? Commanders Surrendering in World War I' in H Afflerbach and H Strachan (eds) *How fighting ends: a history of surrender* (Oxford, OUP, 2012) 279.

One can trust one's life even to a mortal adversary if one believes in their commitment to shared norms such as laws of war that would secure one's protection. In the case of the Indigenous signing of the treaties, there is some evidence to support a similar belief in the existence of shared norms strong enough to build a bridge of trust.

There are I think two possible bases of shared normative ground that Indigenous leaders may have judged sufficient to support genuine entrusting to the Canadian state even in the face of overwhelming difficulty. The first was a belief in a shared sense of the value of the rule of law. The second was the belief in a shared understanding of reverence for the divine as a party to the obligations on both sides.

To see what evidence there might be to support these possibilities, I will look to Peter Erasmus, the translator of the negotiations leading up to the signing of Treaty 6 at Fort Carlton, Saskatchewan as documented in his book *Buffalo Days and Nights*.[36] This source is not free from controversy.[37] Nevertheless, it is some evidence of the Indigenous perspective on the potential reasons for trusting the agents of the Canadian state at the time. Here again, I will quote at length. Let's begin with a speech by Cree Chief Mista-wa-sis:

> I speak directly to Poundmaker and The Badger and those others who object to signing this treaty. Have you anything better to offer our people? …
>
> I, for one, think that the Great White Queen Mother has offered us a way of life when the buffalo are no more. Gone they will be before many snows have come to cover our heads or graves if such should be …
>
> The Great Queen Mother, hearing of the sorrows of her children sent the redcoats … I ask you why those few men could put to flight those bad men who for years defiled the whole of the southern Indian nations? …
>
> It was the power that stands behind those few redcoats that those men feared … the power that is represented in all the Queen's people, and we the children are counted as important even as the Governor who is her personal speaker.
>
> The Police are the Queen Mother's agents and have the same laws for whites as they have for the Indians.[38]

Next Chief Star Blanket said:

> For my part, I think that the Queen Mother has offered us a new way and I have faith in the things my brother Mista-wa-sis has told you … Surely the Indians can learn the ways of living that made the white man strong and able to vanquish all the great tribes of the nations … I will accept the Queen's hand for my people.[39]

The Queen's credibility seems to have been buttressed by at least some Indigenous experience of the North West Mounted Police (the redcoats) as willing and able

[36] See n 30 above.

[37] R Brown, A Acorn, D Lindberg, J Nichols, E Pentland, B Roe 'Roundtable: *Buffalo Days and Nights*, Peter Erasmus and Henry Thompson' (2019) 57:1 *Alta Law Rev* 145.

[38] Erasmus, n 14, 247–48

[39] Ibid 250.

to offer equal protection of just laws to Indigenous people and settlers alike. The symbolic power and presumed decency of the Queen Mother is seen as corroborated by the real power and experienced decency of the redcoats. This seems to support the possibility that a shared commitment to the values of the rule of law would provide a solid reason for Indigenous trust.

Religion and ceremony also played a role in the Indigenous sense that there was sufficient shared ground to support a decision to extend genuine trust despite desperate circumstances. We saw in the previous section how the agents of the Canadian state invoked God as an important presence in ensuring the solemnity of the treaties. Indeed, the Lieutenant Governors cited their own trust in God's beneficence as a reason for both sides to have confidence in entering into the treaties.[40]

It is easy to see how the state agents' references to God as a kind of spiritual third party guarantor of the treaty promises resonated and inspired confidence in the Indigenous people, given the centrality of spirituality to their culture and the connections between Indigenous religious ceremony, truth telling and promise keeping. The Indigenous party assembled for the negotiation of Treaty 6 engaged in a peace pipe ceremony that was of the utmost significance within Indigenous spiritual traditions. Referring to the sacredness of ceremony at the time of the making of the treaties, Erasmus writes:

> these ceremonial practices had a deep significance to the tribes and can only be explained as a solemn approach to a vital and serious issue for discussion …
>
> Few people realize that those so-called savages were far more deeply affected and influenced by their religious beliefs and convictions than any comparable group of white people, whose lip service to their religion goes no deeper than that.[41]

The Canadian Government's Treaty Research Report published in 1985, talking about the significance of ceremony to the Indigenous understanding of the solemnity of the treaties, says this:

> The purpose of this tradition is that the Indians have utmost and absolute belief in the sacredness of the pipe. In the presence of the pipe, only the truth must be used and any commitment made in its presence must be kept.[42]

Indigenous spiritual traditions underpinned a sense of the solemnity of the treaties, the sacredness of the promises, the absolute obligation to truth and good faith in negotiating and concluding those obligations. For the Indigenous parties it was as if the pipe ceremony inducted a sacred and spiritual third party guarantor into the treaty relationship to ensure the truth of the undertakings and the performance of the obligations. It is easy to see therefore how they would have assumed that the religious invocations on the part of the agents of the Canadian state secured a

[40] See quotations accompanying nn 13 and 15.
[41] See n 30 Erasmus, 240.
[42] Treaty Research Report – Treaty Six (1876), Indigenous and Northern Affairs, Canada, www.aadnc-aandc.gc.ca/eng/1100100028706/1100100028708.

similar solemnity and sacredness for their own part. They would have understood that a shared reverence for the deity secured shared normative common ground.

Even where an adversary seeks to dominate one, even where that adversary has engineered one's destitution, their commitment to values and principles outside that quest for domination could motivate that party to honour their word and follow through on their stated commitments. Thus despite the difficulties amounting to duress that Indigenous people faced, and despite the likely participation of at least some agents of the Canadian state in bringing about those difficulties, despite even the ways in which the Canadian state clearly stood to benefit from Indigenous destitution, it was still open to the Indigenous parties genuinely to trust the bona fides of the Canadian state. It was not unreasonable for Indigenous people to view the state agents' commitment to the ideals of the rule of law and to reverence for God as good enough reasons to trust even if they suspected that their professed claims to feelings of loving kinship were insincere.

IV. The Betrayal

> Let us not pretend to doubt in philosophy what we do not doubt in our hearts.[43]

Both in the immediate aftermath of the signing of the treaties and in the decades following, the Canadian state completely disregarded its undertakings. In this section I will pair historical facts about those failures to honour treaty promises with an examination of another perennial philosophical question about trust. What is it about trust that makes its breach an occasion for feelings of betrayal rather than mere disappointment?[44] As we shall see, the reasons for this sense of betrayal attaching to breaches of trust are built upon what we have already observed about the emotional flavour of trust and the way in which trust can be based on a belief in shared values.

Noting the widespread disregard by the Canadian state of its treaty obligations, Jill St Germain describes a gathering of Cree chiefs to address the issue of breaches in 1884, seven years after the signing of Treaty 6.

> the chiefs were now prepared to accept that they had erred in giving Canada the benefit of the doubt and that Canada's persistent indifference in the implementation of its treaty promises was not a failing of ignorance but a manifestation of deliberate duplicity. This was a shocking revelation of the solemnly sworn treaty relationship, but having digested it, the Crees could now address the problem of Canadian insincerity.[45]

[43] CS Peirce, 'Some Consequences of Four Incapacities' (1868) 2, *Journal of Speculative Philosophy* 140–57, www.peirce.org/writings/p27.html.

[44] For a good discussion of a number of philosophers on this point see ES Hinchman, 'On the Risks of Resting Assured: an assurance theory of trust' in P Faulkner and T Simpson (eds) *The Philosophy of Trust* (Oxford, OUP, 2017).

[45] J St Germain, *Broken Treaties: United States and Canadian Relations with the Lakotas and the Plains Cree, 1868–1885* (Lincoln, University of Nebraska Press, 2009) 313.

With the full benefit of the massive redistribution of wealth wrought by the Indigenous ceding of territory in hand, the state proceeded to confine Indigenous people to reserves often far smaller than what they had agreed to and to renege on their reciprocal obligations to promote the welfare of Indigenous people; the provision of agricultural implements, seeds and such like as well as medical care and relief in times of famine.[46]

Perhaps the most devastating failure of trustworthiness of the Canadian state was in relation to the education of Indigenous children. The state had agreed to set up schools on reserve when bands judged it appropriate for their children to learn to read and write. The language of Treaty 6 reads, 'Her Majesty agrees to maintain schools for instruction in such reserves hereby made as to Her Government of the Dominion of Canada may seem advisable, whenever the Indians of the reserve shall desire it.'[47] In a nightmarish bait and switch, the Canadian government instead enacted a legal framework for and committed to a practice of forcing Indigenous children into residential schools.[48] Rather than the instruction being optional for those bands who desired it as agreed, the state abducted Indigenous children and forcibly confined them in residential schools far from their reserves. The explicit purpose of the schools was to destroy Indigenous culture and language and to assimilate indigenous people into settler society.[49] Prime Minister John A MacDonald arguing before the House of Commons in favour of the legislation in 1883 said this,

> When the school is on the reserve the child lives with its parents, who are savages; he is surrounded by savages, and though he may learn to read and write his habits, and training and mode of thought are Indian. He is simply a savage who can read and write.[50]

The solution was to coerce Indigenous children into residential schools. There was no way to contest this drastic interference with liberty as a matter of right. There was no way to contest it at all. The Report of the Canadian Truth and Reconciliation commission outlines the myriad abuses and atrocities, including physical and sexual abuse, deliberate malnutrition and medical experimentation that comprised the attempted cultural genocide that was the residential schools.[51]

[46] Ibid and see n 2 above and see also Bill Waiser, 'History Matters: Treaty 6 Promises were quickly broken', http://thestarphoenix.com/opinion/columnists/history-matters-treaty-six-promises-were-quickly-broken.

[47] See text of Treaty 6, www.aadnc-aandc.gc.ca/eng/1100100028710/1100100028783.

[48] 57–58 Victoria, Chapter 32, An Act to Further Amend the Indian Act Assented to 23 July 1894, s 11. See in particular s 138(2). In general see National Centre for Truth and Reconciliation, 'Honouring the Truth, Reconciling for the Future: Summary of the Final Report of the Truth and Reconciliation Commission of Canada' Truth and Reconciliation Commission of Canada, 31 May 2015, www.toronto.ca/wp-content/uploads/2019/05/8e6e-Honouring-the-Truth-Reconciling-for-the-Future-Executive-Summary.pdf.

[49] Ibid.

[50] Ibid.

[51] Ibid.

The residential school system existed for over 100 years, to the catastrophic detriment of the Indigenous people of Canada.[52]

The question hardly bears asking, given the state's inhumanity here. But let's ask it. What can we observe about trust in this context to shed light on why a sense of betrayal rather than mere disappointment is an appropriate response to a breach? First, recall the declarations of love used to persuade Indigenous people to trust. Where a belief that one is loved acts as reason for trusting, trust entails a vulnerability greater even than vulnerability to a breach in relation to the objects of one's trust. Trusting on the surety of a declaration of love risks having to shift from a belief that one's well-being is highly valued to an awareness that one's well-being is of little or no significance to the other. Here the shift required was even more drastic; from a (requested) belief in the love of the Queen and her agents to a hard awareness of the Queen's indifference and her agents' hatred. The implementation of the residential school system as a method of doing away with Indigenous culture is a clear case of hatred, at least if we follow Aristotle's understanding that hatred is the desire for the non existence of the other.[53] The necessary reorientation of understanding of one's place in a relationship occasioned by a breach of trust; the realisation not only that one has erred in relying on the other but that one has erred in believing oneself to be an object of the others loving concern is what takes the emotional register out of mere disappointment or even outrage at inhumanity and into the register of betrayal.

Let's turn now to the Indigenous party's belief in a shared commitment to the rule of law as a reason for trusting to the Canadian state. We saw in the last section that a core aspect of the rule of law that mattered to Indigenous people was equal protection of the law. They wanted a criminal process that would value Indigenous lives and would not turn a blind eye to the murder of Indigenous people by whites. A sense of the integrity of the redcoats appears, at least on Erasmus's account, to have been an important piece of evidence supporting the Indigenous belief that the Crown was committed to a rule of law that included Indigenous people as full citizens. Yet equal protection of Canadian law eluded and has continued to elude Indigenous people. Even today it is difficult to see the Canadian state, and indeed the Royal Canadian Mounted Police, as fully committed to protecting Indigenous people from white violence. The grossly improbable acquittal of white farmer Gerald Stanley on the charge of murder of Indigenous man Colton Boushie by an all-white jury in 2018 in Saskatchewan, along with other high-profile acquittals of white people on charges of murder of Indigenous people in the face of cogent evidence of guilt, are seen by many as sad proof that the Chiefs who trusted the Canadian state's commitment to the rule of law were sorely deceived.[54]

[52] Ibid.

[53] Aristotle, *The Rhetoric* (350 BCE) Translated by W Rhys Roberts, http://classics.mit.edu/Aristotle/rhetoric.html.

[54] K Roach, *Canadian justice, indigenous injustice: the Gerald Stanley and Colten Boushie case* (Montreal, McGill-Queens University Press, 2019).

A robust commitment to the rule of law would also argue for a framework for effective enforcement for legal agreements. Yet there was scant possibility for Indigenous people to enforce the state's treaty obligations through the late nineteenth and much of the twentieth century.[55] It was not necessarily that no common law rights that the treaties gave rise to could be enforced by the courts, but there were layers and layers of difficulty in trying to do so. The structure of legal and civil society on the prairies prevented almost all access to a civil judicial system for Indigenous people.[56] In 1927 the Canadian government went further to formalise the restrictions on Indigenous people's access to the protections of the rule of law. They enacted section 141 of the Indian Act in an effort to prevent Indigenous access to legal institutions.[57] The section shattered any remaining illusions of the Canadian state as committed to a notion of the rule of law where Indigenous people would have full legal membership. The section made it an offence, punishable by imprisonment, to raise money to pursue a claim on behalf of an Indigenous band or to accept money to represent an Indigenous band advancing any claim on behalf of the band.

We are a long way now from the Lieutenant Governors' assurances of the love and generosity of the Crown. So what light does all this shed on the question of why breaches of trust are occasions for feelings of betrayal rather than mere disappointment? We can turn again to James Sákéj Youngblood Henderson who notes that respect for and faith in the rule of law runs deep in Indigenous culture. He writes, 'Typically, Indigenous answers to the question about the value of the legal system display a deep continuity in Indigenous teachings. These teachings imply a profound trust in knowledge and justice; a trust that most law schools and legal professionals do not share.'[58] The sense of betrayal then here comes from the disruption of the belief in shared moral ground. One of the many differences between the two peoples was a difference in the sincerity of their trust in the very idea of justice through law.

The possibility of trust depends on the possibility of intersubjective accord – the possibility that separate people could hold in common an understanding and intention – that they could hold the same sincerity of commitment to shared values. When a belief in that common understanding, intention and commitment turns out to be false, the reorientation required causes pain over and above the pain of disappointed expectation. There is the additional pain of broken human connection; the additional shock of the failure of that intersubjective accord. We can get help here again from the Indigenous notion of wahkohtowin which is

[55] J Timothy S McCabe, *The Law of Treaties Between the Crown and Aboriginal Peoples* by (LexisNexisCanada, 2010).

[56] J Borrows and M Coyle (eds), *The Right Relationship: reimagining the implementation of historical treaties* (Toronto, UTP, 2017) 86.

[57] The Indian Act 1927 s 141.

[58] JSY Henderson, 'Postcolonial Indigenous Legal Consciousness' (2002) 1 *Indigenous Law Journal* 1, 27.

fundamentally about relatedness. The breach of trust can be a disavowal of relatedness. And the pain of broken relation, that pain of betrayal, is separate from and in addition to the pain of misplaced expectation.

Furthermore, the eventually obvious falsehood of any Indigenous belief that shared devotion to God might be a guarantee of trustworthiness on the part of the agents of the state – the idea that each party's invocation of the sacred at the time of the signing of the treaties might provide a robust foundation for trust – reveals more about why the breach of trust was an occasion for feelings of betrayal over and above disappointment. The Indigenous understanding of the sacred embodied in the pipe ceremony marked, as we have seen, a sense of supremely heightened obligations in relation to truth telling and promise keeping. The idea of the sacred itself helps explain both the notion of trust and feeling of betrayal. In invoking the sacred at the moment of promise making one pledges, as much as is humanly possible, continuity between the present and future self. Invocation of the sacred is a means of straining the will to its uttermost to get it to extend beyond the present moment in relation to another. Here the breach of trust entails a kind of profanity which once again requires on the part of the one who trusted a larger kind of reorientation and a deeper kind of pain than that of mere disappointed expectation.

V. The Denial

> It's discouraging to think how many people are shocked by honesty and how few by deceit.[59]

Despite this long history of betrayal, Canadian state agents continue to describe their relationship with Indigenous people as a relationship of trust. Canadian law relating to Indigenous rights is replete with references to 'the integrity of the Crown', 'the honour of the Crown', 'the duty of honour and good-faith of the Crown' and the status of the Crown as a fiduciary in relation to Indigenous people.[60] In *R v Sparrow*, for example, the Supreme Court of Canada speaks of 'The special trust relationship and the responsibility of the government vis-à-vis aboriginals'.[61] The Department of Justice Canada's website on Indigenous relations states, 'The Government of Canada recognises that it must uphold the honour of the Crown, which requires the federal government and its departments, agencies, and officials to act with honour, integrity, good faith, and fairness in all of its dealings with Indigenous peoples.' This lavish but vague rhetoric of trust and trustworthiness

[59] N Coward, *Blithe spirit: an improbable farce in three acts* (London, Methuen Drama, 2002).
[60] See n 1 above.
[61] *R v Sparrow* [1990] 1 SCR 1075.

endures despite ongoing inhumanity,[62] ongoing breaches of treaty obligations,[63] and ongoing failures of equal protection of the law for Indigenous people in Canada.[64] One is prompted to wonder how state actors continue to manage the cognitive dissonance, the incongruity, the ubiquitous language of trust and equally ubiquitous breaches of trust that characterise this relationship. Is it just a case of shameless dishonesty coupled with blind self-congratulation?

To investigate this, let's turn to a final conceptual point about trust raised by Annette Baier. Baier understands trust as having a three-place predicate, 'A trusts B with valued thing C.' She says 'there will be an answer not just to the question, Whom do you trust? but to the question, What do you trust to them? – what good is it that they are in a position to take from you, or to injure?'[65] Baier notes that it will not always be easy to specify that third value but she argues that presuming that one needs to do so will be helpful in clarifying our understanding of trust.

Baier is right about the importance of specifying the third place predicate. But I would argue further that it is ethically preferable for that third place to specify not the value B is trusted with, but rather what B is trusted *to do*. Of course, this recommends a contractarian kind of narrowing and confining of our understanding of trust. And that might well mean less trust overall. But that narrowing is ethically important when, as here, the relation has all the epistemic problems associated with paternalism.[66] When A trusts B with value C and B believes that safeguarding value C requires that B impose his understanding of C because B knows more than A about the true meaning of C, B can keep on believing he's trustworthy even when he's not. But if we require specificity not about what value B has been entrusted with but rather what B has been trusted *to do* it's easier to nail down the truth about betrayal.

The Canadian state's continued confidence in its own trustworthiness vis-à-vis Indigenous people rests on its belief it was entrusted with the welfare of Indigenous people and that safeguarding that welfare with integrity entailed also deciding what was best for Indigenous people. The grand narrative of trust at the bottom of colonialism in Canada lies in the notion of progress. Indigenous peoples and settlers alike, so the story goes, could trust that settler culture, under the sovereignty of the Canadian state, could deliver progress as a *sine qua non* of all,

[62] At the date of publication many Indigenous communities, even those in close proximity to settler towns, still have no clean water. See Human Rights Watch website, 'Canada: Blind Eye to First Nation Water Crisis' 2 October 2019, www.hrw.org/news/2019/10/02/canada-blind-eye-first-nation-water-crisis. This problem is exacerbated by the Covid-19 pandemic. See Council for Canadians website, 'Safe Water for First Nations', https://canadians.org/fn-water.

[63] See *Beardy's & Okemasis Band #96 and #97 v Her Majesty the Queen in Right of Canada*, 2015 SCTC 3.

[64] See n 2 above *First Nations Child and Family Caring Society of Canada v Attorney General of Canada (Representing the Minister of Indian Affairs and Northern Development Canada)*.

[65] See n 3 above Baier, 236.

[66] Ibid, 247–48. Baier resists the contractarian tenor of much philosophical discussion of trust in part because she sees that focus as orienting us toward trusting white male business elites of equal power. But, as here, contractual relations can be relations of vastly unequal power and shot through with paternalism.

including Indigenous, welfare. To be trustworthy in its stewardship of Indigenous as well as settler welfare the state needed to support economic growth within capitalism, progress in science, transportation, technology, medicine, architecture and the like. On their own, Indigenous people could never hope for this kind of advancement. The breaches of treaty promises, however unfortunate, ought to be overlooked by intelligent Indigenous people of reciprocal good faith because they were necessary to bring about that better world from which Indigenous people now benefit. Those breaches of promise do not mean that Indigenous people's trust was misplaced. The superior world in which Indigenous people are invited to participate redeems the trustworthiness of the Canadian state. There is a sense of its own meta-trustworthiness at the core of the state's positive self-understanding. Indigenous people are unfair to nitpick about the specific failures of promise keeping when, from a higher vantage point, one can see how much better off they are now than they ever would have been without us given the possibilities open to them in the sophisticated settler society.

The layers of error in this kind of thinking are many. But what this narrative reveals for our purposes is that it is possible, within relations of domination and paternalism, for there to be a gigantic difference in the parties' perspective on the question of whether trust has been breached because of equivocation and slippage of meaning on the content of that third place predicate. If we insist on greater specificity in the objects of trust, as the terms of the treaties attempted to do, we make at least some progress toward consensus about whether the trustee has been trustworthy, whether they have acted with moral decency or not.

VI. Conclusion

The language of trust continues to dominate the relationship between Indigenous people and the Canadian state. Indeed, the Report of the Canadian Truth and Reconciliation Commission set up to provide a form of restorative justice for the wrongs of the residential schools is itself something of a reinvestment in the language of trust. The report states for example

> The destructive impacts of residential schools, the Indian Act, and the Crown's failure to keep its Treaty promises have damaged the relationship between Aboriginal and non-Aboriginal peoples. The most significant damage is to the trust that has been broken between the Crown and Aboriginal peoples. That broken trust must be repaired. The vision that led to that breach in trust must be replaced with a new vision for Canada; one that fully embraces Aboriginal peoples' right to self-determination within, and in partnership with, a viable Canadian sovereignty.

Philosopher Onora O'Neill reminds us that trust itself is of no value in the absence of trustworthiness.[67] Trustworthiness has to come first. Yet, it's hard to begin to

[67] Onora O'Neill, *A Question of Trust* (Cambridge, CUP, 2002).

imagine how Canada might resurrect trustworthiness as a foundation for trust in its relationship with Indigenous people when the whole of settler society literally sits on a foundation of untrustworthiness and betrayal. But there is some hope in the fact that, like the treaties themselves, the Calls to Action contained in the report of the Truth and Reconciliation Commission fill in that third place predicate with 95 specific things that need *to be done* to begin to build evidence of trustworthiness and a foundation for future trust.[68]

References

Aristotle, 'Rhetoric' (350 BCE) Rhys Roberts W. (trs), http://classics.mit.edu/Aristotle/rhetoric.html.

Baier A, 'Trust and Anti-Trust' (1986) 96 *Ethics* 231.

Borrows K and Coyle M (eds) *The Right Relationship: reimagining the implementation of historical treaties* (Toronto, UTP, 2017).

Brown R, Acorn A, Lindberg D, Nichols J, Pentland E, and Roe B 'Roundtable: *Buffalo Days and Nights*, Peter Erasmus and Henry Thompson' (2019) 57 *Alberta Law Review* 145.

Council of Canadians, 'Safe Water for First Nations', https://canadians.org/fn-water.

Coward N, *Blithe spirit: an improbable farce in three acts* (London, Methuen Drama, 2002).

de Montaigne M, 'Whether the governor of a besieged fortress should go out and parley.' In *Michel de Montaigne: the complete essays*. A.M. Screech Translator (London, Penguin Books, 1991).

Dempsey, HA, *Big Bear: the end of freedom* (Regina, University of Regina Press, 2006).

Department of Justice Government of Canada, 'Principles respecting the Government of Canada's relationship with Indigenous peoples' (2018), www.justice.gc.ca/eng/csj-sjc/principles-principes.html.

Duhame, R (1964). 'Copy of Treaty No. 6 between Her Majesty the Queen and the Plain and Wood Cree Indians and other Tribes of Indians at Fort Carlton, Fort Pitt and Battle River with Adhesions' Ottawa: Queen's Printer and Controller of Stationery. IAND Publication No. QS-0574-000-EE-A-1, www.rcaanc-cirnac.gc.ca/eng/1100100028710/1581292569426#chp1.

Erasmus P and Thompson H, *Buffalo Days and Nights* (Calgary, Glenbow Institute, 1999).

Gunn A, 'Ottawa has spent more than $5 million in legal fees fighting complaints about First Nations child welfare' *The Chronicle Herald* (Halifax, 30 January 2020), www.thechronicleherald.ca/news/canada/ottawa-has-spent-more-than-5-million-in-legal-fees-fighting-complaints-about-first-nations-child-welfare-405103/.

M Harris, 'How Should We Relate to Each Other Politically? Love and Trust as Relational Ethics in the Political Realm' in this volume.

Heagerty, JJ, *Four centuries of medical history in Canada: and a sketch of the medical history of Newfoundland*, 1879–1946. Vol 1 (Toronto, The Macmillan Co, 1928).

Henderson JSY 'Postcolonial Indigenous Legal Consciousness' (2002) 1 *Indigenous Law Journal* 1.

Henderson JSY 'The Indigenous Law Foundation of the Victorian Treaties', Talk delivered at Edmonton, University of Alberta Faculty of Law, March 6th, 2018.

Hinchman ES, 'On the Risks of Resting Assured: an assurance theory of trust' in P Faulkner and T Simpson (eds) *The Philosophy of Trust* (Oxford, OUP, 2017).

Houston CS and Houston S, 'The first smallpox epidemic on the Canadian Plains: In the fur-traders' words' (2000) 11 *Canadian Journal of Infectious Diseases and Medical Microbiology* 112–15.

[68] Truth and Reconciliation Commission of Canada: Calls to Action, http://nctr.ca/assets/reports/Calls_to_Action_English2.pdf.

Hubbard T, 'Buffalo Genocide in Nineteenth Century North America: "Kill, Skin, and Sell"' in AL Hinton, A Woolford, J Benvenuto (eds.) *Colonial Genocide in Indigenous North America* (Duke University Press, 2014).
Human Rights Watch, 'Canada: Blind Eye to First Nation Water Crisis' (2 October 2019), www.hrw.org/news/2019/10/02/canada-blind-eye-first-nation-water-crisis.
Johnson HR, *Firewater: how alcohol is killing my people (and yours)* (Regina, University of Regina Press, 2016).
Jones K, 'Trust as an affective attitude' (1996) 107 *Ethics* 4.
Jones KF, 'Trust and Terror' in P DesAutels and M Urban Walker (eds) *Moral psychology: feminist ethics and social theory* (Lanham, Rowman & Littlefield, 2004).
McCabe JTS, *The Law of Treaties Between the Crown and Aboriginal Peoples* (LexisNexisCanada, 2010).
Miller J, Ray AJ, Tough F, *Bounty and Benevolence: a history of Saskatchewan treaties* (Montreal, McGill-Queens, 2000).
Morris A, *The treaties of Canada with the Indians of Manitoba and the North-West Territories, including the negotiations on which they were based, and other information relating thereto* (Toronto: Belfords, 1880).
O'Neill O, *A Question of Trust* (Cambridge, CUP, 2002).
Peirce CS, 'Some Consequences of Four Incapacities' (1868) 2, *Journal of Speculative Philosophy* 140, www.peirce.org/writings/p27.html.
Rae B 'Is It a Divorce or Marriage? Two versions of a treaty narrative' *Walrus Talks* (23 April 2015), https://thewalrus.ca/tv-is-it-a-divorce-or-marriage-two-versions-of-a-treaty-narrative/.
Roach K, *Canadian justice, indigenous injustice: the Gerald Stanley and Colten Boushie case* (Montreal, McGill-Queens University Press, 2019).
Showalter D, 'By the Book? Commanders Surrendering in World War I' in H Afflerbach and H Strachan (eds) *How fighting ends: a history of surrender* (Oxford, OUP, 2012).
Stearn EW and Stearn AE, *The effect of smallpox on the destiny of the Amerindian* (Boston, Bruce Humphries, 1945).
St Germain J, *Broken Treaties: United States and Canadian Relations with the Lakotas and the Plains Cree, 1868–1885.* (Lincoln, University of Nebraska Press, 2009).
Taylor, JL (1985) 'Treaty Research Report – Treaty Six (1876), Indigenous and Northern Affairs, Canada' Treaties and Historical Research Centre, www.rcaanc-cirnac.gc.ca/eng/1100100028706/1564413507531.
Taylor MS, 'Buffalo Hunt: International trade and the virtual extinction of the North American Bison' (2007) National Bureau of Economic Research Working Paper 12969 Cambridge, MA.
Truth and Reconciliation Commission of Canada. 2015. *Truth & reconciliation: calls to action*, http://trc.ca/assets/pdf/Calls_to_Action_English2.pdf.
Truth and Reconciliation Commission of Canada. 2015 *Honoring the Truth, Reconciling for the Future: Summary of the Final Report of the Truth and Reconciliation Commission of Canada*, www.toronto.ca/wp-content/uploads/2019/05/8e6e-Honouring-the-Truth-Reconciling-for-the-Future-Executive-Summary.pdf.
Waiser B, 'History Matters: Treaty 6 Promises were quickly broken' *Star Phoenix* (Saskatoon, 12 September 2017), http://thestarphoenix.com/opinion/columnists/history-matters-treaty-six-promises-were-quickly-broken.
Whitehouse Strong D, '"Everything Promised had been Included in the Writing": Indian reserve farming and the spirit and intent of treaty six reconsidered' (2007) 27 *Great Plains Quarterly* 25.

Cases

Beardy's & Okemasis Band #96 and #97 v Her Majesty the Queen in Right of Canada [2015] SCTC 3.
Delgamuukw v British Columbia [1997] 3 SCR 1010.

First Nations Child and Family Caring Society of Canada v Attorney General of Canada (Representing the Minister of Indian Affairs and Northern Development Canada) [2016] CHRT 2; [2016] CHRT 10; [2017] CHRT 14; [2018] CHRT 4.
Lax Kw'alaams Indian Band v Canada (Attorney General) [2011] 3 SCR 535.
R v Sparrow [1990] 1 SCR 1075.
R v Badger [1996] 1 SCR 771.

Legislation

Indian Act 1927, s 141.
The Vaccination Act 1853, http://navigator.health.org.uk/content/united-kingdom-vaccination-act-1853-made-vaccination-against-smallpox-compulsory.
57–58 Victoria, Chapter 32, An Act to Further Amend the Indian Act Assented to 23 of July, 1894, s 11.

8

Public Trust(s)

ACHAS K BURIN*

I. Introduction

Scholarship about property is dominated by private property. The possibility and, indeed, the existence of common property does not often receive an airing. Inconveniently, however, common property persists. This chapter focuses on one instance of common property, a legal doctrine known as 'the Public Trust'.[1] The doctrine of Public Trust provides, broadly, that the government holds public spaces such as roads, parks, beaches, squares and waterways on trust for the public's benefit. Some semblance of this idea has been with us from Roman times, and its variants are found across the common law world.

This chapter argues that trust is an enabling condition for the existence of common property. Common property is, by definition, a resource available to others. Using it means associating with other people, which gives rise to risk and vulnerability. Trust permits cooperation in the face of risk. Furthermore, trust is necessary in order to have property that is *truly* common, which is to say, available to everyone while privileging none over another. Trust should form part of explanations of common property, whereas accounts of property are currently framed predominantly in terms of right. At its lowest, trust complements rights-based accounts of common property. At its highest, trust rivals the accounts of property rights. Property scholars should be open to the possibility that a new perspective could progress the literature and the possibility of explanations being multifaceted rather than unitary.

The next subsection sets out the legal doctrine of Public Trust. The subsection after it establishes the account of trust that this chapter invokes, one defended by

* Enormous gratitude is due to Ana Laura Edelhoff, Arushi Garg, Benjamin Kindler and – most of all – the editors of this volume for their invaluable input. Without them, the chapter could not have been written.

[1] Two homologous streams of scholarship should be distinguished from the inquiry in this chapter. In the philosophical literature, the phrase 'public trust' is used as a shorthand for the idea that the public places trust in institutions. Separately, the phrase is used by fiduciary government theorists, who believe that the private law relationship of trustee-beneficiary illuminates the relations between the government and the governed. This chapter says nothing about those two literatures. Nor should it be read as taking any position on trusts or fiduciary law more generally.

Amy Mullin. Section II then examines why trust has been absent from discussions of property. The reason is a long history of assuming that cooperative behaviour was impossible, and private property was our only recourse. This idea found expression in Garrett Hardin's famous 'tragedy of the commons'. However, shortcomings of his thesis spurred research in the social sciences which pointed to the role trust plays in facilitating coordination. Section III makes the central argument that trust explains how common property is possible. The presence of irreducible uncertainty in public space, arising out of common property's availability to others, means that cooperative behaviour can only be secured by something like trust. Section III also responds to an objection that law displaces any role for trust. Finally, Section IV considers a second challenge to my argument. One objection to rights-based accounts of property is that an egalitarian distribution of rights does not, *in practice*, ensure egalitarian access to property. A similar type of challenge can be made against trust. Section IV argues that trust can overcome this challenge.

Section V concludes that even if a system of private property is one answer to a coordination problem, it is only *one* answer. However, many people have lost sight of this due to disciplinary myopia. Garrett Hardin inherited the preoccupation of his discipline with rational self-interest; legal scholars likewise inherited the suffocating association of the word 'property' with the concept of private property and right. Trust provides an alternative way of understanding common property that is at least as plausible as rights-based accounts.

A. The Public Trust

One way the Public Trust troubles the pre-eminence of private property is simply through its widespread existence. Britain's previous colonies all have their own takes on trust doctrine in general and the Public Trust in particular. Public Trusts are prevalent in the United States, having been inherited from Britain.[2] They also appear in Canada,[3] New Zealand,[4] Australia,[5] and the modern-day United Kingdom.[6] Given that the specific content of the legal doctrine varies between jurisdictions, a gloss of its common features is all that this chapter aspires to.

[2] *Illinois Central Railroad Company v Illinois* 146 US 387 (1892); *Hague v Committee for Industrial Organization*, 307 US 496 (1939), 515; *Frisby v Schultz*, 487 US 474 (1988), 481. Each US state has its permutation of the doctrine.

[3] *SW Properties Inc v Calgary (City)* (2003) 222 DLR (4th) 430, [19]; *The Queen in Right of Canada v Committee for the Commonwealth of Canada* (1987) 36 DLR (4th) 501, 509f, (1991) 77 DLR (4th) 385, 393d–f.

[4] *Man O'War Station Ltd v Auckland CC* [2000] 2 NZLR 267, [22].

[5] *Bathurst City Council v PWC Properties Pty Ltd* [1998] HCA 59, [48]–[49].

[6] *Ex Parte Lewis* (1888) 21 QBD 191, 198; *Secretary of State for the Environment v Baylis and Bennett* (2000) 80 P&CR 324, 332; *R(Beresford) v Sunderland County Council* [2004] 1 AC 889, [87]. Gray and Gray interpret these cases as giving rise to a public trust: K Gray and S Gray, *Elements of Land Law*, 5th edn (OUP, 2008), 10.7.3.

This will be sufficient for our purpose, which is to investigate the role of trust in the spaces subject to the Public Trust.

In law, a trust is a relationship that arises when one person (the *trustee*) has an obligation to deal with property they control for the benefit of others (called *beneficiaries*).[7] The beneficiaries can enforce those obligations even though they are not regarded in law as the 'owners' of the property. The trustee must manage or use the property for any specific purpose established by the terms of the trust. They must also comply with duties imposed by the general law. The trustee is accountable to the beneficiaries for the exercise of powers and duties. In the specific context of the Public Trust, the trustee is a government body, whereas the beneficiaries are the general public. Public space is the resource subject to the Public Trust, eg, parks, roads, waterways, playgrounds, and beaches.

One commentator on the Public Trust made a claim which he intended to be dismissive but is, in fact, suggestive.

> The word 'trust' has various meanings. In ordinary discourse, it has to do with confidence in others. In law, it describes an arrangement under which the legal and equitable title to property are held by different persons. The public trust doctrine has far more to do with the former than the latter meaning.[8]

This chapter investigates this assertion, made by James Huffmann, that the ordinary notion of trust has explanatory potential for the Public Trust (understood in its technical, legal sense). Huffmann's dismissiveness flows from his political and economic commitments.[9] The motivation for it can be seen when applying the idea of a trust to roads, beaches, and the like. The result is that the government must deal with land in a way that is consistent with its obligations to the general public, who are the beneficiaries of the Public Trust. This, in summary, is the idea of the Public Trust. It poses a distinct challenge to paradigms of private property held dear by some lawyers and neoclassical economists. It has been called 'a jarring exception of uncertain dimensions, [which] posits that some resources are subject to a perpetual trust that forecloses private exclusion rights'.[10]

In contrast to the idea of private property as exclusive control over a resource, the trust facilitates plural ownership.[11] By contrast with the idea of private ownership as unrestricted power to use and dispose of property, the trust imposes obligation and constraint. Today, discourse about 'property' is largely coextensive

[7] This definition is modelled on Article 2 of the Convention on the Law Applicable to Trusts and Their Recognition. It will not satisfy everyone. For other definitions, see *Re Scott* [1948] SASR 193, 196 and *Re Marshall's Will Trusts* [1945] Ch 217, 219.

[8] James Huffmann, 'Fish Out of Water: The Public Trust Doctrine in a Constitutional Democracy' (1989) 19 Envtl L 527, 534.

[9] Ibid, at 534, 552.

[10] Joseph Kearney and Thomas Merrill, 'The Origins of the American Public Trust Doctrine: What Really Happened in *Illinois Central*' (2004) 71 U Chi L Rev 799, 800.

[11] Carol Rose, 'The Comedy of the Commons: Custom, Commerce and Inherently Public Property' (1986) 53 U Chi L Rev 711, 711–12.

with discourse about private property. However, the association of the word 'property' with private property need not be automatic. The Public Trust here is common property.[12] Non-private types of property are frequently said to be under-theorised.[13] The next subsection sets out an account of trust that helps us theorise common property.

B. What is Trust?

The account of 'trust', which I assume here, although I cannot argue for it in depth, is a version of Annette Baier's account as refined by successive feminist scholars. If a defence of the account is needed, it is in Amy Mullin's 'Trust, Social Norms and Motherhood'. On this account,

> Trust involves both beliefs and emotional attitudes in which the truster interacts with the trusted one in a way that assumes the one trusted is intrinsically and not merely instrumentally committed to [what is usually] a particular social norm governing the trusted one's behaviour in a certain domain.[14]

Mullin's account has three attractive features. First, it unifies the phenomenon of trust between intimates and non-intimates. This is because social norms apply to intimates as well as strangers. If we do not want our notion of trust to become too friable, it is desirable to make sense of its use across different contexts. Within public space, lots of people interact constantly. Many will never have met before and may never cross paths again. Mullin's account illuminates the sense in which these people trust each other, a sense elaborated upon with examples in Section III.

Second, Mullin can distinguish trust from reliance. Reliance is the mere prediction that certain acts will occur. The perceived motivation of the trusted person is what distinguishes trust from reliance. Some authors, such as Diego Gambetta, conceive of trust very similarly to reliance. This alternative view dubbed a 'risk assessment' view of trust, holds that trust is the level of subjective probability at which an agent assesses that another agent will perform a particular action, where that action affects the agent's own behaviour, and the agent cannot monitor the other.[15] The account that I favour maintains that trust obtains when the trusted person is perceived to have a specific type of motivation for their commitment

[12] There is no space to discuss a full taxonomy of property types. However, many would agree with my classification of the Public Trust as common property, eg, Christopher Rodgers, 'Towards a Taxonomy for Public and Common Property' (2019) 78(1) CLJ 124, 132, 146–147 and John Page and Ann Brower, 'The Four Dimensions of Public Property' in Heather Conway and Robin Hickey (eds), *Modern Studies in Property Law* (Hart 2017) 303. Both articles acknowledge that such classes are not watertight anyway.

[13] Page and Brower, ibid, 296.

[14] Amy Mullin, 'Trust, Social Norms, and Motherhood' (2005) 36(3) *Journal of Social Philosophy* 316, 325. Words in square brackets added to gloss Mullin's view so that it conforms more closely to mine.

[15] Diego Gambetta, 'Can We Trust Trust?' in Diego Gambetta (ed), *Trust: Making and Breaking Cooperative Relations* (Blackwell, 1988) 217.

to a norm governing their behaviour. Risk assessment views are insensitive to the trusted one's motivation.

A third attractive feature of Mullin's account is that it makes room for the possibility that trust can be morally good but does not insist it always is. Social norms may coincide with what morality requires, but they need not. They sometimes coincide in surprising ways, as will be seen in the example of evacuating an overcrowded train station in Section III below. Mullin's view can also accommodate the converse case, namely those situations where trusting and/or being trustworthy is not good (eg, in abusive relationships, in mafioso gangs, etc).

In flagging up distinctive features of Mullin's account, this brief sketch indicates points of divergence between different accounts of trust. There are a number of ways that we could categorise trust accounts: moral or amoral,[16] cognitive or noncognitive,[17] emphasising disposition, affect or motive,[18] as resting on a one-, two- or three-place predicate (this latter question within philosophy relates to how trust is formalised into a proposition),[19] and so on. I have suppressed many complexities. There could be degrees of trust,[20] thicker or thinner forms of trust,[21] generalised and particular types,[22] or prototypical and non-prototypical types.[23] Space precludes discussing these complexities further. Despite the rich literature, trust has been neglected in property scholarship. The following section suggests why this might be and why it is regrettable.

II. How Have We Thought about Trust in Relation to Property?

Given that there are prevalent doubts about whether common goods can be the subject of rights, the dearth of alternatives to rights-based heuristics for understanding property is surprising. Among the most pressing doubts is *compossibility*.[24] This is the argument that a necessary precondition for qualifying as a right is that right-holders must be able to exercise their rights to the

[16] Marc Cohen and John Dienhart, 'Moral and Amoral Conceptions of Trust with an Application to Organizational Ethics' (2013) 112 *Journal of Business Ethics* 1.

[17] Laurence Becker, 'Trust as Noncognitive Security about Motives' (1996) 107(1) *Ethics* 43.

[18] Karen Jones, 'Second-Hand Moral Knowledge' (1999) 96(2) *Journal of Philosophy* 55, 68.

[19] Eric Uslaner, *The Moral Foundations of Trust* (Cambridge UP, 2002) (one-place); Paul Faulkner, 'The Attitude of Trust is Basic' (2015) 75(3) *Analysis* 424 (one- and two-place); Russell Hardin, 'Conceptions and Explanations of Trust' in Karen Cook (ed), *Trust in Society* (Russell Sage, 2003) 8, 12–16 (three-place). See also Margaret Walker's capacious 'mixed account', which takes in all of these and a four-place relation in *Moral Repair* (Cambridge UP, 2006) 27, 82–83.

[20] For example, Hardin (n 19) 13.

[21] Robert Putnam, *Bowling Alone* (Simon & Schuster, 2000) 136–37.

[22] Uslaner (n 19).

[23] Carolyn McLeod, *Self-Trust and Reproductive Autonomy* (MIT Press, 2002) 11–15.

[24] Hillel Steiner, *An Essay on Rights* (Blackwell, 1994).

fullest degree. Where resources are scarce and finite, it may be impossible to satisfy the claims of all right-holders. If correct, compossibility is fatal to rights in common property. Rather than delving into the extensive debate on rights,[25] this chapter instead seeks to break new ground. If rights-based accounts fail, we need to know how the Public Trust persists in so many different countries. Even if rights-based accounts succeed, they still need to be supplemented by trust. As argued below, trust is always relevant under conditions of risk and uncertainty. Trust, as an alternative or supplement to theories of right, is well-motivated. We can see this by drawing on social scientists' work.

A seminal paper, entitled 'The Tragedy of the Commons' by Garrett Hardin,[26] has courted controversy since it was published 50 years ago. Hardin suggested that cooperation between self-interested individuals in respect of common resources was impossible because it would be rational for each one to take more than his share. The worry is that rights, even if compossible in principle, would inevitably be abused in practice. The common property would be wasted, to the detriment of all. His example, a pasture subject to overgrazing, captured the public imagination, and the phrase he coined, 'the tragedy of the commons', passed into popular currency.

Hardin's theory met with a compelling rejoinder in the 1980s. In a series of empirical studies, Elinor Ostrom demonstrated the workability of self-managed commons using real-world examples.[27] She highlighted the lack of fit between the predictions of simplistic models and data gathered through fieldwork.[28] At the same time, experimental research in economics showed that self-interested free-riding did not occur in the way models predicted.[29] The research indicated that the explanation lay in variables that standard models did not take into account, 'non-standard behaviours'[30] like trust.[31]

This prompted economists to investigate trust further. The resultant idea is that interpersonal interactions are a resource known as 'social capital'. Although 'social capital' is not consistently defined, some widely-accepted definitions posit

[25] Entries in the debate include Neil MacCormick, 'Rights in Legislation' in Peter Hacker and Joseph Raz (eds), *Law, Morality and Society* (OUP, 1985); Denise Réaume, 'Individuals, Groups, and Rights to Public Goods' (1988) 38(1) University of Toronto Law Journal 1; Jeremy Waldron, 'Can Communal Goods Be Human Rights?' in his *Liberal Rights: Collected Papers 1981–1991* (Cambridge University Press, 1993); Andrei Marmor, 'Do We Have a Right to Common Goods?' (2001) 4(2) *Canadian Journal of Law & Jurisprudence* 213.

[26] Garrett Hardin, 'The Tragedy of the Commons' (1968) 162 *Science* 1234.

[27] Elinor Ostrom, *Governing the Commons: the Evolution of Institutions for Collective Action* (Cambridge University Press, 1990) 23.

[28] Elinor Ostrom, 'Toward a Behavioural Theory Linking Trust, Reciprocity and Reputation' in James Walker and Elinor Ostrom (eds), *Trust and Reciprocity: Interdisciplinary Lessons from Experimental Research* (Russell Sage Foundation, 2003) 23–26.

[29] James Andreoni, 'Why Free Ride? Strategies and Learning in Public Goods Experiments' (1988) 37 *Journal of Public Economics* 291 and literature cited therein.

[30] Ibid, 292, 301.

[31] Ostrom, 'Linking Trust, Reciprocity and Reputation' (n 28) 34.

that trust is constitutive of social capital because it facilitates coordination[32] (including between strangers),[33] and/or is a measurable proxy for social capital more generally.[34] Trust is thought particularly salient to social dilemmas involving public goods.[35] In sum, social science research strongly suggests that trust carries explanatory potential for the Public Trust – instead of, or in addition to, rights.

Section III deals with a possible objection that it is not trust doing the work, that people just rely on the law. Section IV turns to discuss the twin problems of women's safety in public space and suspicion of men (especially Black men and lower-class men) in those same spaces. The objection might be that I am changing the subject. 'Sure', an economist might say, 'we recognise that safety is a public good and procuring it a social dilemma[36] … but surely that is a different problem?' Was I not supposed to be providing an account of trust among users of common property? Should I not be explaining how trust can help us to share our things nicely?

That is exactly what I am doing. We should be suspicious of the hold that paradigms have over us. The Public Trust is a modern, urban example of common-goods-holding that is so familiar that it has gone virtually unnoticed. Garrett Hardin's legacy made us think of extractive, common-pool resources as the only kind of common property. He took a subset of common property and inappropriately generalised his theory around it.[37] Hardin came from a tradition that began with Hugo Grotius. Grotius is credited as the first modern theorist of property.[38] He believed all things were originally held in common, but private property became necessary because coordination was too inconvenient under conditions of mounting complexity and/or discord.[39] Newer research from the social sciences shows how a system of private property is but one answer to a 'social dilemma' or coordination problem. We should be open to a new perspective advancing our understanding and the possibility of explanations being multifaceted rather than unipolar. The next section argues that the significance of the explanatory role for trust lies in the irreducible uncertainty that comes with the availability of common property to other people.

[32] Putnam, *Making Democracy Work* (Princeton UP, 1993) 167.

[33] Kim Sønderskov, 'Different Goods, Different Effects: Exploring the Effects of Generalized Social Trust in Large-N Collective Action' (2009) 140 *Public Choice* 145.

[34] For example, Stephen Knack and Philip Keefer, 'Does Social Capital Have an Economic Payoff? A Cross-Country Investigation' (1997) 112(4) *The Quarterly Journal of Economics* 1251.

[35] Sønderskov (n 33); Ostrom, 'Linking Trust, Reciprocity and Reputation' (n 28).

[36] Ostrom, 'Linking Trust, Reciprocity and Reputation' (n 28) 20.

[37] Ostrom, *Governing the Commons* (n 27) 3, 7.

[38] Adam Mossoff, 'What is Property? Putting the Pieces Back Together' (2003) 45 Arizona LR 371, 379.

[39] Hugo Grotius, *De Jure Belli ac Pacis* (1625), Book II, chs 2–3; Stephen Neff (ed), *Of War and Peace* (Cambridge UP, 2012) 92–94, 105.

III. Can the Public Trust?

It is not difficult to accept that trust may facilitate coordination between a small group of common-good-holders, all of whom know each other well. Yet, it is not immediately obvious how trust could facilitate coordination between disparate people when it comes to the Public Trust. In fact, trusting strangers is not as counterintuitive as it first appears. Pioneering studies of trust within philosophy abound with examples. Annette Baier, Onora O'Neill, Karen Jones, Trudy Govier and Martin Hollis all use illustrations of behaviour in communal spaces – sharing the roads,[40] getting the train,[41] or falling asleep in public.[42] Trust is often invisible because it is unconscious, implicit, and pervasive.[43] Distrust is more accessible to us in everyday experience. For that reason, it is a helpful analytical tool. It makes visible the role that trust otherwise plays, for we exhibit trust even as we exhibit distrust: like asking a fellow passenger on a train to keep an eye on our belongings while we go to the bathroom. Our fellow passenger, a stranger, is selected by us to keep further unknown strangers at bay. Writers on trust have treated it as a desideratum if their analyses can extend to show how trust obtains between non-intimates, even where intimate trust was the primary focus of the work.

It is more evident that trust is often desirable. Trusting each other improves our phenomenological experience. Distrust is mentally exhausting and physically labour-intensive. Trust reduces for us the complexity of the world we move through.[44] The flip side is, of course, that if we do not place our trust well, the risks materialise. However, that there are risks and that we go about our business with some awareness of them does not go to show there is no trust. This chapter recognises full well that when out on urban pavements, you cannot avoid stepping on cracks. What it argues is that our proximity to other people already implies a certain level of trust in strangers. Daily interactions between strangers chime with Mullin's account of trusters assuming trusted ones are intrinsically committed to social norms governing their behaviour.

This does not merely occur when the probability of others defecting is low. We trust even when the stakes are high for us or for the people we love. Take as an example the common resource of the highway. When we call the emergency services, we trust in the unselfishness of road-users to get out the way of the sirens and flashing lights. The last thing that we expect from others in such a situation is the self-interest that Garrett Hardin envisaged. If self-interest were what we expected, then there would be no point in calling the ambulance – we would take

[40] Onora O'Neill, *A Question of Trust* (CUP, 2002), 11, 12; Trudy Govier, *Social Trust and Human Communities* (McGill-Queen's UP, 1997) 31; Martin Hollis, *Trust Within Reason* (Cambridge UP, 1998) 1.
[41] O'Neill (n 40) 11; Annette Baier, 'Trust and Antitrust' (1986) 96 Ethics 231, 234. Govier (n 40) 115 and Walker (n 19) 84 mention air travel.
[42] Baier (n 41) 234; Hollis (n 40) 10.
[43] Govier (n 40) 45.
[44] Niklas Luhmann, *Trust and Power: Two Works* (Howard Davis et al (tr), Wiley, 1979) 7, 10.

matters into our own hands and drive to the hospital ourselves. However, this is not what most of us do.

This is not the only instance where reactions based on a rational assessment of the probability of others defecting could result in death. For example, the *London Evening Standard* discovered in 2008 that at least one London Underground station is closed and evacuated each week due to overcrowding and the danger of crush injuries.[45] The network transports upward of three million people a day, and something as minor as maintenance work or a signal failure can cause disruption on a grand scale. Under these conditions, coordination becomes vital (literally). As no trains leave the platform yet commuters pour in, space diminishes. On one of these occasions, a newspaper reported that passengers fell over one another at the top of escalators as they fought for space and that a commuter was 'screaming' for fear they would be crushed to death.[46]

Facilitating coordination between passengers is crucial at such times. The network operator could coordinate through its authority (eg, by making announcements over the loudspeaker), but it may not respond quickly. If a stampede is not to ensue, commuters must trust that the authority will get them out safely. Trusting the network operator to take charge, rather than adopting a get-out-and-every-man-for-himself approach, meant that the screaming passenger did not begin a full-fledged panic. The crowd-control measures eventually implemented included turning off the escalators, blocking entrances and evacuating the station single file.[47] Behaviours ordinarily thought to be mere civility (making way, queueing, taking one's turn) prevented crush injuries even after the authority took over and an evacuation plan was in place. This is a situation where social norms (of civility) coincide with the demands of morality.

While this example (repeated in identical form many times over the past decades) does not reflect well on London infrastructure, it is certainly not farfetched. Nor is it an example of a small group of intimates using an extractive common-pool resource. Rather, it exhibits a form of trust that allows people to get to work safely in an everyday urban environment. This is an instance of trusting other people in their use of a resource – space – that is finite yet available to all. It also shows that an attitude that starts out as reliance (that the trains will run to timetable) may become one of trust as the stakes increase. I introduce the example to head off a possible objection from a risk assessment theorist of trust. It is not the case that we only trust because the likelihood of others defecting is low.

[45] Katharine Barney, 'Stations shut each week because of Tube crush' (*London Evening Standard*, 22 February 2008), www.standard.co.uk/news/stations-shut-each-week-because-of-tube-crush-6662102.html.

[46] Hannah Al-Othman and Ross Lydall, 'Victoria Line delays: Commuter panic as emergency sparks "crush" to leave Seven Sisters station' (*London Evening Standard*, 15 February 2016), www.standard.co.uk/news/transport/evacuation-sparks-crush-at-seven-sisters-station-a3180321.html.

[47] 'Battle of Waterloo: Rush hour descends into chaos and "dangerous overcrowding" (*Daily Express*, 8 August 2017), www.express.co.uk/news/uk/838313/Waterloo-station-London-chaos-rush-hour-travel-commute-dangerous-overcrowding.

So, what is the relevance of high stakes when talking about trust in relation to common goods? It is that trust involves vulnerability.[48] We are vulnerable when there is risk, as risk assessment views identify. However, these are not usually risks whose probability we can determine, accurately or at all. There may be no alternative courses open to us, even if we could. Rather, trust is relevant where there is irreducible uncertainty.[49] This is how it can explain the possibility of common property. By definition, a commons is available to others. It follows that association between users of common property is likely. 'Association' here covers two things. It involves users interacting with other users in person. It also involves dealing with others' impact on the resource and any consequences this may have for oneself. These are conditions for uncertainty and vulnerability. Users of common property are vulnerable to other agents in themselves, as well as to others' effect on the resource. Trust facilitates coordination under such conditions.

Thus my argument is not that trust has explanatory potential for the Public Trust because every interaction in our rich and complex public life involves trust, nor is it that every agent in our rich and complex society trusts. We will find both trust and reliance in public life (and many other things besides), but trust is an enabling condition for common property even when there are high stakes. Once we understand this, we see that private property is not the only solution to coordination problems.

A. Is this Just Reliance on Law?

There is, however, a worry that occurs when we are talking about non-intimate relations more strongly than it might with intimates. The worry is that people just rely on legal norms rather than trusting each other to abide by social norms.[50] This is a familiar worry with common property, especially because of the hangover tendency to see private property, governmental regulation and self-management as independent and mutually exclusive solutions. When we cash this worry out, however, it tends to recede. Before moving on to another objection in the next section, I canvass three versions of this claim and provide some responses.

One way to refine the claim is to ask which laws are said to have this effect. It is presumably mandatory criminal laws against bodily injury and property damage that give impetus to the idea that reliance, not trust, undergirds public interactions. Nobody seriously thinks there are laws requiring you not to panic if you cannot get out of the subway. The worry must then be about a subset of interactions or

[48] Baier (n 41) 239.

[49] Guido Möllering, *Trust: Reason, Routine, Reflexivity* (Elsevier, 2006) 8.

[50] For example, Putnam (n 21) 136; Larry Ribstein, 'Law v Trust' (2001) 81 Boston U LR 553, 555, 570; McLeod (n 23) 30; Lon Fuller, *The Problem of Social Order* (Duke UP, 1981) 76; Francis Fukuyama, *Trust: The Social Virtues and the Creation of Prosperity* (The Free Press, 1997) 27, 311.

discrete aspects of them. Let us, therefore, examine whether law necessarily or contingently precludes trusting.

The first way law could be said to exclude trust is the view that law is essentially coercive.[51] Russell Hardin (not Garrett Hardin, this time) compares trust to acting at gunpoint. For him, 'Part of what is wrong when I coerce you to do what I 'trust' you to do is that such an act violates the sense that trust as a concept has no meaning in a fully deterministic setting'.[52] Trust is relevant under conditions of irreducible uncertainty, as I said. Law does not eliminate uncertainty. This is because some actions are unregulated. Even when actions are regulated, there is always the risk that someone could breach a law. Laws are not guaranteed to be enforced. Someone who is trusted enjoys some discretion, however, constrained.[53] Law cannot shrink this sphere of discretion to nothing. As HLA Hart argued, laws are disanalogous to the commands of a gunman.[54]

There is a second worry about law that may arise from Mullin's account of trust. In her account, the truster takes the one trusted to have an intrinsic commitment to a social norm. Does law undercut the trusted one's motive? No. It is perfectly possible to act in accordance with the law without having the requisite commitment to legal norms. Even where a social and a legal norm demand the same thing, Mullin's account of trust leaves space for the possibility that someone could be motivated by the intrinsic commitment to a social norm without being intrinsically committed to a legal norm with the same content. (For example, a nudist may disagree with public indecency laws yet still be a trustworthy babysitter because they are committed to the social norm that people should be clothed in front of children not raised as nudists. A parent hiring the sitter knowing their views on the law would still trust them in Mullin's account.) Laws can coexist alongside social norms without displacing them.

A third different worry is that law may render trust otiose by serving an identical function to trust. As Raz notes, some laws have a coordinating function.[55] A classic example, highly relevant to our context, is the requirement to drive on the left-hand side of the road in Britain. However, laws like this do not exhaust the need for assurance. Take the hashtag *#JoinThePact* which encourages road-users to make a public commitment on social media not to drink-drive. There is room for this expression of trustworthiness despite laws against driving over a certain blood-alcohol limit. Laws can even help us place our trust well. I have always been struck by rule 111 of the British Highway Code, which exhorts you not to trust the signals of other drivers but to establish for yourself whether the way is clear to proceed.

[51] Expressed in eg, Ribstein (n 50) 562, 563, 582.
[52] Hardin (n 19) 4.
[53] Baier (n 41) 236, 237; Govier (n 40) 111, 128.
[54] HLA Hart, *The Concept of Law*, 2nd edn (Clarendon Press, 1961) 47–48, 77–78.
[55] Joseph Raz, *Ethics in the Public Domain* (Clarendon Press, 1994) 330–34.

This points to the plausible idea that laws could undermine *or* promote trust: that it is a contingent matter. Russell Hardin thinks that law creates conditions in which trust develops. He says we feel reassured about people's motivations in the little things when we lose our fear over the big things, like threats to life and limb. Many other scholars have likewise alluded to trust being facilitated by a regulatory backdrop.[56] At the same time, one hears these various claims that law 'crowds out' trust. Certainly, the law has the capacity to reduce trust, but we should turn to empirical research and principles of institutional design to find out when it actually does so. The many scholarly disciplines interested in trust all contribute to enriching our understanding of it.

IV. How Much Can Trust Explain about Common Property?

One objection that can be levelled against rights-based accounts of common property is this. An egalitarian distribution of (compossible) rights does not guarantee egalitarian access to common property in reality. While Garrett Hardin worried about people taking too much, others worry about people taking too little. Not everyone feels safe or welcome using public space. This section considers an objection that trust does not fare better than rights in the extent to which it explains the possibility of property that is *truly* common, ie available to all, while privileging none. Such a challenge is mounted by Shay Welch. Welch says, 'thin social trust cannot overcome cooperation problems consequent of oppression'.[57] Although she does not develop this criticism in detail, I take it that Mullin's account (and therefore mine) count as 'thin social trust' in her view. This section provides a possible defence against the challenge that 'thin social trust' resolves only a subset of coordination problems.

Let us call this the *therapeutic challenge*. The term 'therapeutic challenge' is appropriate because Welch's point is that thin social trust cannot help society rise above its existing levels of trust. These levels have come about due to long-standing oppression of certain groups by other groups. In the case of a street subject to a Public Trust, formal availability to all may reduce to variable accessibility to different groups, brokered by levels of trust. This might indicate that trust is limited in the extent to which it can explain the possibility of common property. If that is the case, then so be it. However, I think there is more to be said. The therapeutic challenge gets at intriguing paradoxical aspects of trust itself.

[56] Ostrom, 'Linking Trust, Reciprocity and Reputation' (n 28) 62; Govier (n 40) 33, 118; Mullin (n 14) at her footnote 4; Walker (n 19) 32, 84; Frank Cross, 'Law and Trust' (2005) 93 Georgetown LJ 1457.

[57] Shay Welch, 'Transparent Trust and Oppression' (2013) 16(1) *Critical Review of International Social and Political Philosophy* 45, 57.

In order to demonstrate the paradoxical aspects, here are some statements about trust that many regard as true. Trust is self-reinforcing.[58] Trusters are blind to evidence of untrustworthiness. This means trust has a dark side, as illustrated by abusive relationships. Yet it is thought to be a good, or to bring goods with it, even though we know trust is violated all the time. Trust is often unconscious. Given that trust is unconscious and frequently broken, you might conclude there is a lot of unjustified trust around. This suggests a problem that needs curing by trusting only the trustworthy or (under more realistic conditions without full information on risk) trusting less. However, that prescription forgoes the goods that come with trusting and the good that trusting can do for the trusted person.[59] How much, when, and whom should we trust? Call this the *optimality problem*.

There is another paradoxical aspect to trust; call it the *bootstrap problem*. The bootstrap problem is this: If trust and distrust are self-perpetuating and self-confirming, then we have an impasse. How can trust pull itself up by its own bootstraps? Social scientists express it as a worry about societies entering 'steady states' which impede progress toward higher (more optimal?) levels of trust. Thus Welch's therapeutic challenge gets at some deep questions about trust itself. I want to consider the challenge as it applies to a prominent issue in public space. This is the question of women's safety and suspicion toward minority-ethnic or lower-class men.

Brent Staples describes his experience of arriving in Chicago for the first time and having a young woman flee him in the street. In his article, 'Black Men and Public Space', he says: 'It was in the echo of that terrified woman's footfalls that I first began to know the unwieldy inheritance I'd come into – the ability to alter public space in ugly ways'. He acknowledges that the threat to women is 'not a hallucination' and so takes extraordinary measures to increase his perceived trustworthiness. 'On late-evening constitutionals, … I whistle melodies from Beethoven and Vivaldi and the more popular classical composers … Virtually everybody seems to sense that a mugger wouldn't be warbling bright, sunny selections from Vivaldi's *Four Seasons*'. Anthony Walton, writing on the same theme, describes a dispiriting occasion when the measures he took to hike up his perceived trustworthiness were unsuccessful. It was then that he saw: 'I am often treated the same as a thug, [and] no amount of conformity, willing or unwilling, will make me the fabled American individual'.[60] Laurence Thomas, an African-American philosopher who has written about trust, sums up: 'I rarely enjoy what is properly called the public trust of whites'.[61]

[58] Baier (n 41) 197; Govier (n 40) 36–40 discusses psychological research on this point.

[59] Govier (n 40) 133.

[60] Anthony Walton, 'Willie Horton and Me' (*New York Times*, 20 August 1989), www.nytimes.com/1989/08/20/magazine/willie-horton-and-me.html.

[61] Laurence Thomas, 'Next Life I'll Be White' (*Toronto Globe & Mail*, 16 August 1990) reproduced in Govier (n 40) 123.

All three men carry a similar burden of jacking up their perceived trustworthiness, but it appears that Staples discharges it more effectively than Walton or Thomas. Although Walton complains that his actions were doomed to be ineffectual, it seems to me that all three men have a valid complaint regardless of their skill at discharging it, namely having to carry the burden at all. Staples recognises a mirror-image burden that women carry, namely that their vulnerability requires them to place trust well. Everyone wants the world to be a better place, but exhortations to 'trust more'[62] or to 'be trustworthy'[63] are burdensome for individuals. Even if these exhortations are intelligible to begin with (they assume trust can be willed), they may be too much to ask given personal or group histories of oppression. As Karen Jones observes, the social climate, the domain of competence and the particular risk modulate whether one should trust in a particular situation.[64] Public life is filled with these inconvenient instances of multiply-oppressed groups whose interests in using public space are apparently pitted against one another.

Can trust realistically make common property accessible to all such groups, or is Welch correct to say that 'thin social trust cannot overcome cooperation problems consequent of oppression'? In one sense, she is right. It is right that trust cannot do all the work *alone*. We should not forget the enormous contribution of public administration and urban design to creating the 'feel' of a neighbourhood.[65] Is it right, though, that thin social trust cannot do any of the work ever? That is a strong claim and, I think, a false one. To see why, I examine Shilpa Phadke's 'Reflections on Loitering and Gendered Public Spaces'.

Phadke is concerned with women's access to public space in India, where highly-publicised rape cases led to government officials recommending that women avoid 'hostile' spaces.[66] Additionally, there was a clamour to clean up streets and remove undesirables, including lower-class men, sex workers and migrants. These are calls to limit the use of a common resource. Phadke's counter-proposal, inspired by women's protests, calls women to 'loiter' in public space. This is to assert their claim to take up that space and simultaneously fill it with 'friendly bodies whose presence might counter the threat perceived to be emanating from unfriendly bodies'.[67] Activists will thereby be doing the opposite of what Brent Staples lamented – namely, by their presence, changing public space in ways that make it less 'ugly'. Instead, women's presence impresses upon popular imagination what an ideal cityscape would look like to them. If Phadke's suggestion is tenable, then it provides a counterexample to Welch's therapeutic challenge. It is an example of thin social trust capable of overcoming a coordination problem consequent on oppression.

[62] Uslaner (n 19) 4; Jones (n 18), 72. Contrast Govier (n 40) 43 and O'Neill (n 40) 64.

[63] Govier (n 40) 48.

[64] Jones (n 18), 71; Walker (n 19) 87.

[65] See eg, Jane Jacobs, *The Death and Life of Great American Cities* (Vintage 1992); Shilpa Phadke, 'Unfriendly Bodies, Hostile Cities: Reflections on Loitering and Gendered Public Space' (2013) 39 *Economic and Political Weekly* 50, 53, 54.

[66] Phadke, ibid, 50–51.

[67] Ibid, 54.

Phadke is, of course, acutely aware of risk. For her, the question is how to weigh the values of freedom, comfort and safety. Freedom, comfort and safety are distributed unequally between women. Some activists might more lightly carry the burden of trusting so that they can 'loiter'. It is demanding less to ask them to bear it on behalf of others. It is to these more privileged women that Phadke primarily directs her work. She does not argue that there is an obligation to loiter, just the supererogatory option. (Further, there exist 'friendly bodies' who are not women, nor indeed activists – street hawkers and students were frequently mentioned by the respondents to her research. The burden is not all on women.).

Phadke also underscores that weighing safety above all things incurs concomitant losses to the possibility of pleasure, something that women may also be hesitant to claim. This chimes with literature on trust – trust is relevant under conditions of ineradicable risk, and without it, there are many goods forgone. The novelty of Phadke's approach is that it does not recommend reducing risk. Phadke ventures that 'the more complex and multidimensional a space, the more comfortable it is likely to be for women'.[68] Although she does not take herself to be addressing the literature on trust, her conclusion is supported by writers who study it, including Bo Rothstein, Thomas Pettigrew and Hugh Forbes.[69] To generalise hugely, they posit that under appropriate conditions, contact between dissimilar groups increases social trust. By asking those women who are more able to trust to flaunt their trust in public space, association between different groups can take place.

Taking Phadke's research and these studies on trust, it seems radical loitering can overcome the bootstrap problem. Shay Welch might object that it is not a true counterexample because the optimality problem remains. Is it asking too much to make oneself vulnerable, even optionally? Phadke is adamant that 'what women need in order to access public space is not conditional safety but the right[70] to take risks'.[71] I take her to concede that the optimality problem remains, but she de-problematises it by accepting the inevitability of risk and inciting women to political activism. She makes the case for a subset of people to collectively change the situation for everyone, friendly and 'hostile' bodies alike. The possibility of intentional collective action is rarely proposed in the philosophical literature on

[68] Ibid, 56.

[69] Bo Rothstein, *Social Traps and the Problem of Trust* (CUP, 2005) 99; Thomas Pettigrew, *Racially Separate or Together?* (McGraw Hill, 1971) 275; Hugh Forbes, *Ethnic Conflict: Commerce, Culture and the Contact Hypothesis* (Yale UP, 1997) 23.

[70] Phadke uses the words 'claim' and 'right' in ways that may grate on legal/philosophical scholars. I have generally reproduced or paraphrased her work without interrogating her use of terms. It is notable that even in work as thoughtful as hers, we see the word 'property' used to mean private property without any glimpse of an idea that streets could be common property and the 'right' (if so it is) might be a proprietary one. See her sentence, for example, that 'loitering envisages an inclusive city where people have a right to city public spaces, creating the possibility for all to stake a claim not just to the [private] property they own, nor to use the [private] ownership of property as grounds for being more equal citizens, but to claim undifferentiated rights to public space'. (Phadke et al, 'Why Loiter? Radical Possibilities for Gendered Dissent' in Melissa Butcher and Selvaraj Velayutham (eds), *Dissent and Cultural Resistance in Asia's Cities* (Routledge, 2009)).

[71] Phadke (n 65) 51.

trust, but it is preferable to the exhortations directed at individuals. The therapeutic challenge fails; thin social trust makes possible truly common property despite the existence of distrust consequent on oppression.

V. Conclusion

Discourse about property focuses on private property to such an extent that the word 'property' is coterminous with private property. This chapter looked at a neglected yet widespread instance of common property, namely the Public Trust. The Public Trust is longstanding and pervasive across the Commonwealth, yet legal and philosophical scholarship offers little explanation for how this is possible.

Although common property is under-theorised, there is a rich interdisciplinary scholarship on trust which should inform it. I drew on that literature. Research in social science motivated this argument that trust is explanatory of common property, instead of, or as well as, notions of right. Experimental and empirical research in economics showed that trust facilitates cooperation in the face of coordination problems, even among strangers. Trust is relevant under conditions of irreducible uncertainty. By definition, a commons is available to others and, therefore, association with others is likely. Trust makes common property possible under these conditions of vulnerability.

The interdisciplinary scholarship helped address objections too. Philosophical work on the nature of law allowed me to counter some misunderstandings about it necessarily 'crowding out' trust. Shilpa Phadke's scholarship from the perspective of cultural studies furnished a counterexample to Shay Welch's objection from a philosophical perspective. Trust is needed in addition to any formal entitlement to access public space in order to ensure property is truly common. It can fulfil this function even under real-world conditions involving multiple oppressed groups.

One of the great joys of scholarship on trust is that it shows why we should not be so anxious to balkanise academic inquiries. Often academia achieves rigour at the regrettable price of esotericism. Interdisciplinarity challenges this; it allows that a full explanation of a phenomenon could be more multifaceted than our desire for conceptual neatness would dictate. In the absence of such a realisation, the possibility and existence of the Public Trust would be an enduring puzzle.

References

Andreoni, James, 'Why Free Ride? Strategies and Learning in Public Goods Experiments' (1988) 37 *Journal of Public Economics* 291.

Baier, Annette, 'Trust and Antitrust' (1986) 96 *Ethics* 231.

Becker, Lawrence, 'Trust as Noncognitive Security about Motives' (1996) 107(1) *Ethics* 43.

Cohen, Marc and Dienhart, John, 'Moral and Amoral Conceptions of Trust with an Application to Organizational Ethics' (2013) 112 *Journal of Business Ethics* 1.

Cross, Frank, 'Law and Trust' (2005) 93 *Georgetown Law Journal* 1457.
Faulkner, Paul, 'The Attitude of Trust is Basic' (2015) 75(3) *Analysis* 424.
Forbes, Hugh, *Ethnic Conflict: Commerce, Culture and the Contact Hypothesis* (Yale University Press 1997).
Fukuyama, Francis, *Trust: The Social Virtues and the Creation of Prosperity* (The Free Press 1997).
Fuller, Lon, *The Problem of Social Order* (Duke University Press 1981).
Gambetta, Diego, 'Can We Trust Trust?' in Gambetta, Diego (ed), *Trust: Making and Breaking Cooperative Relations* (Blackwell 1988).
Govier, Trudy, *Social Trust and Human Communities* (McGill-Queen's University Press 1997).
Gray, Kevin and Gray, Susan, *Elements of Land Law*, 5th edn (Oxford University Press 2008).
Grotius, Hugo, *De Jure Belli ac Pacis* (1625), Book II, chs 2 and 3; Neff, Stephen (ed), *Of War and Peace* (Cambridge University Press 2012).
Hardin, Garrett, 'The Tragedy of the Commons' (1968) 162 *Science* 1234.
Hardin, Russell, 'Conceptions and Explanations of Trust' in Cook, Karen (ed), *Trust in Society* (Russell Sage 2003).
Hart, HLA, *The Concept of Law* (Clarendon Press 1961).
Hollis, Martin, *Trust Within Reason* (Cambridge University Press 1998).
Huffmann, James, 'Fish Out of Water: The Public Trust Doctrine in a Constitutional Democracy' (1989) 19 *Environmental Law* 527.
Jacobs, Jane, *The Death and Life of Great American Cities* (Vintage 1992).
Jones, Karen, 'Second-Hand Moral Knowledge' (1999) 96(2) *Journal of Philosophy* 55.
Kearney, Joseph and Merrill, Thomas, 'The Origins of the American Public Trust Doctrine: What Really Happened in *Illinois Central*' (2004) 71 *University of Chicago Law Review* 799.
Knack, Stephen and Keefer, Philip, 'Does Social Capital Have an Economic Payoff? A Cross-Country Investigation' (1997) 112(4) *The Quarterly Journal of Economics* 1251.
Luhmann, Niklas, *Trust and Power: Two Works* (Davis, Howard et al (tr), Wiley 1979).
MacCormick, Neil, 'Rights in legislation' in Hacker, Peter and Raz, Joseph (eds), *Law, Morality and Society* (Oxford University Press 1985).
Marmor, Andrei, 'Do We Have a Right to Common Goods?' (2001) 4(2) *Canadian Journal of Law & Jurisprudence* 213.
McLeod, Carolyn, *Self-Trust and Reproductive Autonomy* (MIT Press 2002).
Möllering, Guido, *Trust: Reason, Routine, Reflexivity* (Elsevier 2006).
Mossoff, Adam, 'What is Property? Putting the Pieces Back Together' (2003) 45 *Arizona Law Review* 371.
Mullin, Amy, 'Trust, Social Norms, and Motherhood' (2005) 36(3) *Journal of Social Philosophy* 316.
O'Neill, Onora, *A Question of Trust* (Cambridge University Press 2002).
Ostrom, Elinor, *Governing the Commons: the Evolution of Institutions for Collective Action* (Cambridge University Press 1990).
Ostrom, Elinor, 'Toward a Behavioural Theory Linking Trust, Reciprocity and Reputation' in Walker, James and Ostrom, Elinor (eds), *Trust and Reciprocity: Interdisciplinary Lessons from Experimental Research* (Russell Sage Foundation 2003).
Page, John and Brower, Ann, 'The Four Dimensions of Public Property' in Conway, Heather & Hickey, Robin (eds), *Modern Studies in Property Law* (Hart 2017).
Pettigrew, Thomas, *Racially Separate or Together?* (McGraw Hill 1971).
Phadke, Shilpa, 'Unfriendly Bodies, Hostile Cities: Reflections on Loitering and Gendered Public Space' (2013) 39 *Economic and Political Weekly* 50.
Phadke, Shilpa et al, 'Why Loiter? Radical Possibilities for Gendered Dissent' in Butcher, Melissa and Velayutham, Selvaraj (eds), *Dissent and Cultural Resistance in Asia's Cities* (Routledge 2009).
Putnam, Robert, *Making Democracy Work* (Princeton University Press 1993).
Putnam, Robert, *Bowling Alone* (Simon & Schuster 2000).
Raz, Joseph, *Ethics in the Public Domain* (Clarendon Press 1994).
Réaume, Denise, 'Individuals, Groups, and Rights to Public Goods' (1988) 38(1) *University of Toronto Law Journal* 1.

Ribstein, Larry, 'Law v. Trust' (2001) 81 *Boston University Law Review* 553.
Rodgers, Christopher, 'Towards a Taxonomy for Public and Common Property' (2019) 78(1) *Cambridge Law Journal* 124.
Rose, Carol, 'The Comedy of the Commons: Custom, Commerce and Inherently Public Property' (1986) 53 *University of Chicago Law Review* 711.
Rothstein, Bo, *Social Traps and the Problem of Trust* (Cambridge University Press 2005).
Sønderskov, Kim, 'Different Goods, Different Effects: Exploring the Effects of Generalized Social Trust in Large-N Collective Action' (2009) 140 *Public Choice* 145.
Steiner, Hillel, *An Essay on Rights* (Blackwell 1994).
Uslaner, Eric, *The Moral Foundations of Trust* (Cambridge University Press 2002).
Waldron, Jeremy, 'Can Communal Goods Be Human Rights?' in his *Liberal Rights: Collected Papers 1981–1991* (Cambridge University Press 1993).
Walker, Margaret, *Moral Repair* (Cambridge University Press 2006).
Welch, Shay, 'Transparent Trust and Oppression' (2013) 16(1) *Critical Review of International Social and Political Philosophy* 45.

9

On Voluntary Associations and New Avenues for Research on Social Trust

NELI DEMIREVA

I. Introduction

The focus of this chapter is on the almost perennial question of the association between organisational involvement and social trust. Social trust can be described as an expectation of the goodwill of people and the honouring of their commitments (Freitag and Bauer, 2013). More specifically, I consider the well-trodden paths and new avenues that social scientists should take in order to investigate whether we can have too much of something good, and whether pervasive cuts to associations should be lamented because they really impair our ability to trust and for society to function properly. Furthermore, the debate on the factors that augment or undermine social trust will benefit from theorisation and empirical testing and, using Britain as an example, I outline a possible agenda for future research in this area.

A lamentation on the death of bowling alleys provides the narrative thread in Putnam's seminal work 'Bowling alone' (Putnam, 2000). Not all scholars agree however that voluntary community involvement through organisations ensures the smooth functioning of modern societies. In *The Rise and Decline of Nations*, Mancur Olson has argued that Britain's long-term economic decline is the result of the existence of a multitude of interest groups that help to dilute and decentre public policy in dangerous ways (Olson, 2008). Thus, excessive rent-seeking behaviour, which can be described as voluntary associations[1] diverting public

[1] Community organisations is a term widely used in the UK literature (Olson, 2008) to describe voluntary associations that are based in a specific locality and provide services to residents in a local area. Community centre usually denotes the building or the meeting space in which the activities of the organisation take place, but in some cases the term can be used to refer to the organisation itself. The coverage area of such organisations however can vary widely and some may represent one specific neighbourhood, while others cover several boroughs or a city. It is common for the US literature to use the terms voluntary associations, organisations and community involvement somewhat interchangeably (Putnam, 2000). Participation in such organisation can also be referred to as community/voluntary involvement, civic organising, associational life or civicness.

resources to support the causes they are interested in, eg women's health care or the protection of biodiversity (Fukuyama, 2001), can undermine the overall public good, especially if these organisations do not represent real public interests but rather the 'excessive politicisation that we can have of public life, which can either distort public policy or lead to deadlock' (Fukuyama, 2001: 12). Yet, Fukuyama (2001) concludes that it is surely worse to have too little of voluntary involvement than too much.

Voluntary associational involvement is often part of political agendas, which is an important aspect almost completely disregarded in the empirical research on the topic. This chapter will provide evidence of the necessity for taking the local context into account in which organisations exist and function, using British community organisations as an example. In 2010, David Cameron was eager to announce plans for the establishment of a Big Society initiative that should have heralded a further expansion and strengthening of the vibrant voluntary sector in communities around Britain. In reality, however, community organisations saw their budgets severely cut while at the same time associations have had to deal with increasing expectations from within the community of the services they can provide, usually to the most vulnerable in localities blighted by multi-layered disadvantage (O'Hara, 2015). A story of declining associational involvement usually focuses on individualisation processes that divest the individual from their community. Often, I would argue, there can be several factors at play; yet, research that connects the micro and macro context including the local and national funding climate is nascent.

In the following sections, I overview the wider literature on the link between associational involvement and social trust and present some of the issues that have been raised throughout it. I discuss the nature of associations in Britain and the importance of considering their local embeddedness, and present evidence of the impact of cuts on the British voluntary sector. The chapter will conclude with a discussion of new and not so new but important directions for research on social trust and voluntary associational involvement.

A systematic and wide-ranging analysis that aims to identify the link between voluntary associations and trust remains very much needed. Voluntary involvement continues to be touted as paramount to efforts to sustain and nurture a vibrant, socially healthy, and trusting society. It frequently features as public policy goal, while cuts to community organisations are widely feared and despised. Yet, there is scope for more robust evidence on the interconnection between joining and trusting. This essay attempts to outline a way forward for this important research strand.

II. Voluntary Associational Involvement and Social Trust: The Evidence

Given the very loose way in which authors have used these foundational concepts – social trust and associational involvement – it is important to provide a definition at the outset of this chapter. When social trust is referred to, we usually distinguish between particularised trust (such as trust in relations, friends and neighbours), generalised trust (trust in strangers) and trust in groups (such as the ethnic group to which one belongs) (Freitag and Bauer, 2013). Defined very broadly, voluntary associations represent a formal group of members who are not financially remunerated and are joined together by a variety of interests: be it social, political, cultural, sports, religious, industry, occupational or professional (Tschirhart and Gazley, 2014). It is often hypothesised that regular interactions with others – friends, family, neighbours – in organisations in which involvement is voluntary can cement trust in fellow human beings through the facilitation of a general sense that individuals can be relied upon to fulfil their social duties (Welch et al, 2007). In particular, the opportunity for and establishment of formal ties within voluntary associations is often theorised to have unparalleled benefits to social and political cohesion. Lipset (1959: 63) summarises vividly these purportedly positive effects: 'they inhibit the state or any single source of private power from dominating all political resources, they are a source of new opinions, they can be the means of communicating ideas, particularly opposition ideas, to a large section of the citizenry, they train men in political skills and so help to increase the level of interest and participation in politics' (Lipset, 1959).

Putnam et al (1993) distinguishes between associations' *internal* effects on their members and the possible *external* effects on the political system. Internally, associations can be seen as *schools of democracy* because of their educational aspect – they teach members at the micro-level how to be better part of the community, one that cooperates better and trusts more. According to Putnam et al (1993: 89–90), 'associations instil in their members habits of cooperation, solidarity and public-spiritedness'. This important effect of socialisation, as schools are often seen as agents of socialisation, ensures that the members of the community organisation become citizens with the right *habits of the heart* (Newton, 2001, Newton, 1997) – citizens who are ready to extend their goodwill to others. Externally, voluntary associations can be viewed as alternative sources of influence. They provide institutional links between the members and the political system and occupy the role of intermediaries (Putnam et al, 1993).

One of the key debates in the literature on associational involvement and social trust focuses on the causality of the relationship. It is indeed difficult to establish a causal link (reciprocal or not) between trust and organisational life. Robert Putnam (2000), colloquially, refers to this stumbling block in the following way: 'The causal arrows among civic involvement, reciprocity, honesty and social trust are as tangled as well-tossed spaghetti. Only careful, even experimental, research will be able to sort them apart definitively … We need to recognize that they form a coherent syndrome.' (Putnam, 2000: 145).

Empirically, several studies have sought nevertheless to disentangle that *spaghetti bowl*.[2] Early attempts usually focused on the direction and the size of

[2] The literature focuses particularly on trust as the cementing blocks of societies (Putnam, 2000).

the observed effect – something that subsequent studies mostly ignore. Brehm and Rahn (1997) find stronger support for the influence of group involvement on generalised trust than the reverse although they do report the existence of a 'tight reciprocal relationship' between the two (pp 1112–13). The reciprocity is contested by Claibourn and Martin (2000) who using youth and parent samples claim that reverse causality has been overstated and report only a negligible substantive effect of trust on voluntary involvement.

In a seminal study, Stolle (2001) raises the issue of self-selection confounding both the results as well as their interpretation. For example, it is possible that those who join voluntary associations in the first place are more civic-minded. Establishing the causal connection is difficult because longitudinal data on the topic hardly exists. Stolle (2001) creates a mock panel by comparing the values and behaviours of new members of an organisation with those of long-time members in an attempt to partially account for selection issues. The conclusion reached by Stolle (2001) is that it is less than clear that greater organisational participation translates into greater civic involvement in the larger society proxied by voting in local elections and engagement with community issues. Looking at three countries, Stolle (2001) observes some positive association in the United States and Germany but quite a weak link between organisations and civicness in Sweden, where there is actually a negative relationship between length of membership in voluntary associations and community engagement outside of the group. Importantly, the results suggest that generalised trust and openness to strangers do not increase with longevity of group membership. Thus, the results seem to suggest that there are no especially positive long-term benefits to associational involvement that translate to society at large.

McPherson, Smith-Lovin and Cook (2014) argue that formal ties – social ties within voluntary organisations – create trust in specific people – other members of the organisation who can be quite similar socially, ethnically and culturally – rather than trust in a generalised other. Similar sentiments are expressed in Uslaner (2002) and Uslaner and Brown (2005), who urge us not to be too quick to assume that generalised trust will be positively influenced by civic and organisational involvement. Uslaner (2002: 120) puts it aptly: 'If you put a bunch of misanthropes in a room and have them sing, they will still be Scrooges (and they may sound sour notes). The linkage between voluntary associations and trust is likely the other way around: Trusting people show up in choral societies (and other organizations) – and there is substantial evidence for this.' Thus, in a similar way to Stolle (2001), Uslaner (2002) argues that trusting people are more likely to join voluntary associations than non-trusting people. Trust can thus be seen as an affective attitude and the people that display it are perhaps more likely to be outgoing and involved in associations (Jones, 1996). The main reason we frequently observe voluntary associations to accommodate more trusting, more open and more civic-minded people is self-selection, not the magical *rainmaker* powers of associational life. Simply put, 'good neighbours make good fences' (Uslaner, 2002: 123).

There is also the question about the diversity within voluntary associations. The positive effect of voluntary involvement is often attributed to exposure and association with diverse others (Glanville et al, 2009, Farkas and Lindberg, 2015, Stolle, 2001). Evidence that membership can be homogenous across individual and socio-economic dimensions such as education, age or race essentially indicates low odds of inter-group contact (Uslaner, 2002). Other voices on this point, however, argue that organisations can be homogeneous on one dimension such as age but heterogeneous on others such as ethnicity and gender (Putnam, 2000); and membership in multiple associations matters (Wollebaek and Selle, 2002).

Recent research continues to paint a highly polarised picture of the impact of voluntary associations on trust. Using the Social Capital Community Benchmark Survey, Glanville (2016) finds that involvement in voluntary association facilitates the development of trust by connections to dissimilar others although the effect is small.

In contrast, using data from panel studies from Switzerland, the UK, Netherlands and Australia, Van Ingen and Bekkers (2015) find little support for the hypothesis that civic engagement creates and augments generalised trust. According to this study if any such evidence exists (the authors only find such evidence with Swiss data), it is confined to small, short-term effects, which however do not last – civic engagement may bring trusting individuals together, but it has limited impact upon generalised trust in the long run, it seems. The UK data indeed provides no evidence to support a causal association of voluntary engagement and trust. A similar conclusion is reached by Van der Meer and Van Ingen (2016) who suggest that voluntary associations should be categorised as *pools of democracy* rather than schools of democracy; that is to say, they provide opportunities for individuals involved with a variety of issues to come together, rather than create a learning effect.

Some studies find strong evidence for the rainmaker hypothesis, that is to say, the ability of associational life to offer larger societal benefits. The issue of reverse causality can remain however unsettled and the embeddedness of communities within regions may matter. For example, Kriesi and Baglione (2003) find that even distrusting individuals can be more likely to join interest groups if they live in a country where generalised trust is higher, which attests to an overall importance of the climate in which individuals are embedded.

The number of associations in which the individual takes part as well as the type of associations is probably an important piece in the social capital puzzle. Paxton (2007) produces a large-scale, comprehensive examinations of the factors contributing to generalised trust across 31 nations and observes that multiple membership of organisations promotes trust both at the individual and country levels, while isolated membership – membership in a particular type of association is not conducive to the formation of generalised trust. This means that there will be associations which are detrimental to some social capital outcomes at the national level. The finding resonates with concerns of scholars such as Sigrid Rossteutscher (2002), who believe that associations may result in a political climate that is anti-democratic and potentially detrimental to societal governance. The examples used by Rossteutscher (2000) are nationalist associations in turn of the century Germany, which albeit representing a free associational expression of the citizenry, served to amplify authoritarian and nationalist voices. Similarly, scholars have worried about the potential isolation from the mainstream society within ethnic associations (Koopmans, 2016) with a multicultural agenda serving to create parallel communities rather than a unique whole.

Certainly, with a growing diversification of societies, there is a proliferation of ethnic associations. Fennema and Tillie (2001) raise concerns that ethnic voluntary organisations may operate as exclusive bodies which can limit connectivity with the broader community. Even if this does not result in ethnic strife, such lack of connectivity in civil society may lower society's reserve of trust. With longitudinal data, Wiertz (2016) establishes some concerning trends. Using unique panel data from the Netherlands Longitudinal Life Course Study (NELLS), Wiertz (2016) finds that all ethnic groups are equally likely to join voluntary organisations; yet, ethnic minorities are more likely to leave such organisations than are Dutch natives, which accounted for their overall lower involvement rates. The existence of strong ethnic sorting across organisations of different ethnic composition and the lack of contact to outgroups leads Wiertz (2016) to conclude that the potential of voluntary associations as pathways to social integration is limited and that concerns that ethnic organisations can contribute to the generation of ethnic enclaves are not without grounds.

Still ethnic organisations can have important societal functions that cannot be disregarded. Fennema and Tillie (2001) ask for ethnic associations to be seen as *primarily* political opportunity structures rather than exclusively cultural phenomena. Indeed, political organising may ensure the political integration of ethnic minorities. One can argue that the articulation of interests and aggregation of values of which Putnam speaks (1993) – the essence of voluntary involvement – is of great civic importance that ultimately contributes to a stable democracy. Civil society can be a means of balancing (a check on) the power of the state. It can protect individuals from the state's power (Fukuyama 2001) by making sure that groups and the interests of the individuals they comprise are represented. The existence of a diverse range of associations can be considered a sign of democratic pluralism. Thus, the presence of community organisations is a value in itself (Wollebaek and Selle 2002) as it ensures the representation of groups and can be important outlet for the views and issues of vulnerable minority individuals. I would argue that this is particularly true of local community centres that act as a focal meeting point for residents in a neighbourhood but are also a means for signalling societal concern for different groups and vulnerable others. Associational life may not be futile even if some of its supporters are passive: the mere existence of an organisation can convey a sense of political efficacy and societal recognition that extends both to the members of the organisation and those outside of it (Wollebaek and Selle 2002). Furthermore, organisations may be important diffusers of information whose power to connect members may facilitate for example employment opportunities and thus alleviate certain burdens on the state.

Clearly, the literature has been dominated by attempts to establish the empirical existence of a relationship between trust and community involvement. Yet, similarly to the debates on social capital that remain loose and mired by vague propositions, the mechanisms that theorise the link between trust and voluntary associations are not fully fleshed out. There is lack of suitable longitudinal data, different types of organisations are not really discussed, as well as different types of social trust – great many of these studies are concerned only with the link between generalised trust and organisational involvement. Moreover, there is almost no consideration of the embeddedness of organisations in a variety of different localities and no account of factors that can be related to their existence such as political climate, deprivation and funding cuts. The following sections of this chapter will use British voluntary associations as an example and will illustrate that local area embeddedness is not just a side aspect of associational life – it is a cornerstone feature of associations related to their creation and continued existence.

III. Voluntary Associations in Britain: Expansion and Diversification

The history of voluntary associational life in Britain is one of community organising, the creation of community centres that are usually deeply rooted in a local area and aim to address specific problems that this community faces. As this section will show voluntary community involvement can be the result of the concern of individual residents with a societal issue specific to their locality, however, large-scale organising requires a vision, passion and crucially funding which may transcend individual attempts for neighbourhood improvement. Three main organisations represent historically the voluntary involvement in Britain – the National Council of Voluntary Organisations, the Federation of Residential Settlements and the Educational Settlements Association.

The Settlement Movement, originating in the 1880s, placed emphasis upon the need of the urban poor for social justice and equality. Some of the early pioneers were Samuel Barnett, Canon of Westminster and his wife Dame Henrietta Barnett. Samuel who is represented with the figure of a sower on his memorial in the south choir aisle of Westminster Abbey – 'laboured unceasingly to unite men in the service of God' and steered the movement towards challenging the barriers of class and hierarchical distinctions. This became a founding principle of the Federation of Residential Settlements, which adopted in its core structure the Barnetts' vision of bringing together men and women to work for social betterment and the common good. The Federation formally established in the 1920s still represents the network of University Settlements founded in 1884 (Abel, 1979). Currently named the British Association of Settlements and Social Action Centres (BASSAC), it merged in April 2011 with the Development Trusts Association (DTA) to form Locality – a new hub for community organisations in the UK, responsible for the operation of large community centres in more than 60 urban areas (Locality, 2020). Although small in terms of associated centres, the settlement movement has had huge impact upon associational involvement world-wide, particularly in Japan and the US. Toynbee Hall, created in 1884, provided a residential place for future leaders who would live and work as volunteers in London's East End – social pioneers such as Clement Attlee and William Beverage were both residents of Toynbee Hall. In addition, the settlement movement encouraged research on poverty and the connection between academia and ordinary citizens. Oxford House, which also opened doors in 1884 (and still exists as a youth club) operated as a mini Oxford college in Bethnal Green; and its residents, usually students of an Oxford college, assisted with the establishment of youth clubs, acted as lawyers for the destitute and taught adult education classes (Shepherd, 2010).

The Educational Settlements Association, established in the 1920s, bore certain resemblance to the Federation but also conspicuous differences. The organisations that comprised the association were primarily non-residential. Arnold S Rowntree, its President, described its mission as 'education in the community'; and together with the Workers Educational Association and the Young Men's Christian Association, the association implemented a variety of continuous education strategies (Davies and Freeman, 2003).

The aforementioned three major and very influential initiatives operated alongside smaller yet important outfits that deserve a mention. The Social Service clubs were formed around the miners' strikes of 1926/27 and aimed to provide a space for critical gatherings. These were later repurposed as educational centres and activity clubs. Village halls in town and rural areas continue to function and to bring sociability equally to cities full of busy workers and to farmland with dwellings frequently several miles apart. Village halls historically have represented local residents to local and national governments. The growth of Women's Institutes from 1915 originally centred on the women's contribution in the war effort and subsequently played a major role in the suffragette movement (Morris, 1983).

Currently, many of these organisations continue to exist, albeit to some extent in a rebranded format. There is a strong focus on services aimed at the needs of the local community and the recognition of disadvantage. In recent years, a proliferation of food banks has been witnessed, which has added to the landscape of voluntary organisations in Britain. Whereas soup kitchens had existed for quite some time, the proliferation of food banks can be traced to the period after the economic crisis in 2008. The Trussell Trust, a Christian social action charity and a non-governmental organisation that coordinates the network of community-run (food bank) franchises in the UK, reports a multi-fold increase in the need for food parcels: in 2009–10 Trussell Trust food banks were operating in 29 local authorities across the UK; by 2013–14, the number had risen to 251 (Trust, 2014). Such voluntary organisations have become vital to efforts of sustaining the local communities and alleviating poverty that frequently surpass the commitment of local or national governments to a destitute area (Loopstra and Lalor, 2017, Loopstra et al, 2015).

The diversification of the British society has been reflected in a growing number of organisations which focus on the needs of different migrant and minority groups. These are widely seen as part and parcel of the multiculturalist agenda of successive British governments. Such community organisations and the centres associated with them provide a space in which members can discuss their roots and engage in cultural practices. Accountability in terms of outreach to the general public is often expected of them (Buettner, 2008). Thus, the support received by the organisation is also support for the continuing incorporation in the mainstream and usually takes the form of funding for outreach events. Will Kymlicka (2010) talks of the 'samosa revolution' that many of these centres have instigated in Britain by organising various food festivals. At the same time, they can also be seen by the minority community as complicit in the undermining of a political agenda of recognition (Vertovec, 1996). The situation can be further complicated if the migrant and minority community centres are believed to be part of 'enclaves' by mainstream papers such as the *Daily Mail*, a potential breeding ground for reactionary ideas and sentiments which help foster exclusion and division (Mail, 2013).

Nevertheless, community organisations can play important role in bringing migrants and minorities closer to the mainstream and this is an aspect of associational involvement largely ignored in the literature on the topic. By providing educational opportunities usually closer to a learner's home, with staff known to the residents, and offering services such as day care, local community centres have operated as important information hubs to migrants and their families who may lack knowledge of the ways in which the mainstream receiving society operates. In effect, they are an integral part of the conception of the localised community. The research of Glanville and Paxton (2007) and Freitag and Traunmüller (2009) shows that trust within more localised domains, such as family, neighbours and co-workers produces higher levels of trust in generalised others. Strategically placed, local community centres can be important mediators of this relationship. Such environmental brokerage of trust can recompense for country of origin differences in norms, values and beliefs on the part of migrants – differences related to generalised trust that should not be underplayed. For example, research by Delhey and Newton (2011) shows that there are considerable cross-country variations in perceptions of who the generalised other is or who the phrase 'most people' captures.

Community centres periodically reappear on political agendas as elements of different integration strategies. Recently, the All Party Parliamentary Group on Social Cohesion has recommended that: 'local authorities in areas whose population normally includes significant numbers of new immigrants should establish welcome centres for new arrivals. These centres should offer immigrants joined-up access to public services, language classes and cultural orientation initiatives'. Furthermore, 'the Home Office should consider whether an adequate number of welcome centres are available to new arrivals seeking to live and work in a particular area of the country when allocating region-specific visas' (APPGR Report 2017: 47). In fact, as we have seen, such organisations have existed continuously for some time; yet, their presence in governments' hearts and minds is much less stable. And as we will see in the next section, some of these institutions might be particularly vulnerable to funding cuts.

IV. Funding Cuts and their Impact upon Communities in Britain

The role of policy on voluntary involvement and its impact upon social outcomes has been little investigated. As discussed in the previous section, many organisations depend for their existence on funding, usually provided from local or national government funds in Britain. There are indications that measures of austerity have led to the complete disappearance of certain types of institutions, and the proliferation of others. The main body of research on the impact of austerity in Britain focuses on food insecurity and the ominous rise of food banks since the financial crisis. In *Austerity Bites*, Mary O'Hara (2015) builds a bleak picture:

> Food banks unquestionably became one of the most visible totems on the austerity landscape – what one voluntary sector chief executive remarked was fast becoming 'the new normal'. So common had they become by December 2012 that the UK Prime Minister, David Cameron, lauded food bank volunteers as exponents of his 'Big Society' initiative, but critics countered that they represented nothing short of a return to a 'Dickensian' model of welfare, where the state retreats from its most basic responsibilities and charities and churches are left to pick up the pieces (O'Hara, 2015).

O'Hara further castigates the now largely forgotten Big Society programme of David Cameron that had at its heart the devolvement of power to local communities. The programme envisioned that community organisations will team up with local authorities in order to become primary service providers in local areas. In the reality of funding cuts, local authorities saw their budgets greatly reduced – and so did local charities and service groups (O'Hara, 2015).

The funding cuts seem to have affected disproportionally the most vulnerable. Loopstra et al (2018) show that the use of food banks is higher in more deprived local authorities and these with higher rates of disability and lone parenthood. Loopstra et al (2015) furthermore ascertain that the increased use of food banks is the result of economic sanctioning levied on the unemployed, and austerity, rather than food banks creating their own demand. Lambie-Mumford (2013) studied the Trussell Trust food bank and their emergency intervention model. At the centre of the model is indeed the local community – food is donated by local people, collected through neighbourhood churches, schools and supermarkets, stored locally and distributed to the most vulnerable within the community. Her respondents describe poignantly the impact of cuts to local organisations and services:

> because of the local government cuts, we've faced very substantial reductions in our funding, so the way that we used to, erm, what we used to do was work a different scheme, er, which was funded through our, through grant funding that we had previously, so we were in a position where we were stuck, financially, we were trying to think of creative ways in which we could continue to support families and that was the basis on which I thought we would give this [food bank] a try' (Lambie-Mumford, 2013: 81).

Thus, almost overnight, local voluntary organisations found themselves largely responsible for service provision at the area level while facing considerable and pervasive cuts.

Research shows that deprived areas in particular experienced a sharp decrease in services since 2010, and they are markedly composed by less trusting individuals although long-term analysis of the impact of austerity on social indicators is still very much needed (Lupton and Fitzgerald, 2015) as well as analysis that will consider the differences in types of community organisations. Incorporating the policy aspect in parallel to attempts of addressing the under-theorisation of mechanisms in the literature and the variety of methodological challenges is a key to our understanding of the factors and conditions under which social trust is augmented.

V. New Avenues for Research and Discussion

In *Bowling Alone*, Robert Putnam (2000) establishes a useful and viable framework for the study of matters of societal engagement and trust that is still very valid and relevant today to any research on the impact of the decline in associational involvement. His original starting point has been to address any nostalgic claims of the better days of the past by 'counting things' (2000: 22). To adapt this guiding principle to the concerns of the present chapter means that we need to establish first whether there are particular areas in which there has been pronounced decline in trust, and sociability and ascertain whether this decline can be linked to the absence or the diminished number of voluntary associations alongside a range of other individual and structural factors.

An important avenue forward is given to us by studies of segregation that map changes within communities by creating typologies and tracing the factors associated with varying circumstances (examples of studies in the US, see Sharkey (2013), Crowder and South (2012, 2011, 2008) and in the UK, Catney (2017, 2016)). I would advocate that we need to construct a similar typology of social vulnerability. Research on the relationship between involvement and social trust has been largely divorced from the residential and local area context. This is an important omission. The local area provides both the opportunity for involvement through exposure and of actual contact – between members in an organisation. A longitudinal view at the local level is much needed and it should take into consideration a whole host of phenomena – socio-economic opportunities, deprivation, crime, internal and external migration at the local level in which individuals and communities are embedded. This is essential, as the most vulnerable and least trusting are often found to be concentrated in disadvantaged neighbourhoods and regions with greater economic turnover, prolonged unemployment, bad jobs, and poorer employment prospects. The British Household Panel Study and its successor Understanding Society are excellent data for such a mapping exercise.

The BHPS is a household panel that started in 1991 and it was replaced by the much larger Understanding Society Panel in 2009, which still includes the original BHPS respondents as well. Yearly variations in local conditions can be used to explain social and political trust, community engagement, bridging social ties, and Labour Force Survey information can provide an understanding of changing economic circumstances of communities and regions.

Then, there is the problem of categorising different associations. Research has primarily looked into voluntary associations without distinguishing between different types of organisations. There is a whole spectrum of community organising that can be quite complex (Paxton, 2007; Bernhagen and Maloney, 2010). A lack of understanding of the differences between membership organisation – a proliferation of studies with 'unintegrated set of disparate findings, in dire need of compelling theory' (Knoke, 1986: 2) – has always been cited as a problem in the social capital literature. Several useful classifications have been developed. Paxton (2007) distinguishes between connected and isolated associations. Connected organisations are associations that are linked to other associations through cross-memberships. Isolated associations are organisations who essentially have isolated members. The first type seems to be particularly important for the generation of trust at societal level. Bernhagen and Maloney (2010) take into account the internal democratic procedures of an organisation and demonstrate that many organisations that are commonly and unambiguously classified as voluntary or civil society organisations in fact operate with hierarchical business principles in place. Although they find that the democratic characteristics of organisations are only marginally related to individual political participation, and individuals involved in different organisations display similar behaviour regardless of the level of democratisation of these institutions, this distinction merits further attention. It is possible that more hierarchical organisations are perceived as more professional by central government and therefore worthy of continuous subsidy and support. Further work in this area is needed and classification of organisations will form an integral part of any mapping exercise of voluntary associations.

More empirical work needs to be done that also examines in depth geographical patterns – do we witness cuts across all communities, or are the most deprived local areas disproportionally affected? Research suggests that vulnerable local areas, areas with high levels of unemployment, presence of single mothers and crime may have witnessed greater withdrawal of social support than others (Loopstra et al, 2015, 2017).

A decline in voluntary organisations might also represent a survival of the fittest and most adaptable institutions. A changing landscape of associational involvement creates methodological challenges that will be difficult to surpass. In *Bowling Alone*, Putnam asks: 'Are club meetings really less crowded today than yesterday or does it just seem so? … Are friendly poker games less common now, or is it merely that we ourselves have outgrown poker? League bowling may be passé, but how about softball and soccer?' (2000: 24). There could be decline in demand. The great expansion of the educational system in Britain, in particular, of higher education, has perhaps resulted in reduced relevance of centres for continuous learning, or in a more competitive environment in which just the most vibrant and energetic establishments survive. A limitation of any research set in the present is that the counterfactual cannot be explored. For example, since its foundation in 1889 as the Morley Memorial College for Working Men and Women, Morley College has operated continuously providing music education to adults in Waterloo and Lambeth, one of the first institution of its kind to admit both men and women on an equal footing (Richards, 2013, Poole, 2011). Other similar institutions have however disappeared. A research that aims to understand the different fortunes of organisations will need to involve the voices of the people that have constituted the beating heart of these organisations – both the ones that survived and the ones that did not. This is a serious methodological challenge that merits sustained research effort. Oral histories might provide us in the first instance with a way of understanding how local residents rationalise what has happened to their communities over time; and membership lists can be used to trace potential study participants.

It is possible that online community involvement and virtual engagement are superseding more dated physical forms of organising, or that at least a combination of virtual and physical social organising exists. Research on online organising and its relationship to generalised trust is nascent. Fan and Lederman (2018) investigate online health communities and show that trust is built through a knowledge of how contributors interact with others and the ways in which they have responded to fellow community members. Similarly to exchanges in the real world, trust in online communities seems dependent not only upon the actual information and facts shared (which the authors describe as the building of cognitive trust), but emotions and affections may also have an impact – expression of emotions sanctioned by the online community towards certain events or individuals can be seen as a sign of trustworthiness, much as happens in face-to-face interactions (Hieronymi, 2008).

The distinction between active and passive membership of a community organisation, and non-membership, is also important as trust can be considered exogenous to passive membership (Sønderskov, 2011). Some studies claim that affiliations, even passive ones, may contribute to a sense of identification with a cause and commitment to it (Wollebaek and Selle, 2002) and may affect both active and passive supporters because social capital does not necessarily stem only from face to face interactions but also through the sense of affinity to an idea that is important to the self and to others. Community organisations can be seen as repositories of trust, especially at the local level which encourage political efficacy, cooperation for common purposes, and thus foster a sense of shared belonging to something important. Thus, according to Wollebaek and Selle (2002) they may have come to resemble Anderson's (2006) idea of an imagined community, a concept referring to a social system that have transcended face-to-face contact but ensures social solidarity. Not all social scientists agree however with this representation of voluntary organisations as imagined communities. Sønderskov (2011), for example, rejects this notion and the referral to the ritualistic framework of community organisations. Instead, according to Sønderskov, social solidarity is represented in the community organisation through the establishment of relationships that acknowledge the existence of multitude of groups and interests in a society, and which may influence supporters, active or passive, and non-supporters alike through their presence. Community organisations, one can argue, become places where collective action is enacted, practised and cemented as counter to our individualistic nature focused on the self. Collective action is by no means guaranteed and even if community organisations do not necessarily bring members of disparate groups together, the existence of these social brokers reconfirms a commitment to the recognition of the vulnerable or groups in need of support. Social capital is not easily created or even shaped by public policy (Fukuyama, 2001); however, in eliminating and discontinuing funding to community organisations, one can argue that some of the radii of trust in which human beings naturally select themselves are reduced and eliminated.

Whereas it might be difficult to claim that a voluntary organisation per se is an imagined community in Anderson's way (2006), the notion can really be extended to the community centres that host the organisation. Such centres often resort to flags, logos and signs to demarcate their presence. The physical presence of a socially constructed space can serve to augment community sense and belonging. Food banks and soup kitchens can represent the impoverishment of society and the increasing gap between rich and poor, and at the same time, they enact a societal commitment to its most vulnerable members. Their visibility – to members/recipients and non-members alike – is a statement.

In *Bowling Alone*, Putnam (2000) argues that the challenge of studying the evolving social climate is analogous to some extent to the challenges faced by meteorologists (presciently) studying global warming: since inferences almost by definition are bound to be imperfect, one needs to triangulate between several sources. I would argue that a multi-method paradigm is very much needed that would consider the embeddedness of individuals in their communities, and the society as a whole. There is clearly scope for more important work to be done on the impact of formal organisations and their relationship to trust especially in a funding climate that considers them dispensable.

References

Abel, E K (1979). 'Toynbee Hall, 1884–1914.' *Social Service Review* 53: 606–32.

Anderson, B (2006). *Imagined Communities: Reflections on the Origin and Spread of Nationalism*. Verso Books.

Bernhagen, P and Maloney, W A (2010). 'Civil Society Organizations as 'Little' Democracies?' *Civil Society and Activism in Europe. Contextualizing Engagement and Political Orientations* 100–26.

Brehm, J and Rahn, W (1997). 'Individual-Level Evidence for the Causes and Consequences of Social Capital.' *American Journal of Political Science* 999–1023.

Buettner, E (2008). 'Going for an Indian: South Asian Restaurants and the Limits of Multiculturalism in Britain.' *The Journal of Modern History* 80: 865–901.

Catney, G (2016). 'The Changing Geographies of Ethnic Diversity in England and Wales, 1991–2011.' *Population, Space and Place* 22: 750–65.
Catney, G (2017). 'The Complex Geographies of Ethnic Residential Segregation: Using Spatial and Local Measures to Explore Scale-Dependency and Spatial Relationships.' *Transactions of the Institute of British Geographers.*
Claibourn, M P, Martin, P S (2000). 'Trusting and Joining? An Empirical Test of the Reciprocal Nature of Social Capital.' *Political Behavior* 22: 267–91.
Crowder, K, Hall, M and Tolnay, S E (2011). 'Neighborhood Immigration and Native Out-Migration.' *American Sociological Review* 76: 25–47.
Crowder, K, Pais, J and South, S J (2012). 'Neighborhood Diversity, Metropolitan Constraints, and Household Migration.' *American Sociological Review* 77: 325–53.
Crowder, K and South, S J (2008). 'Spatial Dynamics of White Flight: The Effects of Local and Extralocal Racial Conditions on Neighborhood Out-Migration.' *American Sociological Review* 73: 792–812.
Daily Mail (2013), www.dailymail.co.uk/news/article-2332998/One-country-religions-telling-pictures-The-pews-churches-just-yards-overcrowded-mosque.html.
Davies, J and Freeman, M (2003). 'Education for Citizenship: The Joseph Rowntree Charitable Trust and the Educational Settlement Movement.' *History of Education* 32: 303–18.
Delhey, J, Newton, K and Welzel, C (2011). 'How General is Trust in "most people"? Solving the Radius of Trust Problem.' *American Sociological Review* 76: 786–807.
Fan, H and Lederman, R (2018). 'Online Health Communities: How do Community Members Build the Trust Required to Adopt Information and Form Close Relationships?' *European Journal of Information Systems* 27: 62–89.
Farkas, G M and Lindberg, E (2015). 'Voluntary Associations' Impact on the Composition of Active Members' Social Networks: Not an Either/Or Matter.' *Sociological Forum* 30 (4): 1082–1105. Wiley Online Library.
Fennema, M and Tillie, J (2001). 'Civic Community, Political Participation and Political Trust of Ethnic Groups.' *Multikulturelle demokratien im Vergleich.* Springer.
Freitag, M and Bauer, P C (2013). 'Testing for Measurement Equivalence in Surveys: Dimensions of Social Trust across Cultural Contexts.' *Public Opinion Quarterly* 77: 24–44.
Freitag, M and Traunmüller, R (2009). 'Spheres of Trust: An Empirical Analysis of the Foundations of Particularised and Generalised Trust.' *European Journal of Political Research* 48: 782–803.
Fukuyama, F (2001). 'Social Capital, Civil Society and Development.' *Third World Quarterly* 22: 7–20.
Glanville, J L (2016). 'Why does Involvement in Voluntary Associations Promote trust? Examining the Role of Network Diversity.' *Sociological Inquiry* 86: 29–50.
Glanville, J L and Bienenstock, E J (2009). 'A Typology for Understanding the Connections Among Different Forms of Social Capital.' *The American Behavioral Scientist* 52 (11): 1507–30.
Glanville, J L and Paxton, P (2007). 'How do We Learn to Trust? A Confirmatory Tetrad Analysis of the Sources of Generalized Trust. *Social Psychology Quarterly* 70 (3): 230–42.
Hieronymi, P (2008). 'The Reasons of Trust.' *Australasian Journal of Philosophy* 86 (2): 213–36.
Jones, K (1996). 'Trust as an affective attitude.' *Ethics* 107 (1): 4–25.
Knoke, D (1986). 'Associations and interest groups.' *Annual Review of Sociology* 12 (1): 1–21.
Koopmans, R (2016). 'Does Assimilation Work? Sociocultural Determinants of Labour Market Participation of European Muslims.' *Journal of Ethnic and Migration Studies* 42 (2): 197–216.
Kriesi, H and Baglioni, S (2003). 'Putting Local Associations into their Context. Preliminary Results from a Swiss Study of Local Associations.' *Swiss Political Science Review* 9: 1–34.
Kymlicka, W (2010). 'The Rise and Fall of Multiculturalism? New Debates on Inclusion and accommodation in Diverse Societies' *International Social Science Journal* 61 (199): 97–112.
Lambie-Mumford, H (2013). '"Every Town should have One": Emergency Food Banking in the UK.' *Journal of Social Policy* 42 (1): 73–89.
Lipset, S M (1959). 'Political Man: The Social Bases of Politics.' In R A Dahl, I Shapiro and J A Cheibub (eds), *The Democracy Sourcebook.*

Locality (2020). About.
Loopstra, R, Fledderjohann, J, Reeves, A and Stuckler, D (2018). 'Impact of Welfare Benefit Sanctioning on Food Insecurity: A Dynamic Cross-Area Study of Food Bank Usage in the UK.' *Journal of Social Policy* 47 (3): 437–57.
Loopstra, R and Lalor, D (2017). 'Financial Insecurity, Food Insecurity, and Disability: The Profile of People Receiving Emergency Food Assistance from The Trussell Trust Foodbank Network in Britain.' *London: the Trussell Trust.*
Loopstra, R, Reeves, A, Taylor-Robinson, D, Barr, B., McKee, M and Stuckler, D (2015). 'Austerity, Sanctions, and the Rise of Food Banks in the UK.' *Bmj*, 350: h1775.
Lupton, R and Fitzgerald, A. (2015). 'The Coalition's Record on Area Regeneration and Neighbourhood Renewal 2010–2015.' *Social Policy in a Cold Climate Working Paper*, 19.
Morris, R J (1983). 'Voluntary Societies and British Urban Elites, 1780–1850: An Analysis.' *The Historical Journal* 26: 95–118.
Newton, K (1997). 'Social Capital and Democracy.' *The American Behavioral Scientist* 40 (5): 575–86.
Newton, K (2001). 'Trust, Social Capital, Civil Society, and Democracy.' *International Political Science Review* 22: 201–14.
O'Hara, M (2015). *Austerity Bites: A Journey to the Sharp End of Cuts in the UK*. Policy Press.
Olson, M (2008). *The Rise and Decline of Nations: Economic Growth, Stagflation, and Social Rigidities*. Yale University Press.
Paxton, P (2007). 'Association Memberships and Generalized Trust: A Multilevel Model across 31 Countries.' *Social Forces* 86 (1): 47–76.
Poole, A G (2011). 'The Citizens of Morley College.' *Journal of British Studies* 50: 840–62.
Putnam, R D (2000). *Bowling Alone: The Collapse and Revival of American Community*. New York, London: Simon & Schuster.
Putnam, R D, Leonardi, R and Nanetti, R Y (1993). *Making Democracy Work: Civic Traditions in Modern Italy*. Princeton, NJ: Chichester, Princeton University Press.
Richards, D (2013). *Offspring of the Vic: A History of Morley College*. Routledge.
Roßteutscher, S (2002). 'Advocate or reflection? Associations and political culture.' *Political Studies* 50: 514–28.
Sharkey, P (2013). *Stuck in Place: Urban Neighborhoods and the End of Progress Toward Racial Equality*. University of Chicago Press.
Shepherd, J (2010). 'Squires in the Slums: Settlements and Missions in Late Victorian London.' Oxford, UK: Oxford University Press.
Smith, J A, McPherson, M and Smith-Lovin, L (2014). 'Social Distance in the United States: Sex, Race, Religion, Age, and Education Homophily among Confidants, 1985 to 2004.' *American Sociological Review* 79 (3): 432–56.
Sønderskov, K M (2011). 'Does Generalized Social Trust Lead to Associational Membership? Unravelling a Bowl of Well-Tossed Spaghetti.' *European Sociological Review* 27 (4): 419–34.
Stolle, D (2001). 'Clubs and Congregations: The Benefits of Joining an Association.' In K S Cook (ed.) *Trust in Society*. New York: Russell Sage Foundation.
Trust, T (2014). Below the Breadline, www.trusselltrust.org/wp-content/uploads/sites/2/2016/01/below-the-breadline-the-trussell-trust.pdf.
Tschirhart, M and Gazley, B (2014). *Advancing Scholarship on Membership Associations: New Research and Next Steps*. Los Angeles, CA: Sage Publications.
Uslaner, E M (2002). *The Moral Foundations of Trust*. Cambridge University Press.
Uslaner, E M and Brown, M (2005). 'Inequality, Trust, and Civic Engagement.' *American Politics Research* 33: 868–94.
Van Ingen, E and Bekkers, R (2015). 'Generalized Trust Through Civic Engagement? Evidence from Five National Panel Studies.' *Political Psychology* 36 (3): 277–94.
Van Ingen, E and Van Der Meer, T (2016). 'Schools or Pools of Democracy? A Longitudinal Test of the Relation Between Civic Participation and Political Socialization.' *Political Behavior* 38: 83–103.

Vertovec, S (1996). 'Multiculturalism, Culturalism and Public Incorporation.' *Ethnic and racial studies* 19: 49–69.
Welch, M R, Sikkink, D and Loveland, M T (2007). 'The Radius of Trust: Religion, Social Embeddedness and Trust in Strangers.' *Social Forces* 86: 23–46.
Wiertz, D (2016). 'Segregation in Civic Life: Ethnic Sorting and Mixing across Voluntary Associations.' *American Sociological Review* 81: 800–827.
Wollebaek, D and Selle, P (2002). 'Does Participation in Voluntary Associations Contribute to Social Capital? The Impact of Intensity, Scope, and Type.' *Nonprofit and Voluntary Sector Quarterly* 31 (1): 32–61.

PART III

Trust, Evidence, Authority and the Law

10

Trust, Trustworthiness and Credibility in Relation to Testimonial Evidence at Common Law

WILLIAM TWINING

This chapter briefly examines some concepts and key distinctions in discourse about evidence and testimony in legal contexts, mainly in common law jurisdictions.[1] It is concerned with the credibility of witnesses and of witness statements made in court or extra-judicially. It is not concerned with the law of trusts, which is best treated as a distinct legal field. It suggests that while trust and trustworthiness are not terms of art in modern law, some standard distinctions in legal discourse may be suggestive in respect of these concepts.

In the discourse about evidence in legal contexts, the most important distinctions are between materiality, relevance, weight (or probative force) and admissibility.[2] All of these have meaning in the context of an *argument* involving inferential reasoning from evidence in respect of a particular case (as a whole or some part of it).

Material facts (sometimes referred to as facts in issue, *ultimate probanda*) are the propositions that a party must prove or negate in order to win their case.[3] These are prescribed by *substantive law*.[4] For example, the law of murder prescribes the several elements each of which the prosecution must prove beyond reasonable doubt to obtain a conviction; for example, the victim is dead, the cause of death was an unlawful act, the act was committed by the accused, the accused acted with

[1] There are historical and intellectual links between and among common law and civil law jurisdictions in relation to theorising about evidence in legal contexts. Here it is best to treat Anglo-American theorising as distinct, especially in relation to systems of criminal and civil procedure. For a useful summary see Damaska (1997).

[2] For a short glossary of the main terms in discourse about evidence at common law see Anderson et al, *Analysis* (2005) 379–87.

[3] 'A fact in issue is a fact the correctness of which the tribunal, under the law of the case must be persuaded' (Wigmore, 1935: 7).

[4] Materiality is governed by substantive law, in this case the law of murder, which varies in detail across jurisdictions.

criminal intent, and without lawful justification or excuse. These 'facts in issue' (*probanda*) are analogous to hypotheses in an empirical enquiry.

Relevance is a word of relation: A is relevant to B; that is it either tends to support or tends to negate directly or indirectly one or more material facts.[5] The test of relevance is governed by ordinary inferential reasoning in the particular circumstances of the case, not by formal legal rules. As James Bradley Thayer said: 'The law has no mandamus on the logical faculty'.[6]

Similarly, subject to minor exceptions, questions *of weight or probative* force are not governed by formal rules, but by ordinary 'common sense' reasoning.[7] In the judicial context, an item of evidence is either relevant or irrelevant. If irrelevant it is not *admissible*, ie it cannot be considered or used by the fact-finder. *Admissibility* is governed by the exclusionary rules of the law of evidence. Of the four concepts, the law of evidence strictly speaking only covers admissibility. The most important criterion of exclusion is covered by logic rather than law: evidence is excluded as irrelevant because it cannot form part of an argument in the circumstances of the case.[8] The bulk of the surviving law of evidence deals with exclusion of otherwise relevant evidence for a variety of reasons of policy, such as state security or client-lawyer confidentiality or improperly obtained confessions whether or not they might be true.[9]

Testimony of witnesses and real evidence are the two main types of evidence.[10] 'Real evidence' refers to physical objects, for example seized drugs or weapons, which may be presented as evidence if they are relevant and admissible and authentic. The focus of this chapter is on direct evidence given orally by a witness under oath in open court. The main concepts relating to testimonial evidence are

[5] '"Relevant evidence" means evidence having a tendency to make the existence of any fact that is of consequence [ie material fact] to the determination of the action more probable or less probable than it would have been without the evidence.' (US Federal Rules of Evidence 401.)

[6] Thayer (1898: 314). Several classic writers, notably JH Wigmore, used the phrase 'logic and general experience' to refer to the test of both relevance and weight. Eg, the subtitle of Wigmore's *Principles of Judicial Proof*, (1913) was *'as Given by Logic, Psychology and General Experience'*.

[7] The distinction between relevance and weight is controversial. I here adopt the view that relevance/irrelevance is binary, but questions of weight are relative on a spectrum of probabilities (not necessarily mathematical). But some people talk of 'more relevant'/'less relevant'. This is different from the concept of 'potentially relevant' where judgement is suspended pending more evidence or clarification of what is being argued.

[8] On a tendency by some modern American judges to blur the distinction between admissibility and weight, see Haack (2014: 307).

[9] Other associated concepts include believability, reliability and plausibility. Evidence theory struggles, not always successfully) to keep separate logos (inferential reasoning from evidence) and pathos (rhetoric, persuasion, plausibility). For example, *cogency* refers to the strength of an argument. Plausibility is not a term of art in legal contexts. It may refer to a witness, a story or an item of testimony. It cuts across pathos and logos. Sometimes it has a negative connotation, for example, ' he is plausible (or his story is plausible). In a recent book Orna Alyagon Darr usefully links the concept of plausibility (in the eyes of judges) to background generalisations that provide warrants for inferences in ordinary practical reasoning, in this instance the stock of beliefs about sex and sexuality of largely expatriate judges dealing with alleged sex offences during the period of the Palestine Mandate. The examples may be esoteric, but the analysis is of general significance for Evidence theory and practical reasoning (Darr, 2018).

[10] Other types, for example documentary and demonstrative evidence are not considered here.

competency, credibility, compellability and corroboration. Here we are mainly concerned with the first two.[11]

The history of competence in English law is illuminating. Under the old law of evidence, starting in the sixteenth century, many classes of witness were treated as incompetent, that is they were unable to testify in court. These classes included spouses, infants, non-Christians, convicted felons and even the parties themselves. Technically a witness could only be competent if they were able to swear an oath in a prescribed form. The main rationale for excluding classes of witness was untrustworthiness, but this was mixed in with bias, self-interest, and external factors such as preservation of harmony between spouses.

Early in the nineteenth century Jeremy Bentham launched a sharp attack on all the competency rules under the heading 'trustworthiness of witnesses'. His central point was that these artificial rules undermined 'rectitude of decision' by excluding more good evidence than bad and that the credibility of a witness or any particular item of evidence could be *tested* by a range of internal and external 'securities for the trustworthiness of testimony,[12] the most powerful of which is cross-examination.

Bentham's focus was on untrustworthiness. He ranked *grounds of suspicion* under four heads.

> 1. that the fact spoken of [the evidence] is circumstantial rather than direct; 2. the information in question is not delivered immediately from the source of the information (e.g. hearsay evidence); 3. the evidence in question is not collected or delivered under securities for trustworthiness in the best mode; 4. the person who is the source of the information is exposed to some assignable cause of suspicion affecting the trustworthiness of his statements.[13]

The context is Bentham's thesis that the danger of deception should not be a proper ground for *exclusion* of evidence. It is important to note that the first three of his grounds for suspicion relate to specific evidence in a particular case, but the third allows for some doubt about the general credibility of a particular witness.

Bentham's argument won the day, but in a slow and piecemeal fashion of which he would have disapproved. During the nineteenth century nearly all of the rules of competency were abolished piecemeal, though not entirely because

[11] There is now no general *requirement* of corroboration under English Law although mutually supporting or convergent evidence is, of course, epistemically very important in practice; compellability of witnesses is tangential to questions of trust and trustworthiness.

[12] This is the title of Book II of his five-volume *Rationale of Judicial Evidence* (edited by JS Mill, 1827). His main discussion is in Book II Vol 1 pp 259–606. An annotated edition of the *Rationale* is currently being prepared by the Bentham Project at UCL, but the Mill edition is still a reliable text.

[13] The internal securities relate to desirable qualities of testimony. Bentham's list was: 1. Particularity; 2 Recollectedness; 3. Unpremeditatedness; 4. Suggestedness; 5. Unsuggestedness; 6 Interrogatedness; 7. Distinctness (in point of expression); 8. Permanance, expressed by permanent signs, eg by writing. The list of external securities was: 1. Punishment; 2. Oath; 3. Infamy; 4. Interrogation; 5. Reception in the viva voce, or ready-written form; or both; 6. Notation; 7. Publicity; 8. Counter-evidence; 9. Investigation. His elaborate analysis over 300 pages suggests overkill, but it contains a wealth of specific insights well ahead of his time.

of Bentham's direct influence.[14] Remarkably, it was not until 1898 that the accused in criminal cases were allowed to testify on their own behalf.[15] The various rationales for their retention mixed in trustworthiness with such considerations as the sanctity of marriage, reliability, honesty, self-interest, and the power of the oath. Today the rules excluding witnesses hardly survive, and there is a general presumption of competence. Suspicions about individual witnesses are dealt with under credibility rather than competence in the context of particular cases.

Thus the history of the development of common law evidence discourse has shown a strong tendency to move from focusing on exclusion of general types of evidence (eg hearsay) and classes of witness (eg women, children, convicted felons, the accused) towards admitting most relevant evidence and types of witness and testing credibility in the particular circumstances of a specific case. The tendency has been to move away from generalised mistrust of types of evidence and witnesses, to subject particular testimony to various tests of credibility in the particular context and to give more discretion (trust?) to judges and juries to do their best in each case. The modern mantras for decision include 'Decide on the basis of the evidence presented in this case', 'Judge the act, not the actor', 'Exclude relevant evidence if its prejudicial effect outweighs its probative value in the circumstances of this case'. The surviving exclusionary rules, much diminished, concretise and create a diminishing number of exceptions to these 'general principles'.

The English law of evidence has changed almost beyond recognition since Bentham wrote, mainly but not entirely in the direction he advocated, especially in substituting discretion in place of technical rules; much of his argument has been confirmed, extended and refined, including by psychological and other research; and today most of it reads like common sense. Nevertheless, this remarkable analysis still deserves attention, not least for its systematic approach and many particular insights.

Today we would distinguish between (1) general credibility of a class of persons; (2) the general credibility of a particular person; and (3) the credibility of a particular evidentiary proposition testified to by one or more witnesses in a specific case. The historical tendency has been to switch the focus from (1) to (3), in short from general to particular.

Today trustworthiness is not a term of art. It has been replaced by credibility, which relates to weight and is a relative matter not generally governed by rules. It is important to distinguish between a credible witness and a credible evidentiary proposition. The best modern account of the latter is by David Schum, a psychologist who draws on extensive psychological literature. He distinguishes between *veracity* (a witness believing that what she says is true), *bias*, and *observational sensitivity*.[16] An honest witness may be mistaken because of conscious

[14] For a detailed account see Allen, *The Law of Evidence in Victorian England* (1997).
[15] Criminal Evidence Act 1898.
[16] Schum's main work is explored at length in his major work, *Evidential Foundations of Probabilistic Reasoning* (1994/2001), but is succinctly restated in Anderson et al (2005: 63–77).

or unconscious bias, or because of the conditions under which they observed an event or because of defects in their capacity to observe, such as myopia or intoxication. All of these credibility attributes are time- and context-dependent. According to Schum, because there are no usable statistical records of these attributes of witnesses, '[t]here is no discipline outside of law in which a more extensive effort has been made for impeaching and supporting witness credibility.'[17] Drawing on the legal literature Schum developed an extensive analysis of the variety of different items that may serve as ancillary evidence bearing on the attributes of credibility of ordinary witnesses. These are summarised in Figure 10.1.[18]

Figure 10.1 Ancillary Evidence Concerning Attributes of Witness Credibility

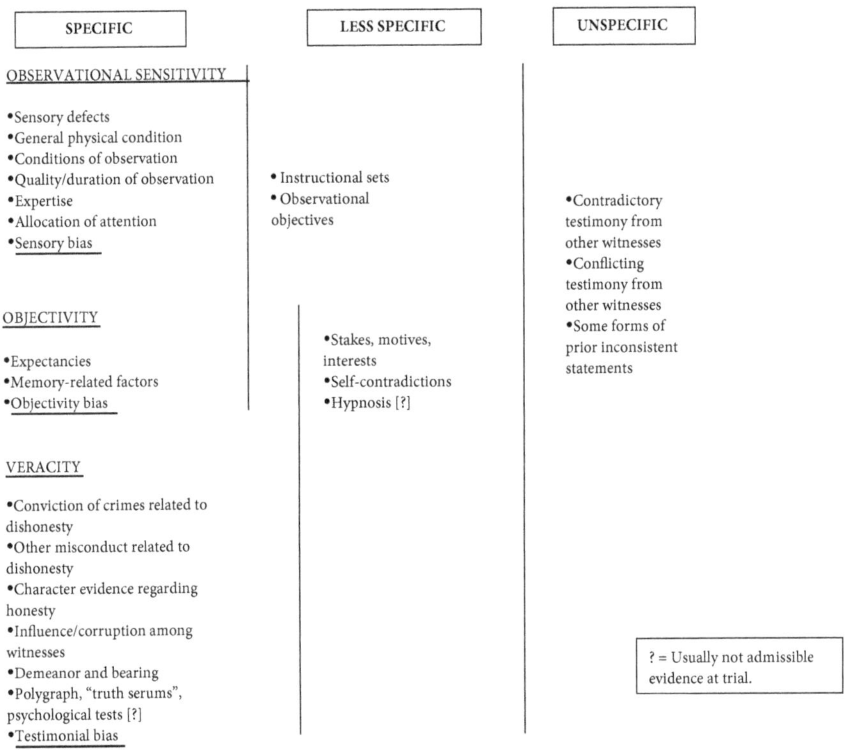

Source: T Anderson, D Schum and W Twining, *Analysis of Evidence* (Cambridge University Press, 2005) p 68

[17] Anderson et al (2005: 67).

[18] 'Each item listed is a form of ancillary evidence bearing on the credibility of ordinary witnesses, but only some, not all, of these forms of ancillary evidence can be uniquely associated with one of the three credibility attributes we have discussed.' This table summarises Schum's elaborate analysis in his main work, *Evidential Foundations of Probabilistic Reasoning* (1994/2005: ch 7). A more succinct account is given in Anderson et al (2005: 67–70).

Two general points emerge from this analysis. First, the concept of credibility is much wider than the concept of trustworthiness. While we may consider that veracity is an aspect of the trustworthiness of a witness or even a witness statement,[19] it is stretching the concept of trust to say of a witness 'she cannot be trusted to remember what she saw, because it was dark, the event was 200 yards away and she is myopic' or of a particular statement, that 'it cannot be trusted because of confirmation bias'. Such statements are doubtful or unbelievable or unreliable[20] rather than untrustworthy. Moreover, trust relates more clearly to character and relationships (ethos), while the law is more concerned with the accuracy of particular statements. Of course, in ordinary discourse words like 'trust' are loosely extended in such ways, but for purposes of analysis it is useful to distinguish between credibility and its various aspects on the one hand and trust or trustworthiness on the other.

Second, Schum's analysis confirms Bentham's point that the law makes use of many devices to test the credibility of witness evidence; it does not need very much to rely on trust. It also reinforces and extends the point that in the common law attention is more focused on specific statements in a particular context rather than general attributes of a person or kinds of evidence.

Two enclaves of the legal literature illustrate the complexities of credibility in legal contexts: eyewitness identification evidence and expert evidence. There is a large psychological literature on the reliability of eyewitness identification evidence which is very important in many criminal cases. The thrust of this literature is to show that this kind of evidence is generally unreliable, with 'the honest but mistaken witness' playing a major role, because of defects of memory, observational capacity, objectivity (bias), articulation, confirmation bias and so on. However, the circumstances of this kind of identification are extremely variable, so that it is misleading to say that all such identification is unreliable.[21] Because of this the common law has held back from making corroboration a blanket requirement for the admissibility of such evidence; rather the judge should direct juries on 'the special need for caution' and to examine closely 'the circumstances in

[19] There is an extensive literature on lying, which inter alia suggests that it is a difficult art, often requiring more skill than truth-telling. In this view the Cretan Liar Paradox is based on a naïve premise. As deviant lovers know, the accomplished liar hides a little untruth in a thicket of truth.

[20] 'Reliability' has caused some confusion in the context of scientific evidence (Haack, 2014: 200–01), but I do not pursue that here. Consider further the statement: 'My watch can be relied on/trusted to be 10 minutes slow'. Is not 'trusted' in this context best interpreted as ironic or sarcastic? Haack shows that the concept of 'reliability' is problematic in the context of litigation. In respect of scientific evidence it is ambiguous. Her main argument in this chapter is that there is a profound difference between scientific enquiry and advocacy enquiry and the latter is less reliable, even in respect of forensic science (which is generally conducted for the police or the prosecution) (ibid: xxiii).

[21] *R v Turnbull* [1977] QB 224, CA, eg RZ at 688. Lord Devlin treated an instance of 'clear recognition in a good light of a family member, work colleague, or close associate' as exceptional (Devlin P (Lord Devlin) (1976) *Report on Evidence of Identification in Criminal Cases* HC 338 (London) (1976) (The Devlin Report); *cf* the hypothetical example used in *R v Turnbull* [1977] QB 224 CA, discussed in Roberts and Zuckerman, op cit: 686–87. See also, W Twining, *Rethinking Evidence* (2006: ch 6) for a critique of the literature.

which identification by each witness came to be made'.[22] This brings out the point that suspected lying is only one aspect of the reasons for rejecting the credibility of a witness statement. In common law countries 'neutral' court-appointed experts are used sparingly, compared to the practices in civil law countries.[23] A major reason for this is that in so-called 'adversarial' proceedings the parties typically choose what witnesses to call and the latter are subject to examination and cross-examination. This can lead to 'the battle of experts' which sometimes involves, as Judge Learned Hand put it, setting 'the jury to decide, where doctors disagree'.[24]

Furthermore the common law has been concerned that experts should not usurp the role of the jury in deciding on the facts of a case. As a result under the 'ultimate issue rule', experts have not been allowed to present conclusions on facts. The demise of this artificial and widely disregarded rule has been long expected, but it still survives and has further complicated the topic.[25] However, one can come away with some basic points. First, trust and trustworthiness are not terms of art in respect of scientific evidence, nor are they helpful. Credibility or believability do the work much better, because they can be tested in different ways in which veracity is just one aspect. The legal controversies are much more complex and esoteric than public debates about mistrust in science and expertise. For example, it is doubtful that the legal literature can throw much light on climate change denial.

To sum up: there is a very rich literature on evidence and proof in legal contexts that may be relevant to particular enquiries about trust and trustworthiness in other contexts. Credibility of witnesses is a topic of particular interest. However, much depends on whether trust, trustworthiness and reliability are interpreted in moral terms or more broadly. In law veracity is only one of the tests of credibility.

Historically the common law has moved jerkily from emphasis on the untrustworthiness of classes of witness and evidence to testing the truth of particular evidentiary propositions in a given context and to a much lesser extent the general credibility of a particular witness. Insofar as being 'trustworthy' or 'trusting' a person involves generalisation, this goes against law's concern with particularity in respect of evidence. One might say that the common law moved away from *ethos* (the witness's general credibility and character) in the direction of *logos* (appeal to logic and reason and evidence). Insofar as the concept of 'trustworthiness' involves a moral dimension, this goes contrary to the concern of law to subject particular testimonial propositions to rigorous testing, which is almost the antonym of

[22] *R v Turnbull*, 228–30.

[23] Haack (2014).

[24] Hand (1901: 54). This article is still well worth reading.

[25] Susan Haack calls one section of her study of scientific evidence '[a]n epistemological swamp: the sinking sands of litigation-driven and evidentiary reliability'. Haack (2014: 195–201). Scholars interested in trust should treat this as a warning to steer clear of this topic, except perhaps those who are interested in mistrust of science or expertise. Haack's primary concern here is with the complexities of the common law, rather than trust in science or scientists.

taking something 'on trust' or taking 'a leap of faith', both of which suggest absence of evidence.

References

Allen, C (1997). *The Law of Evidence in Victorian England*. Cambridge: Cambridge University Press.
Anderson, T J, Schum, D and Twining, W (2005). *Analysis* of Evidence (2nd edn). Cambridge: Cambridge University Press.
Bentham, J (1827). *Rationale of Judicial Evidence*. J S Mill (ed), Edinburgh: Hunt and Clarke.
Damaska, M (1997). *Evidence Law Adrift*. New Haven: Yale University Press.
Devlin, P (Lord Devlin) (1976) *Report on Evidence of Identification in Criminal Cases* HC 338 (London). The Devlin Report.
Haack, S (2014). *Evidence Matters: Science, Proof and Truth in Law*. New York: Cambridge University Press.
Hand, L (1901) 'Historical and Practical Considerations Regarding Expert Testimony', 15. *Harvard Law Review* 40–58.
Roberts, P and Zuckerman, A (2010). *Criminal Evidence* (2nd edn). Oxford: Oxford University Press.
Schum, D (1994). *The Evidential Foundations of Probabilistic Reasoning*. New York: John Wiley, Evanston: Northwestern University Press.
Thayer, J B (1898). *A Preliminary Treatise on Evidence at Common Law*. Boston: Little Brown.
Twining, W (2006). *Rethinking Evidence* (2nd edn). Cambridge: Cambridge University Press.
Wigmore, J H (1935). *A Students' Textbook of the Law of Evidence*. Chicago: The Foundation Press.
Wigmore, J H (1937). *The Principles of Judicial Proof, as Given by Logic, Psychology and General Experience* (3rd edn 1937 sub. nom., *The Science of Judicial Proof*). Boston: Little Brown.

11

Fabricating Authenticity

Trust and Trustworthiness in the History of Culture, from Late Antiquity to the Middle Ages

GIULIANO MORI

I. Authenticity, Trustworthiness, Trust

One of the significant risks faced in analysing trust relationships is that of supposing that such relationships should always result from a certain party's encounter with a counterpart thought to be trustworthy. A staggering number of historical examples contradicts this notion showing us that the choice between trusting or not trusting someone or something is often influenced by considerations that have little to do with the perceived or actual trustworthiness of one's counterpart.

This essay aims to explore the grey area that surrounds the relationship between trust and trustworthiness. In this analysis, I will consider trust from the point of view of cultural and intellectual history, focusing on the period from late Antiquity to the close of the Middle Ages. Rather than analysing cases in which trust is placed in a certain person or group of people in an unmediated fashion, I will analyse cases in which trust in a certain person or group is mediated by an object or text. In these terms, objects or texts can be trusted if believed to be true and transparent, reflecting the intentions (or indeed the essence) of the person who is the ultimate object of one's mediated trust.[1]

Textual or material mediation is crucial in late antique and medieval trust relationships since it is the main channel through which *auctoritas* (authority) is transmitted. The notion of *auctoritas* is a very nuanced one, but in few words, it can

[1] These considerations are not confined to late antique and medieval culture. On the contrary, they are still crucial, eg, for the juridical and constitutional debate on the role of interpretation. *Cf* inter alia: RM Dworkin, 'Social Sciences and Constitutional Rights: The Consequences of Uncertainty' (1977) 6/1 *Journal of Law and Education* 3, 3–12; RM Dworkin, 'The Arduous Virtue of Fidelity: Originalism, Scalia, Tribe, and Nerve' (1997) 65/4 *Fordham Law Review* 1249, 1249–68; TAO Endicott, *Vagueness in Law* (Oxford, Oxford University Press, 2000); J Raz, *Between Authority and Interpretation: On the Theory of Law and Practical Reason* (Oxford, Oxford University Press, 2009).

be regarded as concerning the prestige and authoritativeness of a famous person's words, theories, or injunctions. *Auctoritas* intertwines both authority and authorship: a written or oral tradition that belongs to this field is considered authoritative because of the respected status accorded to its author due to their prominent position in politics, religion, science, etc. It follows that authority normally implies authenticity. In other terms, a given account generally loses its *auctoritas* if it is shown as falsely attributed to an authoritative author.

This bundle of interwoven notions is inextricably connected to trust as it was conceived in the period analysed in this essay. Late antique and medieval culture generally embraced an authority-based criterion of truth, according to which *auctoritas* was essentially synonymous with trustworthiness. Moreover, as a consequence of the connection between authority and authenticity, trustworthiness gradually became associated with authenticity. For these reasons, I will hereafter use the expression 'authenticity/trustworthiness' to indicate the conviction that in order to be trustworthy, something had to be vouched for by authentic authority, that is, by an authoritative position authentically associated with its authoritative author. This conviction became commonplace in the first centuries AD. Late antique culture accordingly developed a keen eye for textual and documentary authenticity, which was rare in the pre-Christian era.[2]

To better understand how the notions of authority, authenticity and trustworthiness generally interacted in the late antique and medieval period, let us consider a standard eleventh-century papal bull. For instance, the bull issued by Leo IX in 1049 confirming the privileges (*privilegia*) granted by his predecessor to the bishopric of Toul, in Lorraine. The structure of the bull is rather straightforward. The first line indicates the bull's author and its addressees: 'Pope Leo, servant of the servants of God, to all the orthodox prelates of the Holy Roman Church, and all the devotees of the true religion and the true faith, present and future'. In the central part of the text, the pope cites his authority (*nostra apostolica auctoritate* and *sancti Petri auctoritate*) to confirm the privileges granted to the bishopric, namely 'twenty-two *mansi* and a half in … the town of Poussay, with the right to command [*cum banno et districtu*], and everything we possess there'. Before closing the bull, those who should not obey the authoritative decision of the pope are condemned to eternal punishment, while eternal glory is promised in exchange for obedience. At the foot of the bull is the signature of the pope, and the *rota*

[2] How and when precisely ancient culture developed a notion of authorial and intellectual property is the object of many interesting analyses. For a general introduction to the topic, *cf inter alia*: A D Baum, *Pseudepigraphie und literarische Fälschung im frühen Christentum: Mit ausgewählten Quellentexten samt deutscher Übersetzung* (Tübingen, Mohr Siebeck, 2001); B D Ehrman, *Forgery and Counterforgery: The Use of Literary Deceit in Early Christian Polemics* (Oxford, Oxford University Press, 2013) chs 4–5; A Grafton, *Forgers and Critics: Creativity and Duplicity in Western Scholarship* (Princeton, Princeton University Press, 1990) 19–20; RM Grant, *Heresy and Criticism: The Search for Authenticity in Early Christian Literature* (Louisville, KY, Westminster J Knox Press, 1993); W Speyer, *Die literarische Fälschung im heidnischen und christlichen Altertum: Ein Versuch ihrer Deutung* (Munich, Beck, 1971) ch B.I.

containing his name and his motto (*Misericordia Domini plena est terra*). The whole document is dated and completed with the papal seal.[3]

Both the incipit and explicit of the bull, together with the *rota* and seal, are aimed at authenticating the document, certifying that it is issued under the direct authority of the pope. These elements allowed the addressees of the bull to assess its authenticity. Once assured of the authenticity of the bull, its addressees were also assured of its authority and thus–under the authority-based criterion of truth–of its trustworthiness. The addressees of the bull could then trust the document as the actual expression of the will of the pope.

As shown by the analysed bull, the logical correlation between authority, authenticity, trustworthiness, and trust seems to follow a precise direction: the authenticity of the authority cited by the bull proves the trustworthiness of the document, which in turn causes its addressees to trust the bull as the true will of the pope. Based on this example, one would suppose that, for late antique and medieval culture, trustworthiness was requisite for trust. The logical priority of trustworthiness over trust characterised the reception of many documents from late Antiquity throughout the Middle Ages. However, it fails to explain the possibility of trusting something/someone notoriously untrustworthy. Most importantly, if we posit that trustworthiness is the logical antecedent and requisite for trust, we are forced to brand all the cases in which untrustworthiness was met with trust as sheer aberrations. However, the history of these 'aberrations' suggests a different interpretation.

Reasons of political, economic, or philosophical convenience were often crucial for the creation of epistemic premises that would allow for trust to be established regardless of authenticity/trustworthiness. However, as shown in the following paragraphs, in most of these cases, inauthenticity/untrustworthiness was not simply disregarded. On the contrary, trust placed in a tradition that in the first instance was found to be inauthentic/untrustworthy often caused the same tradition to acquire authenticity/trustworthiness, although only in the second instance. In other words, the 'process' that led from authenticity/trustworthiness to trust could be reversed, leading from trust to authenticity/trustworthiness.

II. Canonical and Apocryphal Authority

Within the early Christian environment, one of the most significant consequences of the redefinition of the authority-based criterion of truth in terms of authenticity was the diffusion of a cultural attitude that tended to link authenticity/trustworthiness very closely on the one hand and moral truth on the other.[4]

[3] Leo IX, *Epistolae et dectreta pontificia*, 16 [Migne, *PL* 143.614–16].

[4] For a survey of various scholarly interpretation on this theme, *cf* B M Metzger, 'Literary Forgeries and Canonical Pseudepigrapha' (1972) 91/1 *Journal of Biblical Literature* 3, 16–19.

As Ehrman puts it, in most cases, the author and the content were assessed in tandem: the authentic/trustworthy authority of an author established the truthful character of the content and the doctrinal soundness of the content proved the authentic/trustworthy authority of the author.[5] One could thus agree with Torm's classic interpretation, according to which pseudepigraphic materials in early Christianity were either taken as authentic and thus highly considered or exposed as inauthentic and thus disregarded and censored.[6]

However, the process of identification between author and content did not always work in the direction suggested by Torm. While in some cases, the orthodoxy of the content was extrapolated from the authenticity/trustworthiness of its author, at times, the strongest element in favour of the authenticity of a given account was the orthodox character of its content.[7] This content-based method of authentication can be described as 'an organoleptic way of finding that the books are genuine'–in other terms, a possibly spurious letter of the Apostles is authentically apostolic and to be trusted as such if it produces in the audience the same effect that an authentic apostolic letter is supposed to produce.[8]

The content-based method of authentication adopted by early Christians also explains why, in the first centuries AD, inauthenticity and heresy were closely associated. If a piece of writing was deemed heretical, it was also generally considered inauthentic, although a posteriori.[9] An example of this trend is provided by Athanasius of Alexandria's *Epistola festalis*, 39. Once laid down the Canon of both Old and New Testament, Athanasius rejects as untrue all inauthentic (apocryphal) works, which he considers 'the inventions of heretics, who write them whenever they wish, and then attribute to whichever age is more convenient for them, so that, by having them considered ancient, they could deceive innocent and simple people'.[10] Pseudepigraphy (ie apocryphal, inauthentic literature) is rejected because it is heretical and only as such inauthentic/untrustworthy. Heresy also provides a reason for inauthenticity/untrustworthiness: looking to advance their lies, heretics

[5] *Cf* Ehrman, *Forgery and Counterforgery* 86, 91.

[6] *Cf* FE Torm, *Die Psychologie der Pseudonymität im Hinblick auf die Literatur des Urchristentums* (Gütersloh, C Bertelsmann, 1932) 19.

[7] *Cf* inter alia: Metzger, 'Literary Forgeries' 15. Baum suggests that in late antiquity, authorial authenticity was exclusively assessed based on content (*cf* Baum, *Pseudepigraphie* 3–4). I do not think this is the case; rather, I believe we should see the process of authentication (of author and content) as working possibly in both directions: from the author to the content and from the content to the author. This interpretation is also espoused by other scholars, such as Ehrman (*cf* Ehrman, *Forgery and Counterforgery* 87).

[8] A Johns, 'Lay Assaying and the Scientific Citizen' (2016) 160/1 *Proceedings of the American Philosophical Society* 18, 22.

[9] *Cf* TL Wilder, *Pseudonymity, the New Testament and Deception: An Inquiry into Intention and Reception* (Lanham MD, University of America Press, 2004) 146–47.

[10] Athanasius, *Epistolae heortasticae*, 39 [Migne, *PG* 26.1440]. *Cf* in this regard: AY Reed, 'Pseudepigraphy, Authorship, and the Reception of "The Bible" in Late Antiquity' in L DiTommaso and L Turcescu (eds), *The Reception and Interpretation of the Bible in Late Antiquity: Proceedings of the Montréal Colloquium in Honour of Charles Kannengiesser, 11–13 October 2006* (Leiden, Brill, 2008) 467–69, 471.

usurp the names of respectable figures to deceive the general population into believing them. Athanasius' bias was by no means exceptional. A few years later, for instance, very similar stances were adopted by Epiphanius of Salamis, whose *Panarion* (ca 374–77) stressed that heretics usurped the name of the Apostles and other authorities to spread their untruthful writings.[11]

It is obvious that by assessing authenticity/trustworthiness by the standard of orthodoxy, religious texts were at risk of suddenly becoming inauthentic/untrustworthy in parallel with the ever-shifting criteria of heresy espoused by the Christian community. This was the case, eg, with the *Gospel of Peter.* In the late second century, Bishop Serapion of Antioch permitted the use of the *Gospel* in the Syrian community of Rhossus. A few years later, Docetist heresiarchs cited the *Gospel of Peter* as the main authority in support of their doctrine. On a second visit to the parish of Rhossus, around the year 200, Serapion of Antioch re-examined the book and found it to be inauthentic.[12] Although the text had not changed, the *Gospel of Peter* had lost its authenticity/trustworthiness because, as demonstrated by its heretic use, it could no longer be trusted. Regardless of all considerations concerning the political disingenuousness motivating sudden reappraisals such as Serapion's, the reception of the *Gospel of Peter* demonstrates that in some instances, rather than being produced by trustworthiness, trust was the very rationale for trustworthiness. In other words, trust in the orthodoxy of a given text could establish the trustworthiness and authenticity of the text itself, while distrust exerted the opposite effect, causing distrusted works to be branded as untrustworthy and inauthentic, of course, a posteriori.

That being said, there were cases in which the spuriousness of given texts was too patent to be denied, therefore making it impossible for trustworthiness to be established (even a posteriori) under the criterion that equated trustworthiness and authorial authenticity. Some texts, however, were perfectly orthodox in content, thus calling for a theoretical justification that could account for their trustworthiness in spite of their pseudepigraphic nature. In such cases, late antique authors often turned to the notion of 'inspirational authenticity' to endow spurious texts of warranted orthodoxy with trustworthiness, in spite of their authorial inauthenticity.[13] According to this notion, the source of inspiration could be distinguished from the material compiler(s) of a text and prioritised. The content of a text could be considered authentic/trustworthy insomuch as it transparently reflected the true message of its source of inspiration rather than the intention of its material compiler.[14]

[11] *Cf* Epiph. *Adv haeres.* 30.15; 30.23; 38.2; 39.5.

[12] *Cf* Metzger, 'Literary Forgeries' 14.

[13] On the topic of inspiration in pseudepigraphic writings, *cf inter alia*: K Aland, 'The Problem of Anonymity and Pseudonymity in Christian Literature of the First Two Centuries' (1961) 12/1 *The Journal of Theological Studies* 39, 44; Baum, *Pseudepigraphie* 140; W Speyer, 'Fälschung, pseudepigraphische freie Erfindung und "echte religiöse Pseudepigraphie"' in K von Fritz (ed), *Pseudepigrapha I: Pseudopythagorica; Lettres de Platon; Littérature pseudépigraphique juive* (Geneva, Fondation Hardt, 1972) 342.

[14] *Cf* Reed, 'Pseudepigraphy'475–76.

By considering them inspired by the teachings of the Apostles or by the words of Jesus, even documents such as the *Constitutiones Apostolorum*, the *Didascalia Apostolorum*, and the *Testamentum Domini nostri Jesu Christi* could be considered authentic and trustworthy even though they had not been penned by Jesus or by the Apostles.[15] Similarly, in the Jewish milieu, the texts attributed to Moses and Enoch could be deemed authentic/trustworthy since they appealed to Moses and Enoch as conduits of God's message rather than as material authors (a notion that was rekindled in the seventeenth century by scholars such as Richard Simon).[16]

Inspirational authenticity was clearly a last resort in the process whereby trust in the orthodoxy of a given text could cause it to acquire authenticity/trustworthiness a posteriori. Indeed, claims of inspirational authenticity were not universally accepted. Yet, on both sides of the opposition between orthodoxy and heresy, believers held pseudepigraphic works of their choosing or even of their own fabrication to be inspirationally authentic although materially inauthentic. Therefore, we can ask to which degree inspirational authenticity could be cited in defence of pseudepigraphic works whose inspiration was considered inauthentic by almost everyone except their authors.

The example of Salvian of Marseilles' (ca 400–80) *Thimothei ad ecclesiam libri IV* is revealing in this regard. Questioned by Salonius, the bishop of Genoa, about the authenticity of the work's attribution to Timothy, Salvian defends the compiler of Timothy's *ad ecclesiam* without explicitly confessing to the authorship of the forgery. He accuses of dullness the critics who judge a book by the author (*cuius legant*) instead of the content (*quid legant*) and cites both the orthodoxy of the content and the authenticity of the author's inspiration in an attempt to establish the trustworthiness of the booklet.[17] 'You ask me, my dearest Salonius, why the booklet *Ad ecclesiam*, which is written by someone in our time, is ascribed to Timothy', writes Salvian: 'whoever wrote [it] wanted to remain unknown and to conceal his identity in order to prevent a work that contains many commendable notions to be put aside due to the [obscurity of] its author'.[18]

In these few lines, Salvian describes at the same time the main problem concerning an authority-based criterion of truth and the solution that was often adopted by late antique authors. More specifically, Salvian is concerned about the tendency to associate trustworthiness and authoritativeness too closely since–he believes–such tendency damages lesser-known yet perfectly orthodox writers. To circulate their works, these authors need to attribute their own pieces to somebody who is better known (and more authoritative). However, if they do so to spread orthodox doctrines, their works–Salvian holds–are to be accepted as trustworthy,

[15] *Cf* Aland, 'The Problem of Anonymity' 44; Speyer, *Die literarische Fälschung* 28.

[16] *Cf* Reed, 'Pseudepigraphy' 477.

[17] *Cf* Baum, *Pseudepigraphie* 49; PF Beatrice, 'Forgery, Propaganda and Power in Christian Antiquity: Some Methodological Remarks' (2002) 33 *Jahrbuch für Antike und Christentum. Ergänzungsband* 39, 44; K Schreiner, 'Zum Wahrheitsverständnis im Heiligen- und Reliquienwesen des Mittelalters', (1966) 17 *Saeculum* 131, 155; Wilder, *Pseudonymity* 194.

[18] Salvianus, *Epistolae*, 9 [Migne, *PL*, 53.169–74].

although they are authentic only inasmuch as they reflect an authoritative, divine inspiration, rather than being authentically attributed to an authoritative author.[19]

Salvian's stance was, of course, quite extreme. While many could have accepted the inspirational authenticity of a 'Pauline' epistle compiled by someone as a written record of Paul's oral teachings, few would have accepted Salvian's argument. However, Salvian's *Thimothei ad ecclesiam libri IV* and the Pastoral Epistles attributed to Paul differed in the extent to which their authentic/trustworthy status was accepted, rather than in the way such status was conceived. In both cases, trust in a work's content motivated an attempt to establish the work's trustworthiness, but since this was equated with authenticity, inspirational authenticity had to be cited to counterbalance or justify formal inauthenticity. Trusted works whose inspirational authenticity was accepted could finally be considered trustworthy, although authentic in inspiration rather than in authorship. In Speyer's terms, these works were understood as 'echte religiöse Psedepigraphie' and thus pertained to the category of 'Pseudepigraphie ausserhalb der Fälschung'.[20]

III. Inauthentic Documents in the Early Middle Ages

As demonstrated by the history of pseudepigraphic works in the first centuries AD, the relationship between trustworthiness and trust did not necessarily imply the logical antecedence of trustworthiness. A very similar attitude towards the notion of trust is revealed by the role of documents in the Middle Ages.

Medieval culture, like the culture of late Antiquity, was centred around an authority-based criterion of truth that mostly conceived authenticity as a requisite for authority and trustworthiness. Late Antiquity and Middle Ages can also be compared in terms of the sheer quantity of inauthentic documents fabricated. However, while the first centuries brought forth a plethora of pseudepigraphic texts, in the Middle Ages, inauthenticity mostly fell under the category of diplomatic forgery, although encompassing other aspects of medieval culture, including religious pseudepigraphy.[21] The Carolingian period was particularly prone to forgery and inauthenticity.[22] The MGH edition of the *Diplomata* of Charlemagne's reign, eg, contains 262 documents, nearly 100 of which are counterfeited.[23]

[19] *Cf* Ehrman, *Forgery and Counterforgery* 94–95, 548; Wilder, *Pseudonymity* 194–96.

[20] *Cf* Speyer, *Die literarische Fälschung* 49; Speyer, 'Fälschung, pseudepigraphische freie Erfindung' 331–36.

[21] For one of the most complete analyses of the diffusion of forgery and falsehood in the Middle Ages, see *Fälschungen im Mittelalter: Internationaler Kongress der Monumenta Germaniae Historica, München, 16–19 September 1986*, MGH, Schriften 33, 5 vols (Hannover, Hahnsche Buchhandlung, 1986).

[22] *Cf* inter alia: G Constable, 'Forgery and Plagiarism in the Middle Ages' (1983) 29 *Archiv für Diplomatik Schriftgeschichte Siegel- und Wappenkunde* 1, 29.

[23] *Cf* H Fuhrmann, 'Die Fälschungen im Mittelalter: Überlegungen zum mittelalterlichen Wahrheitsbegriff' (1963) 197/3 *Historische Zeitschrift* 529, 532.

However, the apex of the diffusion of inauthentic documents was reached in the eleventh and twelfth centuries, the 'golden age of Mediaeval forgery'.[24]

The reasons that led medieval authors to produce inauthentic documents are many but can mostly be related to two general factors: political turmoil on the one hand and the insistence on documentary evidence as a means to establish truth on the other. Rapidly changing political contexts induced individuals and especially institutions to produce unquestionable evidence to certify and possibly increase the extent of their privileges. Evidence of this kind was needed to lay claim to what institutions considered their due and oppose contrary claims advanced by other parties.[25]

In this context, many if not the majority of the documents produced were inauthentic. However, the kind of diplomatic forgeries that circulated in the Middle Ages was not always the same. In some cases (in fact, not too many), institutions and individuals produced inauthentic documents in support of statements that they knew to be untrue. In other cases, inauthentic documents were produced in order to replace older authentic documents that had been lost or destroyed. For the most part, however, diplomatic forgeries aimed to produce documentary confirmation of privileges received in the past that, in origin, had not been documented. In these cases, medieval authors forged papers in order to certify by documentary authority something they trusted as true due to their own historical memory or the narratives that circulated in their own community. Certain individuals or institutions would thus forge documents to provide something they trusted with the trustworthiness necessary for it to be trusted by other individuals or institutions as well.[26] In Eco's terms, 'mediaeval [forgers] falsified to reconfirm trust in something (an author, an institution, a current of thought, a theological truth) and to advocate a certain [notion of] order'.[27]

Let us consider a few examples of this type of forgery. An early instance of false documents produced to support something considered true is provided by the Symmachian forgeries of the sixth century, which originated in connection to the proceedings against Pope Symmachus, who was accused of various crimes by the partisans of antipope Laurentius. The supporters of Symmachus produced an array of inauthentic documents to prove that no one could judge the Bishop of Rome and certainly not an assembly of other bishops. This stance was perfectly in line with a practice reflected by papal Decretals in the West and discussed in Dionysius Exiguus' Canon. Based on this trusted tradition, the Symmachian forgers fabricated documents about trials against popes and bishops of the past in order to ground a de facto practice in the historical and juridical tradition of the Church, so furnishing it with further authority.[28]

[24] *Cf* EAR Brown, 'Falsitas pia sive reprehensibilis: Medieval Forgers and Their Intentions' in *Fälschungen im Mittelalter* 1:118; Constable, 'Forgery and Plagiarism' 12–13.

[25] *Cf* Brown, 'Falsitas pia sive reprehensibilis' 1:118.

[26] *Cf* U Eco, 'Tipologia della falsificazione' in *Fälschungen im Mittelalter* 1:71, 1:73.

[27] Eco, 'Tipologia della falsificazione' 1:82.

[28] *Cf* P Landau, 'Gefälschtes Recht in den Rechtssammlungen bis Gratian' in *Fälschungen im Mittelalter*, 2:16–17. On the need to provide historical evidence, *cf* H W Goetz, 'Fälschung und

In the eleventh and twelfth centuries, the desire to support claims trusted as truthful motivated most of the diplomatic forgeries produced in monastic milieus, especially in the scriptoria of French and Italian monasteries, such as Montecassino, Banzi, Pisticci, and Montescaglioso.[29] A particularly revealing set of examples was studied by Brühl in his analysis of the false documents fabricated in connection to the chancery of Roger II of Sicily.[30] In most cases, these were produced by monasteries to obtain some form of compensation for the abuses suffered at the hands of the Normans. For instance, in the forged diploma classified in Capsar's register as †230 and probably modelled after an authentic diploma, the king of Sicily gives back to the monastery of Banzi its castle, which had been taken away from the monastery by the Normans. Now, although this document is materially inauthentic, the historical fact it refers to, that is, the restitution of the 'castellum Bancie', had actually taken place. We know that by 1153 the castle had been returned to the monastery.[31]

This kind of falsehood, which aimed at attesting circumstances that were considered historically true, did not merely concern diplomatic forgery in the strict sense. A similar attitude also characterised many of the eleventh- and twelfth-century death-bed testaments, in which prominent figures of the time put forth a variety of admonishments. In this case, too, forgeries were usually carried out in line with what was perceived as the true message of the dying man's will.[32] Falsification, in such instances, usually aimed at heightening the effect of the testator's words and providing subsequent events with a justification based on the dispositions of a precedent will. Very rarely, these falsifications aimed to provide authority to facts and interpretations that were not trusted to be in line with the testator's intentions.[33]

The best-known example of medieval diplomatic forgery is provided by the pseudo-Isidorian Decretals, an enormously influential collection that mingled inauthentic papal letters and authentic conciliar canons ranging from the pontificate of Anacletus I (ca 79–92) to that of Gregory II (715–31).[34] In fabricating their canonical collection, the pseudo-Isidorian author(s) largely based themselves on an earlier compendium, the *Hispana gallica augustodunensis*. In the form available to them, the *Hispana gallica* was the corrupt version of an original Visigothic collection of papal Decretals and conciliar decrees from Nicea (325) to Seville (619).

Verfälschung der Vergangenheit: Zum Geschichtsbild der Streitschriften des Investiturstreits' in *Fälschungen im Mittelalter*, 1:187–88.

[29] *Cf inter alia*: C Brühl, *Diplomi e cancelleria di Ruggero II* (Palermo, Accademia di scienze lettere e arti di Palermo, 1983) 138, 145; M Chibnall, 'Forgery in Narrative Charters' in *Fälschungen im Mittelalter* 4:331; Constable, 'Forgery and Plagiarism' 8; P De Leo, 'Falsi, falsari e istituzioni medievali: Tra le carte di archivi dell'Italia meridionale' in *Fälschungen im Mittelalter*, 4:11–12.

[30] *Cf* Brühl, *Diplomi* 79–118.

[31] *Cf* Brühl, *Diplomi* 82–83.

[32] *Cf* HEJ Cowdrey, 'Death-Bed Testaments' in *Fälschungen im Mittelalter* 4:703.

[33] *Cf* Cowdrey, 'Death-Bed Testaments' 4:723–24.

[34] *Cf* H Fuhrmann, 'The Pseudo-Isidorian Forgeries' in D Jasper and H Fuhrmann (eds), *Papal Letters in the Early Middle Ages* (Washington, Catholic University of America Press, 2001) 137.

These materials were re-edited by the pseudo-Isidorian forgers, who carefully altered many elements of the legislation preserved by the *Hispana gallica*. The partly restyled and falsified documents were taken from the *Hispana gallica* and then pieced together with another set of documents, both authentic and inauthentic.[35]

The pseudo-Isidorian forgery was carried out quite carefully: inauthentic materials were interpolated in a body of authentic documents collected from earlier 'authorities'. Besides, even the pieces that were completely inauthentic were composed by the pseudo-Isidorian author(s) by assembling sentences and texts taken from authentic legal sources, Biblical commentaries, and histories. In this way, the pseudo-Isidorian author(s) concealed their forgeries in a particularly efficient way: both because their procedure did not formally differ from the customary habit of producing new canonical collections by piecing together old and new materials, and because, by avoiding as much as possible to write anything of their own, they sensibly decreased the risk of committing detectable errors.

The immediate aim of the pseudo-Isidorian collection is apparently to demonstrate that the politics of the emperor clashed with the tradition of the Church. For this reason, early detractors of the collection, such as Flacius Illyricus (1520–75) and the Magdeburg Centuriators, concluded that the pseudo-Isidorian forgeries must have originated in Rome, in a milieu close to the pope. Recently, however, it has become evident that the Roman milieu cannot be held responsible for producing the pseudo-Isidorian texts. According to Fuhrmann, the pseudo-Isidorian author(s) reacted to a political situation that led, between 818 and 845, to the deposition of many bishops in the Frankish Empire and the secular trial of clerics. Therefore, the main objective of the Decretals would have been to shield suffragan bishops from secular power. Even the increase in the pope's power that resulted from an application of the Decretals would have served, then, the end of protecting bishops.[36] Further clarification on the origin of the pseudo-Isidorian Decretals came from Zechiel-Eckes' discovery of three annotated manuscripts that linked the forgers to the abbey of Corbie. In his analysis, Zechiel-Eckes proposed to date the Decretals to the period immediately following the Synod of Thionville (835), in which Ebo, the Archibishop of Reims, and other opponents of Louis the Pious were forced to recant and drop the accusations previously levelled at the emperor, who deposed them from their sees. According to this interpretation,

[35] For a general analysis of the pseudo-Isidorian Decretals, see in particular: H Fuhrmann, *Einfluß und Verbreitung der pseudoisidorischen Fälschungen: Von ihrem Auftauchen bis in die neuere Zeit*, MGH, Schriften 24, 3 vols (Stuttgart, Hiersemann, 1972); Fuhrmann, 'The Pseudo-Isidorian Forgeries' 136–95; W Hartmann and G Schmitz (eds), *Fortschritt durch Fälschungen?: Ursprung, Gestalt und Wirkungen der pseudoisidorischen Fälschungen. Beiträge zum gleichnamigen Symposium an der Universität Tübingen vom 27 und 28 Juli 2001*, MGH, Studien und Texte 31 (Hannover, Hahnsche Buchhandlung, 2002); K Zechiel-Eckes, 'Ein Blick in Pseudoisidors Werkstatt: Studien zum Entstehungsprozeß der falschen Dekretalen', (2002) 28/1 *Francia* 37, 37–90.

[36] *Cf* Fuhrmann, 'The Pseudo-Isidorian Forgeries' 141–43; A Marchetto, 'La "fortuna" di una falsificazione: Lo spirito dello Pseudo-Isidoro aleggia nel nuovo Codice di Diritto Canonico?' in *Fälschungen im Mittelalter* 2:408.

the pseudo-Isidorian Decretals could be ascribed to some opponents of Luis in Corbie, perhaps to Paschasius Radbertus.[37] The purpose of the Decretals would hence be to censure Luis' politics and especially to demonstrate that Canon law did not allow the emperor to depose bishops.

Despite all these different interpretations, one can perceive a consistent pattern in the use of the Decretals in the Middle Ages.[38] Early canonists were somewhat unwilling to consider the whole pseudo-Isidorian collection as a trustworthy tradition. However, they realised that substantial sections of the Decretals were perfectly in line with the tradition of the Church and could thus be trusted as a source of bona fide juridical knowledge. Consequently, they provided these sections of the Decretals with the necessary trustworthiness by including them in their own authoritative Canons. Even Gratian derived from the Decretals about 375 chapters of his own Canon, 300 of which were largely preserved in the 1917 Code of Canon Law. In Landau's terms: 'the theological forger inspired the canonical jurist'.[39]

The production and the reception of the greatest medieval collection of diplomatic forgeries invite comparison with the politics of trust surrounding late antique pseudepigraphic texts. Not only were the Decretals produced to support with legal authority/trustworthiness an interpretation that was de facto considered standard and in line with the tradition of the Church, but also the reception of the pseudo-Isidorian forgeries reflected trust in some sections, which were considered inspired by legitimate considerations and hence worthy of being proved trustworthy, although a posteriori.

IV. Authenticating Relics in the High Middle Ages

The medieval conception of authenticity as a guarantee of authority and trustworthiness did not concern merely documentary authenticity but also material authenticity. This problem was felt with unique urgency by medieval culture due to its religious undertones. In particular, material authenticity was relevant for assessing relics, which played a central role in medieval society, both in devotional and political terms. Relics were sought by private individuals, either as religious

[37] K Zechiel-Eckes, 'Auf Pseudoisidors Spur: Oder, Versuch, einen dichten Schleier zu Lüften' in Hartmann and Schmitz (eds), *Fortschritt durch Fälschungen?* 1–28. The hypothesis of a later date of composition has been recently defended by E Knibbs (*cf* E Knibbs, 'Ebo of Reims, Pseudo-Isidore, and the Date of the False Decretals' [2017] 92/1 *Speculum* 144, 154–64, 177–81). Hinen suggested instead that the pseudo-Isidorian Decretals might have been produced as early as 831 (*cf* S Heinen, 'Pseudoisidor auf dem Konzil von Aachen im Jahr 836' in K Ubl and D Ziemann (eds), *Fälschung als Mittel der Politik?: Pseudoisidor im Licht der neuen Forschung. Gedenkschrift für Klaus Zechiel-Eckes*, MGH, Studien und Texte 57 [Wiesbaden, Harrassowitz Verlag, 2015] 120–24).

[38] For a detailed analysis of the reception of the pseudo-Isidorian Decretals, see Fuhrmann, *Einfluß*.

[39] P Landau, 'Gratians unmittelbare Quellen für seine Pseudoisidortexte' in Hartmann and Schmitz (eds), *Fortschritt durch Fälschungen?* 176.

souvenirs or as a symbol of power. Moreover, relics were required for the foundation of new places of worship.[40]

The huge demand for relics could be satisfied by fraudulent means alone.[41] Authentic relics were stolen, sold on the 'black market', and dissected into tiny pieces that were then redistributed. Even these practices, however, did not come near to meeting the demand of the market. As a consequence, medieval society became flooded with false relics. Prior to the French Revolution, fourteen holy prepuces were worshipped in continental Europe; there were also three holy umbilical cords, four spears of Longinus, three crowns of thorns, two heads of Saint John the Baptist, and full pints of Mary's tears.

In spite of this anatomical nightmare, medieval culture did not take relic authenticity lightly. The unlawful commerce of false relics was sarcastically described by authors such as Chaucer and Boccaccio, and the doctrinal consequences of the spread of inauthentic relics were widely discussed in the theological milieu, throughout the Middle Ages and up to the seventeenth century.[42] Miracle claims were carefully investigated, and the highest ranks of the Church generally tried to circumvent the risk of idolatrous worship that was connatural to the spread of false relics.[43] Ninth- and tenth-century bishops discouraged the cult of relics they deemed possibly inauthentic and, according to Herrmann-Mascard, since the mid-eleventh century, the Church had disciplined a practice of relic authentication, which, by the end of the thirteenth century, had become a requisite for relic worship.[44]

[40] *Cf* P Boussel, *Des reliques et de leur bon usage* (Paris, Balland, 1971) 57; E Bozóky, *La politique des reliques de Constantin à Saint Louis: Protection collective et légitimation du pouvoir* (Paris, Beauchesne, 2007); PRL Brown, *The Cult of the Saints: Its Rise and Function in Latin Christianity* (Chicago, University of Chicago Press, 1981) 12; Constable, 'Forgery and Plagiarism' 14; PJ Geary, *Furta Sacra: Thefts of Relics in the Central Middle Ages* (Princeton, Princeton University Press, 1978) 61–62, 158; T Granier, '"Si quilibet lector idoneus affuisset, incunctanter ad rei veritatem pertigissemus": Identifier et authentifier les reliques (IXe-XIIe siècle)' in C Leveleux-Teixeira (ed), *Experts et expertise au Moyen Âge: Consilium quaeritur a perito. XLIIe Congrès de la SHMESP, Oxford 31 mars–3 avril 2011* (Paris, Publications de la Sorbonne, 2012) 57; AK Harris, 'Gift, Sale, and Theft: Juan de Ribera and the Sacred Economy of Relics in the Early Modern Mediterranean' (2014) 18/3 *Journal of Early Modern History* 193, 212–14; N Herrmann-Mascard, *Les reliques des saints: Formation coutumière d'un droit* (Paris, Klincksieck, 1975) 106–7, 110–11; V Saxer, *Le culte de Marie Madeleine en occident: Des origines à la fin du Moyen Âge* (Auxerre and Paris, Société des Fouilles Archéologiques et des Monuments Historiques de l'Yonne, 1959) 263–64; Schreiner, 'Zum Wahrheitsverständnis im Heiligen- und Reliquienwesen' 131; J Sumption, *Pilgrimage: An Image of Mediaeval Religion* (Totowa, NJ, Rowman and Littlefield, 1975) 29.

[41] *Cf inter alia*: P J Geary, *Living with the Dead in the Middle Ages* (Ithaca, Cornell University Press, 1994) 185; Sumption, *Pilgrimage* 35–36.

[42] *Cf* G Chaucer, 'The Canterbury Tales' in LD Benson (ed), *The Riverside Chaucer* (Boston, Houghton Mifflin, 1987) 6.C.335–51, 6.C.943–55; G Boccaccio, *Decameron*, ed V Branca (Turin, Einaudi, 1980) 6.10.1, 6.10.34–36, 6.10.43–49, 6.10.53.54.

[43] *Cf* C Walker Bynum, *Christian Materiality: An Essay on Religion in Late Medieval Europe* (New York, Zone Books, 2011) 168, 212–13; J Rubenstein, 'Liturgy against History: The Competing Visions of Lanfranc and Eadmer of Canterbury', (1999) 74/2 *Speculum* 279, 281, 294–97; K Schreiner, '"Discrimen veri ac falsi": Ansätze und Formen der Kritik in der Heiligen- und Reliquienverehrung des Mittelalters', (1966) 48/1 *Archiv für Kulturgeschichte* 1, 11–13; Schreiner, 'Zum Wahrheitsverständnis im Heiligen- und Reliquienwesen' 163; Sumption, *Pilgrimage* 27.

[44] *Cf* Herrmann-Mascard, *Les reliques des saints* 81, 108, 137.

The best-known example of the concern with relic authenticity is provided by Guibert of Nogent's (1055–1124) *De sanctis et eorum pigneribus*. Guibert was aware that many if not most of the relics venerated in Europe were inauthentic. These false relics posed a great risk for true faith. First, in Guibert's terms: 'what is more sacrilegious than to revere as divine something that is not divine?'[45] Secondly, inauthentic relics lacked the power to act as a medium between the devotees' invocations and God, thus effectively nullifying prayers.[46] Thirdly, extreme cases of relic forgery, such as that of Jesus' alleged milk tooth or foreskin, insinuated heretical positions that clashed with the dogma asserting that Jesus was resurrected with his body, ie, with all the parts thereof.[47] For all these reasons–Guibert contends–it would be better to leave holy and ordinary remains undisturbed and to do without relics altogether.[48] However, granted that relic worship is not condemnable per se, bishops should at least expend a critical effort to distinguish between authentic and inauthentic relics, sanctioning exclusively the worship of relics that they trust to be undoubtedly authentic.[49]

The measures suggested by Guibert to oppose the spread of false relics were not always applied too intransigently. Even authors, such as Caesarius von Heisterbach, held that God would operate miracles through false relics (thus making them virtually 'true') as long as they were trusted to be authentic relics and worshipped as such.[50] A certain laxness in the standards of relic authenticity was somewhat unavoidable given the lack of conclusive methodologies to distinguish between authentic and inauthentic relics. This lack produced a twofold effect. On the one hand, it encouraged a non-interventionist attitude, criticised by Guibert and embodied, eg, by Innocent III, who referred to the debated issue of Jesus' prepuce(s), concluding that it is better to consider divine something worldly than vice versa.[51] On the other, the lack of conclusive authentication criteria favoured the upsurge of other kinds of methodologies. Most were more or less patently

[45] Guibert of Nogent, *De sanctis et eorum pigneribus*, ed RBC Huygens, Corpus Christianorum: CM 127 (Turnhout, Brepols, 1993) A29.624D–A30.625C. *Cf* also: K Guth, *Guibert von Nogent und die hochmittelalterliche Kritik an der Reliquienverehrung* (Augsburg, Winfried-Werk, 1970) 75–77, 109; C Morris, 'A Critique of Popular Religion: Guibert of Nogent on "The Relics of the Saints"' in GJ Cuming and D Baker (eds), *Popular Belief and Practice: Papers Read at the Ninth Summer Meeting and the Tenth Winter Meeting of the Ecclesiastical History Society*, (Cambridge, Cambridge University Press, 1972) 56–57; H Platelle, *Présence de l'au-delà: Une vision médiévale du monde* (Villeneuve d'Ascq, Presses universitaires du Septentrion, 2004) 126.

[46] *Cf* Rubenstein, 'Liturgy against History' 60, 126–27; Schreiner, 'Discrimen veri ac falsi' 32.

[47] *Cf* Guibert of Nogent, *De sanctis et eorum pigneribus* A1.607D-A1.608D, A73.651A–A74.651B, A77.653A–A78.653B, A93.662C–A94.663B. *Cf* in this regard: Rubenstein, 'Liturgy against History' 140–41.

[48] *Cf* Guibert of Nogent, *De sanctis et eorum pigneribus* A35.628B–A35.628C; Guth, *Guibert von Nogent* 91–92.

[49] *Cf* Herrmann-Mascard, *Les reliques des saints* 90.

[50] Caesarius of Heisterbach, *Dialogus miraculorum: Dialog über die Wunder*, ed N Nösges and H Schneider, 5 vols (Turnhout, Brepols, 2009) 8.69. In this regard, *cf* also: Schreiner, 'Discrimen veri ac falsi' 4; Schreiner, 'Zum Wahrheitsverständnis Im Heiligen- Und Reliquienwesen' 141, 149; Sumption, *Pilgrimage* 36.

[51] *Cf* Innocentius III, *De sacrificio missae* (Migne, *PL* 217.876–77).

grounded in the notion that authenticity/trustworthiness can be established based on generalised trust.

This is the case, for instance, with *authenticae*, small slips of parchment attached to relics that contained the name of the saint to which the relic was attributed. Generally, relics accompanied by *authenticae* were considered trustworthy. However, these 'documents' could be used to solve doubts about the specific saint to which a certain relic was to be attributed but did not prove anything concerning the authenticity of the relic itself. Rather, they transferred the issue of trust from material relics to the 'tradition' recorded in the *authentica*: if the traditional attribution recorded in the *authentica* was trusted, that is, if the relics had been traditionally trusted to be authentic, they were to be considered authentic/trustworthy.[52]

A different process was at stake in authentication by miracle, which Guibert accepted as a reliable proof of authenticity.[53] In principle, authentication by miracle was grounded in the assumption that an authentic, holy relic had the power to operate miracles since it worked as a conduit on earth of the supernatural power of the saint to which it belonged.[54] In these terms, authentication of relics by miracle was epistemologically akin to the canonisation of saints, which generally required some miraculous evidence of sanctity.

Yet, while both saints and relics could cause miracles spontaneously, when doubts were raised about the authenticity of allegedly holy remains, miracles could also be elicited. The practice of eliciting miracles from relics was based on a widespread conviction that authentic relics would not only prove incorruptible but also defend themselves against acts of vandalism. Walker Bynum records, for instance, the account of a tumbler containing St Anthony's relics, which remained intact after being thrown out of a window by some heretic.[55]

The easiest way to elicit a miracle from a relic was to cast it in the fire.[56] By these means, it would have been possible to distinguish ordinary remains, which would burn to ashes, from authentic/trustworthy relics, which would instead resist the flames in the same way that saints were not subject to purgatorial fires.[57] This method of authentication had a precedent in the medieval judicial use of the

[52] With regard to *authenticae*, cf: P Bertrand, 'Authentiques de reliques: Authentiques ou reliques?' (2006) 112/2 *Le Moyen Age* 363, 363, 367–70; P Cordez, 'Gestion et médiation des collections de reliques au Moyen Âge: Le témoignage des authentiques et des inventaires' in JL Deuffic (ed), *Reliques et sainteté dans l'espace médiéval* (Saint-Denis, Pecia, 2006) 34–35; Geary, *Living with the Dead* 203–4; Herrmann-Mascard, *Les reliques des saints* 119–23, 127.

[53] *Cf* Guth, *Guibert von Nogent* 73–74, 81–84; Rubenstein, 'Liturgy against History' 127.

[54] *Cf* Michele Ferrari, 'Lemmata sanctorum: Thiofrid d'Echternach et le discours sur les reliques au XIIe siècle' (1995) 151 *Cahiers de Civilisation Médiévale* 215, 215–20; Geary, *Living with the Dead* 202; R Landes, *Relics, Apocalypse, and the Deceits of History: Ademar of Chabannes, 989–1034* (Cambridge MA, Harvard University Press, 1995) 211; Platelle, *Présence de l'au-delà* 126; Schreiner, 'Discrimen veri ac falsi' 23–24.

[55] *Cf* Bynum, *Christian Materiality* 136–37.

[56] *Cf* Sumption, *Pilgrimage* 39–40.

[57] *Cf* T Head, 'Saints, Heretics, and Fire: Finding Meaning through the Ordeal' in S A Farmer and BH Rosenwein (eds), *Monks and Nuns, Saints and Outcasts: Religion in Medieval Society. Essays in Honor of Lester K. Little* (Ithaca, Cornell University Press, 2000) 230, 234–35; T Head, 'The Genesis

ordeal by fire, which was employed in extreme circumstances either to guarantee the trustworthiness of one's declaration of faith or, as a last resort, to settle cases of adultery and disputed paternity, that is, cases in which one could not count upon reliable witnesses.[58]

One of the first to apply the ordeal by fire to relics was probably Egbert, Archbishop of Trier (d 993). According to the records, during the construction works for the Church of St Eucharius, the remains of a certain St Celsus were found in a late antique sarcophagus. There was, however, no account of an early Christian saint by the name of Celsus, except for the inscriptions on the sarcophagus. To confirm the holiness of the relics (and the sanctity of Celsus, whose remains had been propitiously unearthed), Egbert decided to try the relics by fire.[59] The ritual is described by Theodoricus of Saint Eucharius in the *Historia inventionis sancti Celsi*: 'having taken a piece of very thin cloth in front of all the Clergy, [Egbert] wrapped it around a knuckle of the holy finger and cast it on the live coals in the thurible, where incense burnt for a whole hour during which he recited the mystical Canon in its entirety. [The finger] remained intact and untouched by the fire'.[60]

A clear description of a similar ritual is provided by the anonymous *Historia inventionis corpori sancti Prisci*. According to the author of this piece, in order to solve doubts about the authenticity of St Priscus, a high prelate ordered that a large fire be lit in front of the altar 'and, with litanies and prayers, he placed a small fragment of St Priscus' head in the fire before the eyes of the presbyter Nicholas and other good men'. The miracle then takes place in front of the archpriest, the priest, and other reliable witnesses: 'the more [the fire] was fanned, the more it was extinguished; then the holy relics started resounding in the fire, inspiring great awe in the bystanders'.[61]

The case of St Celsus and St Priscus is by no means exceptional. Accounts of authentication by fire were fairly common in medieval hagiographic literature: eg, we find similar records in the *Vita sancti Wistani* in the *Chronicon abbatiae de Evesham*, in Leo of Ostia's *Chronica monasterii Casinensis*, and the anonymous *Vita Menwerci*.[62] In some cases, the highest ranks of the Church seemed somewhat reluctant to put relics to the test of fire.[63] However, from the sixth to the twelfth

of the Ordeal of Relics by Fire in Ottonian Germany: An Alternative Form of "Canonization"' in G Klaniczay (ed), *Procès de Canonisation Au Moyen Âge: Aspects Juridiques et Religieux* (Rome, École française de Rome, 2004) 21.

[58] *Cf* R Bartlett, *Trial by Fire and Water: The Medieval Judicial Ordeal* (Oxford, Clarendon Press, 1986) 2, 19–22, 26, 29.

[59] *Cf* Head, 'Saints, Heretics, and Fire' 221–23.

[60] Theodoricus of Saint Eucharius, *Historia inventionis sancti Celsi* 22 (Bolland, *AS* February 3, 406).

[61] *Historia inventionis corporis sancti Prisci* 13 (Bolland, *AS* September 1, 218).

[62] *Cf* WD Macray, 'Life and Miracles of S. Wistan' in WD Macray (ed), *Chronicon abbatiae de Evesham, ad annum 1418* (London, Longman Roberts and Green, 1863) 335–36; Leo of Ostia, *Chronica monasterii casinensis*, ed H Hoffmann, MGH, SS 34 (Hannover, Hahnsche Buchhandlung, 1980) 2:23; *Vita Meinwerci episcopi*, ed H Hoffmann, MGH, SS Rer Germ 59 (Hannover, Hahnsche Buchhandlung, 1921) 209.

[63] *Cf Historia inventionis corporis sancti Secundini* 6–7 (Bolland, *AS* February 2, 531); Honorius III, 'Grave et indignum …' in F Gaude (ed) *Bullarum, diplomatum et privilegiorum sanctorum romanorum pontificum* (Turin, Franco e Dalmazzo, 1857) 3:389.

century, authentication by fire was overall perceived as one of the most reliable methods of relic authentication. Accounts of relics that resisted and even extinguished the flames were widespread and, although some of these were probably fictional, authentication by fire was certainly practised to a relatively large extent.[64]

I have dwelt upon the case of relic authentication by fire because, unlike other cases analysed in this essay, it suggests that the establishment of authenticity/trustworthiness was required by trust and logically antecedent to it. However, in order to fully understand this practice, we need to ask a naive, yet fundamental question. Namely, how to explain the fact that allegedly authentic relics reportedly resisted fire? Of course, one may suppose that all accounts of relics that did not burn or even extinguished the flames were purely fictional or fraudulent and reflected political aims utterly dissociated from the quest for religious authenticity. However, this explanation is excessively reductionist. Not only does it fail to take into account a genuine concern with relic authenticity, but also incorrectly equates reality and perception.

As suggested by Head, the results produced by the act of burning that lay at the heart of relic authentication by fire were not an either/or. The doctrinal presupposition upon which authentication by fire operated was as follows: sinners and heretics are turned into ashes; ordinary people burn, although not completely; and saints burn only minimally if at all. This spectrum of burning implies that the extent of the damage sustained by a relic could not be assessed automatically but rather required a measure of subjective interpretation. The point was not whether a relic had or had not burnt, but whether it had *really* burnt. One can imagine, therefore, that, given a priori trust in a certain relic's authenticity, the 'assessor' would have been led to interpret a partially yet not significantly burnt relic as being completely intact, without intention to deceive.

The subjective element implied by the interpretation of the authentication ritual by fire emerges from some accounts of the practice. For instance, in the *Chronica boemorum*, Cosmas of Prague (c 1045–1125) records that, when the abbess of St George was gathering holy relics in a reliquary, she was stopped by the bishop, who was sceptical about the sanctity of a certain martyr Ludmila, from whose tunic the abbess had obtained a strip of cloth. The abbess objected that the relic of St Ludmila had produced many miracles over the years and the bishop decided to try the relic by placing it on a pile of burning coals: 'Marvellous thing, a little smoke and a small flame appeared around the piece of cloth, but scarcely damaged it. And this too proved to be evidence of a miracle, that due to the great heat, the cloth could not be taken out of the flames for a long time, and when it was recovered it seemed as intact and whole as if it had been woven on that same day'.[65] The sanctity of Ludmila and the authenticity of her relic are hence proved by the fact that the relic is scarcely (*minime*) damaged by fire (rather than not damaged at all). Besides, once taken out of the flames, the piece of cloth is judged to be intact as if it had just been woven, although the author admits it had been somewhat if minimally burnt.

[64] *Cf* Herrmann-Mascard, *Les reliques des saints* 134–35.

[65] Cosmas of Prague, *Die Chronik der Böhmen*, ed B Bretholz and W Weinberger, MGH SS Rer Germ NS 2 (Berlin, Weidmannsche Buchhandlung, 1955) 3:11.

The case of Ludmila's relic is extremely significant since it sheds light on the 'process of trust' that characterised authentication by fire. As she demonstrates objecting to the bishop's doubts, the abbess of St George trusts a priori the sanctity of Ludmila and the authenticity of her remains. Compelled to prove the authenticity/trustworthiness of the relic for it to be trusted by everyone else, she is called to interpret the dubious result produced by the ordeal and, in good conscience, she perceives the relic as being essentially intact, thus miraculously proving its authenticity/trustworthiness. Yet, it is clear, the interpretation of this proof is utterly dependent on the a priori trust placed by the abbess in the sanctity of Ludmila and the authenticity of her relic.

The authentication of St Ludmila's relic suggests an interpretation that can be taken as emblematic of the whole argument of this essay. In late Antiquity and the Middle Ages, instead of being a prerequisite for trust, trustworthiness was often established based on a priori trust in the veracity or wholesomeness of given items or accounts. This inversion of the 'natural relationship' between trustworthiness and trust characterises most of the analysed instances of falsification and authentication.

In the early centuries AD, trust in the wholesomeness of religious texts was required in order to warrant their authenticity/trustworthiness; on the contrary, distrust in their religious value was enough to make them inauthentic/untrustworthy regardless of their authorship. Most diplomatic forgeries in the Middle Ages answered the need to provide an official mark of trustworthiness for those claims that were sincerely trusted as true, although a priori. Finally, even in cases where authenticity/trustworthiness was genuinely regarded as a prerequisite for trust, the outcome of authentication procedures was largely determined by a priori trust, as demonstrated by the abbess of St George.

As shown by these examples, official acts aimed at establishing something as authentic/trustworthy (eg, the canonisation of texts and saints, authentication of relics, production of official documents) were almost invariably based on a priori trust in the veracity or wholesomeness of the claims, accounts, and objects in question. Rather than being dependent on authenticity/trustworthiness, in most cases, trust was thus dependent, in the first place, on psychological, political, religious, and social considerations largely unrelated to the actual authenticity/trustworthiness of the accounts and objects examined. In brief, not only was it possible and, indeed, common to distrust things or notions that were authentic/trustworthy, but it was also possible to trust things that were inauthentic/untrustworthy.

References

Primary Sources

Athanasius, *Epistolae heortasticae*, Migne: *PG* 26 (Paris, JP Migne, 1857) 1339–1450.

Boccaccio, G, *Decameron*, ed V Branca (Turin, Einaudi, 1980).

Caesarius of Heisterbach, *Dialogus miraculorum: Dialog über die Wunder*, ed N Nösges and H Schneider, 5 vols (Turnhout, Brepols, 2009).

Chaucer, G, 'The Canterbury Tales' in LD Benson (ed), *The Riverside Chaucer* (Boston, Houghton Mifflin, 1987).
Cosmas of Prague, *Die Chronik der Böhmen*, ed B Bretholz and W Weinberger, MGH SS Rer. Germ. NS 2 (Berlin, Weidmannsche Buchhandlung, 1955).
Epiphanius, *Panaria eorumque anacephalaeosis*, ed D Petau, 2 vols (Berlin, A Ascher, 1859–61).
Guibert of Nogent, *De sanctis et eorum pigneribus*, ed RBC Huygens, Corpus Christianorum: CM 127 (Turnhout, Brepols, 1993).
Historia inventionis corporis sancti Prisci, Bolland: *AS* September 1 (Paris, Apud Victorem Palme, 1868) 216–19.
Historia inventionis corporis sancti Secundini, Bolland, *AS* February 2 (Paris, Apud Victorem Palme, 1864), 531–35.
Honorius III, 'Grave et indignum …' in F Gaude (ed) *Bullarum, diplomatum et privilegiorum sanctorum romanorum pontificum* (Turin, Franco e Dalmazzo, 1857) 3:389.
Innocentius III, *De sacrificio missae*, Migne: *PL* 217 (Paris, JP Migne, 1853) 763–968.
Leo IX, *Epistolae et dectreta pontificia*, Migne: *PL* 143 (Paris, JP Migne, 1853) 591–794.
Leo of Ostia, *Chronica monasterii casinensis*, ed H Hoffmann, MGH, SS 34 (Hannover, Hahnsche Buchhandlung, 1980).
'Life and Miracles of S. Wistan' in WD Macray (ed), *Chronicon abbatiae de Evesham, ad annum 1418* (London, Longman Roberts and Green, 1863) 335–37.
Salvianus, *Epistolae*, Migne: *PL* 53 (Paris, JP Migne, 1847) 157–74.
Theodoricus of Saint Eucharius, *Historia inventionis sancti Celsi*, Bolland: *AS* February 3 (Paris, Apud Victorem Palme, 1865) 402–6.
Vita Meinwerci episcopi, ed H Hoffmann, MGH, SS Rer. Germ. 59 (Hannover, Hahnsche Buchhandlung, 1921).

Studies

Aland, K, 'The Problem of Anonymity and Pseudonymity in Christian Literature of the First Two Centuries' (1961) 12/1 *The Journal of Theological Studies* 39.
Bartlett, R, *Trial by Fire and Water: The Medieval Judicial Ordeal* (Oxford, Clarendon Press, 1986).
Baum, AD, *Pseudepigraphie und literarische Fälschung im frühen Christentum: Mit ausgewählten Quellentexten samt deutscher Übersetzung* (Tübingen, Mohr Siebeck, 2001).
Beatrice, PF, 'Forgery, Propaganda and Power in Christian Antiquity: Some Methodological Remarks' (2002) 33 *Jahrbuch für Antike und Christentum. Ergänzungsband* 39.
Bertrand, P, 'Authentiques de reliques: Authentiques ou reliques?' (2006) 112/2 *Le Moyen Age* 363.
Boussel, P, *Des reliques et de leur bon usage* (Paris, Balland, 1971).
Bozóky, E, *La politique des reliques de Constantin à Saint Louis: Protection collective et légitimation du pouvoir* (Paris, Beauchesne, 2007).
Brown, EAR, 'Falsitas pia sive reprehensibilis: Medieval Forgers and Their Intentions' in *Fälschungen im Mittelalter: Internationaler Kongress der Monumenta Germaniae Historica, München, 16.-19. September 1986*, MGH, Schriften 33, 5 vols (Hannover, Hahnsche Buchhandlung, 1986) 1:101–119.
Brown, PRL, *The Cult of the Saints: Its Rise and Function in Latin Christianity* (Chicago, University of Chicago Press, 1981).
Brühl, C, *Diplomi e cancelleria di Ruggero II* (Palermo, Accademia di scienze lettere e arti di Palermo, 1983).
Chibnall, M, 'Forgery in Narrative Charters' in *Fälschungen im Mittelalter: Internationaler Kongress der Monumenta Germaniae Historica, München, 16.-19. September 1986*, MGH, Schriften 33, 5 vols (Hannover, Hahnsche Buchhandlung, 1986) 4:331–46.
Constable, G, 'Forgery and Plagiarism in the Middle Ages' (1983) 29 *Archiv für Diplomatik Schriftgeschichte Siegel- und Wappenkunde* 1.

Cordez, P, 'Gestion et médiation des collections de reliques au Moyen Âge: Le témoignage des authentiques et des inventaires' in JL Deuffic (ed), *Reliques et sainteté dans l'espace médiéval* (Saint-Denis, Pecia, 2006) 33–63.

Cowdrey, HEJ, 'Death-Bed Testaments' in *Fälschungen im Mittelalter: Internationaler Kongress der Monumenta Germaniae Historica, München, 16.-19. September 1986*, MGH, Schriften 33, 5 vols (Hannover, Hahnsche Buchhandlung, 1986) 4:703–24.

De Leo, P, 'Falsi, falsari e istituzioni medievali: Tra le carte di archivi dell'Italia meridionale' in *Fälschungen im Mittelalter: Internationaler Kongress der Monumenta Germaniae Historica, München, 16.-19. September 1986*, MGH, Schriften 33, 5 vols (Hannover, Hahnsche Buchhandlung, 1986) 4:11–34.

Dworkin, RM, 'Social Sciences and Constitutional Rights: The Consequences of Uncertainty' (1977) 6/1 *Journal of Law and Education* 3.

Dworkin, RM, 'The Arduous Virtue of Fidelity: Originalism, Scalia, Tribe, and Nerve' (1997) 65/4 *Fordham Law Review* 1249.

Eco, U, 'Tipologia della falsificazione' in *Fälschungen im Mittelalter: Internationaler Kongress der Monumenta Germaniae Historica, München, 16.-19. September 1986*, MGH, Schriften 33, 5 vols (Hannover, Hahnsche Buchhandlung, 1986) 1:69–82.

Ehrman, BD, *Forgery and Counterforgery: The Use of Literary Deceit in Early Christian Polemics* (Oxford, Oxford University Press, 2013).

Endicott, TAO, *Vagueness in Law* (Oxford, Oxford University Press, 2000).

Fälschungen im Mittelalter: Internationaler Kongress der Monumenta Germaniae Historica, München, 16.-19. September 1986, MGH, Schriften 33, 5 vols (Hannover, Hahnsche Buchhandlung, 1986).

Ferrari, M, 'Lemmata sanctorum: Thiofrid d'Echternach et le discours sur les reliques au XIIe siècle' (1995) 151 *Cahiers de Civilisation Médiévale* 215.

Fuhrmann, H, 'Die Fälschungen im Mittelalter: Überlegungen zum mittelalterlichen Wahrheitsbegriff' (1963) 197/3 *Historische Zeitschrift* 529.

Fuhrmann, H, *Einfluß und Verbreitung der pseudoisidorischen Fälschungen: Von ihrem Auftauchen bis in die neuere Zeit*, MGH, Schriften 24, 3 vols (Stuttgart, Hiersemann, 1972).

Fuhrmann, H, 'The Pseudo-Isidorian Forgeries' in D Jasper and H Fuhrmann (eds), *Papal Letters in the Early Middle Ages* (Washington, Catholic University of America Press, 2001) 136–95.

Geary, PJ, *Furta Sacra: Thefts of Relics in the Central Middle Ages* (Princeton, Princeton University Press, 1978).

Geary, PJ, *Living with the Dead in the Middle Ages* (Ithaca, Cornell University Press, 1994).

Goetz, HW, 'Fälschung und Verfälschung der Vergangenheit: Zum Geschichtsbild der Streitschriften des Investiturstreits' in *Fälschungen im Mittelalter: Internationaler Kongress der Monumenta Germaniae Historica, München, 16.-19. September 1986*, MGH, Schriften 33, 5 vols (Hannover, Hahnsche Buchhandlung, 1986) 1:165–88.

Grafton, A, *Forgers and Critics: Creativity and Duplicity in Western Scholarship* (Princeton, Princeton University Press, 1990).

Granier, T, '"Si quilibet lector idoneus affuisset, incunctanter ad rei veritatem pertigissemus": Identifier et authentifier les reliques (IXe-XIIe siècle)' in C Leveleux-Teixeira (ed), *Experts et expertise au Moyen Âge: Consilium quaeritur a perito. XLIIe Congrès de la SHMESP, Oxford 31 mars-3 avril 2011* (Paris, Publications de la Sorbonne, 2012) 49–58.

Grant, RM, *Heresy and Criticism: The Search for Authenticity in Early Christian Literature* (Louisville, KY, Westminster J Knox Press, 1993).

Guth, K, *Guibert von Nogent und die hochmittelalterliche Kritik an der Reliquienverehrung* (Augsburg, Winfried-Werk, 1970).

Harris, AK, 'Gift, Sale, and Theft: Juan de Ribera and the Sacred Economy of Relics in the Early Modern Mediterranean' (2014) 18/3 *Journal of Early Modern History* 193.

Hartmann, W and G Schmitz (eds), *Fortschritt durch Fälschungen?: Ursprung, Gestalt und Wirkungen der pseudoisidorischen Fälschungen. Beiträge zum gleichnamigen Symposium an der Universität Tübingen vom 27. und 28. Juli 2001*, MGH, Studien und Texte 31 (Hannover, Hahnsche Buchhandlung, 2002).

Head, T, 'Saints, Heretics, and Fire: Finding Meaning through the Ordeal' in SA Farmer and BH Rosenwein (eds), *Monks and Nuns, Saints and Outcasts: Religion in Medieval Society. Essays in Honor of Lester K. Little* (Ithaca, Cornell University Press, 2000) 220–238.

Head, T, 'The Genesis of the Ordeal of Relics by Fire in Ottonian Germany: An Alternative Form of "Canonization"' in G Klaniczay (ed), *Procès de Canonisation Au Moyen Âge: Aspects Juridiques et Religieux* (Rome, École française de Rome, 2004) 19–37.

Heinen, S, 'Pseudoisidor auf dem Konzil von Aachen im Jahr 836' in K Ubl and D Ziemann (eds), *Fälschung als Mittel der Politik?: Pseudoisidor im Licht der neuen Forschung. Gedenkschrift für Klaus Zechiel-Eckes*, MGH, Studien und Texte 57 (Wiesbaden, Harrassowitz Verlag, 2015) 97–126.

Herrmann-Mascard, N, *Les reliques des saints: Formation coutumière d'un droit* (Paris, Klincksieck, 1975).

Johns, A, 'Lay Assaying and the Scientific Citizen' (2016) 160/1 *Proceedings of the American Philosophical Society* 18.

Knibbs, E, 'Ebo of Reims, Pseudo-Isidore, and the Date of the False Decretals' (2017) 92/1 *Speculum* 144.

Landau, P, 'Gefälschtes Recht in den Rechtssammlungen bis Gratian' in *Fälschungen im Mittelalter: Internationaler Kongress der Monumenta Germaniae Historica, München, 16.-19. September 1986*, MGH, Schriften 33, 5 vols (Hannover, Hahnsche Buchhandlung, 1986) 2:11–49.

Landau, P, 'Gratians unmittelbare Quellen für seine Pseudoisidortexte' in Hartmann and Schmitz (eds), *Fortschritt durch Fälschungen?: Ursprung, Gestalt und Wirkungen der pseudoisidorischen Fälschungen. Beiträge zum gleichnamigen Symposium an der Universität Tübingen vom 27. und 28. Juli 2001*, MGH, Studien und Texte 31 (Hannover, Hahnsche Buchhandlung, 2002) 161–89.

Landes, R, *Relics, Apocalypse, and the Deceits of History: Ademar of Chabannes, 989–1034* (Cambridge, MA, Harvard University Press, 1995).

Marchetto, A, 'La "fortuna" di una falsificazione: Lo spirito dello Pseudo-Isidoro aleggia nel nuovo Codice di Diritto Canonico?' in *Fälschungen im Mittelalter: Internationaler Kongress der Monumenta Germaniae Historica, München, 16.-19. September 1986*, MGH, Schriften 33, 5 vols (Hannover, Hahnsche Buchhandlung, 1986) 2:397–411.

Metzger, BM, 'Literary Forgeries and Canonical Pseudepigrapha' (1972) 91/1 *Journal of Biblical Literature* 3.

Morris, C, 'A Critique of Popular Religion: Guibert of Nogent on "The Relics of the Saints"' in GJ Cuming and D Baker (eds), *Popular Belief and Practice: Papers Read at the Ninth Summer Meeting and the Tenth Winter Meeting of the Ecclesiastical History Society*, (Cambridge, Cambridge University Press, 1972) 55–60.

Platelle, H, *Présence de l'au-delà: Une vision médiévale du monde* (Villeneuve d'Ascq, Presses universitaires du Septentrion, 2004).

Raz, J, *Between Authority and Interpretation: On the Theory of Law and Practical Reason* (Oxford, Oxford University Press, 2009).

Reed, AY, 'Pseudepigraphy, Authorship, and the Reception of "The Bible" in Late Antiquity' in L DiTommaso and L Turcescu (eds), *The Reception and Interpretation of the Bible in Late Antiquity: Proceedings of the Montréal Colloquium in Honour of Charles Kannengiesser, 11–13 October 2006* (Leiden, Brill, 2008) 467–90.

Rubenstein, J, 'Liturgy against History: The Competing Visions of Lanfranc and Eadmer of Canterbury', (1999) 74/2 *Speculum* 279.

Saxer, V, *Le culte de Marie Madeleine en occident: Des origines à la fin du Moyen Âge* (Auxerre and Paris, Société des Fouilles Archéologiques et des Monuments Historiques de l'Yonne, 1959).

Schreiner, K, '"Discrimen veri ac falsi": Ansätze und Formen der Kritik in der Heiligen- und Reliquienverehrung des Mittelalters', (1966) 48/1 *Archiv für Kulturgeschichte* 1.

Schreiner, K, 'Zum Wahrheitsverständnis im Heiligen- und Reliquienwesen des Mittelalters', (1966) 17 *Saeculum* 131.

Speyer, W, *Die literarische Fälschung im heidnischen und christlichen Altertum: Ein Versuch ihrer Deutung* (Munich, Beck, 1971).

Speyer, W, 'Fälschung, pseudepigraphische freie Erfindung und "echte religiöse Pseudepigraphie"' in K von Fritz (ed), *Pseudepigrapha I: Pseudopythagorica; Lettres de Platon; Littérature pseudépigraphique juive* (Geneva, Fondation Hardt, 1972) 331–366.
Sumption, J, *Pilgrimage: An Image of Mediaeval Religion* (Totowa, NJ, Rowman and Littlefield, 1975).
Torm, FE, *Die Psychologie der Pseudonymität im Hinblick auf die Literatur des Urchristentums* (Gütersloh, C Bertelsmann, 1932).
Walker Bynum, C, *Christian Materiality: An Essay on Religion in Late Medieval Europe* (New York, Zone Books, 2011).
Wilder, TL, *Pseudonymity, the New Testament and Deception: An Inquiry into Intention and Reception* (Lanham, MD, University of America Press, 2004).
Zechiel-Eckes, K, 'Auf Pseudoisidors Spur: Oder, Versuch, einen dichten Schleier zu Lüften' in Hartmann and Schmitz (eds), *Fortschritt durch Fälschungen?: Ursprung, Gestalt und Wirkungen der pseudoisidorischen Fälschungen. Beiträge zum gleichnamigen Symposium an der Universität Tübingen vom 27. und 28. Juli 2001*, MGH, Studien und Texte 31 (Hannover, Hahnsche Buchhandlung, 2002) 1–28.
Zechiel-Eckes, K, 'Ein Blick in Pseudoisidors Werkstatt: Studien zum Entstehungsprozeß der falschen Dekretalen', (2002) 28/1 *Francia* 37.

12

The Legal Significance of Theories of Public Trust in Science: An Illustration from Italy

FEDERICO BRANDMAYR

I. Introduction

In October 2012, a court in the city of L'Aquila in central Italy sentenced seven earth scientists and civil protection experts to six years in prison for manslaughter. The judge found that they had made carelessly reassuring statements about seismic risk in the area just a few days before a deadly earthquake hit the city in 2009. The case is a complex one and continues to puzzle those who explore its intricacies. At least two narratives of the case exist.[1] According to the first, the inhabitants of the city (Aquilani), frightened by the numerous shocks that were hitting the city during the weeks before the quake, were relieved that the Italian authorities had sent to L'Aquila the uppermost scientific advisory body to explain what was going on. They had placed their trust in these experts, and the experts had reassured them, only to be contradicted a few days later, when a quake killed more than 300 people. The subsequent trial, in which many Aquilani joined as plaintiffs, corrected this injustice by punishing both experts and government officials, who had acted negligently and carelessly.[2]

[1] For detailed analysis of early interpretations of the case, see M Yeo, 'Fault lines at the interface of science and policy: Interpretative responses to the trial of scientists in L'Aquila' (2014) 139 *Earth-Science Reviews* 406–19.

[2] See eg D Ropeik, 'The L'Aquila Verdict: A Judgment Not against Science, but against a Failure of Science Communication', *Scientific American Guest Blog* (22 October 2012); M Portanova, 'Grandi rischi, la scienza non c'entra. I sismologi 'condannati' dalla politica', *Il Fatto Quotidiano* (23 October 2012), considering that the sentence was 'not about science,' and highlighting a series of clumsy political ploys to reassure the general public in L'Aquila and prevent disorder; J Etienne and T Palermo, 'The L'Aquila earthquake case is not 'science on trial'. It is a challenge to the way public officials communicate risk', *LSE EUROPP Blog* (1 November 2012); A Donovan and C Oppenheimer, 'Resilient science: The civic epistemology of disaster risk reduction' (2016) 43.3 *Science and Public Policy* 363–374; AJ Imperiale and F Vanclay, 'Reflections on the L'Aquila trial and the social dimensions of disaster risk', *Disaster Prevention and Management* (4 December 2018); P Pietrucci and L Ceccarelli, 'Scientist Citizens: Rhetoric and Responsibility in L'Aquila' 22.1 *Rhetoric and Public Affairs* 95–128.

According to the other narrative, the trial testifies to the profound ignorance people have of the workings of science. Earthquakes are complex phenomena and there is no certainty about their evolution and occurrence. When the experts came to L'Aquila in 2009 to speak about seismic risk, they were asked questions that the very best science of the Earth could not answer. After the earthquake struck, people reacted in frustration by blaming scientists, using them as scapegoats. The trial thus reveals the profound ignorance, distrust, and even hostility people can have towards science in Italy, and possibly in other countries as well.[3]

In sum, the L'Aquila trial has been and still is interpreted through a narrative of betrayed trust on the one hand, and a narrative of ignorance fuelling distrust on the other. Regardless of whether the risk assessment carried out by the defendants was or was not negligent, it is certain that many people, frightened as they were of the shocks, placed their trust in the experts. The commission that met in L'Aquila not only represented the Italian state taking care of its citizens, but was also made up of scientific experts, possessing a special knowledge and recognised as the best specialists in their field. Many Aquilani were arguably willing not only to act according to their advice, but also to believe that their advice was right, grounded as it was in the laws of nature themselves.[4] And there is little doubt, on the other hand, that distrust of state institutions and of official experts ran high in L'Aquila after the earthquake.[5]

Yet these narratives simplify and omit too much. What happened in L'Aquila in 2009 was a tangled imbroglio in which different social logics, including state authority, scientific knowledge, decision-making under uncertainty, local culture, and institutional trust, collided spectacularly. The trial mirrored this complexity. The 800-page sentence was the result of a lengthy process involving an extensive preliminary investigation, dozens of lawyers, prosecutors, judges, and witnesses, over 30 court hearings, and thousands of pages of briefs, legal opinion, and expert reports. Many different knots had to be untangled in order to reach a decision: whether the defendants had acted in a formal capacity, whether what they had said

[3] See eg P Odifreddi, 'Scienza o onniscienza?', *Il non-senso della vita 3.0 Blog* (23 October 2012), linking the event to the omnipresence of magical and religious thinking in the country and claiming that 'both the accusation and the sentence against the experts are typical expressions of the contradictory and twisted attitude Italians have towards science'; J Kluger, 'Scientific Illiteracy: Why the Italian Earthquake verdict is Even Worse than it Seems', *Time* (24 October 2012), blaming widespread scientific illiteracy for the outcome of the trial and connecting the sentence to other examples of 'junk science', including anti-vaccination, homophobia, and climate change denial; M Halpern, 'Italian Scientists Jailed for Failing to Predict an Earthquake', *Union of Concerned Scientists Blog* (22 October 2012), remarking that the sentence was 'coming from the home country of Galileo', bitterly adding that perhaps 'some things never change'; 'Shock and law: The Italian system's contempt for its scientists is made plain by the guilty verdict in L'Aquila' (2012) 490 *Nature* 446, claiming that 'the Italian system's contempt for its scientists [was] made plain by the guilty verdict in L'Aquila' and exhorting the scientific community to promptly challenge the decision.

[4] See A Benessia and B De Marchi, 'When the earth shakes … and science with it. The management and communication of uncertainty in the L'Aquila earthquake' (2017) 91 *Futures* 35–45.

[5] See JJ Bock, 'The second earthquake: how the Italian state generated hope and uncertainty in post-disaster L'Aquila' (2017) 23(1) *Journal of the Royal Anthropological Institute* 61–80.

was consistent with the consensus in earth science, and whether they had actually influenced the population in a way that was conducive to death and injury. All these issues were extensively argued in front of the court and supported with many different pieces of evidence. This process did not stop in 2012. It continued over two levels of appeal, and ended in November 2015 with a decision of the Supreme Court of Cassation, Italy's Supreme Court, that kept much of the argumentative framework of the first sentence but acquitted six of the seven defendants.

In this chapter, I focus on a particular aspect of the case that has not received much attention: I examine the way in which trust in science and in official expert bodies was framed, exemplified, and theorised during the proceedings. Trust was a crucial element of the trial: as will be explained below, the prosecution had to prove that there was a causal connection between what the seven defendants said and what some of the victims did. Prosecutors had to show that some of the inhabitants of L'Aquila who died or were injured in the earthquake had listened to the defendants, that the defendants' (negligent) message contained a clear instruction about what to do, that the victims had trusted them, and that the line of action indicated in the message led them to die in the quake.

Whether people trust scientists was one of the crucial questions addressed during the L'Aquila trial, one among many that make it particularly thought-provoking. In some respects, there is nothing extraordinary about the trial: it can be considered a case dealing with alleged professional negligence and malpractice, which is something not uncommon after a disaster, especially one that is anthropogenic in origin. The case is unusual, however, in that the professionals at the bar were mainly academics rather than practitioners, and in that they had not been involved in the operation of a technical device or system. Instead, they had been summoned to provide local authorities and the general population with expert advice about seismic risk in central Italy, and the contested conduct mainly consisted of speech acts that they had performed (or had omitted to perform).

In what follows, I will show how what Gary Edmond called the 'law-set' (ie judges, prosecutors, attorneys, expert and lay witnesses, and defendants) negotiated the meaning of trust, how they assessed (social and behavioural) scientific evidence about trust in science, and how their arguments were used to support or oppose certain legal outcomes.[6] Three major theories of public trust in science were advanced during the trial. I call them the secular church theory (according to which scientists exert a quasi-religious form of authority over the public), the two-step flow theory (according to which scientific communication is distorted by journalists and opinion leaders), and the emotional brain theory (according to which in situations of uncertainty people follow their intuitions rather than scientific evidence). These three theories might be found in other legal cases involving experts as defendants and in broader political debates about the role of science in society or in which scientific advice play a prominent role.

[6] G Edmond, 'The law-set: The legal-scientific production of medical propriety' (2001) 26(2) *Science, Technology, & Human Values* 191–226.

The chapter is structured as follows. In section II, I present some background information on the 2009 L'Aquila earthquake and the meeting the seven defendants attended a few days earlier. In section III, I delve into the complexities of the trial and the three legal decisions that followed it, focusing on the role of trust in the arguments presented by the prosecutors and defendants in support of their cause. In section IV, I reconstruct the different theories of public trust in science that were advanced by three expert witnesses. In section V, I show how the three theories were assessed and used by the first instance and appeal judges, while the conclusion explores their relevance beyond the L'Aquila trial.

II. The 2009 Earthquake and the Meeting of the L'Aquila Seven

In March 2009, most Aquilani were frightened. Tremors had been rattling the city for several months, and appeared to be growing in number and intensity. The city had been severely damaged in deadly earthquakes in 1461 and 1703, and many believed that the tremors were harbingers of a strong shock. Cracks appeared on many buildings, including hospitals and halls of residence. Most buildings of the city were not designed to resist a strong earthquake. A local amateur seismologist, Giampaolo Giuliani, had agitated the population further by making several short-term predictions of an imminent earthquake hitting the area as shown by measurements of radon gas emissions. He was personally in contact with and alerted the mayors of L'Aquila and other nearby towns in the western side of the Abruzzo region. People used vans equipped with loudspeakers to warn the inhabitants of an imminent quake (some say they were associated with Giuliani, others that they were burglars who aimed at profiting from the panic). Some people, especially students attending the local university whose family lived far from L'Aquila, left the region, or considered doing so.[7]

On 30 March, the authorities tried to re-establish order in the city. Giuliani was cited for instigating alarm (*procurato allarme*) and the local section of the Italian Department of Civil Protection (DCP) issued an ambiguous press release stating: 'No more shocks are expected [*non si prevedono altre scosse*]. Any other piece of information of different content is to be considered false and unfounded.'[8] Ironically, that same day the strongest tremor since the start of the seismic swarm (a technical concept now part of the vernacular) was registered. No injuries were reported, but fear lingered among city residents. The mayor issued an order for schools to be closed the following day and many people started sleeping in their

[7] For a good descriptive account of the events before and during the trial, see AJ Imperiale and F Vanclay, 'Reflections on the L'Aquila trial and the social dimensions of disaster risk' (2019) 28.4 *Disaster Prevention and Management* 434–445.

[8] L'Aquila Court, Sentence n° 380 (2012), p 149. There are several abridged and translated versions of the sentence circulating online. I used the non-abridged Italian version, which runs to 943 pages.

cars and spending as much time as possible outside of their homes. The head of the DCP, Guido Bertolaso, decided to summon in L'Aquila a meeting of the agency's advisory body, the National Commission for the Forecast and Prevention of Major Risks (CMR) and phoned the head of the local section of the DCP, to arrange it. This telephone conversation, which was wiretapped at the time because Bertolaso was under investigation for an unrelated corruption case, is revealing of his ideas about what was going on in L'Aquila. Bertolaso believed that the seismic swarm was not increasing the odds of a strong earthquake. As a matter of fact, he believed that such odds were reduced because small shocks were discharging the total amount of energy contained in the earth ('better to have one hundred 4 Richter scale shocks than silence because one hundred shocks help to liberate energy [*liberare energia*] and there will never be the shock that hurts, do you understand?'[9]). But he also believed that the L'Aquila region had a very high seismicity so that a strong earthquake could happen at some point in time. Thus, according to Bertolaso it was important to tell the Aquilani that the situation they were experiencing was business as usual: that is, a relatively high seismic risk compared to other regions of Italy, but a very low absolute chance of a strong earthquake.

The reasons for holding the meeting were twofold: first, to rectify the clumsy press release by stating that scientists and civil protection officials are no more able to predict when shocks *will not* happen than they are able to predict whether and when they *will* happen ('you must tell your staff not to write press releases saying that other shocks will not happen because this is bullshit, you must never say such things when you talk about earthquakes'); secondly, refute the predictions made by Giuliani as groundless by stating that there are no significant correlations between radon emissions and seismic activity ('[My deputy Bernardo De Bernardinis and I] have decided to hold a meeting there in L'Aquila about this story of the seismic swarm in order to shut up any imbecile, calm down any conjectures, worries, etcetera'). The meeting was intended by Bertolaso as a 'media event' (*operazione mediatica*) to reassure the Aquilani, and had to be advertised as a pedagogic event in which 'the best scientists in the field of seismology' would have explained what was going on.[10]

The meeting, held on 31 March from 6.30 pm in the Abruzzo Region Headquarters in L'Aquila, was widely advertised as a meeting of the 'CMR experts', meant to 'provide the Abruzzo citizens with all the information available to the scientific community on the seismic activity'. It was attended by 16 people, including the seven defendants. Most attendants were members of the DCP, the prefecture, and the local government. Apart from De Bernardinis, deputy head of the DCP, the other six defendants held permanent research positions as seismologists or earthquake engineers, as well as other roles in private and public organisations associated with the management of seismic risk.[11] Four of them were

[9] Ibid, 151.
[10] Ibid, 150–51.
[11] The defendants were Franco Barberi, Enzo Boschi, Gian Michele Calvi, Bernardo De Bernardinis, Mauro Dolce, Claudio Eva and Giulio Selvaggi.

full members of the CMR. The meeting, which lasted less than an hour, centred on the seismic swarm, Giuliani's predictions, seismic risk in the area, and the precautionary measures to be taken. A recurring claim was that earthquakes cannot be predicted, that seismic swarms are not precursor phenomena (ie they do not increase the odds of a strong quake), and that a strong earthquake was possible but very unlikely. The meeting was followed by a public press conference. Several people who attended the meeting gave interviews to local news stations. In one of these interviews, actually conducted before the meeting, De Bernardinis stated that the people of L'Aquila, accustomed as they are to living in a high seismicity area, 'should be prepared to live with this situation.' 'There is no danger', he added, supporting this statement with the claim that the 'scientific community' was telling him that, on the contrary, it was 'a favourable situation thanks to the constant discharge of energy [*scarico di energia*].'[12]

A few days later, on the night of 5 April and early morning of 6 April, three tremors struck L'Aquila. The first two, respectively at 10.48 pm and 12.39 am, were relatively weak and produced no damage, despite being felt by, and wakening, many inhabitants. The third, at 3.32 am, killed 309 people and injured over 1,500.

III. The Trial of the L'Aquila Seven, or: Can Scientific Communication Kill?

A. A Negligent Assessment?

In the months following the earthquake, an investigation started after local lawyers and prosecutors filed a suit against the DCP and the CMR, alleging that they had violated their duties of civil protection. The local prosecutor issued indictments against the seven participants at the meeting and, after the approval of the investigating judge, a trial started in September 2011. They were charged with multiple manslaughter (*omicidio colposo plurimo*) and bodily harm (*lesioni colpose*), acting in conspiracy with each other (*cooperazione colposa*) as members of the CMR. The crimes were imputed to negligence (*negligenza*), carelessness (*imprudenza*), and incompetence (*imperizia*), rather than malice and intention (*dolo*). After 31 court hearings, judge Marco Billi returned a guilty verdict and sentenced them to six years in prison. Billi found that the seven acted in a formal capacity in L'Aquila as members of the CMR, either because they were named members (*membri nominativi*) of the commission or because they were invited participants without voting rights. He stated that in L'Aquila on 31 March 2009 the seven defendants acted as civil servants, state functionaries or government officials (*funzionari pubblici*), and not as scientists or researchers.[13] He contrasted their statements

[12] Ibid, 109.

[13] On this point, see F Brandmayr, 'When Boundary Organisations Fail: Identifying Scientists and Civil Servants in L'Aquila Earthquake Trial' (2021) 30.2 *Science as Culture* 237–260.

during the meeting and in interviews with claims made by the defendants in their published scholarly work on risk assessment and seismic phenomena (as well as with other authoritative sources), and reached the following conclusions: i) the defendants had made claims unsupported by the scientific consensus (notably the claim that a seismic swarm reduces the likelihood of a strong quake by discharging energy); ii) they had severely understated the risk (eg by claiming that a strong earthquake was very unlikely and by overlooking worrying information about the vulnerability of buildings in the region); iii) their risk assessment had been sloppy (eg by making the meeting last less than an hour); iv) they had failed to consider how the authorities and the public would interpret their message (eg by not refuting the idea according to which the impossibility of earthquake prediction means that people can be reassured).

These imputations of scientific and administrative misconduct were the subject of fierce debate and meticulous scrutiny during the trial. Concerning the idea of a favourable discharge of energy, several earth scientists were called to testify as expert witnesses. Most of them agreed that while low-intensity tremors technically *release* energy, this does not amount to a favourable *discharge* of energy in the way suggested by De Bernardinis and possibly by other CMR experts (notably Franco Barberi, a volcanologist). The arguments advanced to refute this idea generally pointed to the fact that since magnitudes are based on a logarithmic scale, a magnitude 4 earthquake releases a negligible quantity of energy compared to that released by a magnitude 6 earthquake (and, more generally, to the energy stored in an active fault zone). Bertolaso testified that he mentioned the theory of the favourable discharge of energy 'dozens of times' to various earth scientists (including some of the defendants) and that 'nobody ever raised any objection about that'.[14]

Adding to the confusion, the defendants' lawyers showed, by interrogating other scientists and by producing documentary evidence, that the expression 'discharge of energy' was commonly used by seismologists when communicating with the public. The defence claimed that seismic swarms are 'neutral phenomena', meaning that they neither increase nor decrease the chances of a strong quake. However, according to several earth scientists who gave expert testimony, the consensual position in seismology is that they increase the likelihood of a major quake. For example, Russian seismologist Vladimir Kossobokov stated that 'the situation on 31 March 2009 pointed to a danger 100 times higher than normal'.[15] Others argued that the consensual position has evolved in recent years thanks to the study of recent swarms. Italian seismologist Warner Marzocchi claimed that he

[14] L'Aquila Court, Proceeding R.G. TRIB. 448/11, Court Hearing 15 February 2012, p 97.

[15] Court Hearing 7 March 2012, 24. Kossobokov was probably alluding to the conclusions reached by a report published in 2011 by the International Commission on Earthquake Forecasting, appointed by Bertolaso and presided by US seismologist Thomas H Jordan. See TH Jordan, et al, 'Operational earthquake forecasting. State of knowledge and guidelines for utilization' (2011) 54(4) *Annals of Geophysics*. The authors of the report stated that according to their models the probability of a strong earthquake was 100 times more likely than a normal situation (ie with no seismic swarm). However, they added that, in absolute terms, the one-day probability of a L'Aquila-size event following 30 March was still 'much below 1%' (p 343).

(as well as many of his colleagues) 'changed his mind' after the L'Aquila earthquake and started seeing seismic swarms as potential precursors of major events.[16]

B. Words that Kill: From Negligent Risk Assessment to Negligent Homicide

Putting aside the crucial issue of whether the risk assessment had actually been negligent, how did the prosecution and the judge prove that the defendants had caused the death of many earthquake victims by uttering certain words? The court's reasoning was as follows: according to testimonies and common knowledge, many Aquilani used to stay outside of their homes for several hours after a tremor, and some would sleep in their cars. This was particularly true in the early months of 2009, when tremors were intense and cracks had appeared on many buildings. For the defendants to be found guilty of manslaughter and bodily harm, it was necessary to prove that each victim had decided to stay in their homes after the two tremors that struck L'Aquila on the night of April 5 and early morning of April 6 *because* they had heard the defendants' reassuring statements six days earlier and *instead* of what they would have normally decided to do in line with 'historically consolidated habits' (*consolidate abitudini precauzionali*). To do so, it was necessary to reconstruct the victims' 'decision-making process' (*processo motivazionale*) using their testimonies (if they were still alive) or testimonies given by friends and relatives. Other 'intervening variables' (*fattori condizionalistici alternativi*) had to be controlled for: perhaps a victim had heard and understood the reassuring statements but had never worried about earthquakes, or wanted to wake up early the following day, or had no car in which to sleep.[17] Such factors could have overridden the causal link between the defendants' conduct and the decision of the victims to stay inside their homes.[18]

In the preliminary investigations and in court hearings in which relatives and friends of the victims were called to testify, it emerged clearly that, at least according to the witnesses, many of them had placed their trust in the CMR experts. Ana Paola Fulcheri, a university student residing in the city's hall of residence who was injured in the earthquake, claimed that she declined a friend's offer to sleep in a car because she had come to believe that tremors such as the one that struck L'Aquila at 10.48 pm were actually a good sign:

> Public Prosecutor – The source of this theory?
>
> Witness, Fulcheri A. – For me it was what the CMR had said, the story of the normal seismic swarm, a gradual discharge of energy, so that we didn't expect strong tremors.

[16] Court Hearing 12 January 2012, p 171.

[17] Sentence n° 380, pp 397, 399.

[18] On the intricacies of these causal arguments, see F Brandmayr, 'How Social Scientists Make Causal Claims in Court: Evidence from the L'Aquila Trial' (2017) 42(3) *Science, Technology, & Human Values* 346–80.

> This relieved me a lot, for me it was like … If I feel something, if I'm sick and I go to the doctor, and the doctor tells me not to worry, he runs some tests and tells me: 'You do not need to worry', then I don't worry. I'm relieved, I can't listen to my fears, I trust what my doctor says and the same happened when the CMR said that there was nothing to worry about and I didn't worry because I knew that they … you know I had to trust them, they are the experts.[19]

Similarly, Giordani Linda Giuseppina, an old lady with little formal education, recalled in court a telephone exchange she had after the 10.48 shock with her adult daughter Daniela Visione, who used to be terrified by the tremors, had slept in a car with her children at least two times before the CMR meeting, and was killed in the earthquake:

> Witness, Giordani Linda G. – I call her again immediately, and I say: 'Daniela! Have you felt it?' 'Of course, ma! It's strong!' 'Well, what are you doing, aren't you coming down?' 'No, ma, it's done,' – her words – 'It's done, it has discharged, you know the scientists, we must have trust.' I told myself: 'she has lost her mind.' Yes, I also had trust, but the education I received would have told me to go out.[20]

Lawyer Maurizio Cora, who lost his wife and two daughters, stated in court that 'we had complete trust in these people' because 'they were the highest expression of science in that field at the Italian level and not only in Italy, or so we were told.'[21] Vincenzo Vittorini, a physician who lost his wife and daughter, recalled a telephone call in which he told his worried brother that the seismic swarm raised no danger because it was discharging energy, and explained his trust in the CMR (and his distrust of Giuliani) as follows: 'Since I'm a surgeon I always think that what science tells me is the right thing to believe in, and precisely because of my profession, because of my attitude, I can't believe in rumours, I don't believe those who speak without any factual support.'[22] Testimonies such as these were used by the prosecution to show that the CMR meeting had had a profound impact on the way people of L'Aquila made sense of the swarm and changed dramatically the way they behaved in relation to seismic risk.

IV. Three Theories of Public Trust in Science

Many other witnesses testified to the same effect in the first months of the trial. Yet the prosecutors believed that more was needed to support the claim that the

[19] Court Hearing 9 November 2011, pp 77–78.

[20] Court Hearing 25 January 2012, p 70. Due to several idiomatic expressions it might be helpful to quote the original passage: 'Testimone Giordani Linda G. – "Immediatamente la richiamo, faccio: Daniela, avete sentito?"; "Come no, mà! È forte!" "Embè, che fate non venite sotto?" "No, ma', ha fatto" – la parola sua – "ha fatto, si è scaricato, stanno gli scienziati, dobbiamo avere fiducia." Ho detto: "ma questa si è scemita." Sì, io pure tenevo fiducia, però il sopravvento dell'educazione avuta sarei uscita.'

[21] Court Hearing 30 November 2011, pp 7–8.

[22] Ibid p 77.

defendants' negligent statements had radically altered the decision-making process of some of the victims. The prosecution feared that the Aquilani's behaviour could simply be imputed to their free will or to individual attitudes towards risk. They then appointed a cultural anthropologist working at the University of L'Aquila, Antonello Ciccozzi, as an expert witness (*consulente tecnico*) to provide general evidence of why people might have been influenced by the CMR experts. The prosecution sought a scientific and objective theory (or, in the words of judge Billi, a covering law [*legge di copertura*]) that would provide a causal model to which the specific cases of L'Aquila could be related, thus formalising some implicit assumptions of the reasoning behind the indictment. In doing so, Ciccozzi developed a theory of scientists' place in society and of public trust in science which I call the 'secular church' theory, because it rests on an analogy between the authority of religion and the authority of science. In turn, De Bernardinis' counsel summoned Mario Morcellini, a media sociologist working at Sapienza University in Rome, while one of the other defendants' counsel (Gian Michele Calvi) summoned Stefano Cappa, a neuroscientist working at Vita-Salute San Raffaele University in Milan. I call Morcellini's the 'two-step flow' theory because it rests on the idea that institutional and scientific communication reaches the general public only through the mediation (and distortion) of journalists and opinion leaders. I call Cappa's the 'emotional brain' narrative because it posits that instinctive and emotional factors have priority over rational deliberation in situations of deep uncertainty about the future, such as when people feel earthquake tremors.

These theories tell different stories about the place of science in society. They offer a fuzzy but relatively coherent picture of the relationship between scientists (or experts) and laypeople, selecting certain features and discarding others, in which some sort of explanation is offered to account for their interactions and transformations (answering questions such as: Are people rational? Is the authority of scientists declining? Are highly educated people more or less trustful?). They possess, to some extent and in varying degrees, a sequential and rhetorical structure. But I prefer to call them theories, rather than narratives, because the appeal to scientific studies, objective data and systematic inquiry prevails over the characterisation of social facts in highly biased terms.[23] In the conclusion, I will argue that these theories are used to support and oppose different narratives in political debates in which scientific advice and expertise play a prominent role.

[23] I take inspiration here from various strands of literature, including reflexive works in science and technology studies and public understanding of science, works in the sociology of ideas, and studies emphasising the cultural nature of scientific discourse. See eg S Hilgartner. 'The dominant view of popularization: Conceptual problems, political uses' (1990) 20(3) *Social Studies of Science* 519–39; T Gieryn, *Cultural Boundaries of Science: Credibility on the Line* (Chicago, CUP, 1999); M Bucchi, 'Of deficits, deviations and dialogues: Theories of public communication of science' in M Bucchi and B Trench (eds) *Handbook of Public Communication of Science and Technology* (London, Routledge, 2008); C Camic, N Gross and M Lamont (eds), *Social Knowledge in the Making* (Chicago, CUP, 2011).

A. The Secular Church Theory of Public Trust in Science

According to the first theory advanced in court, science is an extremely powerful institution that commands the attention and respect of most people, similarly to the higher levels of the Catholic Church in pre-modern Europe. People trust scientists because they give incontrovertible explanations for worrying things, and promise to find solutions to the most pressing problems.

The two basic tenets of Ciccozzi's testimony and 40,000-words report are the claim that authority plays a crucial role in social life, and the claim that science is one of the most powerful sources of authority in Western societies. 'In front of authority', he stated in court, 'regression mechanisms activate and subjects have an inclination to self-infantilise, that is to adopt information coming from authority in an a-critical and aprioristic way.' He then specified what sorts of things can exert this form of ascendancy by adding that our general attitude towards authority, 'whether it is science or religion or any other form of constituted power', is that of a 'suspension of judgment'.[24] Science is the most powerful source of authority in modern societies, and as such it shares fundamental features with religious authority in traditional ones. Drawing on Serge Moscovici's theory of social representations, Ciccozzi stated that 'in modern societies … science is invested with an authority equivalent to that of the religious leader in a traditional society.' To offer an illustration, he said that 'the scientist in our culture is like the imam for a traditional Islamic society, that is the indisputable source of authority.'[25]

For Ciccozzi, people are especially prone to seek the protection and comfort provided by authority in situations in which they feel helpless to face or even understand some sort of threat. In L'Aquila, this threat was of course the seismic swarm: 'the city, astonished by a mysterious and disturbing event, reacted in a very human way: with a need for meaning [*richiesta di senso*].'[26] Indeed, 'in such a situation it is obvious that the attention of the city was altogether projected towards a primordial need for meaning. There was a hunger for meaning concerning the interpretation of what was going on.'[27] People were thus particularly receptive to what the CMR experts said and it makes perfect sense that they have been influenced by them. When a lawyer asked what was specifically charged with authority in the CMR meeting, Ciccozzi replied as follows:

> First of all, there was a deployment of qualifications, which had a very broad ceremonial significance, in other words in announcing the arrival of the CMR, appellations of scientificity and prestige were abundantly shown off. But apart from this, the mere fact that a commission of international renown came to [the small and provincial city of]

[24] Court Hearing 11 April 2012, p 18.
[25] Ibid p 15.
[26] A Ciccozzi, 'Rassicurazionismo: antropologia della comunicazione scientifica nel terremoto dell'Aquila'. Expert Witness Report, Proceeding R.G. TRIB. 448/11, L'Aquila Court, 2012, p 5.
[27] Court Hearing 11 April 2012, p 19.

> L'Aquila had an enormous symbolic significance, and was seen as an epiphany, a revelation directly happening on-site.[28]

Ciccozzi added that our society is divided into different groups that may be more or less receptive to different forms of authority. In particular, he claimed that 'it is not by chance that many witnesses who claimed to have placed their faith in the definition, in the diagnosis of the CMR, are the most highly educated witnesses, with a cultural background closer to the scientific world of the CMR.'[29] In his expert report, he develops this contrast further. On the one hand, there is 'the rationalist, typically holding a university degree, trustful of the institutions, for whom it was easy to believe in the CMR and to label certain popular customs as superstitions.'[30] On the other, there are those 'who strongly trust their intuitive side, their spontaneous feelings, and who follow the habits of popular culture sedimented in the collective subconscious that we improperly call "instinct".' Traditionally-minded people 'filtered the accredited CMR evaluations through individual repertoires of local anthropological culture', drawing from a 'generalised suspicion toward institutional culture' and a local folklore according to which 'shocks still mean essentially "warning"', regardless of what the CMR experts said.[31]

Ciccozzi's theory of science was criticised by defence attorneys as overly polemical and distrustful of the institution of science. They attributed a critical component to the theory that undermined its objectivity. Ciccozzi retorted that 'science' should be distinguished from 'the social use of science.'[32] In other words, science as it ought to be does not correspond to science as it is, ie a source of authority that can be used to control and potentially harm large numbers of people.

To sum up, the secular church theory of public trust in science states that science is one of most powerful sources of authority in modern societies, that in situation of uncertainty and existential threat people desperately seek authoritative sources for emotional comfort and cognitive explanation, and that more educated people are more likely to seek guidance from scientific sources.

B. The Two-Step Flow Theory of Public Trust in Science

According to the second theory advanced in court, science is an institution that produces knowledge and informs the broader public about recent discoveries, technological innovations, medical risks and natural hazards. These pieces of information, however, do not reach the public directly, but are rather propagated by a series of mediators, and through this process they are fundamentally altered. Local news people, friends, neighbours, relatives: this diverse range of 'opinion

[28] Ibid pp 35–36.
[29] Ibid p 26.
[30] A Ciccozzi, Expert Report, p 89.
[31] Ibid p 91.
[32] Court Hearing 11 April 2012, p 71.

leaders' shape how the public understand scientific information. This is particularly true in situations of crisis, fear, and uncertainty about the future.

If Ciccozzi's main source was Moscovici, Morcellini's were Paul Lazarsfeld and Elihu Katz, authors of the 1955 book *Personal Influence*, in which they emphasised the role of opinion leaders in consumer and voting behaviour. He summarised the main argument of the book by saying in court that 'between medium and mass, there is the small group'.[33] In his expert report, he wrote that 'the collection and evaluation of risk information form a collective process, which involves the network of which each individual is part'. Information provided by the authorities (scientific or otherwise) tends to be accepted if it is consistent with 'pre-existing beliefs (to avoid cognitive dissonance)' and with 'the judgment of reference groups (to avoid social exclusion)'.[34] In a situation of crisis, people tend be dissatisfied with the information they can get from a few institutional sources, so they turn on their friends, colleagues, relatives, and neighbours to know more: 'interpersonal relations become the touchstone for assessing information'.[35] The key medium is not the television or the newspaper, where institutional information is reported and users are just passive receivers, but the telephone: people call each other and actively evaluate what they read and heard on mass media. Scientists, doctors, and civil authorities have thus little power in determining how people think and act.

But news people, and the media industry in general, also play a major role in shaping how the public perceive scientific knowledge, according to Morcellini. The original message of an institutional spokesperson is often 'broken down in the normal and obvious meat grinder of media industry'.[36] News companies have 'the necessity to produce content', which increasingly leads journalists to 'transform informational reports into outright stories'. Spectacularising the news in this way obviously carries a 'distorting potential' in relation to scientific communication.[37]

Furthermore, modern societies are characterised by a media system which is polyphonic (if not cacophonic) rather than monologic. Information presented 'monolithically', in Orwellian fashion, might lead people to act in a certain way. But, Morcellini added, 'in the Italian situation there is no way for a voice to present itself as the only and most authoritative one, because in a market system there is a juxtaposition of different truths'.[38] He argued that such 'communicational divergence' happened in L'Aquila, since certain newspapers framed the key message of the CMR meeting as one of 'reassurance', while others as one urging people to 'remain vigilant'.[39] The notion that shocks discharge energy

[33] Court Hearing 9 May 2012, p 74.

[34] M Morcellini, 'Relazione. Un'analisi dell'impatto comunicativo durante il terremoto dell'Aquila'. Expert Witness Report, Proceeding R.G. TRIB. 448/11, L'Aquila Court, 2012, p 66.

[35] Court Hearing 9 May 2012, p 78.

[36] Ibid p 125.

[37] M Morcellini, Expert Report, p 25.

[38] Court Hearing 9 May 2012, p 91.

[39] Ibid p 118.

was popularised through various articles summarising the views of scientists (including some who did not attend the 31 March meeting), and became in this way a 'popular slang expression'.[40] De Bernardinis' interview, in which he made the most reassuring and scientifically unfounded claims, was presented by several newspapers as the 'abstract of the meeting', when in fact it had been filmed before it.[41]

Finally, Morcellini claimed that even assuming that people rely on the mainstream media (instead of listening to local opinion leaders) for information, and even assuming that news is presented in a factual and rigorous way, there are still three levels through which what the general public retains is not equivalent to the original message. Firstly, people expose themselves only to certain media, on the basis of their 'cultural expectations', and different media frame news in different ways. Secondly, when people listen or read the news in their medium of choice, they actually grasp only a limited number of ideas, because 'the mind is a very active filter': perception is always selective, and decryption always arbitrary. Thirdly, selectivity does not concern only exposition and perception, but also memory: 'people tend to remember only the information that is compatible with their value system and that is the least distressing for the subject'.[42]

To recapitulate, the two-step flow theory of public trust in science states that in modern, pluralistic societies, scientific communication passes through a series of steps, including journalists and local opinion leaders, that dilute and distort it. What people receive at the end of the process is not only influenced by the operations of these actors, but also by the very agency of the receivers, who selectively focus their attention on certain elements while neglecting others.

C. The Emotional Brain Theory of Public Trust in Science

According to the third theory advanced in court, science is a body of knowledge that inform the decisions of a minority of people only, and only under certain circumstances. Most of the time, and especially in situations of crisis and fear, most people tend to act according to intuitions, heuristics and emotions, which often leads them to irrational and biased choices. Scientific communication might change what people believe (or believe to believe), but can hardly change how people act in concrete situations.

Cappa's testimony relied heavily on recent studies in the fields of neuroscience and social psychology, but also drew on Frank Knight's classic distinction between risky events, 'whose probability can be calculated so that costs and benefits can be foreseen' (eg, rolling dice), and ambiguous events, whose probability is unknown

[40] Ibid p 84.
[41] Ibid p 85.
[42] Ibid pp 95–97.

'because of insufficient of conflictual information'. He stated that in situations of ambiguity:

> the most atavistic structures at the level of the nervous system activate, that is to say the orbitofrontal cortex-amygdala system, those structures that trigger reactions that are automatic, rapid, instinctive and not very permeable to rational analysis, which is triggered by other cortical areas.[43]

According to Cappa, in late March and early April 2009 the Aquilani were in a situation of ambiguity, since the probability of a strong earthquake striking the town was unknown, and conflicting statements were made by ordinary folk, Giuliani, the DCP, the CMR and the broader scientific community. In situations of ambiguity, people's risk aversion activates at varying degrees according to genetic factors, precocious experiences, whether they are tired, hungry or stressed, but these individual variations 'are not very permeable to, let's say, cultural and persuasive factors'.[44] The Aquilani's decision to leave or stay in their homes after a seismic shock was not based on rational calculation of risk according to what they had heard from authoritative sources, such as the CMR experts. Rather, their choices followed from intuitive, emotional reactions that were activated by the very physical experience of the tremor. Consider the following exchange:

> Expert Witness, Cappa, S.: [I]n a situation in which there is a physical signal that is constantly associated with a certain reaction, this physical signal has an extremely intense emotional meaning; as all stimuli are emotional in so far as they are relevant for survival, it is very plausible that this sets in motion the subcortical mechanism of the amygdala circuitry, determining extremely elementary reactions. Basically, in this context the reaction is flight.
>
> Defence attorney, Stefano, A.: But what I'd like to know is if and how much institutional information can influence this mechanism, bearing in mind for example the cultural level of the subject receiving the information.
>
> Expert Witness, Cappa, S.: The evidence we have on this point is rather … is usually referred to as discouraging from the point of view of science. The impact that expert communication has is maybe formally recognised, but is very limited from the point of view of behaviour change.[45]

Asked to evaluate Ciccozzi's expert report, he gave a negative assessment of its central tenet: 'dozens of years of international scientific research on the perception of environmental, physical, and social risk show that there is a stable and clamorous difference between how the man of the street and the specialist technician express judgments of danger, probability of catastrophic events, plausibility of accepting behavioural risks, etc.' 'In evaluations expressed in everyday life,' he added, 'in spite of the formal respect for those who embody the role of scientific

[43] Court Hearing, 16 May 2012, p 72.
[44] Ibid p 73.
[45] Ibid pp 75–76.

and technical expert, what matters are mental processes that follow paths and strategies not always close to the standards of rationality.'[46]

In short, people's brains are wired to ignore long-term safety concerns about earthquakes, and tend to activate only when an earthquake actually happens, causing people to take flight if the stimulus is strong enough. As evidence to back up this claim, he pointed to the inefficacy of anti-tobacco campaigns, which have had an effect only after 40 years and only on certain sections of the population. He also presented the results of a survey conducted at the national level shortly after the L'Aquila earthquake on young students on their beliefs and attitudes about seismic risk. Cappa summarised its findings by stating that 'despite the massive amount of information on the event,' the survey shows 'a lack of awareness and the maintenance of previous habits'. Over 70 per cent of the Italian population is exposed to a significant seismic risk, yet even after a tragedy such as the L'Aquila earthquake only 34 per cent of the respondents have checked the structural conditions of their school. 'These data,' Cappa concluded, 'indicate the limited influence images, interviews and information reported by the media can have.'[47]

To summarise, the emotional brain theory of public trust in science states that in situations of deep uncertainty people 'trust their gut' rather than following the advice of scientific experts. How they behave depend on various factors that are mostly related to genetic make-up, precocious experience, and situational conditions, while cultural influence have little influence.

V. The Assessment and Use of the Theories by the Judges

It is easy to see how Ciccozzi's testimony could be used against the defendants, while Morcellini and Cappa's could be used in their favour. The secular church theory depicts scientists as powerful, as capable of conditioning people's beliefs and acts. It attributes what legal theorists call 'practical authority' to the scientific establishment, in addition to simple 'theoretical authority' that experts are usually considered to have.[48] By contrast, the two step-flow theory and the emotional brain theory suggest, each in its own way, that scientists and experts are quite powerless in the face of news people, reference groups, instinctual reactions, and unreflective habits.

The trial judge was favourable to Ciccozzi's testimony, describing it as 'undoubtedly an anthropological scientific law', and accepting its argument that 'trust in science increases with the cultural level and the propensity to respect rules

[46] S Cappa and E Smeraldi, 'Relazione di consulenza tecnica'. Expert Witness Report, Proceeding R.G. TRIB. 448/11, L'Aquila Court, 2012, p 8. The report was co-authored by Enrico Smeraldi, a psychiatrist who did not testify in court.

[47] Ibid p 10.

[48] See HM Hurd, 'Challenging authority' (1991)100.6 *The Yale Law Journal* 1611–77.

and institutions.'[49] The words of the CMR experts 'had triggered a psychological reaction among the victims', consisting of a 'collective suppression of the "fear of the earthquake"', and a 'total confidence in the CMR evaluations and recommendations, supported by the prestige (*autorevolezza*) of the source.'[50] By applying this general theory to each case brought to the court, the judge found that 29 deaths and four injuries had been caused by the negligent reassurance of the CMR experts, considered as a whole.

The judge dismissed Morcellini's testimony as 'completely unfounded', arguing that victims with very different 'reference groups' had similarly changed their mind on the risk posed by the seismic swarm.[51] Furthermore, Billi claimed that journalists did not distort the message of the defendants, pointing to the case of a journalist who wrote about the CMR meeting in a local newspaper, and subsequently lost his two children. He had been reassured and had reported the reassurances not only to the readers of the newspaper, but also to his family, in a context where there was no need to produce sensational content. 'The message coincided with its reporting', Billi concluded.[52] He also rejected Cappa's testimony by stating that the example of anti-tobacco campaigns actually confirms that institutional communication can have an influence, regardless of the frequency with which it occurs.[53] He added that the Aquilani, before the earthquake, were in the same situation as a person with breathing problems, ie much more receptive to messages about the dangers of tobacco.

In the appeal judgment, issued in November 2014 by the L'Aquila Court of Appeals and upheld by the Supreme Court of Cassation a year later, this interpretation was overturned. The judges found that a scientific 'covering law' was not necessary to establish a causal link between a statement and an action. Instead, 'principles of experience' based on common sense were sufficient. They described Ciccozzi's theory as unscientific, unfalsifiable, biased and ex-post.[54] The appeal judges defined the 31 March meeting as an informal gathering of scientists without any official standing, and singled out De Bernardinis as the only individual who was responsible for informing the Aquilani about seismic risk. By controlling the individual causal attributions made by Billi, they found De Bernardinis causally responsible of the deaths of 13 people as a consequence of the negligent statements he had made. In a way, Ciccozzi's theory was vindicated in that each individual causal connection, made by analysing the testimony of friends and relatives of the

[49] Sentence n° 380, p 689.
[50] Ibid pp 691–692.
[51] Ibid p 665.
[52] Ibid p 652.
[53] Billi's disregard of frequency is linked to his claim that 'covering laws' must simply establish a statistical regularity between two phenomena and need not have a high 'statistical coefficient' (yet alone one equal to 1). To support this claim, he mentions a case in which a cloistered nun had been raped by a soldier during the Bosnian War of 1992–95 and had been infected with HIV. The probability of being infected after only one instance of sexual intercourse is very low, but since no other reasonable counterfactual scenario was conceivable, the court rightly decided that the soldier had caused her to be infected with HIV.
[54] L'Aquila Court of Appeals, Sentence n° 3317, 2014, p 270.

victims, implicitly rested on the idea that institutional authority, especially when surrounded by an aura of scientificity, can shape how people think and act.

VI. Conclusion: The Legal and Political Relevance of Theories of Public Trust in Science

Many lessons can be learned from the L'Aquila trial. One could reflect upon the importance of establishing clearer boundaries between science and politics (and between risk assessment and risk management), of instructing experts to communicate their knowledge more honestly and seriously to broad audiences, or of educating scientists to challenge and correct policymakers when they are wrong. Instead of developing these normative claims, my study suggests that the L'Aquila trial is a strategic case to understand how people talk about science, what they expect from it, what kind of role they think scientists play or ought to play, and what are the practical implications of these views. In other words, the case revealed a host of implicit assumptions, which in certain cases were formalised into genuine theories, about the place of science in society. My analysis of the 'science talks' in the trial focused on theories of public trust in science, which spell out whether scientists exert some kind of influence over the public. These theories were not created out of nothing for the proceeding, their relevance is not limited to the L'Aquila trial, and they do not exhaust how the role of scientists in society can be theorised. They are embedded in different scholarly traditions, and are used, developed and popularised by different disciplines and research networks. There are good reasons to believe that they are present at the folk level among different social groups, as unequally distributed collective representations about the relationship between science and society that I called elsewhere 'public epistemologies'.[55] At the same time, it is not implausible that people draw on them opportunistically and use them as rhetorical instruments to impose a certain definition of the authority of science and promote certain lines of action, as lawyers, expert witnesses, and judges did in the L'Aquila trial. What is, then, the legal, social, and political relevance of these theories of public trust in science?

Scientists, experts, researchers, and technicians are periodically, and perhaps increasingly, named as defendants in lawsuits dealing with risk management, environmental regulation, public health, medical malpractice, scientific misconduct, natural hazards, and industrial disasters.[56] If the L'Aquila case is representative of

[55] See F Brandmayr, 'Public Epistemologies and Intellectual Interventions in Contemporary Italy' (2021) 34 *International Journal of Politics, Culture, and Society* 47–68.

[56] See eg PE Kalb and KG Koehler, 'Legal Issues in Scientific Research' (2002) 287(1) *JAMA* 85–91; D Michael (ed), *Doubt is Their Product. How Industry's Assault on Science Threatens your Health* (Oxford, OUP, 2008); G Markowitz and D Rosner, *Lead Wars: The Politics of Science and the Fate of America's Children*, Los Angeles, University of California Press, 2013; RJ Bretton et al, 'Implications of legal scrutiny processes (including the L'Aquila trial and other recent court cases) for future volcanic risk governance' (2015) 4 *Journal of Applied Volcanology* 18.

such legal disputes, it suggests that the secular church theory of public trust in science is likely to be used as a framework to place blame on experts, while the two-step flow theory and the emotional brain theory will be used to exonerate them. More broadly, science is increasingly under public scrutiny and is the object of the grievances of growing sections of society. Social movements denounce scientists' collusion with unscrupulous private companies. Conservative politicians and activists attack science's supposed left-wing or liberal bias. State administrations demand expert advice on a great variety of issues, pushing them to exaggerate the certainty of their knowledge and provoking reactions from groups that are negatively affected by public decisions. Scientists and their supporters use a variety of arguments in their defence. It is likely that the emotional brain theory and the two-step flow theory of public trust in science are part of this defensive repertoire, while the secular church theory is mainly used by their attackers.

Finally, the three theories are likely to be found in political debates in which a decision about complex, technical issues have to be made. They have distinctive normative implications and point to different policy levers, ie different routes of intervention in order to enact public policies. The secular church theory suggests either to transform how experts advise policymakers, in the direction of a more democratic and genuinely public deliberation over technical issues, or to rebel against technocratic encroachment altogether in the name of local and traditional forms of social life. The two-step flow points to a transformation of the media system in order to promote the transmission of certain key messages, and to intervene at the local level by supporting opinion leaders and grassroots organisations. The emotional brain theory seems particularly adapted to provide justifications for manipulation techniques and 'nudges', ie the exploitation of intuitions and biases to influence people's behaviour without imposing prescriptions or proscriptions, leaving them unaware of this effect.

The L'Aquila trial has deeply divided people both inside and outside the court of law. Among the many issues that have been controversial, the question of whether people trust and how they respond to communication coming from expert bodies and state authorities is highly consequential beyond the case itself. Policy-makers, expert advisors, and lawyers can learn much from this deployment of theories. Perhaps all of them contain some element of truth. But each of them also omits much, and it is through these omissions that they can serve as basis for action and carry different political implications. Appreciating the direction and scope of such normative power, which is common to most social theories of trust, is a first step to gain a truly reflexive understanding of trust itself.

References

Benessia, A and B De Marchi. 'When the earth shakes … and science with it. The management and communication of uncertainty in the L'Aquila earthquake'. *Futures* 91 (2017): 35–45.

Bock, J-J 'The second earthquake: how the Italian state generated hope and uncertainty in post-disaster L'Aquila'. *Journal of the Royal Anthropological Institute* 23(1) (2017): 61–80.

Brandmayr, F 'Public Epistemologies and Intellectual Interventions in Contemporary Italy.' *International Journal of Politics, Culture, and Society* (2021) 34: 47–68.

Brandmayr, F 'How Social Scientists Make Causal Claims in Court: Evidence from the L'Aquila Trial'. *Science, Technology, & Human Values* (2017) 42.3: 346–80.

Brandmayr, F 'When Boundary Organisations Fail: Identifying Scientists and Civil Servants in L'Aquila Earthquake Trial'. *Science as Culture* (2021) 30.2: 237–260.

Bretton, RJ et al, 'Implications of legal scrutiny processes (including the L'Aquila trial and other recent court cases) for future volcanic risk governance', *Journal of Applied Volcanology* (2015) 4: 18.

Bucchi, M 'Of deficits, deviations and dialogues: Theories of public communication of science', in M Bucchi and B Trench (eds) *Handbook of Public Communication of Science and Technology*, London: Routledge, 2008.

Camic, C, N Gross and M Lamont (eds), *Social Knowledge in the Making*, Chicago: CUP, 2011.

Cappa, S and E Smeraldi. 'Relazione di consulenza tecnica'. Expert Witness Report, Proceeding R.G. TRIB. 448/11, L'Aquila Court, 2012.

Ciccozzi, A 'Rassicurazionismo: antropologia della comunicazione scientifica nel terremoto dell'Aquila'. Expert Witness Report, Proceeding R.G. TRIB. 448/11, L'Aquila Court, 2012.

Donovan, A and C Oppenheimer, 'Resilient science: The civic epistemology of disaster risk reduction', *Science and Public Policy*, 43(3): 363–74.

Edmond, G 'The law-set: The legal-scientific production of medical propriety'. *Science, Technology, & Human Values* 26(2), (2001): 191–226.

Etienne, J and T Palermo, 'The L'Aquila earthquake case is not "science on trial". It is a challenge to the way public officials communicate risk'. *LSE EUROPP Blog*. 1 November 2012.

Gieryn, T *Cultural Boundaries of Science: Credibility on the Line*, Chicago: CUP, 1999.

Halpern, M 'Italian Scientists Jailed for Failing to Predict an Earthquake'. *Union of Concerned Scientists Blog*. 22 October 2012.

Hilgartner, S 'The dominant view of popularization: Conceptual problems, political uses'. *Social Studies of Science* 20(3), 1990: 519–39.

Hurd, HM 'Challenging authority'. *The Yale Law Journal* 100(6), 1991: 1611–77.

Imperiale, AJ and F Vanclay, 'Reflections on the L'Aquila trial and the social dimensions of disaster risk'. *Disaster Prevention and Management*, 4 December 2018.

Jordan, TH et al 'Operational earthquake forecasting. State of knowledge and guidelines for utilization'. *Annals of Geophysics* 54(4), 2011.

Kalb, PE and KG Koehler, 'Legal Issues in Scientific Research'. *JAMA*. 287(1), 2002: 85–91.

Kluger, J 'Scientific Illiteracy: Why the Italian Earthquake verdict is Even Worse than it Seems'. *Time*, 24 October 2012.

L'Aquila Court of Appeals, Sentence n° 3317, 2014: 270.

L'Aquila Court. Sentence n° 380, 2012: 1-943.

Markowitz, G and D Rosner, *Lead Wars: The Politics of Science and the Fate of America's Children*, Los Angeles: University of California Press, 2013.

Michael, D (ed), *Doubt is Their Product. How Industry's Assault on Science Threatens your Health*, Oxford: OUP, 2008.

Morcellini, M 'Relazione. Un'analisi dell'impatto comunicativo durante il terremoto dell'Aquila'. Expert Witness Report, Proceeding R.G. TRIB. 448/11, L'Aquila Court, 2012.

Nature. 'Shock and law: The Italian system's contempt for its scientists is made plain by the guilty verdict in L'Aquila'. *Nature*, 490(7421): 446.

Odifreddi, P 'Scienza o onniscienza?'. *Il non-senso della vita 3.0 Blog*. 23 October 2012.

Pietrucci, P and L Ceccarelli, 'Scientist Citizens: Rhetoric and Responsibility in L'Aquila'. *Rhetoric and Public Affairs*, 22(1): 95–128.

Portanova, M. 'Grandi rischi, la scienza non c'entra. I sismologi 'condannati' dalla politica'. *Il Fatto Quotidiano*, 23 October 2012.

Ropeik, D 'The L'Aquila Verdict: A Judgment Not against Science, but against a Failure of Science Communication'. *Scientific American Guest Blog*. 22 October 2012.

Yeo, M 'Fault lines at the interface of science and policy: Interpretative responses to the trial of scientists in L'Aquila'. *Earth-Science Reviews* (2014) 139: 406–19.

13

Why Should Citizens Trust EU Regulatory Expertise?

Legal Warrants, Science and Politics in EU Food Governance

MARTA MORVILLO

I. Trust *Through* Expertise and Trust *In* Expertise in EU Food Governance. Introduction and Outline

Public trust in experts is shaped by ideas and expectations concerning their legitimate role in a given context. Are they expected to be mere knowledge providers or one of many actors involved in more complex and value-laden science-policy issues? Depending on how one answers these questions, the institutional arrangements and legal mechanisms to foster citizens' trust in experts may vary significantly. At the same time, mismatches between normative expectations as to the legitimate role of experts and the actual practices of regulatory expert bodies may lead to tensions and ultimately result in a failure to secure citizen's trust.

The case of EU food governance is emblematic in these regards. The genesis of the current institutional architecture of EU food governance (Regulation 178/2002, the General Food Law, hereinafter GFL)[1] is rooted in the crises that affected EU food governance in the late 1990s, particularly in the BSE crisis, which simultaneously jeopardised citizens' trust and the functioning of the internal market.[2] The act's recitals bear testimony of how fostering public trust ranked high among the European legislator's priorities, the word 'confidence' (used interchangeably with 'trust' in the context of the Regulation)[3] being reiterated multiple times.

[1] Regulation (EC) No 178/2002 of the European Parliament and Council of 28 January 2002 laying down the general principles and requirements of food law, establishing the European Food Safety Authority and procedures in matters of food safety, [2002] OJ L31/1–24.

[2] S Smismans, 'Constitutionalising expertise in the EU. Anchoring knowledge in democracy', in J Priban (ed) *Self-constitution of European Society. Beyond EU polities, law and governance* (London/New York, Routledge, 2016) 187.

[3] The word 'confidence' is used as a synonym of trust in the six language versions considered: *fiducia* (Italian), *confiança* (Portuguese), *confianza* (Spanish), *confiance* (French), *Vertrauen* (German), *vertrouwen* (Dutch).

Interestingly, the trusting subject is almost invariably understood as a consumer[4] and trust is seen as being ensured by open, transparent, and science-based decision-making processes.[5] When the GFL was adopted, much emphasis was indeed placed on sound science as one of the cornerstones of public trust in EU food governance. The scientific basis for food law, in particular, is understood as being independent, transparent, objective and of high scientific quality.[6] In order to secure such a scientific basis, the GFL established the European Food Safety Authority (hereinafter EFSA, the Agency), an ad hoc and EU-level expert body responsible for scientific risk assessments concerning the food chain. According to Article 22(7) GFL, EFSA is to 'serve as a point of reference' for EU food governance 'by virtue of its independence, the scientific and technical quality of the opinions it issues and the information it disseminates, the transparency of its procedures and methods of operation, and its diligence in performing the tasks assigned to it'. From an institutional point of view, EFSA is an independent agency with no direct regulatory powers;[7] its opinions have, however, proved to be highly influential on the Commission's decisions concerning food governance.[8]

Since its inception, EFSA has placed great emphasis on the need to earn – and maintain – public trust in its scientific assessments. In almost 20 years of existence, the Agency has developed comprehensive independence and transparency policies; meaningfully, its mission statement changed in 2016 and now reads 'trusted science for safe food'. The picture is, however, not entirely that of a clear-cut success. First, while the large majority (82%) of EU citizens generally trusts scientists as sources of information on food-related issues,[9] much fewer are aware of the institutional framework governing food risks, particularly the role (and even the existence) of EFSA (19%).[10] Secondly, EU food governance has continued to be struck by repeated crises over the last two decades. Authorisations of genetically modified crops and plant protection products have triggered heated political conflicts, resulting in public contestation, deadlocked decision-making at the EU level, and extensive litigation.[11] Crucially, contestation has targeted both the assessment and the management of risks, equally questioning EU regulators' capacity to pursue the public interest in risk management and the very quality and

[4] Out of six recitals in which the word 'confidence' appears, four mention consumers as the trusting subject; trading partners feature twice; stakeholders, interested parties, and the public, once.

[5] See recitals 18 and 22.

[6] See recitals 18 and 35.

[7] In line with the non-delegation doctrine, as established in case C-9/56, *Meroni v High Authority of the European Coal and Steel Community* [1958] ECLI:EU:C:1958:7.

[8] See section IV.A below.

[9] Eurobarometer Report, *Food Safety in the EU*, April 2019, 45, www.efsa.europa.eu/sites/default/files/corporate_publications/files/Eurobarometer2019_Food-safety-in-the-EU_Full-report.pdf. EFSA commissioned the survey. It should be noted that the questions refer to scientists in general and not to EFSA specifically.

[10] Ibid, 55.

[11] For example, in the case of GMOs, see M Weimer, *Risk Regulation in the Internal Market. Lessons from Agricultural Biotechnology* (Oxford, Oxford University Press, 2019), 115ff.

independence of the scientific assessments on which it is based. The renewal of the marketing authorisation of the pesticide glyphosate has recently challenged EFSA's risk assessment methods (and that of the competent national authorities) and its independence from industry.[12] EFSA's efforts to gain EU citizens' trust have therefore not yet come to an end.

Against this background, this chapter addresses the coessential relationship between expertise and trust in EU food governance from a legal standpoint. In particular, it focuses on how the EU's commitment to securing citizens' trust in its regulatory expertise is reflected and substantiated in the legal framework governing EFSA. How does 'trusted science' look like in EU food governance? In other words, what justifications are put forward in the GFL for citizens to trust EU regulatory expertise?

The following paragraphs address these questions by complementing a conceptual approach with legal analysis: given the institutional nature of regulatory expertise, law plays a prominent role in formalising such justifications and legal analysis therefore provides a relevant complement to conceptual approaches to public trust in expertise. The chapter advances two main claims: first, that the normative expectations as to the role regulatory expertise is to play in a given regulatory setting shape the meaning of 'trusted science'; secondly, that there should be an alignment between such normative expectations and trust-enhancing legal arrangements, as well as between expectations and practices of expert governance. It ultimately shows that EU food governance has suffered from a misalignment in both respects. Recent developments might have the potential to realign normative expectations, legal arrangements, and institutional practices based on a more iterative understanding of the role of regulatory experts in risk regulation.

Section II articulates a theoretical framework for public trust in regulatory expertise, drawing on debates in Science and Technology Studies (STS), philosophy of science, and democratic theory. It locates the relationship between citizens and regulatory experts within three coordinates: the nature of the authority exerted by regulatory expertise; the mechanism of delegation in place between citizens and experts; the role of law as a medium for citizens' trust in regulatory expertise. Section III considers EFSA's tasks, organisation and functioning, as set out in the GFL and analyses the trust-enhancing mechanisms embedded therein. It starts by contextualising the GFL and EFSA within the risk analysis model, based on risk assessment, management, and communication. It shows that, depending on how one understands the relationship between risk assessment and risk management, ie between the respective roles of science and politics, trust in regulatory expertise rests on purely epistemic grounds, or rather on a combination of epistemic

[12] A Arcuri and YH Hendlin (eds) (2020) 'Introduction to the Symposium on the Science and Politics of Glyphosate', *European Journal of Risk Regulation*, 11(3), 411–21; M Morvillo, 'From contestation to accountability in EU pesticides regulation? The case of glyphosate' in A Arcuri, F Coman Kund (eds) *Technocracy and the Law: Accountability, Governance and Expertise*, (London/New York, Routledge, 2021).

and political grounds. It analyses the trust-enhancing mechanisms in the GFL and shows that, although the former were largely prominent in their original formulation, both were present. Section IV juxtaposes such trust-enhancing legal arrangements and EFSA's practices. It argues that, while EFSA's legislative framework is mainly anchored in an understanding of the relationship between politics and expertise along the lines of separation, its practices have gradually blurred such dichotomy and sought to ground public trust in a more iterative understanding of the relationship between science and politics. The 2019 reform of the GFL can also be read in the context of these developments.[13] Section V concludes.

II. 'Knowing for the Many': Regulatory Expertise, Delegation, and Trust

How to understand the relationship between citizens and regulatory experts? What role does trust play in it, and upon what conditions is it premised? Building on debates and concepts developed in STS, philosophy of science, and democratic theory, the following paragraphs seek to set out three coordinates within which to inscribe the relationship between citizens and regulatory experts and the role of trust therein. They represent the theoretical backbone which will guide the analysis and assessment of the GFL in sections III and IV and relate to three key aspects of the triad (experts, citizens, trust) under consideration: the peculiarities of regulatory expertise as trustee; epistemic delegation as an act of trust; the conditions for trust in regulatory expertise.

A. Regulatory Expertise's Dual Authority

EFSA, as independent scientific agencies generally, is an embodiment of regulatory expertise (or regulatory science).[14] In the context of STS literature, regulatory expertise is defined in opposition to research science: while the latter is 'ordered around the extension of knowledge and competence without any [or with limited] regard for practical application',[15] regulatory science is more practice-oriented, its purpose being the production of 'techniques, processes and artifacts that further the task of policy development'.[16] Accordingly, the respective contexts in which the two operate are crucially different. Research science is carried out in a condition

[13] Regulation (EU) 2019/1381 of the European Parliament and the Council of 20 June 2019 on the transparency and sustainability of the EU risk assessment in the food chain, OJ L 231, 6.9.2019, 1.

[14] S Jasanoff, *The Fifth Branch. Science Advisors as Policymakers* (Cambridge MA, Harvard University Press, 1990) 76ff.

[15] B Barnes, D Edge, *Science in Context* (Milton Keynes, Open University Press, 1982) 147, quoted by Jasanoff, *The Fifth Branch*, 76.

[16] Jasanoff, *The Fifth Branch*, 76. From the point of view of the content, the author sees regulatory science as the outcome of three different types of scientific activity: knowledge production, synthesis and prediction (77).

of relative insulation; regulatory science, on the other hand, is produced and validated in regulatory contexts which normally see the involvement of government, industry, and civil society and is, at least in principle, exposed to both scientific and non-scientific (political, judicial) accountability fora.[17]

Regulatory expertise's peculiar collocation, at the crossroads of science and policy, opens up different options as to what its legitimate role should be in a given regulatory context. A more classical, positivistic understanding, premised on the possibility to neatly separate facts and values, and science and politics, sees expertise as a source of uncontested knowledge, exerting epistemic authority by 'speaking truth to power'.[18] Other post-positivistic accounts, premised on the value-laden nature of scientific knowledge and the impossibility of disentangling facts and values,[19] see regulatory expertise as rather operating at the junction of epistemic and political authority.[20] According to both accounts, experts are endowed with the epistemic authority to validate knowledge claims; in addition, the latter sees regulatory experts as also exerting a form of political authority to make such knowledge claims relevant for collective decision-making.[21] Whether one opts for one or the other account has significant consequences on regulatory expertise's relationship with citizens.

B. Epistemic Delegation as an Act of Trust

The relationship between citizens and regulatory experts has been understood as one of epistemic delegation, whereby the delegated object is epistemic power, ie 'the power of a handful of expert actors in a governing institution to *know* for the many'.[22]

[17] Jasanoff, *The Fifth Branch*, 78. In practice, however, regulatory expertise poses serious accountability challenges. See eg, P Weingart, S Maasen (eds) *Democratization of Expertise? Exploring Novel Forms of Scientific Advice in Political Decision-Making* (Dordrecht, Springer, 2005).

[18] See above all RK Merton, 'Science and the Social Order" (1938), in idem, *The Sociology of Science. Theoretical and Empirical Investigations* (Chicago/London, The University of Chicago Press, 1973), 254.

[19] See in particular the Jasanoff's co-production paradigm, S Jasanoff, *The Idiom of Co-Production*, in idem (ed), *States of Knowledge: The Co-Production of Science and Social Order* (London, Routledge, 2004) 2–3, according to which 'the ways in which we know and represent the world (both nature and society) are inseparable from the ways in which we choose to live in it. Knowledge and its material embodiments are at once products of social work and constitutive of forms of social life; society cannot function without knowledge any more than knowledge can exist without appropriate social supports'.

[20] H Strassheim 'Behavioural Expertise and Regulatory Power in Europe' in Weimer, De Ruijter (eds) *Regulating Risks*, 157; see also S Smismans 'Constitutionalising expertise', 186.

[21] The political nature of regulatory expertise' authority is here understood broadly. Namely, it does not entail party politics or commitment to majoritarianism but rather a broader commitment to pursuing the public interest. Such commitment goes hand in hand with the possibility of different views as to what the public interest is also in scientific bodies, ie with the acknowledgement of the value-laden nature of regulatory science. See D Chalmers '"Food for Thought": Reconciling European Risks and Traditional Ways of Life' (2003) 66:4 *Modern Law Review*, 532, 544, in particular fn 72.

[22] S Jasanoff 'Constitutions of Modernity: Science, Risk and Governable Subjects' in M Weimer, A De Ruijter (eds) *Regulating Risks in the European Union: The Co-production of Expert and Executive Power* (Hart Publishing, Oxford, 2017), 25.

If we understand trust as involving 'a judgment, however implicit, to accept vulnerability to the potential ill will of others by granting them discretionary power over some good',[23] epistemic delegation can itself be conceptualised as an act of trust. Both its constitutive elements – vulnerability and its acceptance – are, in fact, present in epistemic delegation. First, delegating the power to know comes with – and from – the acknowledgement of ignorance. From a trust perspective, the information asymmetries between experts and laymen constitute a form of (epistemic) vulnerability. Secondly, epistemic delegation results from a positive judgment as to the acceptance of such vulnerability. It ultimately is a choice concerning the trade-off between the risk of potential harm descending from ignorance, on the one hand, and the benefits of cooperation (or division of labour), on the other.[24]

The existence and implications of epistemic asymmetries, and thus of a form of vulnerability, between citizens and regulatory experts is relatively uncontroversial.[25] The positive judgment as to their acceptance, hence as to the possibility of epistemic delegation, are, on the other hand, often implicit. Identifying the conditions for such positive judgment is crucial in order to understand the grounds on which regulatory expertise can legitimately advance claims to citizens' trust. It is important to keep in mind that the conditions of a positive trust judgment are shaped by the nature of the delegated power. In particular, whether one sees regulatory expertise as exerting solely epistemic authority or rather as also endowed with a degree of political authority has important implications on the object – and hence on the conditions – of delegation. In the former case, the object of delegation is purely epistemic (ie the power to know); it is, therefore, submitted that a positive trust judgment would be based on the fulfilment of purely epistemic conditions. In the latter, the power to know comes with political implications, in so far as citizens delegate experts to know on their behalf and deploy such knowledge in the public interest. Therefore, it is proposed that for citizens to trust regulatory expertise in its dual capacity, they should be given both epistemic and political warrants to trust and, hence, for epistemic delegation to operate.

[23] ME Warren 'Introduction' in ME Warren (ed) *Democracy and Trust* (Cambridge, Cambridge University Press, 1999) 1; for a definition of trust, see also A Baier 'Trust and antitrust' (1986) 96 *Ethics*, 231, 235; K Powys Whyte, RP Crease 'Trust, expertise, and the philosophy of science' (2010) 177:3 *Synthese*, 411, 412.

[24] Warren, 'Introduction', 1.

[25] See eg, Powys Whyte, Crease, 'Trust, Expertise', 413; see also DR De Nicola, *Understanding ignorance. The surprising impact of what we don't know* (Cambridge MA, MIT Press, 2017) 205. Epistemic vulnerability in a democratic system triggers also other sets of concerns, which, however fall beyond the scope of the present contribution: see T Christiano, 'Rational deliberation among experts and citizens' in J Parkinson, J Mansbridge (eds) *Deliberative Systems: Deliberative Democracy at the Large Scale* (Cambridge, Cambridge University Press, 2012) 27ff; C Holst, A Molander, 'Responding to crises – democratic and epistemic worries about expertise' in M Riddervold, J Trondal, A Newsome (eds), *The Palgrave Handbook of EU Crises*, Basingstoke/New York, Palgrave, 2020).

C. Trust in Regulatory Expertise as Institutional and Legally Mediated

The conditions for citizens' trust in regulatory experts are characterised by a certain degree of formalisation. According to Warren's typology of trust relationships in democratic systems,[26] trust in experts is vertical (as opposed to horizontal) in so far as it concerns a relationship between individuals and institutions rather than between individuals.[27] More specifically, it is 'borrowed by institutions that select, certify and regulate performance, and provide motivation for trustworthiness (eg, oversee conflict of interests and negligence)'.[28] The institutional (as opposed to interpersonal) nature of the warrant means that 'judgments on trust depend more upon judgments on the robustness of institutional norms than upon judgments on individuals within institutional roles'.[29] By 'guarantee[ing] transactions and creat[ing] the effects of trust through third party enforcement, e.g. the working of the law',[30] institutional norms, operate as a medium of trust.

Due to the institutional nature of the trust relationship between experts and citizens, law, and in particular, the legal norms governing the structure and functioning of regulatory scientific bodies, can therefore operate as a medium for citizens' trust in a variety of ways. First, it is law that practically frames the channels – and establishes the boundaries – through which expert knowledge participates and informs regulatory processes. Who the experts are, on what issues they ought to be consulted, whether their opinion is binding or not – all key aspects of epistemic delegation – are enshrined in legislation. From this angle, science-based legislation has been correctly depicted as 'legally-embedded-science-based-law'.[31] Secondly, when the law designs how experts are appointed, consulted and involved in regulatory decision-making, it is not operating in a vacuum. By articulating the tasks, organisation, and functioning of regulatory scientific bodies, legal rules make explicit the normative idea – and the normative expectation – placed upon them.[32] Analysing legal rules can, therefore, shed light on how the role of regulatory experts is conceived of in a given institutional context and on how such expectations as to their role are articulated into conditions for citizens to reach a positive judgment as to regulatory expertise' trustworthiness.

[26] ME Warren, 'What kinds of trust does a democracy need? Trust from the perspective of democratic theory' in S Zmerli, TWG Van der Meer (eds) *Handbook on Political Trust*, (Cheltenham, Edward Elgar Publishing, 2017) 34ff.

[27] Ibid.

[28] Ibid.

[29] ME Warren, 'Conclusion' in ME Warren (ed) *Democracy and Trust*, 349.

[30] Ibid.

[31] A Arcuri, 'Glyphosate' in J Hohmann, D Joyce (eds), *International Law's Objects* (Oxford, Oxford University Press, 2018) 11.

[32] Warren 'Conclusion" 350.

i. Epistemic Warrants for Regulatory Expertise

What do such conditions look like? The epistemic dimension of trust in experts, including its conditions, is a relatively well-explored topic in philosophy of science. According to Goldman, an expert in a given domain is 'someone who possesses an extensive fund of knowledge [...] and a set of skills or methods for apt and successful deployment of this knowledge to new questions in the domain'.[33] It is this combination of knowledge and skills that rationally justifies novices' (who do not possess either of the two) trust towards experts in their domain of competence.[34] In particular, Goldman puts forward five sources laymen might resort to in order to rationally ground their trust in experts:

a) arguments presented by the contending experts to support their own views and critique their rivals' views;
b) agreement from additional putative experts on one side or other of the subject in question;
c) appraisal by 'meta-experts' of the experts' expertise (including appraisals reflected in formal credentials earned by the experts);
d) evidence of the experts' interests and biases vis-à-vis the question at issue;
e) evidence of the experts' past 'track records'.[35]

In other words, the conditions for laymen to rationally trust experts entail *openness* about the arguments and disagreements (a and b), *excellence* (c and e) and *independence* (d) of the individual experts.

ii. Political Warrants for Regulatory Expertise

These conditions grounding a rational justification for laymen to trust experts have been conceived in the context of debates concerned with the epistemic dimension of the relationship between laymen and experts. What then about possible conditions capable of accounting also for regulatory expertise's political dimension? Warren's work can once again provide useful insight on this point. In a democratic system, it is argued, citizens should be given 'some reason – a warrant – for thinking that [her] interests are convergent with the trustee's interests'.[36]

[33] AI Goldman, 'Experts: Which ones should you trust?', (2001) 1 *Philosophy and Phenomenological Research*, 85, 92.

[34] Ibid, 86. See also R Foley, 'Egoism in epistemology', in F Schmitt (ed), *Socializing Epistemology. The Social Dimension of Knowledge* (Lanham MD, Rowman & Littlefield Publishers, 1994), 53; T Burge, 'Content preservation', (1993) 102:4 *Philosophical Review*, 457. See, however, J Hardwig, 'The role of trust in knowledge' (1991) 88 *Journal of Philosophy*, 693, according to whom laymen's trust in experts is necessarily blind.

[35] Goldman, 'Experts', 93.

[36] Warren, 'What kinds of trust', 40. Warren's account is much more sophisticated and premised on the idea that 'democracies ... build on good divisions of labour between participation and trust. Trust covers the many areas of collective attachment where interests converge, enabling citizens to direct their scarce participatory resources toward political arenas in which interests conflict' (Ibid, 46). Even where scientific expertise becomes politicised, ie when diverging interests emerge, trust can be ensured through institutional design (Ibid, 48).

Political warrants for citizens to trust regulatory experts should, therefore, be structured around the idea of ensuring that citizens' interests are convergent with those of regulatory experts or, in other words, that regulatory experts operate in the public interest. They could, eg, aim at ensuring that a plurality of expert and lay voices are heard, that normative goals (eg, high level of health protection, sustainability) are embedded in the workings of regulatory expert bodies, and that the public is given quantitatively and qualitatively adequate information (eg, through high transparency and communication standards) so to understand the issues at stake and eventually hold experts accountable.

Building on these two types of warrants – epistemic and political – the next section aims to provide a trust-oriented reading of the institutional mechanisms put in place in the context of the General Food Law to ground citizens' trust in EFSA.[37] On what normative idea of regulatory expertise are they premised? Do they account for both its political and epistemic dimension or solely for the latter? It is submitted that this largely depends on broader normative understandings of the relationship between science and politics in risk regulation.

III. The Features of 'Trusted Science' in EU Food Governance: A Trust-Based Analysis of the 2002 GFL

A. The GFL and the Risk Analysis Model

The GFL represents the framework legislation in the field of EU food governance. While complemented by other sectoral legislative acts, it sets out the 'vision' and the institutional structure upon which the policy area is premised. The genesis of the GFL is rooted in the food crises that occurred in the 1990s, representing an attempt to restore public trust in the EU's ability to effectively regulate food-related risks. In particular, the GFL reacted to the allegations moved against the Commission of 'not respecting scientific standards and being biased by the interests of Member States'.[38] The reform process, which intersected with the adoption of the 2001 White Paper on Governance,[39] culminated in the adoption of the GFL in 2002. It aimed to address the weaknesses shown by the institutional framework for food governance and restore citizen's trust in EU institutions' capacity to assess and manage food-related risks in the public interest. Besides developing a unitary framework for food governance, the GFL introduced two main innovations: in

[37] The analysis focuses exclusively on the GFL, in its quality of framework legislation, enshrining the objectives and principles of EU food governance, and is, therefore, non-exhaustive. Sectoral legislation develops the framework established by GFL further, setting out other specific procedures. See eg, Regulation (EC) No 1107/2009 of the European Parliament and of the Council of 21 October 2009 concerning the placing of plant protection products on the market and repealing Council Directives 79/117/EEC and 91/414/EEC, OJ L 309, 24.11.2009, 1–50.

[38] S Smismans, 'Constitutionalising expertise' 187.

[39] EC Commission, *White Paper on European Governance*, COM (2001) 428.

institutional terms, the establishment of EFSA;[40] in normative terms, it is the first legislative entrenchment at the EU level of the risk analysis model (and, within its framework, of the precautionary principle).[41] Before considering the trust-enhancing arrangements embedded in the GFL, it is necessary to clarify what normative understanding of the role of regulatory expertise, ie what normative expectations, underpins the act.

A good starting point in this endeavour is the risk analysis model, which provides the fundamental framework within which regulatory experts' role can be inscribed. The risk analysis model essentially aims at providing guidance and structure to decision-makers engaged in processes of risk regulation. It was first put forward by the US National Research Council in 1983 in the context of chemicals regulation,[42] and has been since then exported to other policy fields and institutional settings, including the EU. Its current formulation in the GFL comprises three distinct elements: risk assessment, risk management, and risk communication. Risk assessment represents the scientific component of risk regulation and is defined as the 'scientifically based process' consisting of identifying and characterising hazards, exposure assessment and risk characterisation.[43] It is 'based on the available scientific evidence and undertaken in an independent, objective, and transparent manner'.[44] Risk management, on the other hand, is risk regulation's political facet. It consists of the process of 'weighing policy alternatives in consultation with interested parties'; it is informed by risk assessment but can take into consideration 'other legitimate factors' including the precautionary principle, and, if needed, lead to the adoption of protective measures.[45] Risk communication consists of the 'interactive exchange of information and opinions throughout the risk analysis process … including the explanation of risk assessment findings and the basis of risk management decisions'.[46] In institutional terms, risk assessment is entrusted to EFSA, while risk management falls under the remit of the Commission.[47] Risk communication permeates the whole process, and expressly foresees the participation, besides risk assessors and risk managers, of other interested parties, including consumers, businesses and the academic community.[48]

The relationship between risk assessment and risk management has been – and still is – one of the most debated aspects of the risk analysis model. This comes

[40] Art 22ff GFL. All references to legislation refer to the GFL unless otherwise specified.

[41] Arte 6(1). The principle of risk analysis was already reflected in Commission of the European Communities, *Communication from the Commission on the Precautionary Principle* COM(2000) 1, 18. EU Courts have also contributed to embedding the risk analysis model into EU risk regulation and to defining the respective roles of science and politics therein: see Case T-13/99 *Pfizer Animal Health SA v Council of the European Union*, 11 September 2002, para 149ff. See also Alemanno A (2008), 'The Shaping of Risk Regulation by Community Court', 18 Jean Monnet Working Paper 2008.

[42] National Research Council, *Risk Assessment in the Federal Government: Managing the Process*, (Washington DC, National Academy Press, 1983).

[43] Art 1(11).

[44] Art 6(2).

[45] Art1(12); Art 6(3).

[46] Art 1(13).

[47] Art 6(3) and 22.

[48] Art 1(13).

as no surprise, as the relationship between the two ultimately reflects ideas and understandings about the respective roles of science and politics in risk regulation. In its original formulation, the process of risk analysis was conceived of as a linear one, entailing 'a clear conceptual distinction between the assessment and the consideration of risk management alternatives', resulting in an institutional and operational separation between assessors and managers.[49] The underlying assumption is that of the already mentioned possibility of a separation between facts and values and the purely scientific nature of risk assessment: here, regulatory experts are entrusted with a purely epistemic task. While more consolidated, this is, however, not the only reading of the risk analysis model.[50] In the US context, in particular, the linear understanding of risk analysis has been gradually replaced by more iterative approaches, which acknowledge the role of context and values in risk assessment, and hence the presence of a political dimension in the tasks entrusted to regulatory expertise.[51] On what understanding of the risk analysis model, and hence of the relationship between science and politics, is the GFL premised? The answer is not entirely clear-cut.

Several elements in the GFL suggest the endorsement of a linear understanding of risk analysis: first, the express characterisation of risk management as a process 'distinct from risk assessment';[52] secondly, the establishment of EFSA itself, as an independent agency in charge of risk assessments, resonates with ideas of functional separation.[53] Furthermore, in carrying out its tasks, EFSA's action is oriented by 'methodological principles', which resonate with Goldmann's grounds for rational trust in expertise: excellence, openness and independence 'in the expression of its own conclusions and orientations'.[54] The GFL has indeed been deemed to represent a case of 'solidification' of the linear distinction between risk assessment and management into a legal framework.[55]

[49] B Delogu, *Risk Analysis and Governance in EU Policy Making and Regulation. An Introductory Guide* (Dordrecht, Springer, 2016) 39.

[50] See the critique by E Fisher, 'Framing Risk Regulation: A Critical Reflection' (2013) 2 *European Journal of Risk Regulation*, 125.

[51] The main steps in this evolution are represented by: National Research Council, *Science and Judgment in Risk Assessment* (Washington DC, National Academy Press, 1994); National Research Council, *Understanding Risk: Informing Decisions in a Democratic Society*, (Washington DC, National Academy Press, 1996); National Research Council, *Science and Decisions: Advancing Risk Assessment*, (Washington DC, National Academies Press, 2009).

[52] Art 1(12).

[53] See Delogu, *Risk Analysis*, 40. EFSA's mission encompasses the provision of 'independent information' and 'scientific advice and scientific and technical support for the Community's legislation and policies in all fields which have a direct or indirect impact on food and feed safety' (Article 22(2)). More specifically, EFSA's tasks can be divided into three groups: provision of scientific advice (both in the form of 'the best possible scientific opinions' and of technical support) to EU institutions and the Member States; promotion of institutional cooperation and harmonisation of risk assessment methodologies, within and beyond the EU; scientific activity proper, through the collection and analysis of scientific and technical data, the commissioning of scientific studies and the characterisation of new and emerging risks.

[54] See Art 23, in particular (a), (j), (k).

[55] Fisher, 'Framing Risk Regulation', 129.

This neat distinction is, however, muddied by other elements in EFSA's legal regime. First, EFSA itself is structured into a duality of political (management board, executive director, advisory forum), and scientific bodies (scientific committee and scientific panels), so that political concerns are built into the very structure of the Agency.[56] Second, the interconnected, as opposed to strictly separated, nature of the three components of risk analysis is also expressly acknowledged.[57] Third, the objective of securing a high level of protection permeates the whole risk analysis process, including risk assessment, suggesting the latter's permeability to normative considerations.[58] Conversely, several provisions stress the importance of EFSA's risk assessments, and in particular of its opinions, for risk management,[59] suggesting an even clearer permeability of risk management to scientific considerations. Article 22(7) GFL, in particular, lists among the agency's tasks that of providing 'scientific opinions which will serve as the scientific basis for the drafting and adoption of Community measures in the fields falling within its missions'. Already in 2003, this had been seen as conferring a strong 'normative authority' on EFSA, its opinions having the potential to 'structure individual and institutional choices on food safety within the European Union'.[60] In this sense, EFSA's authority can reach beyond the 'mere' assessment of scientific evidence and play an important role in shaping the content of the measures adopted on the basis of its opinions. This fundamental ambiguity is reflected in the trust-enhancing mechanisms embedded in EFSA's legal framework, where epistemic grounds for trust largely prevail, as recounted by section III.B, although in co-existence with a number of elements hinting at the political dimension of regulatory expertise, examined in section III.C. Against this background, section III.D considers EFSA's practices and the innovations introduced by the 2019 reform.

B. Epistemic Warrants for Trust in EFSA

Section II.C identified independence, excellence and openness as epistemic conditions for trust in regulatory expertise. Are they present, and if so, under what legal form, in EFSA's legal framework, as set out in 2002? EFSA's independence is guaranteed both from an organisational and functional perspective. As to the former, appointment rules play a key role. EFSA's executive director is an emanation of the management board only;[61] members of the scientific panels are 'independent scientific experts' appointed by the management board upon the proposal of the executive director, and members of the scientific committee include the

[56] According to Chalmers, 'Food for Thought', 538, the management board is EFSA's 'political guardian', while the scientific committee its 'engine room'.
[57] Art 1(10).
[58] Art 22(3).
[59] Art 6(3).
[60] Chalmers, 'Food for Thought', 540.
[61] Art 26(1).

chairs of the scientific panels and additional experts appointed by the management board.[62] Functionally, the scientific committees' members undertake to 'act independently of any external influence'[63] (as opposed to the executive director and members of the management board and advisory forum, who are expected to act 'independently in the public interest');[64] external influence includes that of the Commission: while its representatives may assist the activities of EFSA's scientific component, they 'shall not seek to influence decisions'.[65] All of EFSA's members must disclose any conflict of interests.[66]

Excellence is explicitly ensured only as to the management board, whose members must 'secure the highest standards of competence' and a 'broad range of relevant expertise'.[67] Openness, too, features as one of the functioning principles of EFSA. From an epistemic point of view, openness aims to ensure the scientific quality of expert advice through an open confrontation of arguments.[68] Broad publication requirements are envisaged for EFSA's scientific components, in particular with regard to scientific opinions and, importantly, to minority opinions,[69] and to possible scientific divergences with other bodies.[70] The scientific committee and the scientific panels' meetings, however, are not to be held in public (by contrast with the management board),[71] but both can, when necessary, organise public hearings.[72]

C. Political Warrants for Trust in EFSA

Political conditions for trust in regulatory expertise, as identified in section II.C include hearing a plurality of voices, the embedding of the relevant normative goals in the workings of regulatory-expert bodies, and transparency, here oriented at ensuring public understanding and accountability.

When examining the GFL provisions governing EFSA, it is possible to identify several rules aimed at ensuring such conditions, primarily, but not exclusively, relating to the management board and the executive director. From an organisational point of view, both the management board's composition and appointment procedure reflect its political facet. Its members, which, as mentioned above, must ensure the highest standards of competence, are appointed by a political institution (the Council) in consultation with another political institution

[62] Art 28(3–5).
[63] Art 37(2).
[64] Art 37(1).
[65] Art 38(8).
[66] Art 37(1–3).
[67] Art 25(1).
[68] See section II.C above.
[69] Art 26(7).
[70] Art 30.
[71] Art 38(2).
[72] Art 28(1).

(the European Parliament) from a list drawn up by the Commission,[73] seeking to ensure the broadest possible geographical distribution.[74] Furthermore, four of its fourteen members 'shall have their background in organisations representing consumers and other interests in the food chain'.[75] From a functional perspective, Article 42 mandates the Authority to 'develop effective contacts' with civil society representatives, including consumers, producers and other interested parties. The presence of a plurality of interests in risk assessment is, therefore, acknowledged and regulated. When it comes to scientific panels specifically, an element of plurality might be represented by the already mentioned provision concerning the disclosure of scientific divergences, highlighting the possibility of scientific disagreements and different approaches to risk assessments. Links between EFSA's risk assessment activities and the GFL normative commitments can also be identified. First, as already mentioned, the executive director and the management board and advisory committee members must 'act independently in the public interest'.[76] Second, and more significantly, the GFL contains provisions aimed at ensuring consistency between EFSA's yearly work programmes and the Community's legislative and policy priorities in the area of food safety[77] and at establishing a communication channel between the Authority (and in particular its executive director) and the European Parliament.[78] Third, as to transparency, understood in its public accountability dimension, several provisions aim at ensuring public access to the documents possessed by EFSA,[79] whether through their proactive publication by EFSA itself, including the agendas and minutes of the scientific committee and the scientific panel's meetings,[80] or as a reaction to access to documents requests. Only the management board is, however, required to meet in public. Lastly, a role is to be played by provisions on risk communication: while being drafted broadly, they provide that 'the public and any interested parties are rapidly given objective, reliable and easily accessible information, in particular with regard to the results of [EFSA's] work'.[81]

The picture outlined above presents several misalignments. At first, notwithstanding a general commitment to a strict separation between scientific and political considerations, EFSA's legal framework seems to present both political and epistemic elements to ground public trust in its regulatory expertise. At a closer look, however, it can be observed that most political arrangements relate to the Agency's management board (and to an extent to its executive director), while trust in the scientific committee and panels seems to be grounded primarily, if not exclusively,

[73] Art 25(1).
[74] Art 25(2).
[75] Art 25(1).
[76] Art 37.
[77] Art 25(8).
[78] Art 26(1 and 2) and (h).
[79] Art 41; on access to documents, see Arts 38–39.
[80] Art 38.
[81] Art 40(2).

on epistemic grounds. Therefore, a more nuanced separation between political and epistemic considerations within EFSA seem to be incorporated in the Agency's legal framework. To what extent has this arrangement evolved since EFSA's inception? The following paragraph considers EFSA's practices and the recently approved reform of the GFL, suggesting that some more explicit shifts in the relationship between epistemic and political grounds for trust might be underway.

IV. Evolving Understandings of 'Trusted Science' in EFSA's Practices and Reform

A. EFSA's Normative Authority in Practice

Section III highlighted some misalignments between the normative expectations the GFL places on EFSA and the legal arrangements it puts in place to secure them. The following paragraphs will briefly recount how such arrangements have been operationalised since EFSA's inception, focusing in particular on the 2019 GFL reform. It is submitted that such developments have led to a further blurring of the lines separating EFSA's epistemic and political authority.

Externally, the Commission has, over the years, relied extensively on EFSA's scientific advice. Chalmers' prediction as to the strong normative authority exerted by EFSA's opinions has proved well-founded, to the point that EFSA's role vis-à-vis the Commission has been described as that of a passenger giving instructions to a blind driver.[82] Several factors may have contributed to the actualisation of EFSA's normative potential. European Courts' case-law has established strict requirements for the Commission to depart from EFSA's scientific assessments. In such cases, the Commission must 'provide specific reasons for its findings by comparison with those made in the opinion', which should be 'of a scientific level at least commensurate with that of the opinion in question'.[83] The Commission has, therefore, a strong (judicial) incentive to follow EFSA's opinions. Furthermore, the Commission's willingness to frame its risk management measures in scientific terms has been interpreted as a symptom of the Commission's reluctance to move from classical, 'transmission-belt' models of public administration towards more deliberative approaches.[84] Finally, EFSA itself has been found to frame its findings in prescriptive terms.[85]

[82] EIL Vos, FA Wendler (2006). 'Food Safety Regulation at the EU Level' in EIL Vos, FA Wendler (eds) *Food Safety Regulation in Europe. A Comparative Institutional Analysis* (Antwerpen-Oxford, Intersentia, 2006), 122.

[83] Case T-13/99, *Pfizer Animal Health SA v Council of the European Union* [2002] ECLI:EU:T:2002:209, para 199.

[84] M Weimer, G Pisani 'Expertise as Justification: the Contested Legitimation of the EU "Risk Administration"', in Weimer and De Ruijter, *Regulating Risks*, 191.

[85] Ibid 133.

Internally, EFSA seems to have developed its understanding of 'trusted science' both in its epistemic and political dimensions and to have undertaken significant efforts in order to develop a closer engagement with the public. The analysis of the press releases reporting on the management board meetings suggests a shift from an initial framing of trust mainly in terms of independence and transparency to a more comprehensive picture. In particular, it is possible to observe the development, on the side of EFSA, of more attention to participation, stakeholder involvement, and public engagement. The first approach can be traced back to statements which link public trust in EFSA to its being independent ('Through EFSA's strengthened rules on Declarations of Interests, the Authority will continue to build a system which helps reinforce trust in its high quality scientific work')[86] and to the transparency of its work ('increase trust by continuing to ensure independence and enhance transparency and openness of its scientific work').[87] A more nuanced picture has started emerging in particular since EFSA's 2020 Strategy.[88] Without abandoning independence and transparency as key conditions, EFSA's 2020 Strategy sees trust as a result of societal engagement in risk assessment.[89] It, therefore, stresses the need to 'prioritise public and stakeholder engagement in the process of scientific assessment', through which 'EFSA aims to enable society to contribute more widely to its risk assessment work and thereby to increase trust'.[90] Trust is therefore increasingly linked to both epistemic and political grounds, in particular to the possibility for the public to have its voice heard, also in the Agency's scientific activities.

B. The GFL Reform: Addressing Misalignments?

The GFL has been reformed in April 2019, responding to both the Regulatory Fitness evaluation carried out by the Commission and the 'glyphosate crisis', which challenged the transparency and independence of the EU's agency science. From the point of view of the content, the GFL reform explicitly aims to enhance the transparency and sustainability of risk assessment.[91] In fact, it addresses most of

[86] www.efsa.europa.eu/en/events/event/52nd-management-board-meeting-efsas-management-board.

[87] www.efsa.europa.eu/en/events/event/55th-management-board-meeting-efsa-management-board; see also www.efsa.europa.eu/en/events/event/56th-management-board-meeting-efsa-management-board and www.efsa.europa.eu/en/events/event/59th-management-board-meeting-efsa-board-adopts-work.

[88] EFSA's public engagement efforts do, however, have a longer history, see eg, the establishment, in 2005, of its Consultative Stakeholder Platform.

[89] In the same vein, see also Bernhard Url's, EFSA's executive director, statement: 'Science gains its robustness from being embedded in society, which we aim to achieve at EFSA through our openness and transparency approach. We have to move from truth to trust.' (www.efsa.europa.eu/en/press/news/151014).

[90] www.efsa.europa.eu/en/events/event/68th-management-board-meeting-board-adopts-efsas-strategy. See also EFSA's 2020 strategy, www.efsa.europa.eu/sites/default/files/corporate_publications/files/strategy2020.pdf.

[91] For a more comprehensive appraisal of Regulation 1381/2019, in the light of the authorisation of glyphosate, see M Morvillo, 'Glyphosate effect: has the glyphosate controversy affected the EU's regulatory epistemology?', (2020) 11:3 *European Journal of Risk Regulation*, 422.

the trust-enhancing arrangements and mechanisms originally envisaged by the GFL. In particular, the GFL reform resonates with the internal and external developments mentioned above, in the sense of, at least partially, reconsidering the balance and the distribution between political and epistemic grounds for trust.

Trust featured as a prominent concern in the GFL reform, however, in a partly different declination than it did in its 2002 version. When comparing the trust-related recitals of the 2019 Regulation to those of the 'old' GFL (see section I above), it can be observed how the range of considerations informing the legislator's view of trust – initially conceived in a market-oriented fashion ('the consumer') – has broadened. More emphasis is now placed on the societal dimension of food governance by reference to the 'general public' as the trusting subject. A similar widening of the legislator's understanding of trust concerns its grounds. While transparency and independence remain central, they are now no longer exclusively linked to the quality and the objectivity of EFSA's work, but also to the accountability of risk assessment 'to the Union citizens in a democratic system'.[92] Risk communication and the public's possibility to understand the science underpinning food regulation is also given more prominence.[93] Read in these terms, the reform could be seen as a sign of a shift from an economic to a democratic view of trust in EU food governance.

While the reform has reinforced both epistemic and political grounds for trust, the latter seem to be its main focus. New epistemic warrants include the establishment of a register of the studies commissioned by private applicants,[94] so to ensure that no unfavourable data is withheld by the applicant and to enhance risk assessments' independence, and the establishment of requirements of scientific excellence and independence also for the members of the scientific panels.[95] Political warrants, on the other hand, target risk assessments' inclusiveness and transparency. As to the former, EFSA's management board's composition has been revised, so to include Member States' representatives (in line with the joint approach to agencies' governance)[96] and give more structure to interested parties' representation.[97] Inclusiveness also concerns the Agency's strictly scientific component. The members of EFSA's scientific panels will now be appointed based on Member States' proposals so to ensure, besides excellence and independence, also geographical balance.[98] Additional public consultations are envisaged,[99]

[92] Recital 12.
[93] Recital 3.
[94] Art 1(6) Regulation 1381/2019, inserting Art 32b into the GFL.
[95] Art 28(5a)(d) as amended by Regulation 1381/2019.
[96] Art 1(4) Regulation 1381/2019, amending Art 25 GFL. See the Joint Statement of the European Parliament, the Council of the EU and the European Commission on decentralised agencies, 2012, www.europa.eu/european-union/sites/europaeu/files/docs/body/joint_statement_and_common_approach_2012_en.pdf.
[97] Art 1(4)(b), amending Art 35 GFL.
[98] Art 28(5a)(a)–(c) as amended by Regulation 1381/2019.
[99] Art 1(4) Regulation 1381/2019, inserting Art 32c into the GFL.

so to broaden the evidentiary basis upon which the agency assesses authorisation dossiers. As to transparency, a new transparency regime is introduced, aimed at extending the range of information disclosed by EFSA (also) through a more careful analysis of the confidentiality claims raised by the applicants with regard to the scientific studies submitted in the context of product authorisation applications.[100]

The innovation that deserves a more careful analysis in this context is, however, that concerning risk communication – further developed with regard to risk assessment, enhancing both the plurality of voices heard and transparency. As already noted, the original GFL provisions on communication were relatively open-ended and mainly focused on the accessibility and dissemination of the relevant information. The 2019 Regulation, by contrast, adopts a much more structured approach to risk communication, setting out its goals,[101] principles,[102] and a general implementation plan[103] to be enacted by both risk assessors (EFSA) and risk managers (the Commission). Risk communication is explicitly linked to trust in risk regulation, including both its contents and its processes:[104] in particular, trust can be achieved through 'awareness and understanding of the specific issues under consideration, including cases of divergences in scientific assessments'.[105] In a similar vein, enhanced participation also features among risk communication's goals, both through the involvement of and exchanging information with interested parties (consumers, business, academic community). The guiding principles of risk communication include 'transparency, openness, and responsiveness'[106] and establish that communication should be 'clear and accessible, including to those not directly involved in the process or not having a scientific background'. It is worth noting that the technical complexity of the issues at stake is not seen as representing an obstacle but rather as placing a burden on EFSA to try and bridge the epistemic asymmetry with citizens ('the public').

In a way, the GFL reform could be seen as an attempt to realign trust-enhancing legal arrangements and regulatory expertise's practices. The ambiguities resulting from, on the one hand, the normative ideas regarding the purely epistemic authority exerted by EFSA, and, on the other hand, the presence in the GFL of elements hinting also at a possible political dimension of its authority, have resulted in a misalignment between such normative ideas and the Agency's practices, with EFSA exerting a form of authority that reaches beyond the purely epistemic domain. Faced with a de facto partial metamorphosis of the delegated object (from purely epistemic to dual), the EU legislator could have opted for further tightening the separation between risk assessment and risk management, in accordance with the normative ideas embedded in the GFL. The 2019 legislative innovations, however,

[100] Arts 38(c) and 39(2) as inserted by Regulation 1381/2019.
[101] Art 1(2) Regulation 1381/2019, inserting Art 8a into the GFL.
[102] Ibid, inserting Art 8b into the GFL.
[103] Ibid, inserting Art 8c into the GFL.
[104] Ibid, inserting Art 8a(e) into the GFL.
[105] Ibid, letter a).
[106] Ibid, inserting Art 8b into the GFL.

seem to take a different direction, namely that of a more iterative understanding of the relationship between the two, in particular by enhancing accountability, communication, and participation tools, ie by providing additional political grounds for trust in EFSA.

V. Concluding Remarks

The previous sections have discussed the grounds for trust in regulatory expertise, with particular regard to EFSA, the expert agency operating at the core of EU food governance. The analysis started from the assumption that the reasons grounding citizens' trust in regulatory experts change depending on what are the normative expectations placed on experts in a given context. It then characterised the relationship between citizens and experts in terms of delegation and argued, first, that such delegation is premised on an act of trust, and second, that the conditions for citizens' acceptance of their epistemic vulnerability, and hence their deference to experts, are shaped by the nature of the delegated power. In particular, experts can be delegated a purely epistemic authority (ie the authority to validate knowledge claims) or rather a dual, political and epistemic, one (in so far as the knowledge they validate is the basis for decision-making). Given the institutional nature of the trust relationship in place between citizens and experts, law plays a key role as a medium for trust: it expresses the normative expectations as to the experts' role and articulates the conditions to ensure public trust. Depending on such normative expectations, grounds for trust can account solely for the epistemic dimension of regulatory expertise, or also for its political facet. Ideally, the two should be aligned, ie there should be a correspondence between the normative expectations as to experts' role and the legal mechanisms put in place to ground public trust in them.

Against this framework, the analysis of the GFL has shown that citizens are given a multiplicity of grounds to trust EFSA, accounting for both the epistemic and, especially after the 2019 reform, the political dimension of the Agency's activities. It has, however, also shed light on a fundamental misalignment between the normative expectations the GFL places upon EFSA, the Agency's practices, and the trust-enhancing legal arrangements in place. The former is premised on a linear understanding of the relationship between science and politics, according to which the two should be strictly separated, regulatory expertise exerting a purely epistemic authority. EFSA's practices, and in particular the influence of its opinions on the adoption of risk management measures, on the other hand, have shown a metamorphosis of the delegated object, from a purely epistemic one to one which contains elements of political authority. In this context, the 2019 GFL reform has strengthened the political grounds for trust in EFSA, by providing additional avenues for participation, transparency and communication. However, it has done so without a reassessment of the paradigm according to which normative expectations are set, ie the strict approach to risk analysis, towards more iterative approaches to the interaction between science and politics. It is submitted that such approaches might better reflect the reality of regulatory expertise in EU food governance and provide a more solid premise on which to ground public trust in EFSA. Iterative approaches to risk analysis are not entirely alien to EU risk regulation and have been adopted in other policy areas, namely, chemicals regulation. Here, risk assessments are entrusted to the European Chemical Agency (ECHA), which, among other arrangements, includes a Committee for Socio-Economic Analysis, in charge of assessing the impact of chemicals-related measures on the social and economic level, thus incorporating non-strictly scientific concerns in risk assessments.

It is beyond doubt that the relationship between science and politics is complex and requires a fine balance between dialogue and autonomy. Such complexity is reflected in the relationship between regulatory expertise and citizens. EU food governance, in particular, has long been a policy area characterised by a high degree of controversy, and it will likely remain such. A better alignment between normative expectations as to experts' role, trust-enhancing legal arrangements, and institutional practices could perhaps contribute to grounding citizens' trust in regulatory expertise on a sounder basis.

Acknowledgments:

My research in this field has been supported by a Marie Skłodowska-Curie grant on 'The Constitutional Place of Expertise' (CONPLEX), funded under the European Union Horizon 2020 research and innovation programme (grant agreement No. 748463). I would like to thank Max van Drunen, Teresa Cabrita, and the volume editors for their valuable feedback on previous versions of this chapter. All mistakes, of course, remain mine.

References

Alemanno A (2008) 'The Shaping of Risk Regulation by Community Court' 18 *Jean Monnet Working Paper*.

Arcuri A and Coman-Kund F (eds) (2021) *Technocracy and the Law: Accountability, Governance and Expertise*, London/New York: Routledge.

Arcuri A and Hendlin YH (eds) (2020) 'Introduction to the Symposium on the Science and Politics of Glyphosate', *European Journal of Risk Regulation*, 11(3), 411–21.

Arcuri A, 'Glyphosate' in Hohmann J, Joyce D (eds) (2018), *International Law's Objects* (Oxford, OUP), 234–46.

Baier A, 'Trust and antitrust' (1986) 96 *Ethics*, 231–60.

Barnes B and Edge DO (eds) (1982), *Science in Context* (Cambridge MA, MIT Press).

Burge T, 'Content preservation' (1993), 102:4 *Philosophical review*, 457–89.

Chalmers D (2003), '"Food for Thought": Reconciling European Risks and Traditional Ways of Life' 66:4 *Modern Law Review*, 532–62.

Christiano T (2012), 'Rational deliberation among experts and citizens' in J Parkinson, J Mansbridge (eds) *Deliberative systems: deliberative democracy at the large scale* (Cambridge, CUP), 27–51.

De Nicola DR, (2017) *Understanding ignorance. The surprising impact of what we don't know* (Cambridge MA, MIT Press).

Delogu B (2016), *Risk Analysis and Governance in EU Policy Making and Regulation. An Introductory Guide* (Dordrecht, Springer).

Fisher E (2013), 'Framing Risk Regulation: A Critical Reflection', 2 *European Journal of Risk Regulation*, 125–32.
Foley R (1994), 'Egoism in epistemology', in F Schmitt (ed), *Socializing epistemology. The social dimension of knowledge* (Lanham, MD, Rowman & Littlefield Publishers), 53–74.
Goldman AI, (2001), 'Experts: which ones should you trust?', 1 *Philosophy and Phenomenological Research*, 85–110.
Hardwig J (1991), 'The role of trust in knowledge', 88 *Journal of Philosophy*, 693–708.
Hohmann J, Joyce D (eds) (2018), *International Law's Objects* (Oxford, OUP).
Holst C, Molander A (2021), 'Responding to crises – democratic and epistemic worries about expertise', in Riddervold M, Trondal J, Newsome A (eds), *The Palgrave Handbook of EU Crises* (Basingstoke/New York, Palgrave), 647–65.
Jasanoff S (1990), *The fifth branch. Science advisors as policymakers* (Cambridge MA, Harvard University Press).
Jasanoff S (2004), 'The idiom of co-production', in Jasanoff S (ed), *States of Knowledge: The Co-Production of Science and Social Order* (London, Routledge) 1–12.
Jasanoff S (ed) (2004), *States of Knowledge: The Co-Production of Science and Social Order* (London, Routledge).
Jasanoff S (2017), 'Constitutions of Modernity: Science, Risk and Governable Subjects' in Weimer M, De Ruijter A (eds) *Regulating Risks in the European Union: The Co-production of Expert and Executive Power* (Oxford, Hart Publishing) 19–36.
Merton RK (1938), 'Science and the Social Order', in Merton RK (ed) (1973), *The Sociology of Science. Theoretical and Empirical Investigations* (Chicago/London, The University of Chicago Press), 254–66.
Morvillo M (2020), 'Glyphosate effect: has the glyphosate controversy affected the EU's regulatory epistemology?', 11:3 *European Journal of Risk Regulation*, 422–35.
Morvillo M (2021), 'From contestation to accountability in EU pesticides regulation? The case of glyphosate' in Arcuri A, Coman-Kund F (eds) *Technocracy and the Law: Accountability, Governance and Expertise*, London/New York: Routledge, 196–222.
Parkinson J and Mansbridge J (eds) (2012), *Deliberative systems: deliberative democracy at the large scale* (Cambridge, CUP).
Powys Whyte K and Crease RP (2010), 'Trust, expertise, and the philosophy of science', 177:3 *Synthese*, 411–25.
Priban J (ed) (2016) *Self-constitution of European Society. Beyond EU polities, law and governance* (London/New York, Routledge).
Riddervold M, Trondal J, Newsome A (eds) (2021), *The Palgrave Handbook of EU Crises*, Basingstoke/New York, Palgrave).
Schmitt F (ed) (1994), *Socializing epistemology. The social dimension of knowledge* (Lanham, MD, Rowman & Littlefield Publishers).
Smismans S (2016), 'Constitutionalising expertise in the EU. Anchoring knowledge in democracy', in Priban J (ed) *Self-constitution of European Society. Beyond EU polities, law and governance* (London/New York, Routledge) 183–200.
Strassheim H (2017), 'Behavioural Expertise and Regulatory Power in Europe' in Weimer M, De Ruijter A (eds) *Regulating Risks in the European Union: The Co-production of Expert and Executive Power* (Hart Publishing, Oxford), 143–64.
Vos EIL and Wendler FA (2006), 'Food Safety Regulation at the EU Level' in Vos EIL and Wendler FA (eds) *Food Safety Regulation in Europe. A Comparative Institutional Analysis* (Antwerpen-Oxford, Intersentia), 65–138.
Warren ME (ed) (1999), *Democracy and Trust* (Cambridge, CUP).
Warren ME (2017), 'What kinds of trust does a democracy need? Trust from the perspective of democratic theory' in Zmerli S, Van der Meer TWG (eds) *Handbook on Political Trust* (Cheltenham, Edward Elgar Publishing), 33–52.
Weimer M (2019), *Risk Regulation in the Internal Market. Lessons from Agricultural Biotechnology* (Oxford, OUP).
Weimer M and De Ruijter A (eds) (2017), *Regulating Risks in the European Union: The Co-production of Expert and Executive Power* (Oxford, Hart Publishing).

Weimer M and Pisani G (2017), 'Expertise as Justification: the Contested Legitimation of the EU "Risk Administration"', in Weimer M and De Ruijter A (eds), *Regulating Risks in the European Union: The Co-production of Expert and Executive Power* (Oxford, Hart Publishing), 167–92.
Weingart P and Maasen S (eds) (2005), *Democratization of Expertise? Exploring Novel Forms of Scientific Advice in Political Decision-Making* (Dordrecht, Springer).
Zmerli S and Van der Meer TWG (eds) (2017), *Handbook on Political Trust*, (Cheltenham, Edward Elgar Publishing).

EU Legislation

Regulation (EC) No 178/2002 of the European Parliament and of the Council of 28 January 2002 laying down the general principles and requirements of food law, establishing the European Food Safety Authority and laying down procedures in matters of food safety, OJ [2002] L 31/1–24.
Regulation (EU) 2019/1381 of the European Parliament and of the Council of 20 June 2019 on the transparency and sustainability of the EU risk assessment in the food chain, OJ [2019] L 231/1–28.
Regulation (EC) No 1107/2009 of the European Parliament and of the Council of 21 October 2009 concerning the placing of plant protection products on the market and repealing Council Directives 79/117/EEC and 91/414/EEC, OJ [2009] L 309/1–50.

EU Case Law

Case C-9/56, *Meroni v High Authority of the European Coal and Steel Community*, 13 June 1958, ECLI:EU:C:1958:7.
Case T-13/99, *Pfizer Animal Health SA v Council of the European Union*, 11 September 2002, ECLI:EU:T:2002:209.

Institutional Documents

Commission of the European Communities, *European Governance a White Paper*, COM(2001) 428.
Commission of the European Communities, *Communication from the Commission on the Precautionary Principle* COM(2000) 1.
US National Research Council, *Science and Decisions: Advancing Risk Assessment*, (Washington DC, National Academies Press, 2009).
US National Research Council, *Understanding Risk: Informing Decisions in a Democratic Society*, (Washington DC, National Academy Press, 1996).
US National Research Council, *Science and Judgment in Risk Assessment* (Washington DC, National Academy Press, 1994).
US National Research Council, *Risk Assessment in the Federal Government: Managing the Process*, (Washington DC, National Academy Press, 1983).

Other

Eurobarometer, *Food safety in the EU*, Special Eurobarometer Report, April 2019, www.efsa.europa.eu/sites/default/files/corporate_publications/files/Eurobarometer2019_Food-safety-in-the-EU_Full-report.pdf.

14

On the EU Legal Principle of Mutual Trust

BIRGIT AASA

I. Introduction

Talking about trust is topical. This is also the case in the European Union (EU), and one might say in recent years more so than ever before. This particular trust-talk in the EU is not only empirical – ie, the quantitatively measured European citizens' trust towards the EU project at large.[1] The intensified talk about trust is legal in its nature, encircling the EU's legal principle of mutual trust.[2]

Besides its predominant economic and political dimensions, the EU is also a constitutional project[3] comprising different organisational principles[4] that structure its functioning. One recent addition to this prominent set of principles that regulate the most basic functioning of the EU as a polity is the principle of mutual trust. This principle is nowhere to be found in the Treaties that constitute the 'constitutional charter'[5] of the EU. It has instead been created and developed in

[1] Although statistically, citizens seem to be trusting the European project more now than in the past few years: the 2019 Eurobarometer shows the highest levels of citizens trust in the EU since 2014, being even higher than their trust in national governments. See: European Commission 05.08.2019 press release 'Spring 2019 Standard Eurobarometer: Europeans upbeat about the state of the European Union – best results in 5 years', https://europa.eu/rapid/press-release_IP-19-4969_en.htm.

[2] From some of the recent contributions, see: Koen Lenaerts, 'La Vie Après l'avis: Exploring the Principle of Mutual (yet Not Blind) Trust' (2017) 54 *Common Market Law Review* 805; Michael Schwarz, 'Let's Talk about Trust, Baby! Theorizing Trust and Mutual Recognition in the EU's Area of Freedom, Security and Justice' (2018) 24 *European Law Journal* 124; Cecilia Rizcallah, 'The Challenges to Trust-Based Governance in the European Union: Assessing the Use of Mutual Trust as a Driver of EU Integration' (2019) 25 *European Law Journal* 37; Ermioni Xanthopoulou, 'Mutual Trust and Rights in EU Criminal and Asylum Law: Three Phases of Evolution and the Uncharted Territory beyond Blind Trust' (2018) 55 *Common Market Law Review* 480.

[3] On the discussions on this and whether and why it makes sense to talk about the EU in constitutional terms there is abundant literature, see eg: Joseph Weiler, *The Constitution of Europe: 'Do the New Clothes Have an Emperor?' and Other Essays on European Integration* (Cambridge University Press, 1999); Kaarlo Tuori, *European Constitutionalism* (Cambridge University Press, 2015); Allan Rosas and Lorna Armati, *EU Constitutional Law: An Introduction*, 3rd edn (Oxford, Hart Publishing, 2018); P Eleftheriadis, 'The Idea of a European Constitution' (2005) 27 *Oxford Journal of Legal Studies* 1.

[4] These are what Marise Cremona calls structural principles – see Marise Cremona, *Structural Principles in EU External Relations Law* (Hart Publishing, 2018).

[5] Case 294/83, *Les Verts – Parti Ecologiste v European Parliament* [1986] ECR 1339, para 23.

the case law of the Court of Justice of the European Union (CJEU). In essence, the principle requires that EU Member States' courts and authorities should not second guess and control each other's decisions on their substance. In the CJEU's own words:

> The principle of mutual trust requires that all EU Member States, save in exceptional circumstances, have to consider all the other EU Member States to be complying with EU law and particularly with fundamental rights recognised by EU law.[6]

The principle of mutual trust has become fashionable, used by the CJEU in an increasing number of cases and expanding contexts, labelled at the same time by academics as both a potential cause and a quick fix for many current underlying problems the EU is facing: be it recent rule of law backsliding,[7] the state of fundamental rights in Europe,[8] Brexit,[9] judicial independence,[10] financial cooperation in the Banking Union,[11] to name a few.

But what about trust? Should a concept such as trust even have a legal and perhaps even a constitutional footing in the EU legal system? The aim of this chapter is to examine how the EU legal principle of mutual trust and the general concept of trust relate to each other. In recent CJEU case law the principle has acquired a clear legal and enforceable character as it is imposed by the CJEU and brings about direct legal obligations on its addressees (usually Member States and their authorities). The examination of trust in mutual trust rehearses a general account of trust and unpacks the CJEU's conception of mutual trust. One point of focus will be the question of how the idea of mutual trust plays out in practice in one recent CJEU judgment, *Liberato*,[12] which concerns judicial cooperation in civil justice matters – a policy area which is often overlooked when talking about the relevance of the principle of mutual trust in judicial practice.[13] The case unveils a paradox about how mutual trust operates as a presumption of compliance in cases of actual non-compliance. This paradox is particularly concerning when assessed through a conceptual analysis of trust, as it fundamentally undermines how trust as a concept functions. It also calls into question the role of the judiciary

[6] Opinion 2/13 [2014] ECLI:EU:C:2014:2454, para 191.

[7] Ernst Hirsch Ballin, 'Mutual Trust. The Virtue of Reciprocity – Strengthening the Acceptance of the Rule of Law through Peer Review' in Carlos Closa, Dimitry Kochenov and Joseph HH Weiler (eds), *Reinforcing rule of law oversight in the European Union* (Cambridge University Press, 2014).

[8] Luc Danwitz, 'In Rights We Trust: The ECtHR's judgment in Romeo Castaño v. Belgium and the relationship between the ECHR and the principle of mutual trust in EU law', VerfBlog, 2019/8/21, https://verfassungsblog.de/in-rights-we-trust/.

[9] Joseph HH Weiler, Daniel Sarmiento; Jonathan Faull, 'An Offer the EU and UK Cannot Refuse: A Proposal on How to Avoid a No-Deal Brexit', VerfBlog, 2019/8/22, https://verfassungsblog.de/an-offer-the-eu-and-uk-cannot-refuse/.

[10] Petra Bárd, Wouter van Ballegooij, 'Judicial Independence as a Precondition for Mutual Trust', VerfBlog, 2018/4/10, https://verfassungsblog.de/judicial-independence-as-a-precondition-for-mutual-trust/.

[11] Elke König, 'Closer International Cooperation as the Basis for Mutual Trust', Single Resolution Board news release on Eurofi article, 2020/04/24, https://srb.europa.eu/en/node/971.

[12] Case C-386/17 *Stefano Liberato v Luminita Luisa Grigorescu* [2019] ECLI:EU:C:2019:24.

[13] See on that also from E Storskrubb who is filling the gap: Eva Storskrubb, 'Mutual Trust and the Dark Horse of Civil Justice' (2018) 20 *Cambridge Yearbook of European Legal Studies* 179.

in controlling compliance with the law and in creating systemic trust in society. Should it even be a role of the judiciary? A Luhmannian account of trust shows how controls and especially judicial controls and accountability suggests it is. The chapter will show how a sharper concept of trust can elevate and illuminate the analytical assessments of lawyers about the principle of mutual trust and reveal its benefits and pitfalls for genuine trust-building in the EU.

II. Starting with Trust

To assess the principle of mutual trust through the lens of trust, we need a clear understanding of the meaning of 'trust'. It is difficult to pin down. That is because trust penetrates diverse social realities, relationships, and disciplines. Paul Bauer, Chiara Destri and Sergio Lo Iacono deal with different accounts of trust in their contributions to this volume. There is an identifiable conceptual core of trust that different theorists from different fields have arrived at. I will present some of the main accounts of trust from various sociological perspectives, which are well equipped to inform the understanding of lawyers in analysing the EU constitutional principle of mutual trust.

Trust is most commonly conceptualised as a three-place relation where trustor A trusts trustee B in doing X.[14] Thus it is relational and object or domain specific.[15] Trust has different conceptual components. It is often categorised as an 'attitude',[16] a 'psychological state'[17] of the trustor. This attitude is manifested in risky, trusting behaviour. As trust involves risks of betrayal and unmet trust for the trustor, trust as an attitude incorporates a 'willingness' to accept such vulnerability to default or betrayal.[18] K Jones has argued that besides the cognitive and behavioural components, there is also an affective dimension of trust.[19] Philosopher Annette Baier has combined all of these elements and argued that trust challenges the usual division of mental phenomena into cognitive, affective, and volitional being all of these: 'it is based on what we believe about another person or agency, it requires that we feel

[14] Russell Hardin, *Trust and Trustworthiness* (Russell Sage Foundation, 2002) 9; Eric M Uslaner, *The Oxford Handbook of Social and Political Trust* (Oxford University Press, 2018) 6.

[15] Although there are also accounts of a more thick trust-relationship 'A trusts B' full-stop in entirety, not conditioning it to a particular aim, task, context or competence, see eg: Jacopo Domenicucci and Richard Holton, 'Trust as a Two-Place Relation' in Paul Faulkner and Thomas Simpson (eds), *The Philosophy of Trust* (Oxford University Press, 2017).

[16] Carolyn McLeod, 'Trust', *The Stanford Encyclopedia of Philosophy* (Fall 2015 Edition), Edward N Zalta (ed), https://plato.stanford.edu/archives/fall2015/entries/trust/.

[17] Guido Möllering, *Trust: Reason, Routine, Reflexivity* (Elsevier, 2006) 7; Denise M Rousseau and others, 'Not So Different After All: A Cross-Discipline View Of Trust' (1998) 23 *Academy of Management Review* 393, 395.

[18] Roger C Mayer and James H Davis, 'An Integrative Model of Organizational Trust' (1995) 20 *Academy of Management Review* 709, 712; Annette Baier, 'Trust and Antitrust' (1986) 96 *Ethics* 231, 236.

[19] Karen Jones, 'Trust as an Affective Attitude' (1996) 107 *Ethics* 4.

safe in their hands, and it usually involves a voluntary act of entrusting, or placing trust.'[20] So trust as a concept comprises cognition (reason), affect (emotion) and the act of placing trust and all three are needed for a complete account of the unitary phenomenon of trust as a human social experience to exist.[21] Emotions can guide or be reasons for actions and the act of placing trust or entrusting can be manifested in a plurality of behaviours or alterations of reality. Without the act of placing trust, the inherent risks entrenched in trust would not materialise and trust would remain hypothetical and inoperative.

Niklas Luhmann was one of the first sociologists to draw up a comprehensive and sophisticated social theory of trust explaining trust from the perspective of its social functions.[22] For Luhmann, trust functions to provide a basis for dealing socially and psychologically with uncertain, complex, and often threatening future possibilities.[23] He argues that the ultimate function of trust is the reduction of social complexity, alongside other mechanisms (functional equivalents) such as law and formal organisation which also serve to reduce the likelihood of a future marked by uncertainty and unpredictability.[24] These functional equivalents differ qualitatively from trust as the latter is in its essence a psychological tolerance of uncertainty whereas law and organisation bring about mastery over events and where such mastery can be assured, trust is no longer necessary.[25] According to Luhmann trust reduces social complexity by going beyond available information by replacing missing information with an internally (psychologically) guaranteed security.[26] Trust makes mental shortcuts to formulate judgments, which give rise to normative expectations of others' behaviour – that is, beliefs about how others ought to behave – and allows for action and cooperation that would not have been possible without it because of the missing information.

Another sociologist, Diego Gambetta, has defined trust in a similar vein as a particular level of the subjective probability with which an agent assesses that another agent or group of agents will perform a particular action, both before he can monitor such action (or independently of his capacity ever to be able to monitor it) and in the context in which it affects his own action.[27] According to Gambetta, when we say we trust someone, or that someone is trustworthy, we implicitly mean that the probability that he will perform an action that is beneficial or at least not detrimental to us is high for us to consider engaging in some form of cooperation with him.[28] It is important to distinguish here between probabilistic reasoning and

[20] Annette Baier, 'What is Trust?' in David Archard and others (eds), *Reading Onora O'Neill* (Routledge, 2013) 177; Annette Baier, *Moral Prejudices: Essays on Ethics* (Harvard University Press, 1994) 132.

[21] J David Lewis and Andrew Weigert, 'Trust as a Social Reality' (1985) 63 *Social Forces* 20, 971–72.

[22] Niklas Luhmann, *Trust and Power* (Wiley, 1979).

[23] ibid 13.

[24] ibid 8, 93.

[25] ibid 15.

[26] ibid 93.

[27] Diego Gambetta (ed), *Trust: Making and Breaking Cooperative Relations* (Basil Blackwell, 1988) 217.

[28] ibid.

the attitude of trust as the former lacks the emotional-affective facets of trust as an attitude and might remove the riskiness of trust altogether when one has a determined probabilistic conviction that the trustee will respond to trust then it might again be another phenomenon, such as mental certainty or confidence. Thus, the probability cannot lead to certainty to maintain the risk of trusting. Gambetta's observations are valuable, as he builds on the time and risk parameters developed by Luhmann and adds to them the notion of control (or rather the impossibility of it) and the quality of the expected behaviour: the optimistic expectation of the not harmful character of the behaviour of others. Both Luhmann and Gambetta tie trust to a situation of risk and vulnerability in a context of irreducible contingency of possible futures, and especially the unpredictability of the future actions of other actors.

But can we have cross-disciplinary agreement on what counts as trust? In this chapter I rely, besides Gambetta, on the following definition of trust:

> Trust is the willingness of a party to be vulnerable to the actions of another party based on the expectation that the other will perform a particular action important to the trustor, irrespective of the ability to monitor or control the other part.[29]

It is a much-cited study on interdisciplinary understandings of trust, and it falls along the lines of Gambetta's conception of trust, which is among the most comprehensive and informative accounts of trust for lawyers, especially in assessing the principle of mutual trust. It is precise and yet at the same time abstract enough to be fruitfully deployed across disciplines and contexts. It allows broad societal usage and go beyond the narrower and morally loaded philosophers' accounts of interpersonal trust.

III. The Principle of Mutual Trust in EU Law

Trust has become a household term also in the EU under the name of the principle of mutual trust. If one takes the definition of trust as a willingness of a party to be vulnerable to the acts of another party important to the trustor without available monitoring or controls, then the principle of mutual trust as a compliance presumption seems something entirely different.

The principle of mutual trust is not completely new in EU law. It was created and used by the CJEU in the early days of internal market integration. In that context, the principle required that Member States should have mutual trust in the product checks and inspections carried out in their respective territories.[30]

[29] Mayer and Davis (n 18) 712.

[30] See eg: Case 46/76 *W. J. G. Bauhuis v The Netherlands State* [1977] ECLI:EU:C:1977:6, para 38, Case C-11/95 *Commission of the European Communities v Kingdom of Belgium* [1996] ECLI:EU:C:1996:316, para 88; Case C-1/96 *The Queen v Minister of Agriculture, Fisheries and Food* [1998] ECLI:EU:C:1998:113, para 47; Case C-102/96 *Commission of the European Communities v Federal Republic of German* [1998]

But if then the principle was only used scarcely and gained no special constitutional status or prominence, it has become more visible and significant in the last couple of years. This was because it was revived and reinforced again by legislators in the early 2000s to cope with the rapidly developing Justice and Home Affairs (now called Area of Freedom, Security and Justice – AFSJ) policy fields, and more recently, with renewed dimensions and normative force, by the CJEU.[31] The principle of mutual trust was employed by the Member States as an underlying rationale to support the principle of mutual recognition in sidestepping harmonisation in the politically sensitive AFSJ policy fields concerning areas of immigration, criminal justice and civil procedure, which cut to the core of national sovereignty, but where significant impediments to the smooth functioning of inter-state cooperation were identified.

But what does it mean to say that the principle of mutual trust is a principle of EU law and what is its place in the hierarchy of EU legal principles? R Dworkin and R Alexy have famously carved out the structural differences of legal rules and legal principles.[32] The main distinctness lying in the way in which they are applied to facts with rules tending to be applied in an 'all-or-nothing' manner, and principles being optimisation requirements subject to weighing and balancing.[33] A Jakab has disputed this distinction by arguing that principles in fact are not logically-structurally or normatively different from rules, but just *very important general rules*[34] with some functional differences from rules. He has called general principles in the context of EU law *very, very important rules*.[35]

Mutual trust has been already called a 'constitutional' principle of EU law by EU law scholars[36] and a principle of 'fundamental importance in EU law' by the CJEU itself.[37] This must make mutual trust also one very important legal principle in EU law. Not all principles of fundamental importance are necessarily constitutional principles of EU law, but they are arguably *more important* than other principles not ascribed with such 'fundamental importance'. While there is still ongoing disagreement on the exact status of mutual trust in the hierarchy of legal principles in the EU legal order, such name calling still arguably locates it high up the EU legal hierarchy. And that bears significance. CJEU Advocate General Bot

ECLI:EU:C:1998:529, para 22; and Case C-5/94 *The Queen v Ministry of Agriculture, Fisheries and Food, ex parte Hedley Lomas (Ireland) Ltd* [1996] ECLI:EU:C:1996:205, para 19.

[31] See besides Opinion 2/13 other recent noteworthy examples: Joined Cases C-404/15 and C-659/15 PPU *Pál Aranyosi and Robert Căldăraru* [2016] ECLI:EU:C:2016:198; Case C-284/16 *Slowakische Republik (Slovak Republic) v Achmea BV* [2018] ECLI:EU:C:2018:158; Case C-64/16 *Associação Sindical dos Juízes Portugueses v Tribunal de* Contas [2018] ECLI:EU:C:2018:117; Case C-216/18 PPU *LM* [2018] ECLI:EU:C:2018:586.

[32] Ronald Dworkin, *Taking Rights Seriously* (Duckworth, 1977); Robert Alexy, *A Theory of Constitutional Rights* (Oxford University Press, 2002).

[33] Robert Alexy, 'Formal Principles: Some Replies to Critics' (2014) 12 *International Journal of Constitutional Law* 511, 512.

[34] Andras Jakab, *European Constitutional Language* (Cambridge University Press, 2016) 377.

[35] ibid, see that definition in fn 29.

[36] See, eg: Lenaerts (n 2) 806.

[37] Opinion 2/13, para 191.

has even compared the status of mutual trust with two of the most well-known and fundamental EU law principles – primacy and direct effect.[38] According to these CJEU doctrines, EU law is superior to any contrary national law and has immediate direct effect in domestic jurisdictions.[39] But unlike primacy and direct effect, the normative content of mutual trust is not self-evident and needs further explanation.

So, what is the rule deriving from the principle of mutual trust and what are its aims and functions? Mutual trust requires Member States (courts, administrative authorities) to trust each other's EU law and fundamental rights abidance and not to control the administrative or judicial decisions taken. In other words, a Member State's court or authority has to take other Member States' decisions in principle at face value and believe that there is such compliance (without requiring additional control or proof).[40] That is the rule deriving from the principle. Such a presumption of compliance implies a blunt prohibition of controls over actual compliance in the vast majority of cases. It is shorthand for omitting control (judicial review) as a general rule. And the presumption often (but not necessarily always) paves the way for the more operational principle of mutual recognition which gives domestic force to extraterritorial (but intra-EU) state acts. These state acts may be qualifications, inspections or certificates, diplomas, judicial decisions in civil or criminal law and they also translate into the main areas where mutual trust and recognition as dual principles are used: internal market, criminal and police cooperation, civil justice cooperation, immigration and asylum policy. The broad law and rights compliance presumption that mutual trust prescribes in these areas may be rebutted by exceptional circumstances only,[41] which ultimately are for the CJEU to delimit and scrutinise.

In defining these limits to mutual trust, ie when such trust is actually not warranted and control mechanisms can be deployed, the CJEU has arguably moved, at least in EU criminal and asylum law, from 'blind trust' to a qualified form of mutual trust which leaves some room for individual assessment and control of actual compliance with EU law and fundamental rights.[42] I will show with the example of the case study in this chapter that this might not necessarily hold true in the civil justice cooperation policy field, in which a blind trust obligation is still prevalent.

Mutual trust ultimately functions as a facilitator of jurisdictional extraterritorial effect allocating judicial and administrative labour among Member States[43]

[38] See to that effect also: Opinion of Advocate General Bot in Cases C-404/15 and C-659/15 PPU *Aranyosi and Căldăraru*, [2016] ECLI:EU:C:2016:140, para 106.

[39] Eleftheriadis (n 3) 2 and references in fn 4.

[40] See again the definition in Opinion 2/13, para 191: 'The principle of mutual trust requires that all EU Member States, save in exceptional circumstances, have to consider all the other EU Member States to be complying with EU law and particularly with fundamental rights recognised by EU law.'

[41] Ibid.

[42] See: Xanthopoulou (n 2).

[43] See on that: Rizcallah (n 2).

in a context of inter-state action and close cooperation under the Union legal framework. Such close and elaborate cooperation is a worthy aim but one can still ask for a more nuanced approach to the principle beyond that of the discussion of mere limits to it (ie in which cases can trust break down and judicial control be allowed). An unqualified obligation to trust has led to tensions and extensive criticism of the CJEU[44] but even a qualified obligation to trust might be problematic from the perspective of genuine trust-building as theories of trust point out that trust cannot be compelled or willed, but must be cultivated and earned.[45] Thus the discussions perhaps should not only revolve around the limits of mutual trust, but also the appropriateness of trust conceptually and its occurrence in legal-constitutional language.

The tensions inherent in the principle of mutual trust regarding the compliance presumption, a lack of judicial control over actual compliance and failure to impose limits on mutual trust are unveiled in the CJEU's *Liberato* judgment.

IV. *Liberato* – Trusting Despite EU Law Infringements

The *Liberato* case[46] is one recent CJEU judgment where the principle of mutual trust was deployed, and it illustrates some of the problems in having a legal obligation to trust in judicial proceedings. It is a parental and matrimonial jurisdiction case in which one Member State court delivered a final decision contrary to EU jurisdictional rules. The facts of the case are the following. Mr Liberato, of Italian nationality, and Ms Grigorescu, of Romanian nationality, were married and living with their child in Italy until their marriage deteriorated and the mother took the child with her to Romania.[47] Separation and divorce, parental responsibility and maintenance proceedings were started by both parents in their respective countries, but Mr Liberato started the proceedings in Italy first.[48] This is important, as per EU law, the court second seized should stay its proceedings and decline jurisdiction in favour of the court first seized if the latter finds according to EU law rules that it has jurisdiction to hear the case.[49] Although that claim was made

[44] See eg: Henning Bang Fuglsang Madsen Sorensen, 'Mutual Trust – Blind Trust or General Trust with Exceptions? The CJEU Hears Key Cases on the European Arrest Warrant' [2016] *Pécs Journal of International and European Law* 56; Thomas Wischmeyer, 'Generating Trust Through Law? Judicial Cooperation in the European Union and the "Principle of Mutual Trust"' (2016) 17 *German Law Journal* 339.

[45] See in a slight disagreement with this: Richard Holton, 'Deciding to Trust, Coming to Believe' (1994) 72 *Australasian Journal of Philosophy* 63, but theories usually explain this away by stressing the different components of trust – ie, one can will herself to rely or *act* as if trusting, but that does not necessarily mean trusting as a psychological state – Möllering (n 17) 22.

[46] Case C-386/17 *Stefano Liberato v Luminita Luisa Grigorescu* [2019] ECLI:EU:C:2019:24.

[47] Ibid, para 17.

[48] Ibid, paras 18–19.

[49] Art 19 of Council Regulation (EC) 2201/2003 of 27 November 2003 concerning jurisdiction and the recognition and enforcement of judgments in matrimonial matters and the matters of parental

in Romanian courts by Mr Liberato to stay the proceedings in Romania because of *lis pendens* in Italy, the Romanian courts dismissed his objection and arrived at a *res judicata* in favour of Ms Grigorescu prior to the diametrically opposing final decision reached in the Italian courts.[50] The mother then applied for enforcement of the Romanian decision in Italy. A dispute over it arrived to the Italian Supreme Court, which sent a preliminary reference to the CJEU. In the preliminary reference the Italian Supreme Court asked whether, due to the fact that the Romanian courts had in its understanding made a manifest error of *lis pendens* provisions of EU law, the recognition sought could be refused on the ground that it was manifestly contrary to public policy.[51]

In its decision, the CJEU did not allow such non-recognition. In arriving to that conclusion, it relied on the principle of mutual trust to explain why Member States' courts decisions on jurisdiction cannot be reviewed and why grounds for non-recognition of such judgments should be kept to the minimum required.[52] The CJEU did not follow its arguably more balanced approach of recent years in criminal and asylum cases but upheld the strong normative ban that Member States courts cannot review each other's judgments in substance because of mutual trust. That held, even when the CJEU itself confirmed the actual breach of EU law norms.[53] Despite the fact that the EU law compliance presumption was rebutted in reality, the CJEU did not allow for a departure from mutual trust and recognition rules and maintained that Italian courts are not allowed to review the jurisdiction of the court second seized despite a claimed error in EU law[54] and thus also cannot apply the public policy ground for refusal expressly provided in the relevant EU legal instruments.[55]

There is a lot to unpack in the judgment. It showcases the ever-lasting fight over jurisdictional authority among EU Member States. It is symptomatic of a broader trend towards jurisdictional nationalism: in cases of disagreement, mobile EU citizens tend to return to their home country to initiate proceedings there. In disputes involving two EU national parties, this often leads to cases being brought in two different Member States and those national courts wanting to hear cases and accord judicial protection to their nationals. Errors in applying jurisdictional rules and parallel proceedings are not rare. There are EU regulations drafted to hinder these situations, but the case law indicates that their effectiveness is at the same time supposedly enforced but in practice hindered by the principle of mutual trust.

responsibility [2003] OJ L338/1 and Art 27 of Council Regulation (EC) 44/2001 of 22 December 2000 on jurisdiction and the recognition and enforcement of judgments in civil and commercial matters [2001] OJ L012/1.

[50] The Romanian courts granted sole custody to the mother and put maintenance obligations on the father, whereas the Italian court granted sole custody to the father, maintenance on the mother and required the immediate return of the child to Italy – see *Liberato*, paras 20–22.

[51] Ibid, paras 29–31.

[52] See in ibid, paras 41, 44, 46, 55.

[53] Ibid, paras 38, 47, 54.

[54] Ibid, paras 51–53.

[55] Ibid, paras 54–55.

The principle of mutual trust functions to endorse one rule of EU secondary law over another. On the one hand, the principle of mutual trust is usually introduced in a judgment for the enhancement of the effectiveness of an EU legal instrument under dispute, in particular one norm from which often concerns the obligation to recognise and enforce other Member State's decisions quasi automatically, without further delays or controls. On the other hand, and in the case of *Liberato*, the CJEU is disregarding other norms from that regulation, namely rules regulating which court has jurisdiction over specific matters. Although EU law has bindingly regulated relevant jurisdictional rules for the settlement of such cross-border situations, the CJEU in effect decides that, even if these rules are not followed, there is not much the national court actually having jurisdiction according to these rules can do. A public policy refusal for the non-recognition of such a decision cannot be granted in the national legal system: the CJEU prohibits it, among other things per mutual trust. Although mutual trust should be about presuming EU law compliance, in cases of non-compliance, neither national courts nor the CJEU can or will not do much. The EU law error is left unaddressed.

Liberato is just one very illustrative case in a line of cases which exemplify how an EU law compliance presumption has become an empty rhetorical device – in cases where EU law has actually not been complied with the CJEU still keeps using the mutual trust disguise to block judicial review over compliance in concrete instances. This is an EU rule of law problem, but it is also problematic theoretically as it might not achieve a more general aim of adhering to the creation of actual trust in the EU between Member States, in particular between Member States' judicial and administrative authorities. This will be argued next by unpacking mutual trust from a trust theoretical perspective.

V. Mutual Trust in the EU Legal Architecture – In the Name of Trust?

What purpose does mutual trust play in the distinct legal architecture of the EU? Is its function comparable to the function of trust in interpersonal relationships or society? This will require some theoretical scrutiny of mutual trust in light of the concept of trust.

It is noteworthy that the CJEU often refers to mutual trust in parallel to discussing the special constitutional structure of the EU, its autonomy, and the sharing of Article 2 TEU values among Member States. The CJEU stresses that sharing such values implies and justifies the existence of mutual trust, and that the EU law that implements those values is respected, inter alia due to another EU law principle of sincere cooperation.[56] Mutual trust is a part of the network of principles that bind

[56] Case C-284/16 *Slowakische Republik (Slovak Republic) v Achmea BV* [2018] ECLI:EU:C:2018:158, paras 33–34.

the EU and its Member States reciprocally, and bind EU Member States to each other.[57] This implies that the CJEU accords to mutual trust an ultimately functionalist aim for wider EU cooperation and integration on the basis of shared values. This is linked to how trust functions in societies.

Mutual trust is *relational*: it is a relationship between actors depictable in a formula 'A trusts B in doing X'. On this view, Member States authorities should trust each other in correctly implementing EU law. In the case of *Liberato* the Italian court had to trust the lawfulness of the judgment of the Romanian court (ie it had to believe that the decision complied with EU law and fundamental rights, as protected under EU law). It must be noted that the trust relationship here has little to do with the belief in the probability of an outcome, as the outcome was already there and in principle controllable. The trust relationship is reciprocal (by definition due to its definition as *mutual* trust, note that trust in interpersonal relations needs not to be reciprocal) and domain specific ultimately captured by the behavioural component of trust – acting on trust by enforcing and recognising the foreign instrument at hand.

Mutual trust is also characteristically an *optimistic belief* – not neutral or pessimistic.[58] This has to do with the quality of the expectation of beneficial or at least not harmful behaviour of others towards the trustor.[59] This is always risky as people can choose (as autonomous actors with discretionary powers) to deflect and not to respond to trust. This is also emblematic of mutual trust in general (as a broad EU law compliance presumption) and in particular the way it plays out in *Liberato* – it can even be said that the way CJEU insists on mutual trust is overly optimistic about Member States' EU law compliance records, reaching to a level of gullibility.

As mentioned, the optimism of the belief causes the inherent *risks* of trust relationships and the *vulnerability* of the trustor. A Baier associates trust with reliance, risks, and vulnerability, emphasising that trusting entails a dependence on another's behaviour, thus a risk and an active or passive placing yourself in a vulnerable position of being harmed by that risk, in other words, trust is an accepted vulnerability to another's possible but not expected ill will (or a lack of good will) toward one.[60] This vulnerability is detectable in mutual trust and in *Liberato* as there is an evident problem with potentially risky and harmful outcomes when the compliance presumption is unfounded both from the perspective of national legal order (enforcing a foreign decision rendered in breach of applicable EU rules) and from the perspective of individual rights (the impossibility of enforcing an opposing Italian decision granting Mr Liberato parental rights). The Italian court was put in

[57] Ibid, para 33.

[58] See to that end again Gambetta's comment on the essence of trust: 'when we say we trust someone or that someone is trustworthy, we implicitly mean that the probability that he will perform an action that is *beneficial or at least not detrimental* to us is high for us to consider engaging in some form of cooperation with him'. See Gambetta (n 27) 217.

[59] ibid.

[60] Baier (n 18) 235.

a vulnerable position of denying an Italian citizen the enforcement of the rendered Italian decision of parental and maintenance rights in favour of the Romanian one. The former had reached a result that was more favourable to its citizen, but which was barred from effect. The individuals concerned are potentially under even greater risks and vulnerability, putting the Member State authorities concerned also in a position of mediating vulnerability and accountability arising therefrom.[61]

Whereas it might be debatable that such nationality-based arguments should deserve consideration in the post-national European integration context, it still cuts to the core of sovereignty and the purpose of courts' constitutional role of rights protection, including the right to a fair and lawful hearing, also in civil proceedings. There is an uncontrollable (and pertinent) risk that besides being proven procedurally illegal, the Romanian judgment could be illegal also in substance. The Italian courts have per mutual trust no means of controlling the legality of the Romanian decision and they have to give it equal domestic force without any such control. This means that ousting judicial review and giving ample deference to a decision of another court are the instantiations of the principle of mutual trust. But decisions can be erroneous, particularly first instance ones which have not had appellate or cassation review. In a worst-case scenario this could mean expanding the effects of a potentially unlawful decision and migrating it from a foreign jurisdiction to the domestic one. As the facts and merits of the case in *Liberato* do not even deny the EU law breach, the risks and vulnerabilities of the supposedly trusting Italian courts (to enforce a foreign decision that breaches EU law) were materialised, without the CJEU giving a potential route of remedy or redress of the error.

The optimistic beliefs and the risks and vulnerabilities that trust entails are instrumental to the ultimate benefit of trust: to open up further possibilities of (cooperative) action that otherwise would be foreclosed. Mutual trust is likewise directly instrumentalised for cooperative purposes – trust is a necessary feature of cooperative ventures.[62] The desired outcome is to support rapid and effective cooperation among Member States. The orientation of mutual trust towards enhancing cooperative action is detectable in *Liberato*. The Italian court and judges are ultimately asked to think the best of their Romanian counterparts EU law compliance record, and through this the CJEU aims to promote effective integrationist measures of cooperation, in its own words 'for the creation of a genuine judicial area'.[63] This facilitates the free movement of judgments among EU Member States as a cooperative venture otherwise hindered by different costly and time-consuming national control and enforcement mechanisms. Thus, trust is employed to augment the possibilities of further integration and cooperation between EU Member States.

[61] See on such a fiduciary account of mutual trust: Schwarz (n 2).
[62] Gambetta (n 27) 217.
[63] *Liberato*, para 41.

While the principle of mutual trust does have many convergent features prevalent in trust theories, there are also notable frictions, which make mutual trust problematic conceptually speaking. These issues relate to the contextual elements of trust being necessary in circumstances of uncertainty and uncontrollability, the role of the judiciary, its unresponsiveness to coercion and the needed rational basis of trust.

First, trust as a concept is inherently tied to situations of uncertainty and uncontrollability as it relates to the mental willingness of vulnerability stemming from the uncontrollable actions of the trustee. The conceptual uncertainty of trust is manifest either by missing information and evidence (*information asymmetry*) or by *time asymmetry* associated with the uncontrollability of the (mostly future, but also uncontrollable past) actions of others as the object of trust. The temporal feature of uncontrollability means that trust is usually an expectation directed at the *future* actions of others we cannot control, as we cannot predict the future.[64] The features of uncertainty and uncontrollability that trust holds conceptually are something that have little place in the context of a courtroom. Judicial control in general, and also the control undertaken in *Liberato*, are not directed at future, but past events. There is also no time lag between the mutual trust decision and the expected behaviour in the case: mutual trust is not directed to the future but concerns events that have already happened in the past – the legality of the already rendered Romanian court decision.

When trust is not necessarily concerned with the future behaviours of others, it can also be directed to past or current actions or intentions, but then it means they have to be *uncontrollable*. P Dasgupta has noted that trust might result not only from our inability to monitor others' behaviour due to a time lag, but also because of the unobservability of some of these actions.[65] This is mostly tied to lacking information. This source of uncertainty is problematic in *Liberato*, as presumably all relevant information and evidence was provided and controlled by both the Italian court and the CJEU, which does not raise the possibility of missing information or having to decide based on informational lacunas. This is the function of judicial review: to scrutinise past decisions or acts and assess their lawfulness. Thus, there is no element of uncontrollability, quite the opposite: judicial review proceedings are all about control and review of facts and evidence relating to these past events. In sum, the principle of mutual trust, generally and in *Liberato*, does not function under the conditions of uncertainty and uncontrollability that we generally associate with the concept. This is not desirable, as EU law compliance should be controlled in judicial proceedings with all surrounding uncertainties removed in these proceedings.

[64] This temporal and control aspect of trust becomes visible very well in the above-cited D Gambetta's trust definition: trust as a particular level of the subjective probability with which an agent assesses that another agent or group of agents will perform a particular action, both *before he can monitor such action* (or independently of his capacity ever to be able to monitor it) and in the context in which it affects his own action. Gambetta (n 27) 217.

[65] Partha Dasgupta, 'Trust as a Commodity' in ibid 53; Barbara A Misztal, *Trust in Modern Societies: The Search for the Bases of Social Order* (Polity Press/Blackwell, 1996) 83.

Then there is the question of the *rationality* of trust. Although it is debated in the literature, whether trust can be fully grounded in rational considerations of the trustworthiness of the trustee and the opposing importance and extent of uncertainty for such rationality,[66] there is still considerable consensus among theorists that trust needs to be at least somewhat grounded in evidence and, most importantly, it is not rational to talk about trust in contexts of contrary evidence of trustworthiness. Karen J Cook has argued that trust is based on reasoned assessment of evidence at hand that lead one to evaluate others as trustworthy.[67] JD Lewis and A Weigert have added that: '[t]rust is based on a blend of knowledge and ignorance'[68] and D Gambetta has explained well this paradox of evidence and uncertainty and the specific nature of trust as a 'peculiar belief predicated not on evidence but on the lack of contrary evidence'.[69] It is not rational to trust the untrustworthy[70] and since the trusting act involves risks and vulnerability for the trustor, he or she cannot trust if there is evidence that clearly triggers the mental attitude of distrust and not mere uncertainty or lack of information that leaves room for the benefit of the doubt.

The functioning of mutual trust in *Liberato* is problematic from a rational perspective, as there are contrary claims giving rise to necessary and rational distrust: non-compliance with EU law was referred to by both the Italian court and the CJEU itself. All available evidence should have logically triggered distrust. There was not much room for doubt or informational gaps that would allow for an optimistic beneficial interpretation for allowing trust. Thus, upholding mutual trust as an EU law compliance presumption was refuted by facts of the case and limits to its functioning should have been placed. This would also have served the integrity and functioning of the EU legal system and rule of law. Yet this was not done by the CJEU, as it still required Italian courts to enforce mutual trust-based recognition and enforcement of an unlawful Romanian judgment. Besides being particularly problematic in the *Liberato* case, I find that here lies also the most fundamental problem with mutual trust when analysed under a trust-theoretical framework. Both conceptually and institutionally, the inbuilt tension that the principle of mutual trust forbids judicial (or administrative) control cuts to the heart of how trust as a concept should not function as these control mechanisms are institutionally designed to overcome uncertainty and uncontrollability which trust inherently requires. Judicial review is almost always an ex post assessment of relevant events, evidence, and law, and the role of the judiciary is to assess

[66] Where economists and rational choice theorists emphasise the calculative nature of trust, philosophers and sociologists have stressed that fully rational and calculative trust is not in fact trust but mere reliance as there is no element of uncertainty and risk – see eg discussion in Möllering (n 17) 26, 80–83. On the need to redefine the very notion of reason to explain trust: Martin Hollis, *Trust within Reason* (Cambridge University Press, 1998).

[67] Karen J Cook, Jessica J Santana, 'Trust and Rational Choice' in Uslaner (n 14) 273.

[68] Lewis and Weigert (n 21) 970.

[69] Gambetta (n 27) 234–35.

[70] Trust is dysfunctional when it is placed in the untrustworthy, just as distrust towards the trustworthy is dysfunctional. See Möllering (n 17) 83.

available evidence, ascertain relevant facts and events to apply the law and legal consequences to these facts and events. This makes trust a dubious concept to be applied in the context of judicial review.

Moreover, N Luhmann has argued for the need for inbuilt and institutionalised mechanisms of distrust to control and support the operation of trust at a systemic level.[71] He notably singled out researchers and judges as two of the professions embodying this institutionalised systemic distrust mechanisms, stressing how imperative it is that members of the academia and judiciary treat the object of their inquiry and claims about trustworthiness with an attitude of distrust, employing methods of control.[72] Hence the practical implications of the principle of mutual trust – to actually inhibit the inherent distrust and control mechanisms of national judicial systems – run counter to the conceptual interrelationships of trust and distrust in a democratic society governed by the rule of law guarded by the judicial branch. It is the aim and purpose of judicial control not to be dismissive and blindly trusting towards claims about lawfulness. The principle of mutual trust frustrates the role of the judiciary to fulfil that role both how it functions in *Liberato* and by mutual trust definition due to the effect of banning meaningful judicial review over other Member States' acts or decisions.

Another source of friction is the fact that the CJEU imposes mutual trust on national authorities – different Member State authorities (mostly judges) *must* trust their corresponding counterparts. This runs counter to trust's property of being *unresponsive to coercion*, that is, although one can be put under a duty to trust, trust itself in its rationality does not respond to such duty on a personal level and this obfuscates this imposition and makes it unfruitful. Notions of freedom, autonomy and discretion are symptomatic of any occurrence of trust conceptually. Trust cannot tolerate coercion on either side of the trust relationship: the trustor cannot be forced to trust, either by external or internal pressures, and the trustee cannot be forced to meet trust, as this rips the meaning of trust involving risks and uncertainty coming from the trustee's choice of action. This autonomous free will is related to external pressures, but there is again an interesting paradox of voluntariness in the internal sense: a trustor cannot cognitively 'choose' or will himself to trust. Trust is not a matter of free will cognitively.[73] In that sense it is similar to belief: you either have it or not, actively choosing to trust or to believe is simply mimicking that does not amount to actual trust or belief.[74] In this dual paradox, trust is at the same time free in the external meaning and determined in the internal one. A common denominator is unresponsiveness to coercion, both internally (by one's will) and externally, and on both the mental state of the trustor and the discretional actions of the trustee. If one is still coerced to mimic or

[71] Luhmann (n 22) 89.
[72] ibid 92.
[73] Misztal (n 62) 84; Möllering (n 17) 22.
[74] Katherine Hawley, *Trust: A Very Short Introduction* (Oxford University Press, 2012) 78–79.

display trust externally, such mimicking remains insincere and not amounting to real trust conceptually.

In the case of mutual trust in *Liberato* there are obvious tensions of imposing trust on the trustor. The CJEU is saying in *Liberato* to the enforcing Italian court that it must trust its Romanian counterpart in asserting jurisdiction and even though the Romanian court's assessment on its jurisdiction was unlawful, it must still act on this imposed trust (the behavioural element of mutual trust: recognition and enforcement of the trust object – the Romanian judicial decision). In a broader context this may well be the agenda behind mutual trust: to create trust by imposing acts of trust (mutual recognition of decisions) in the hope of creating more trust between Member States and Member State authorities in the long term. This can be paralleled with the theoretical account of the so-called therapeutic trust, where the aim is to increase the trust-responsiveness of the trustee by the act of placing trust.[75] But such therapeutic trust requires that the trustee be aware of the trust placed in him.[76] The effect of this, at least in *Liberato*, is therefore doubtful as the trustee has no opportunity to show trust-responsiveness, as the acts under trust consideration have already passed. Thus, there is no need for the future or uncontrollable events orientation of trust – it becomes redundant.

In sum, the functioning of mutual trust in the *Liberato* judgment demonstrates some features of trust, such as relationality, optimistic character, risk and vulnerability and the aim to augment cooperative action but is in stark contradiction with the requirements of uncertainty, uncontrollability, rationality, and the property of trust of being unresponsive to coercion. This has some very important ramifications for EU lawyers in making assessments about the principle of mutual trust, its functioning and place in the EU legal order. The analysis shows how the principle of mutual trust as an EU law compliance presumption fails to handle instances of proven non-compliance and can become an empty signifier. The main takeaway from this is that CJEU judges might have quite a partial conception of trust. CJEU finds trust is something enforceable top down, stripping away its psychological non-coercive character by reducing it to the enforceable acting of trust, which is only one part of trust as a concept (the others being its cognitive and affective components). Coercing national authorities to act on trust, which is in fact not necessarily there, justified or grounded in evidence (or even more, as in *Liberato*, enforced in the context of existing contrary evidence), the CJEU is depriving the judicial branch its control functions grounded in functionally necessary distrust, which, as argued by Luhmann, would allow for actual systemic trust to flourish between actors. In the context of the EU this would mean that allowing and requiring both national courts and the CJEU to control and remedy EU law non-compliance instead of a mutual trust required compliance presumption would foster the creation of trust both horizontally between EU Member

[75] See: HJN Horsburgh, 'The Ethics of Trust' (1960) 10 *The Philosophical Quarterly* 343; Philip Pettit, 'The Cunning of Trust' (1995) 24 *Philosophy and Public Affairs* 202.

[76] Horsburgh (n 75) 346.

States (authorities) and vertically between the EU and its Member States and their respective courts.[77] Member States would have the much-needed confidence that their courts participate in the EU judicial system of controls and remedies and the CJEU will ultimately intervene when EU law is not complied with.

VI. Concluding Remarks – Trust as a Rationale for EU Integration?

This chapter has assessed the principle of mutual trust, and particularly one recent judgment of the CJEU – *Liberato* – through the theoretical lens of the concept of trust and in particular the theories of N Luhmann, D Gambetta and A Baier. The case study has revealed that although from the outset mutual trust as defined and used by CJEU bears some basic resemblance to trust conceptualisations: namely, that it is an optimistic belief in other EU Member States and their authorities complying with their obligations under EU law with the ultimate appealing aim to enhance and hasten EU wide cooperation. This belief brings about both a CJEU imposed obligation to act on that trust (enforce a foreign decision) and puts that Member State (authority) in a risky and vulnerable position, as the trusted actor might not in fact comply with its EU law obligations, as was exemplified with *Liberato*. However, there is a mismatch between the way that the principle operates in the EU legal order and the way trust should operate or the kind of systems and institutional design necessary to foster meaningful trust between cooperating entities. My main critique here draws on the across-the-board agreement in trust scholarship that trust cannot be coerced, thus the CJEU imposed obligation to trust other Member State authorities without deploying substantial control even in cases where the facts lead to the necessity of control (*Liberato*) is in stark conflict with conceptual trust as distilled in the literature. Obviously the CJEU is unable to change actors' beliefs or attitudes, but only to insist on acting on acclaimed 'mutual trust'. But situations where there in fact exists no such trust might create more backlash than the idealistic aim of furthering cooperation and integration. And, most importantly, insisting on a trust derived obligation on national judiciary in a manner as was done in *Liberato* poses the potential threat of undermining the constitutional role of the judiciary, that is the role of distrusting attitudes and methods to create systemic trust in the society as described by Luhmann. In *Liberato*, trust was not a meaningful concept to use, as the actor having to act on that trust (the Italian court) was not deciding in a context of uncertainty and uncontrollability – there were facts and evidence which cultivated distrusting attitudes.

[77] On the conceptualisation and importance of trust between national courts and the CJEU in the EU integration process see: Juan A Mayoral, 'In the CJEU Judges Trust: A New Approach in the Judicial Construction of Europe' (2017) 55 *Journal of Common Market Studies* 551.

I claim that judges should not be under obligations to trust their object of inquiry, even if it concerns their foreign counterparts' EU compliance record. They have to fulfil their professional and functional duty to control and verify, not blindly trust. If needed, the CJEU should step in and find a way to remedy non-compliance, even if it means impairing the effectiveness of an EU regulatory instrument in a case at hand. Remedying such an infringement would probably create in effect more meaningful wide-ranging trust among cooperating authorities, who would more readily collaborate knowing that breaches and errors of implementation would be addressed and remedied in the functioning of the system. Such judicial control and enforcement could hold the true potential for trust-building in the EU legal system instead of mechanisms that function to frustrate such control and undermine the rule of law in the EU.

The observations drawn from trust literature might not bear any legal significance for EU law as an autonomous legal order, as one might say: judges could create any legal principles they deem necessary for the purposes of deciding cases at hand. But it does make a difference when making normative assessments about the substance and function of a legal principle or when assessed relative to its acclaimed aim. If we take the principle of mutual trust at face value to aim at creating more trust in the EU, it might prove inadequate. If the CJEU is to only enforce an empty rhetoric of trust by obliging trusting behaviour on its interlocutors, it might have its own functional merits but only if we understand that we are not creating genuine trust. Although the concept of trust has vast potential in furthering the European project, its concrete usage and functioning should be carefully crafted and theoretically underpinned to better utilise its value.

References

Alexy, R (2002). *A Theory of Constitutional Rights*. Oxford University Press.

Alexy, R (2014). 'Formal Principles: Some Replies to Critics.' *International Journal of Constitutional Law* 12 (3): 511–24.

Archard, D et al (eds) (2013). *Reading Onora O'Neill*. Routledge.

Baier, A (1986). 'Trust and Antitrust.' *Ethics* 96 (2): 231–60.

Baier, A (1994). *Moral Prejudices: Essays on Ethics*. Harvard University Press.

Ballin, E H (2014). 'Mutual Trust. The Virtue of Reciprocity – Strengthening the Acceptance of the Rule of Law through Peer Review.' In Carlos Closa, Dimitry Kochenov and Joseph H H Weiler (eds), *Reinforcing Rule of Law Oversight in the European Union*. Cambridge University Press.

Cremona, M (2018) *Structural Principles in EU External Relations Law*. Hart Publishing.

Domenicucci, J and Holton, R (2017). 'Trust as a Two-Place Relation.' In Paul Faulkner and Thomas Simpson (eds), *The Philosophy of Trust*. Oxford University Press.

Dworkin, R (1977). *Taking Rights Seriously*. Duckworth.

Eleftheriadis, P (2005). 'The Idea of a European Constitution.' *Oxford Journal of Legal Studies* 27 (1): 1–21.

Gambetta, D (ed) (1988). *Trust: Making and Breaking Cooperative Relations*. Blackwell.

Hardin, R (2002). *Trust and Trustworthiness*. Russell Sage Foundation.

Hawley, K (2012). *Trust: A Very Short Introduction*. Oxford University Press.

Hollis, M (1998). *Trust within Reason*. Cambridge University Press.

Holton, R (1994). 'Deciding to Trust, Coming to Believe.' *Australasian Journal of Philosophy* 72 (1): 63–76.
Horsburgh, H J N (1960). 'The Ethics of Trust.' *The Philosophical Quarterly* 10 (41): 343–54.
Jakab, A (2016). *European Constitutional Language*. Cambridge University Press.
Jones, K (1996). 'Trust as an Affective Attitude.' *Ethics* 107 (1): 4–25.
Lenaerts, K (2017). 'La Vie Après l'avis: Exploring the Principle of Mutual (yet Not Blind) Trust.' *Common Market Law Review* 54 (3): 805–40.
Lewis, J D and Weigert, A (1985). 'Trust as a Social Reality.' *Social Forces* 63: 20.
Luhmann, N (1979). *Trust and Power: Two Works*. Wiley.
Mayer, R C and Davis, J H (1995). 'An Integrative Model of Organizational Trust.' *The Academy of Management Review* 20 (3): 709–34.
Mayoral, J A (2017). 'In the CJEU Judges Trust: A New Approach in the Judicial Construction of Europe.' *Journal of Common Market Studies* 55 (3): 551–68.
Misztal, B A (1996). *Trust in Modern Societies: The Search for the Bases of Social Order*. Polity Press: Blackwell.
Möllering, G (2006) *Trust: Reason, Routine, Reflexivity* (1st edn). Elsevier.
Pettit, P (1995). 'The Cunning of Trust.' *Philosophy and Public Affairs* 24: 202.
Rizcallah, C (2019). 'The Challenges to Trust-Based Governance in the European Union: Assessing the Use of Mutual Trust as a Driver of EU Integration.' *European Law Journal* 25 (1): 37–56.
Rosas, A and Armati, L (2018). *EU Constitutional Law: An Introduction* (3rd edn). Portland, Oregon: Hart Publishing.
Rousseau D M et al (1998). 'Not So Different After All: A Cross-Discipline View of Trust.' *Academy of Management Review* 23 (3): 393–404.
Schwarz M (2018). 'Let's Talk about Trust, Baby! Theorizing Trust and Mutual Recognition in the EU's Area of Freedom, Security and Justice.' *European Law Journal* 24: 124.
Sorensen, HBFM (2016). 'Mutual Trust – Blind Trust or General Trust with Exceptions? The CJEU Hears Key Cases on the European Arrest Warrant.' *Pécs Journal of International and European Law* 56.
Storskrubb, E (2018). 'Mutual Trust and the Dark Horse of Civil Justice.' Cambridge Yearbook of European Legal Studies 20: 179.
Tuori, K (2015). *European Constitutionalism*. Cambridge University Press.
Uslaner, E M (2018). *The Oxford Handbook of Social and Political Trust*. Oxford University Press.
Weiler, J (1999). *The Constitution of Europe:'Do the New Clothes Have an Emperor?'and Other Essays on European Integration*. Cambridge University Press.
Wischmeyer, T (2016). 'Generating Trust Through Law? Judicial Cooperation in the European Union and the "Principle of Mutual Trust".' *German Law Journal* 17 (3): 339–83.
Xanthopoulou, E 2018) 'Mutual Trust and Rights in EU Criminal and Asylum Law: Three Phases of Evolution and the 'Uncharted Territory beyond Blind Trust.' *Common Market Law Review* 55 (2): 480.

INDEX

www.ingramcontent.com/pod-product-compliance
Lightning Source LLC
Chambersburg PA
CBHW071301180926
51613CB00001B/101
9781509935253